THE ITALIAN COUNTRY TABLE

Home Cooking from Italy's Farmhouse Kitchens

LYNNE ROSSETTO KASPER

Color Photographs by Dana Gallagher

Design by Stephanie Tevonian
Black-and-White Photographs by Lynne Rossetto Kasper

Scribner

SCRIBNER
1230 Avenue of the Americas
New York, NY 10020

DESIGNED BY STEPHANIE TEVONIAN

Set in Adobe Fairfield

Manufactured in the United States of America

1   3   5   7   9   10   8   6   4   2

Library of Congress Cataloging-in-Publication Data
Kasper, Lynne Rossetto.
The Italian country table : home cooking from Italy's farmhouse kitchens /
Lynne Rossetto Kasper ; color photographs by Dana Gallagher.
p. cm.
Includes bibliographical references and index.
1. Cookery, Italian. I. Title.
TX723 .K37 1999
641.5945—dc21   99-37377
CIP

ISBN 0-684-81325-4

To my mother, Elda Fulvini, with all my love,
and to beloved friend,
Jerry Erlich, how I wish you were still here.

CONTENTS

ACKNOWLEDGMENTS

Books like this don't happen without the boundless help and generosity of many people. Among them are several I'd prefer never to have out of my life—my husband, Frank, and dear "sister," Cara De Silva. Among the deepest pleasures of this project has been working with friend and editor, Maria Guarnaschelli. Once again, she is the brilliant midwife and advocate who never stops striving for something better. My Tuscan cousin, Edda Pollestrini Tosi inspired love of heritage and the land. The extraordinary Judy Graham made this book possible because of her gift of friendship, administrative genius, taste and humor. Friend and partner, Sally Swift, producer of "The Splendid Table" radio show, took on endless extra work so I could do this project. The incisive, unflappable Lois Lee generously tested recipes and worked through tomato frenzies as did the gifted Hallie Harron. Without Beth Dooley's craft and round-the-clock help in getting words down, no deadline would have been met. Jane Dystel is still the paragon of agents in my book. Annateresa Callen is again my Italian fairy godmother, turning my unique Italian grammar into language. Jane Calabria McPeak ferried Italian products over the ocean and did so much more. Nancy Radke helped with Parmigiano-Reggiano and a lot more. Loving thanks to my Tuscan family—Edda, Alcide, Francesca, Antonella, Claudio, Mimmo, Lahlia and Franco. They taught me so much and sent me down so many paths.

In Italy I never want to be without the insight and firsthand agricultural experience of friends Paola Bini of Villa Gaidello and Mario Zannoni of the Consorzio del Formaggio Parmigiano-Reggiano. At Scribner and Simon and Schuster I've had the support and benefited from the talents of publisher Susan Moldow, associate publisher Roz Lippel, publicity director Beth Wareham, publicist Mary Ellen Briggs, art director John Fontana, text compositor Paul Dippolito, copyeditor Judith Sutton and Matt Thornton. Stephanie Tevonian once again designed a book like no other. Photographer Dana Gallagher and stylists Anne Disrude and Betty Alfenito made the pictures I'd been dreaming of come to life.

Thank you Oldways Preservation & Exchange Trust, especially to Sara Baer-Sinnott and Dun Gifford, a vital force in trying to keep artisan traditions and the land safe and making them viable for the future. Thanks, too, to Ann Woods and the Midwest Organic Alliance for helping me comprehend some of the scope of sustainable and organic agriculture. Buon Giorno market in St. Paul has been one of my sources and delights—thanks to all. The Dimmick Inn in Milford, Pennsylvania's staff always made Maria Guarnaschelli and me feel like we had a second home. Great appreciation goes to colleagues who shared their insights—Professor Corrado Barberis, Ed Behr, Fern Berman, Mark Bittman, Carol Field, Marcella Hazan, Nancy Harmon Jenkins, Corby Kummer, Anna Tasca Lanza, Paola Pettrini, Vincent Schiavelli, Nino Settepani, and Mary Taylor Simeti. Special thanks to Fred Plotkin and to Scribner's M. C. Hald who checked and rechecked for perfection.

This book is about Italy's country people—their foods and their stories. These people helped me, and if I have inadvertently omitted anyone, please blame it on lapses of memory, not of appreciation. In Lombardy, thanks to Emma and Gualberto Martini, Nicla and Sergio Zarattini, and to Riccardo Ricci-Curbastro who opened up Franciacorta and Brescia to me along with Gualberto Ricci Curbastro, the Cerveni family, Professor Maurizio Banzola, and Professor Alfredo Bonomi of Val Sabbia. At the Lombardy museum of agricultural history, thanks to Dr. Francesca Picani and Professor Gaetano Forni. In the Veneto Beppo Zoppelli opened doors to Treviso along with Signore Crespan, Piero Tedesco, Dino De Re, Pietro Cescin, Attilio Brino, and Orlandina Cadamuro. In Emilia-Romagna thanks to Rocco Bagnato, Leo Bertozzi and the Consorzio del Formaggio Parmigiano-Reggiano, Dr. Paolo Guidotti Bentivoglio, Signore Capelli, the ever generous, Marco Costanzini, and Professor Claudio Biancardi of the Consorzio dei Productori di Aceto Balsamico Tradizionale di Modena, Don Enso Donatini, Luciano Gentilini, Ettore Guatelli, the Lancellotti family, Gianni and Elio Lusignani, Hermes Malpighi, Giovanna Montevecche, Nano Morandi, Tarcisio Raccagni, Federico Roncasaglia, Ghetti Rondinin, Loris Silingardi and Gianna Spezia. In Marche and Umbria thanks to Giulio Mancini, Claudio Gianbenedetti, Gino Girolomoni and Leonella Lucarini.

In Puglia thanks to Rosalba and Armando Balestrazzi, La Bruna, Peppino Ceci, Concetta Cantoro, Elisabetta Del Monaco, Rina Durante, Enso at La Locanda, Donato Moschettini, Mimo Nadile, Dora and Angelo Ricci, the late Luigi Sada, and the Sozzo family. In Sicily my great appreciation to Rosario Acquaviva, Cattia Cannelle, Francesco Carbone, Luisa di Giovanni, Maria La Rocca, Dr. Mistretta, Giuseppe Modica, Alceste Moscati, Adelina Norcia and Giuseppe Pedone, Gaetano Pirrera, Roberto Puzzo, and Wanda and Giovanna Tornabene. In the Trentino Alto Adige my deep appreciation to Stefano Girelli who went out of his way to introduce me to Trento with Ince Antonucci (who, in turn, shared literature and insights), Mario Arnoldi, and Aldo Bertoluzza. Thanks also to Tiziana Gecchelin Fata, Maria Fedrizzi, Hans Griefsmair, the Goller family, and Martha and Richard Mulser. In Tuscany my gratitude goes to Gabriele Bertucci, Pietro Luigi Biagioni, Dina and Riccardo Boggi, Signore Frati, Lia Giambutti, the Rigoli family.

Thanks also to all the Italian country people I talked to everywhere, who answered my questions and shared their stories. Their names don't appear here, but their sense of life and values does.

INTRODUCTION

Every time I drive down country roads in Italy, I wonder what people are cooking in those farmhouses I pass, what their lives are like, what stories they have to tell. With this book, I set out to find the answers to those questions. I wanted to learn about the home cooking of Italians who live from the land. I wanted to know what country people eat every day when they come together around the table, and what they reminisce about when they talk of the cooking of their parents and grandparents.

For me, these are the elements that make Italian food Italian. It always begins on the land and in the home. That link to the land tied into my longtime interest in organic foods and sustainable agriculture. Were any Italian farmers in those houses talking about these issues? And how were the European Union's new food production laws affecting their lives?

Another part of this curiosity must come from my heritage. I am the granddaughter of Italian immigrants. My grandparents on both sides came to America from Italy at the beginning of the century. My mother's mother was a Tuscan sharecropper's daughter, who married an estate manager's son from a nearby village. I don't think I wanted to acknowledge it at the beginning of the adventures that became this book, but my fascination with the farm and country food wasn't just about finding what I believe is the soul of Italian cooking, it was also the beginning of exploring my own sense of home.

My penchant for spending a lot of time in small, remote areas of Italy shaped this book. In over twenty years of exploring, I still have not seen all of Italy. One friend joked that when I was writing about the Emilia-Romagna region in my first book, *The Splendid Table*, it took me six months just to get out of one country village—I kept discovering more to know. I love to linger in places where life changes slowly. So for this book, instead of, for instance, visiting all of Tuscany's farming areas, I couldn't pull myself away from the region's remote Garfagnana and Lunigiana mountains. Puglia, the region that is the heel of Italy's boot, captivated me for the same reasons. Most people still live from the land and the food always tastes homemade. To me, Puglia is the Tuscany of the South. It has the same kind of unadorned cooking that delivers an immediacy of taste. I dream longingly of Puglia tomatoes—maybe the best I've ever eaten.

Few Americans visit the Alto Adige, the region that sits right up against Austria's border, but border food is fascinating and farm life there is governed by different laws than the rest of Italy—I had to go. And I had to stay in a single village and thoroughly explore its valley and surrounding mountains. There was so much to learn. So this book tells about country life in the places I couldn't leave.

Country life museums all over Italy became one of my doorways into understanding something of how people lived from the land in each area I visited. In the Alto Adige, I found Italy's only outdoor farming museum—a whole village of antique farm buildings brought from all over the region and spanning several hundred years. The museum's director is Hans Griefsmair, a professor and historian who understands country life from firsthand experience. He was raised in the mountains, the son of a local cowherd. One farmhouse he showed me was so welcoming I felt as though I could move right into the kitchen and start cooking. Even the butter churn next to the hearth was alluring, with its decorative carvings. When I told Professor Griefsmair it tempted me to try churning butter, he started reminiscing about how even when food was scarce, his family always had a mound of butter in the middle of the table. I realized that while he was eating butter to survive, in other parts of Italy it was pure luxury.

I told him how I constantly heard people waxing poetic over life in the cowherds' huts you find all over the region in the high mountains. He explained how cowherds were and still are entrusted with an entire village's cows. They herd them up to high pastures for a whole summer of grazing and cheese and butter making.

Italian country life museums can be deeply personal places. Nearly nine hundred miles south of Griefsmair's world, in Sicily, I found the remnants of a museum where a man who was a poet and schoolteacher attempted to touch the sense of home he believed we all share in common. As Antonino Uccello created his farmhouse museum in the country town of Palazzolo Acreide where he was raised, he tried to make tangible his belief that we all long for the innocence, imagined or real, of the past and have a common sense of home. He believed the farmhouse was the key, with its link to the land and universal rhythms of life, death and rebirth. This was not your typical museum. He called it La Casa Museo, the museum of home.

Uccello died in 1979. I never met him—only read about him and heard his story from his admirers. I did visit what's left of Casa Museo, now run by the government. Governments don't search for the kinds of things poets do. If Uccello were alive, he'd probably have been a touchstone for me. But another man filled that place. He lives in a farmhouse in the hills outside the northern Italian city of Parma. His name is Ettore Guatelli. He brought home to me the resourcefulness and ingenuity I found in most country people.

Ettore Guatelli's in his mid-seventies. He's small and sturdily built, wears thick glasses and looks stern when you first meet him. He lives with his two brothers and their families on a rambling hill farm. They all grew up there as the children of a sharecropper. The big house where the landowner lived is across the barnyard.

Thirty years ago, Guatelli bought a pair of pliers his neighbors were getting rid of and from them he built a museum scholars consider a unique study of northern Italian folklife. Without coyness, he just calls it his collection. There is no sign on the buildings about the museum. Carved into the rough wooden door to his house is something to the effect of "Guatelli lives here. If you want him, ring the bell." I rang the bell. It took time, but after a while Guatelli started to tell his story.

After the pliers, he bought more tools and kitchen implements at local farm sales. He said he saw farm people getting rid of objects that revealed how they'd lived. I saw a homemade toy car fashioned from used shoe polish tins and tomato cans.

A toy speedster from Museo Guatelli.

Guatelli held up a pair of shoes repaired again and again. With their soles and top held together with nails, tacks and cord, they were sculpture to my eyes, but they must have been so painful to wear. I held in my arms a copper polenta pot that had been patched with scraps of metal and rivets through two generations of cooking.

In the 1960s, a series of new laws changed the sharecropping system in Italy. Instead of working for a landowner, sharecroppers were encouraged to either buy their land, which some, like Guatelli and his siblings, did, or hire themselves out to the industrial food producers who were buying up acreage from landowning families.

Either way, in Guatelli's part of Italy, the hill country of Parma province in the Emilia-Romagna region, many country people wanted to throw away reminders of the past. Living from the land wasn't

Homemade, repaired shoe from Museo Guatelli.

easy. As Guatelli talked, I was reminded of my friend Paola Bini, whom I met while researching my previous book, *The Splendid Table*. Paola's farm, Villa Gaidello, is about a two-hour drive south of Guatelli's. When Paola inherited her grandmother's farm over twenty years ago and wanted to open a part-time restaurant where the local farmwomen would cook their traditional foods, she discovered the women found more status in working in the village equivalent of a five-and-ten than in making the phenomenal handmade pasta the region is famous for. The only way she could convince them was to pay very high salaries. Finally, when they saw people driving from faraway cities like Milan to eat at Gaidello and raving about the food, they began to appreciate the value of their own heritage. Paola said they had been ashamed of their cooking—it was what peasants did, not people who were affluent and secure.

Guatelli told me the same thing. Some of his neighbors couldn't wait to leave the land. They wanted to live in new, shiny, sterile apartments in town and to work as mechanics at the local garage, or become shopkeepers. Who could blame them? Farming is hard work with no set hours other than the rhythm of the seasons and weather. As Guatelli's collection of the objects of local country life grew, he said, he realized it was turning into a tribute to his people and to how they found solutions to dilemmas and needs by using their hands and their minds. Many of them left the farm eagerly, but Guatelli's collection, which now is crowded into a huge barn and almost his entire house, documents their incredible ingenuity—and their determination to survive, even prosper.

His objects seem to be bursting to tell their stories, maybe because once you break through his reserve, that's the way Guatelli is. He led me into what he calls the kitchen room, where he'd gathered all sorts of kitchen objects. There are cupboards made of hollowed-out tree trunks with shelves hammered into their interiors, and improvised bread ovens a lot like the clay cloches sold in our kitchen shops for baking bread.

He took me over to a collection of homemade cutting boards he'd arranged leaning against a white-washed wall. They were of thick pieces of hardwood cut from local oak trees. They reminded me of the ones I'd seen at my friends' farm in Lombardy. He said in these hills, people always claimed that when a cutting board was worn through, deeply grooved by the rocking motion of the half-moon knife, it was time to marry off your oldest daughter. According to Guatelli, it took about twenty years to wear out a cutting board—just the right age for a firstborn daughter to find a husband. He lifted

a small object from its hanger on the wall and showed me how old coins no longer honored by the government were turned into pasta cutters. Farmers notched them so they'd cut in a zigzag pattern, pierced their centers and secured the coins to hand-carved wooden handles.

The same ingenuity I saw in the tools and toys is at the heart of the food of every good country cook I've ever met. Whatever the land gives, the ingenious cook turns into good eating. Rosalba Ciannamea is this kind of cook—but very different from the farm-

Pasta cutters from Museo Guatelli.

15

women at Villa Gaidello and Guatelli's neighbors in northern Italy. Born and raised in southern Italy's Puglia region, she comes to the kitchen and the land as a student of her own heritage. She is a city woman turned landowner who learns from the farmers working for her and studies the old scrapbooks of her olive estate's turn-of-the-century mistress.

This is one aspect of understanding Italy that, as an American, I find difficult to express. The past is always present in Italy. Italians might revere it, rail against it or just accept it, but the past is always there. People seem to have a oneness with what has come before. The dishes I've eaten time after time at the tables of farmers and country cooks are always linked to heritage. They might be inventive, but they always taste of the place where I'm sitting at the moment.

In the Naples countryside, farmwomen make a casserole of mashed potatoes mixed with salami and peas. Thick slices of mozzarella are buried in its center. Neapolitans love mozzarella. They have some of the best in Italy and it goes on everything—pizza, potatoes, meats, pasta and anything with tomatoes. Far to the north in the Italian Alps, a cowherd's wife explained how she cooks her potatoes in buttermilk and finishes them with tablespoons of browned butter. Why buttermilk? I wondered. Why not? She has quarts of it every day, left over from churning the butter she sells to a local shop. Will the cowherd's wife ever put mozzarella on her potatoes? Probably not. She has no connection to it. It is not part of her world.

This sense of intrinsic "rightness" and the feeling of being connected to what has come before may be what naturally evolves for a people who are irrevocably connected to the land. Land is at the heart of all things Italian. City people almost always seek out a farmer or wine maker they will go to each year for their annual stocking up of wine, salami, hams and sausages. No patch of land behind a city apartment building or private home is ever without some kind of food growing. Everyone farms, even if it's a short row of tomato plants and a few heads of salad greens. The holiday in the country (*soggiorno in campagna*) used to be an institution. In high summer, city families would go to stay on a farm—often a relative's farm, or that of a farmer they knew who rented out rooms. The guest farm is going through a renaissance. Recently the Italian government encouraged the guest farm by offering tax breaks to farmers who create accommodations for visitors. Staying on guest farms was another doorway for me into Italian country life, and it can be yours too. The farmers are usually wonderfully welcoming.

But why Italians' deep connection to the farm? My own theory is that by the time the Industrial Revolution came along in the mid-nineteenth century, Italy had been an agricultural society for about four thousand years. Industry and modern technology are merely the newest wrinkle. Food is the land; it is what the land gives. No wonder "new and improved" rarely succeeds as a food marketing strategy in Italy.

Three Italian expressions brought home to me the commonality I kept feeling among all the country people I met, even though they were so very different from one another. If there are keys to understanding Italy and maybe to what constantly draws so many of us Americans to things Italian, I think they are in this trio of expressions.

"Nostrano," "campanilismo," and "si sposa." Walk through any Italian market and see the produce and the cheeses, the seafood and the dried beans, the new chestnuts and even the sides of lamb with the occasional label "nostrano." Compliment your host at an Italian dinner party on a wonderful dish and hear "nostrano" somewhere in the response. Nostrano literally translates as "local," but it comes from nostro, meaning "ours." When we refer to "local" produce, we essentially mean geography. When an Italian says nostrano, she means from her own part of Italy. The green beans from a farm outside town are nostrano. Local is geography; nostrano is an embrace. Nostrano lays claim to food, saying this is from our land, from our place in the world. Italians are certain the very best foods are theirs, grown from their land, by people in their part of Italy. Nowhere else can equal that. And nowhere else does anything taste quite the same. One secret to know: Food is all about microclimates, changing from place to place—which is why traditional, handmade and local are everything to quality in Italy. The culinary artisan is master, and the cheese is never the same from one side of the hill to the other.

Nostrano helped me to begin to understand campanilismo. The campanile is the bell tower of the church at the center of every Italian village. Within the sound of those bells is the land, home, family and the only people to truly be trusted. The food of this place is as much a part of an Italian's personal identity as family name and individual personality. This is where the eternal mamma cooks, even if her skills are more affectionate imagination than reality. In *nostrano* and *campanilismo* are two keys to Italy's deep regionalism.

Si sposa means "it marries" and is always used in talking about food. This is how a friend in Milan, where Risotto alla Milanese is almost a religion, explained *si sposa* to me: Imagine you are dining in a home in the Milanese countryside. Go to sprinkle a Sicilian sheep cheese over a plate of Risotto alla Milanese and watch your hostess bite back an expletive. Politely she will explain, *"Non si sposa* (it doesn't marry)." These foods come from two entirely different worlds and mentalities—one the northern city of Milan, with its northern European culture; the other from Sicily, an island ninety miles from the coast of Africa with almost as much Arab, Greek and pure Mediterranean influences as Italian ones. One place is hot, the other cold. She could go on. Notice she's not gotten to how they might taste together. She is focusing on why they don't and never will marry. That they will not taste right in the same dish is a foregone conclusion.

We come full circle back to *nostrano, campanilismo* and the notion of what grows together goes together—spiritually and in taste. Even with the expression "go together," perhaps we lose the wonderful intimacy of foods and traditions "marrying." It is for this reason that I think we are so drawn to the Italian table. Without knowing any of this, the direct simplicity of Italy's foods connects us to it all. This brings me back to Ettore Guatelli, whose tribute to his people in his collection of country objects is all about that profound connection Italians feel to the land, family and the will to flourish. As those objects speak to Guatelli, so I believe Italian food speaks to us in a way we can all understand. Somehow Italian food speaks to us of home.

PROLOGUE

The Grape Harvest

It is 1993 and I have begun researching this book by spending the month of October on my cousin's farm in Tuscany, outside the town of Lucca. It is the end of the day of the grape harvest.

The fragrance of just-crushed grapes is seeping through the floor boards, rising from the wine vats in the barn below. At long tables crowded with food, seventy of us are feasting in the hayloft. Every person in this room has participated in this ancient ritual of bringing in the grapes.

From America, we, the children and grandchildren of immigrants from these hills, have returned to be with the children of those who stayed behind—cousins Edda and Alcide. As every year, their friends have gathered to help, traveling from as far away as England and Denmark and as near as the next farm and village. Together we are drinking the wine of last year's harvest as the new wine is starting to ferment beneath us.

Four generations have been working in Edda's farm kitchen to prepare the harvest feast. Since yesterday, plied with strong coffee and biscotti, we family women have been cooking for the harvest party—chopping vegetables and herbs, pounding beef cutlets and rolling pastry. Edda's mother, Amelia, two years shy of one hundred, nods from her chair. Edda's daughter, Antonella, and I share the big cutting board, while Antonella's toddler, Michèle, tries stuffing tiny fistfuls of bread into his mouth, missing half the time. Family is everything to Edda. She is the daughter of my grandmother's brother, and more sister than cousin to my mother since they first met as girls in 1928. That my mother and I have returned along with our husbands means to her that we are all finally together in our rightful home.

Our general is Francesca, Edda's older cousin. Though she adores Edda, Francesca will tell you, shaking her head, that Edda is hopeless in the kitchen. Edda laughs—this is an old story between them. Francesca is the family's legendary cook. "She couldn't cook bad food if she tried," says Edda.

Planted between her two sauté pans, Francesca is frying off mounds of beef cutlets, tossing jokes and gossip at her crew while directing us in our chores. She is cooking in a pressed apron and pearls. "So what would you serve, *la giornalista*, Miss Professional Cook?" Francesca teases me, "What would you make?" Probably a simple buffet, light and casual, I explain. She stiffens. "Lynne, I don't mean to hurt your feelings, but that is barbaric!" She throws out her arms, embracing me, the kitchen, the vineyard, the world at large. "Lynne. From America, from England they come. Our neighbors give up a Sunday; everyone is here to bring in our grapes. A buffet! I would dishonor myself, and Edda and Alcide—disgrace for the family."

Early that morning, Edda had taken me to the Vendémmia (grape harvest) mass. I knelt in the church where my grandmother, Enrichetta Pollestrini, knelt every Sunday until, at nineteen, she left Italy for America to marry my grandfather. Outside the church, the world she came from is all contained within the arc of the crescent-shaped ridge and the valley below. The church looks out from one end of the ridge. Across the valley at the opposite end is the sharecropper's house where Enrichetta, Edda's father and six generations of our family were born. The bread oven where my grandmother baked each week with her mother and sisters still stands next to the house. Bread bakes there still, made by old friends of Edda's, now the house's owners. On the slopes of the little valley between the two ends of the ridge's arc are the olive trees and vineyards my family worked. Crowning the center of the crescent's curve is the walled estate of the landowner who dominated their lives.

In the 1920s, Edda's father, Clementino, emigrated from the ridge to America. For him, the streets were truly paved with gold. He returned to the ridge wealthy and eager to claim his betrothed, and take her back to California. She refused to go: "I cannot leave my church. I cannot leave the hills." It was a refrain I would hear again and again as I traveled in rural Italy, talking with country people. For some it was prefaced with, "I will not leave my mother. I will not leave my village." Always home, family and the land kept them there.

So Clementino stayed, buying the farm over the ridge from where he was born. This son of a sharecropper became a landowner with sharecroppers of his own. He never saw California again; he is buried next to the church. After visiting his grave, Edda and I took the ridge road back home.

In grape harvesting, water and wine do not mix. Rain threatens. Everyone works fast, breaking away grape clusters with anything that cuts—serrated blades of cheap kitchen knives, proper clippers, old scissors. No one stops. Children run snacks of cheese and bread out to the vineyard. My stepfather, son of a farmer from Piacenza and a retired New York businessman, roams the vineyard, a bottle of grappa tucked under one arm, a bottle of water under the other, offering pickers refreshment from the glasses he clenches in his fists.

Back in the kitchen, we are staggering. "We need air!" proclaims Francesca, leading us behind the house to where vegetables and herbs grow beneath the oldest vines, planted there by Clementino himself. Edda calls it the "women's vineyard." The family women have always harvested these grapes alone, perhaps because of their proximity to the kitchen. We begin twisting clusters from the vines. Jokes start. Francesca hums, goes into singing a bawdy song. Her niece and Edda's daughter, Antonella, winks as she starts singing. Sweet cousin Lahlia tries to scowl and look embarrassed. Edda finally leads us back to the kitchen for more coffee and cooking.

The grapes are in. Teenagers are relaying food through the garden and out to the barn's hayloft that Edda converted into a room for celebrations. Wet harvesters clamber up the hayloft stairs, shaking out slickers. A fire blazes on the wide corner hearth. Across the room, the pizza oven is stoked with wood, keeping pastas and meats hot. The ceiling's beams are thick tree trunks, the walls rough plaster. Wide floorboards slope a little east and a little west. Patiently, we bow our heads during the priest's blessing. Then pitchers of wine are being emptied into tumblers. Everyone is passing platters and huge bowls brimming with course after course of antipasti, pasta, beef cutlets, roast chickens, vegetables, salads, tarts, cookies and cakes. The harvest is in. We are together. All of us, friends and relatives, are family on this night. We are all home.

Prologue

My cousin, Edda Pollestrini, bringing in grapes from the women's vineyard.

ANTIPASTI/ LIGHT MEALS

 find it fascinating that many Italians and Americans who are trying to eat a healthier diet are looking back to the way peasants ate in Italy a century ago, while at that time those peasants yearned for the very foods we are turning away from. La Cucina Povera, Poor People's Cooking, is the all-encompassing term for the food that most of the grandparents of today's country Italians lived on. Out of necessity, they ate what the seasons brought them. La Cucina Povera's dishes have us eating lower on the food chain—vegetables, grains and legumes, with meat perhaps as a seasoning, but rarely as the main ingredient.

In America, much of what we find on antipasto tables in Italian restaurants and in the antipasto section of Italian cookbooks comes from La Cucina Povera. The supper of farmers in Italy's countryside is often made up of dishes we think of as antipasti. A bowl of beans left over from yesterday's minestrone is dressed with onion, vinegar, olive oil and a few shreds of home-cured salami for the evening meal. Bruschetta was and is supper in country kitchens—bread toasted over the fire, rubbed with garlic, drenched in olive oil and topped with what's at hand—tomatoes or greens, maybe cheese or prosciutto. But this is not careless food, thrown together for a meal. Good country cooks think out these dishes with all the care they bring to Sunday dinner. These meals are generous in tastes and satisfaction.

Home cooks serve antipasti at the beginning of important meals like Sunday dinners, homecomings, weddings and birthdays. Sometimes it's a single antipasto—Mushrooms Stuffed with Radicchio and Asiago or Roasted Roman Artichokes. Sometimes antipasti arrive in clusters, like a bouquet. Pugliese country cooks are past masters of this style. They set out a mosaic of light dishes, among them, roasted tomatoes, stuffed peppers, mozzarella bundles and potato and arugula salad.

Antipasti open simple meals too, when a small taste of something just feels right. I've sat at supper in Lombardy with cheese makers Emma and Gualberto Martini and watched Gualberto lift his energy after a long day with an antipasto of a few slices of salami before the one-dish main course of Emma's minestrone.

In my first book, *The Splendid Table,* I shared the foods of one of Italy's richest regions, Emilia-Romagna, with its lush cooking that's evolved from a heritage of court food and an abundant farmland. There the antipasto was a course that opened a meal. In this book an antipasto can be the meal. Coincidentally, it was in Emilia-Romagna that I first heard of La Cucina Povera and became curious about it. I didn't know it then, but the poor people's kitchen was a doorway for me into this world of living from the land. Much of the food in this chapter comes from people who are poor in money but rich in good ingredients from their farms, and even richer in imagination and resourcefulness.

Take these recipes and make them into snacks, lunches and suppers. Most of us don't cook multicourse meals anymore, but the word *antipasto* shouldn't limit our pleasure. It certainly doesn't hold back Italy's country people. Grill

Portobello "Steaks" with Holy Oil, break into a loaf of whole-grain bread and make a salad. This is dinner. Nicla Zarattini, a country cook from the farmland south of Lake Garda, does the same thing with her sumptuous Warm Crushed Potatoes with Anchovies. She pointed out that the potatoes even reheat beautifully, so you can do them ahead. Dishes like Shepherd's Salad, with its hot dressing, wilted greens, bits of cheese and plump beans, have been supper for sheepherders all over Italy. Why not for us too? Cycles never end—the seasons turn, and what was old is new again.

SIGNORA BIMBI'S PEPPERS
I Peperoni della Signora Bimbi

Serves 3 to 4; doubles easily

Yellow and red, sweet and juicy, these wedges of roasted peppers are covered with garlic-toasted bread crumbs and leaves of fresh herbs. You can serve them right away, or let the peppers wait at room temperature for about an hour, making them a fine dish for entertaining. The recipe comes from the turn of the century, proving how timeless good food can be. I discovered it in the old scrapbook of a Signora Bimbi, who back then was the mistress of Il Frantoio, an olive estate deep in the Puglia countryside, where I stayed.

Wine Suggestion: A fresh, fruity rosé from Puglia or California

2 *each* large sweet yellow and red
   peppers
8 herbed or oil-cured black olives,
   pitted and chopped
1 tablespoon red wine vinegar
Salt and freshly ground black pepper

1 1/2 teaspoons extra-virgin olive oil
1 small clove garlic, minced
3 tablespoons fresh bread crumbs
1 tightly packed teaspoon *each* fresh
   Italian parsley and basil leaves,
   chopped

1. Using a wood fire, gas flame, grill, or broiler, roast the peppers, turning them so they blister on all sides. Place the peppers in a paper bag and let rest about 30 minutes.

2. Slip off the skin from the peppers, remove the cores, and scoop away their seeds. Cut the peppers into wedges about 3 inches long and 1 1/2 inches at their widest. Toss with the olives and vinegar, adding salt and pepper to taste. Cover and hold at room temperature for several hours.

3. In a small skillet, heat the oil over medium heat. Add the garlic, bread crumbs, and a little salt and pepper. Stirring constantly, toast the crumbs to golden, about 3 minutes. Immediately turn into a bowl. At this point, you can hold the peppers and crumbs separately for several hours. Don't combine them until just before serving, so the bread crumbs are crisp.

4. To serve, arrange the peppers on a platter. Sprinkle with the bread crumbs and herbs and set out for dining.

OVEN-CANDIED SUMMER TOMATOES

Pomodori al Forno

Makes 16 to 32 pieces, serving 4 to 8

My friend Lois Lee claims having these tomatoes on hand is like having money in the bank. I often use them when sun-dried tomatoes are called for, because they are juicier and more luscious. Pieces of ripe summer tomatoes are slow-roasted with olive oil until their edges have a lacy golden crust and the tomatoes taste like candy. They are heavenly on pasta.

The idea for these tomatoes came from Sicilian writer Corrado Sofia, who in his memoir recalls how the women on his father's farm used to make them in the leftover heat of the bread oven after the loaves came out. That is why in this recipe you keep turning the oven down as the tomatoes bake, to re-create the effects of a gradually cooling bread oven.

➤ *Cook to Cook:* Use *only* ripe, delicious summer tomatoes (see Oven-Roasted Canned Tomatoes, p. 29, for out-of-season roasting). Be sure to "ripen" the roasted tomatoes at room temperature for 4 to 6 hours before eating. Store them covered in the refrigerator up to 6 days. They freeze beautifully for 3 months—and sometimes taste even better for it.

2 to 2½ pounds delicious ripe medium-sized tomatoes (not plum tomatoes, unless they are extremely flavorful)

1 cup robust extra-virgin olive oil
Salt

1. Preheat the oven to 400°F. Core the tomatoes and halve vertically. Do not seed. Leave small tomatoes in halves; cut slightly larger tomatoes into 4 wedges, medium ones into 6, and large into 8. In a half-sheet pan, or two 2½-quart shallow metal baking pans (not glass or enameled metal), arrange the tomato wedges cut side up, about ½ to 1 inch apart. Coat the tomatoes with the oil. Sprinkle with salt.

2. Bake 30 minutes, then lower the heat to 350°F and bake another 30 minutes. Turn the heat down to 300°F and bake 30 more minutes, or until the edges are slightly darkened. If the edges are not yet colored, turn the heat down to 250°F and bake another 10 to 15 minutes. Remove the tomatoes from the oven. Cool 20 minutes. Transfer them to a shallow glass or china dish and pour their oil over them. Let mellow, uncovered, at room temperature 4 to 6 hours.

3. Layer the tomatoes in a storage container, pouring in their oil, and refrigerate. Or freeze the tomatoes in their oil in sealed plastic containers up to 3 months.

4. Serve at room temperature.

THE WOMEN AND THE BREAD OVEN

In Tuscany, outside the walled town of Lucca, is the farm of my cousin Edda. Now in her early seventies, she recalls the big bread oven that stood in the farmyard between her house and the row houses where the sharecroppers lived. From the 1920s until the early '60s, they farmed her father's land for him. She and the sharecroppers' wives all shared the one oven on the property. None of them had ovens in their homes.

Edda says it was like living in a small town with a single village oven. Every Saturday, she and the wives gathered in the farmyard for the bread baking. The night before they would have all kneaded bread until very late—a week's worth of bread, as many as fifteen big loaves. They carried the risen breads out to the oven on long boards. Edda remembered how they all laughed and gossiped. "We swapped recipes. We minded each other's children. We talked about our men.

"After we pulled the loaves out of the oven, we slipped in the other dishes we'd made. The oven stayed hot for hours, so we used the heat to roast and bake the dishes we loved but could only make once a week—tarts, roasted vegetables, baked polenta. One woman put in a chicken with black olives, tomatoes and peppers that I could never quite duplicate. My mother always gave me a pan of pears in wine to put into the oven. My father loved that dish."

Wherever I went in Italy, I heard the same stories. Women cooked in bread ovens the same way from Sicily to way up north in the Alto Adige. When it was a communal oven like Edda's, the oven was where women came together each week. Several told me they didn't miss the work, but they did miss the gatherings.

Edda's bread oven is gone now. It came down in the early 1970s, when they modernized the farm. A swing for Edda's grandchildren stands where the oven was. The sharecroppers are long gone too, their row houses now rented out as apartments. Edda and her neighbors buy bread at the store. Everyone has an oven in the kitchen. Edda loves her central heating, her freezer and new gas stove. When I get her talking about when she was a young woman, she always says more or less the same thing: "You can't imagine the difference from back then to today. Lives were hard for us in ways that don't exist anymore. But we don't laugh the way we used to, and people don't sing anymore when they work in the fields."

Every time I stay with Edda, I walk past the swings on the way from my apartment in the old row houses to her house. I know how hard life was in the days of the bread oven. The deprivation for many was heartwrenching. Yet almost always, as I walk past the swing, there's a moment when I think I can still hear the laughter and smell the bread.

OVEN-ROASTED CANNED TOMATOES

Pelati al Forno

Makes 16 to 32 pieces, serving 4 to 8

Amazing things happen to canned tomatoes when you roast them with olive oil, garlic and herbs. Imagine little scarlet medallions of tomato flecked with herbs, tasting almost brazenly meaty and sweet. Make these tomatoes when fresh ones are out of season. No fresh Roma tomato can touch them. Eat the roasted tomatoes on their own, on bread and bruschetta, with salads, beans, polenta and risotto, or toss them with pasta (see Broken Bridegrooms with Roasted Tomatoes, page 139).

➤ *Cook to Cook:* Surprisingly, I've found certain domestic canned tomatoes taste richer than most Italian imports. Yes, the San Marzano tomato is legendary, but it's nearly impossible to find any good-tasting ones in a can in America. Trust me, it's true. I use whole peeled tomatoes (not necessarily plum types) from the organic producer Muir Glen, or Hunt's, Contadina or Red Pack (take care not to get their tomatoes packed in puree; you want only tomato juice).

2 28-ounce cans peeled whole tomatoes, drained, halved, and seeded (preferably Muir Glen, Hunt's, Contadina, or Red Pack)
1/2 to 2/3 cup extra-virgin olive oil
14 large fresh basil leaves, torn

2 4-inch branches fresh rosemary
1/2 medium red onion, cut into 1/4-inch dice
5 large cloves garlic, coarsely chopped
Salt and freshly ground black pepper

1. Preheat the oven to 300°F. Spread out the tomatoes in a large shallow pan (a half-sheet pan is ideal) and sprinkle with the other ingredients, turning to coat them with oil. Bake 2 1/4 to 2 1/2 hours, basting and turning the tomatoes several times. They're done when their color deepens to dark scarlet and they taste mellow and very rich. Don't let them brown, nor allow the garlic to brown—it'll turn bitter.

2. Transfer the tomatoes and their oil to a glass or china bowl. Let them mellow at room temperature up to 6 hours. The flavors will ripen in this time.

3. Refrigerate the tomatoes up to 4 days, or freeze up to 3 months. Serve the tomatoes at room temperature, or tossed with hot pasta.

Antipasti / Light Meals

TUSCAN WHITE BEANS WITH RED ONION AND SALAMI

Fagioli Toscani con Cipole Rosse e Salame

Serves 6 to 8

The local pizzeria in the wine town of Castellina in Chianti always has this salad on its antipasto table. It's a Tuscan favorite. The cook simmers the beans the way Tuscans love them—with handfuls of sage. He dresses them with garlic, homemade vinegar, olive oil from local farmers, onion and salami. Chianti makers who eat here all the time arrive early for the help-yourself, all-you-can-eat antipasto spread, because when the beans are gone, they're not offered again that day. The trick to cutting back on oil in this dish is to dress the beans while they're warm with vinegar, garlic, salt and pepper so they absorb all their flavors. Later, right before serving, finish the salad with a little Tuscan oil.

➤ **Cook to Cook:** These big white dried beans resemble oversized lima beans. They're called *corona, bianco di Spagna* or *bianco grande* in Italian, and *soisson* in French. Find them in Italian or specialty food stores. Do not substitute Greek gigante; they taste grassy instead of meaty. An American organic pinto bean makes an excellent replacement.

Cacciatora ("hunter's") salami are small dried sausages easily carried around the neck of farmers when they go hunting. If unavailable, use about 2$^1/_2$ ounces of a good-quality salami made without hot pepper. Taste before buying if possible.

**Wine Suggestion: A young light-bodied Chianti like Santa Cristina
or Ceregio Sangiovese di Romagna**

1 pound dried large white beans (see Cook to Cook for types) or organic pinto beans	About $^1/_2$ cup white or red wine vinegar
Water	Salt and freshly ground black pepper
4 large cloves garlic, crushed, plus 1 large clove garlic, minced	$^1/_2$ medium red onion, cut into thin slivers
$^1/_2$ tightly packed cup fresh sage leaves	$^1/_2$ cacciatora salami (2.5 ounces), cut into thin sticks
	Robust extra-virgin olive oil

1. Rinse the beans, turn them into a medium bowl, and cover with very hot tap water. Soak for 1 hour.

2. Drain the beans and place in a 4-quart saucepan. Add fresh water to cover by 2 inches, the crushed garlic, and the sage. Cook until the beans are tender but not falling apart—45 minutes to over an hour, depending upon the beans' freshness.

3. Drain and toss the hot beans with ½ cup vinegar and the minced garlic, seasoning to taste with salt and pepper. Cool, then fold in the onion and salami and taste to see if the beans need more salt or pepper. Do not refrigerate unless holding them for more than 6 hours.

4. Just before serving, sprinkle the beans with a few spoonfuls of olive oil. Taste for more vinegar, seasonings, and oil. Serve at room temperature.

VARIATIONS

White Bean Puree for Bruschetta (page 34) or raw vegetables: Puree leftover bean salad with a little extra-virgin olive oil and water to a thick, creamy consistency. For each cup of bean salad, use about 2 teaspoons olive oil and 2 tablespoons warm water. Season to taste and serve at room temperature.

Tuscan Bean Salad with Tuna: Another classic. Shortly before serving, add to the salad a 6- to 7-ounce can of tuna fish packed in olive oil, drained. Olive oil-packed tuna is found in specialty food stores, some supermarkets, and Italian groceries.

A New Way of Measuring Fresh Herbs

Instead of approximating the amount of fresh herb leaves needed for a measurement in a recipe—and ending up with too much or too little—use this method:

Tightly pack herb leaves into the required tablespoon, cup, etc., until they're level with the rim. Then wash, dry, and chop the leaves. You'll have an accurate measure.

RICH MAN'S ANTIPASTO
Antipasto dei Ricchi

Serves 8 to 12; doubles and halves easily

If you want to taste two of Italy's most extraordinary creations in a way you'll not easily forget, drizzle a little artisan-made balsamic vinegar over small chunks of an excellent Parmigiano-Reggiano cheese. Serve the cheese with drinks or as a savory finale to a special dinner. For my taste, nothing, not even caviar, marks an event as magnificently. Here's a resounding example of foods from the same area being meant for each other—what Italians call "*si sposa,*" or "it marries."

Only one area of the world has the combination of microclimates and the mentality of ingenuity and genius to produce these foods—the neighboring provinces of Modena and Reggio in northern Italy's Emilia-Romagna region. Families there have made the cheese for seven centuries and the vinegar for over a millennium. For celebrations or to impress someone important, they take a wedge of Parmigiano, break out bite-sized chunks, streak them with their precious aged, liqueur-like balsamico and pass them with drinks.

➤ *Cook to Cook:* Never buy Parmigiano-Reggiano without sampling it first. Taste for big, mouth-filling character, hints of cream, hay, roasted meat and flint and a lingering aftertaste that is pleasing. Saltiness, bitterness and sharpness are all flaws. For true artisan-made balsamic vinegar worthy of this dish, look for one of two designations on the label: Aceto Balsamico Tradizionale di Modena or Aceto Balsamico Tradizionale di Reggio-Emilia. (See pages 386 and 383 for more information on Parmigiano and balsamic.)

Wine Suggestion: A sparkling white from Franciacorta like Bellavista, Ca' del Bosco or Ricci Curbastro

A 2- to 4-pound wedge Parmigiano-Reggiano cheese, at room temperature

$^1/_4$ to $^1/_2$ cup artisan-made balsamic vinegar (see Cook to Cook)

1. Set the cheese on a serving platter. With a knife (stubby Parmigiano knives with almond-shaped blades are sold in kitchen shops), break out 1- to $1^1/_2$-inch chunks of cheese: Parmigiano-Reggiano is never actually cut; it is "opened," meaning

you dig your knife about an inch into the cheese, then use it like a wedge to release a chunk. This way you protect its uniquely rough texture, which is important to the way you taste the cheese. Pile the chunks on the cheese wedge, letting some cascade onto the plate. The cheese can be prepared up to 6 hours before serving. Cover with plastic wrap and keep at room temperature.

2. Just before serving, perhaps even in front of your guests, drizzle enough balsamic vinegar over the cheese to streak each chunk generously. Everyone eats this with their fingers. Do have napkins handy.

SICILIAN FARMER'S BRUSCHETTA

Bruschetta del Contadino Siciliano

Serves 6 to 8

Toasted slices of rough country bread rubbed with garlic and moistened with olive oil have captivated all of us here in America. We love the way we can add whatever toppings we like, and how good the combination of bread, garlic and oil tastes on its own. In Rome, Lazio, the Abruzzo and southern Italy, this garlic bread is called *bruschetta* (from *bruciare*, to burn or toast). In Tuscany and Umbria, they call it *fett'unta* (from *fetta*, meaning slice, and *unta*, meaning anointed).

Sicilian farmers turn slices of bruschetta into a meal by topping them with oregano, hot pepper, cheese, onion and tomatoes. When I serve these with a salad, I like to use a sweet and creamy-tasting fresh cheese like a sheep's or cow's milk ricotta to contrast with the salad dressing's vinegar. Otherwise, I top the bread with thin slivers of medium-aged sheep cheese.

➤ *Cook to Cook:* Use a rustic loaf, chewy and full of whole grains, made without sweetening. Medium-aged sheep cheeses you can find in the U.S. are Fiore Sardo, Pecorino di Pienza, Pecorino di Castello or Pecorino Toscano or domestic sheep cheeses like Love Tree Farms or La Paysanne. For a fabulous fresh sheep's milk ricotta, look for Old Chatham Sheepherder's ricotta.

Wine Suggestion: Corvo Rosso from Sicily

8 ¹/₂-inch-thick slices chewy, crusty country bread

2 cloves garlic, split

About ¹/₂ cup robust extra-virgin olive oil

Several generous pinches of dried oregano

Salt

Pinch of hot red pepper flakes

¹/₂ pound Italian cheese—sheep's or cow's milk ricotta, mozzarella, fresh goat cheese, or medium-aged sheep cheese (see Cook to Cook)

¹/₂ medium red onion, thinly sliced into rings

About ¹/₂ cup mixed torn leaves fresh basil and Italian parsley (optional)

4 to 6 Oven-Roasted Canned Tomatoes (page 29), sun-dried tomatoes, or fresh tomatoes, chopped

1. Toast the bread over a wood fire, grill it on top of the stove, or toast it under the broiler. Rub it with garlic (for milder garlic flavor, rub it on the bread before toasting) and moisten lightly with the olive oil. Sprinkle each slice with a little oregano, salt, and red pepper flakes. You could cut each slice into 3 or 4 pieces.

2. Top each slice with a generous layer of cheese. Put several onion rings on the cheese. Sprinkle with a few torn herb leaves and pieces of tomato. Serve at room temperature.

OTHER BRUSCHETTA TOPPINGS

Put out several of these with a platter of toasted bread for a bruschetta buffet or course unto itself:

- Fresh arugula, dandelion, or other greens
- Sliced onions or scallions
- Sliced salami, prosciutto, or coppa
- Tomato Sauce (pages 122 to 128)
- Melting Tuscan Kale (page 277)
- Roasted Peppers and Greens from gemelli recipe (page 78)
- White Bean Puree (page 31)

BRUSCHETTA AND TASTING THE NEW OIL

Farm families harvest olives in the fall and winter, taking them to local mills for crushing into oil. There's almost always an open fire next to the mill to warm cold hands and to make bruschetta, thick slices of toasted bread. Making bruschetta is a ritual, part of tasting the new oil, and a favorite pick-me-up after a day of picking and hauling olives in the cold weather. As the fresh oil pours from the mill's spigot, usually the first thing farmers do is rub a little of the oil between their palms, warming it and inhaling its fragrance. Next they taste it from a spoon, sucking in air while the oil is in their mouths. This helps them discern the oil's individual flavor elements—its fruit, acidity, pepper, sweetness and other qualities.

Finally, they toast thick slices of bread, homemade or store-bought, over the flames, then soak the slices in the brand-new oil. No holding back here. There's no dainty brushing on the oil—they pour it over the bread. When you've tended olive trees for a year and are cold to the bone from picking olives all day, you want to eat your oil, not toy with it. Later, at home on their tables, farmers embellish bruschetta by rubbing it with garlic before pouring on the oil. They top it with what they like—slices of salami, tomato, onions, cheeses, peppers or salad greens.

Antipasti / Light Meals

GRILLED POLENTA "BRUSCHETTA"

Bruschetta di Polenta Grigliata

Serves 6 to 8

My hostess at a country party in the Veneto region served these. She playfully referred to them as bruschetta of the Po, telling me most people in the Veneto grew up eating more polenta than bread, so why not a bruschetta of polenta? I like the crust that forms on polenta when it's grilled. Leftover polenta also becomes a real asset in this recipe. You can keep the grilled slices warm in a low oven. Season them with a rub of garlic and some olive oil, and top with whatever you feel like eating—salad greens, tomato sauce, cheese, salami or raw vegetables. The polenta can be cut into 1-inch squares for serving with drinks.

Wine Suggestion: A simple fizzy white like Prosecco di Valdobbiadene

Polenta made with 1 cup cornmeal as described on page 172, cooled
Extra-virgin olive oil
Salt and freshly ground black pepper
2 large cloves garlic, split

SOME IDEAS FOR TOPPINGS (OPTIONAL)
Sliced tomatoes
Thinly sliced red onion
Cheeses
Fresh herbs

Salami, coppa, or prosciutto
Oven-Candied Summer Tomatoes (page 27) or Oven-Roasted Canned Tomatoes (page 29)
Roasted Vegetables (page 286)
Tomato Sauces (pages 122 to 128)
Salad Greens (pages 299 and 300)
Melting Tuscan Kale (page 277)
White Bean Puree (page 31)
Adriatic Grilled Shrimp (page 266)

1. Pack the polenta into a loaf pan or shape it into a log. Wrap and refrigerate until cold, or up to 3 days.

2. To grill, slice the polenta about ½ inch thick. Anticipate 1 slice per antipasto serving, 3 slices per supper serving. Lightly film a large sauté pan, griddle, or gridded skillet with olive oil. Heat it over medium-high heat. Grill the polenta slices about 2 minutes per side, or until browned and crusty. Season lightly with salt and pepper when you turn each slice.

3. Remove the slices to a serving platter and rub with the cut side of a garlic clove. Moisten each slice with ½ teaspoon to 1 teaspoon olive oil. Serve warm this way, or cover each slice with a topping.

▼ ▼ ▼ ▼ ▼ ▼ ▼ ▼ ▼ ▼ ▼

CANTALOUPE WITH BLACK PEPPER, OIL AND VINEGAR

Insalata di Melone

Serves 4 to 6

A melon salad is not a typical opening to a meal in Italy. I certainly didn't expect it when I stayed at Le Frise, a guest farm in the mountains of northern Lombardy. Gualberto Martini and his wife, Emma, make goat cheeses in the farmhouse, which is reached only by a dirt cow path cut into the nearly vertical mountainside. They prepare meals on weekends for diners and take in guests. Emma dresses chunks of melon with black pepper, vinegar and olive oil. She presents the melon on a bed of pale green curly endive and snips dark green chives over the salad at the last moment. Few things taste better with fresh goat cheese.

This is party food—lovely to look at, light and different. Eat it on its own, or with the Fresh Cheese Ovals with Herbs and Spices (page 40) Emma always serves with it. It's a new way to open special dinners in the summer and fall, and a natural for buffets. The two dishes are also an imaginative fruit and cheese lunch, or cheese course instead of dessert at a dinner party.

Wine Suggestion: A white Tocai Friulano, perhaps by Schiopetto

½ of a 2½- to 3-pound ripe
   cantaloupe, seeds removed
Several pale green leaves from the
   center of a head of curly endive
DRESSING
Salt and freshly ground black pepper
2 teaspoons fruity extra-virgin olive oil

2 teaspoons white wine vinegar
2 teaspoons snipped fresh chives or
scallion tops
2 thin slices soppressata, cut into thin
   strips (optional)

1. With a melon baller, scoop out 1-inch balls from the melon and turn into a medium bowl. Line an 8-inch white serving plate with the greens.

2. Sprinkle the melon with salt and pepper to taste. Gently toss with the oil, then the vinegar. Spoon onto greens, scatter the chives and optional salami over the melon, and serve.

WHAT IS A COUPLE LIKE YOU
DOING IN A PLACE LIKE THIS?

Some guests come to Le Frise goat farm just for dinner on weekends, others spend the night and hate to leave. I am one of the latter. The setting is tranquil, the scenery lovely. The farm lies about an hour east and north of Milan. It sits on a steep mountainside at the opening of the Camonica Valley (Val Camonica) near Italy's border with Switzerland. The old stone farmhouse seems to lean back against the mountain. Wildflowers are everywhere. The barn and garden are set on the small patch of level ground beyond the house. Encouraged by Italy's Agriturismo movement, Emma and Gualberto Martini bought and restored Le Frise in the late 1980s. Italians have always taken vacations on farms, but now the government agri-tourism movement makes taking in paying guests more profitable for the farmers by giving them tax breaks. Agritourism brings city people to the farm and allows the farmer to sell his products directly to the consumer, therefore sidestepping some of the European Union's new laws that are changing traditional food production and distribution systems.

Forty minutes and a world away from Le Frise's mountainside is the Lombardy plain, with its eight-lane highways, cities, factories and smog. At Le Frise, my morning begins with the sound of the clattering of small hooves across cobblestones. Gualberto is herding his goats past the farmhouse to the steep meadows where they graze all day. Gualberto and Emma make goat cheese rivaling that of France, which they sell to fancy restaurants and shops in the Lombardy and Veneto regions.

The Martinis' farmer neighbors wonder why a well-educated middle-class couple chose to raise goats. Emma's an art restorer. She grew up in the village at the bottom of the moun-tain but studied in Venice and Rome. Gualberto is the son of a forest ranger. He grew up in these mountains with the goatherds as his friends, then went to Milan to train as a veterinarian. He likes goats. He says they're inquisitive and smart. Yet for their neighbors, the goatherd is at the lowest end of the local social and economic scales. In the Val Camonica, goats are raised for meat, never for cheese. Most of the farmers have never tasted the sorts of cheeses produced at Le Frise, so a couple making goat cheeses and tak-ing in guests is a puzzle to them. The Martinis

Emma and Gualberto Martini of Le Frise farm.

Goats grazing at Le Frise.

remind me of my friends in Puglia who are restoring an olive estate. Rosalba Ciannamea and her husband, Armando Balestrazzi, like Emma and Gualberto, didn't grow up on a farm but came to country life by choice, wanting to live on the land. Some of their neighbors think they are a little crazy too.

At nightfall, after the goats are milked and bedded down, we all gather at the kitchen table—Emma, Gualberto and their friends Luciana and Franco. Emma cooks here every day. She does meals for fifty and sixty people. Her artistic sense shows up everywhere you look. In one corner, logs burn on the waist-high hearth she restored. Three walls are lined with thick countertops of cut stone supported on brick columns, reminiscent of the designs you can see in sixteenth-century engravings of kitchens. The farmhouse is almost that old. Emma leans her cutting boards—thick and handmade, their centers worn to smooth bowls by years of chopping—against the wall, displaying them like paintings. Wooden bowls carved by mountain shepherds hold drying chestnuts. Little green and red apples, with the occasional wormhole, dry on a woven mat under the window.

We dig into the Martinis' cheese, spreading it on crusts of bread. He pours wine made by their friends. Emma passes a platter of melon chunks on greens, dressed with black pepper and chives. We hand around a stick of salami, each of us cutting off what we want. Butter churned by a neighbor sits on a bright blue plate. The talk starts and stops with wisecracks and opinions, politics and comparing notes on how we live.

Did I know these mountain valleys resisted Christianity? That back in the Middle Ages local women who healed their families with herbs and charms were burned as witches? People believed in magic back then, and those women were seen as the conduits of spirits and dangerous forces. When Luciana points this out as early feminism, we all talk at once. Franco scoffs. Luciana counters. We talk about power and danger. Somehow the conversation turns to how people living up the mountain still cure mountain goat with spices and air-drying. I could spend days here. I could even get to like goats.

FRESH CHEESE OVALS WITH HERBS AND SPICES

Caprino Fresco con Erbe e Spezie

Serves 4 to 6 as an antipasto, 3 to 4 as a light meal

Goat cheese makers Gualberto and Emma Martini gave me the recipe for this colorful new way of serving fruit and cheese. Along with their Cantaloupe with Black Pepper, Oil and Vinegar (page 37), they set out a plate of little ovals of fresh goat cheese, some coated in fresh green chives, others rolled in toasted, crushed black poppy seeds and a few in sweet red paprika. Emma arranges the ovals in a nest of zucchini and carrot sticks dressed with olive oil and vinegar.

Wine Suggestion: A white Schiopetto Collio Sauvignon or Graziano Pra Soave Classico

CHEESE AND SALAD

2 6-inch zucchini, cut into ¹/₈ by 2¹/₄-inch strips

3 small carrots, peeled and cut into ¹/₈ by 2¹/₄-inch strips

3 scallions, cut on the diagonal into long ovals

6 ounces creamy fresh goat cheese

1 generous tablespoon poppy seeds

²/₃ cup finely snipped fresh chives or scallion tops

1 generous tablespoon sweet Hungarian paprika

DRESSING

Salt and freshly ground black pepper

1 tablespoon fruity extra-virgin olive oil

1 tablespoon white wine vinegar

1. Combine the zucchini, carrots, and scallions and refrigerate until ready to serve. Using two teaspoons or your fingers, shape the cheese into 10 ovals about 1¹/₂ inches long. Refrigerate until shortly before assembling.

2. Toast the poppy seeds in a small pan over medium heat 4 minutes, or until aromatic. Reserve.

3. Close to serving time, place the chives (setting aside a generous tablespoon for garnish), paprika, and poppy seeds in three small saucers. In a bowl, toss together the carrot mixture with salt and pepper to taste, and the olive oil. Blend in the vinegar. Mound the vegetables on a 12-inch round platter, arranging a nest in the center.

4. Roll the cheese ovals in the flavorings to coat: 3 or 4 in the chives, another 2 or 3 in the paprika, and the remaining 3 or more in the poppy seeds. Arrange in the nest. Sprinkle the reserved chives over the zucchini-carrot mixture and onto the platter's rim. Set out with small pieces of rough country bread.

TOMATO-MOZZARELLA SALAD WITH PINE NUTS AND BASIL

Insalata di Pomodori e Mozzarella

Serves 6 to 8 as an antipasto, 4 as a main dish

This salad resounds with the intense fragrances and flavors of southern Italy. It's a new approach to an old favorite. Thick-sliced tomatoes with mozzarella and basil are spiced with a mixture inspired by the Arab influences in southern Italy: a blend of toasted pine nuts, onions, currants and garlic tarted up with fresh lemon juice. The tomatoes and mozzarella take to these flavorings beautifully. Have the salad for supper or for a buffet.

Wine Suggestion: A young Puglia rosé like Alezio Rosato, Copertino Rosato or Brindisi Rosato

3 tablespoons fresh lemon juice
1 large clove garlic, minced
1/8 teaspoon freshly ground black pepper
Generous pinch of hot red pepper flakes
1/2 medium red onion, cut into 1/4-inch dice
1 tablespoon currants
Salt

2 tightly packed tablespoons fresh basil, leaves torn
1/4 cup plus 3 tablespoons toasted pine nuts

TOMATOES AND MOZZARELLA

6 medium ripe tomatoes, sliced vertically about 1/2 inch thick
3/4 pound fresh mozzarella packed in liquid, sliced 1/4 inch thick
About 3 tablespoons extra-virgin olive oil

1. In a small bowl, combine the lemon juice, garlic, the two peppers, onion, currants, and salt to taste. Let stand 20 to 30 minutes.

2. Just before assembling the dish, stir the basil and all but 1/2 teaspoon or so of the pine nuts into the onion mixture.

3. Alternate the slices of tomato and cheese on a plate, lightly seasoning each tomato slice with a little salt. Sprinkle each mozzarella slice with a teaspoon or so of the onion mixture. Sprinkle the entire dish with the reserved pine nuts, the olive oil, and any leftover pine nut and onion mixture. Serve at room temperature.

ROMAN SALAD

Puntarelle

Serves 4 to 6 as an antipasto or side dish

This salad is a Roman classic: curls of pale greens, tart and snappy in an anchovy dressing. It's definitely a dish for anchovy lovers; the dressing sings out its flavors—there is no masking here. In Rome, the salad is simply called Puntarelle, named for its main ingredient, the thick, asparagus-shaped hollow stalks of green that hide in the center of heads of Catalonia chicory. The stalks need the chill of a Roman winter to crisp and turn tender. Cooks there slice them into long strips and temper their bite a little by crisping in ice water. The pale green strips curl and coil in the cold water. Puntarelle are occasionally available here, but sometimes that name is used for the outer leaves of Catalonia chicory and not the inner stalks required for this salad. Lacking puntarelle, we can blend the pale inner leaves of escarole or curly endive with Belgian endive. The blend echoes puntarelle's character.

Serve the salad as a prelude to poached fish (page 270), or grilled meats (pages 246 and 253). I like it for supper with Sicilian Farmer's Bruschetta (page 34), or just with coarse whole-grain bread to sop up the dressing and a mild Roman sheep cheese like Cacio di Roma for dessert.

➤ *Cook to Cook:* This salad is simple and quick, but be sure to allow 2 hours for soaking the greens in ice water. Dry thoroughly before tossing. Allow the anchovy and garlic to mellow for 5 minutes in the vinegar.

Look for salted anchovies in specialty stores and Mediterranean groceries. They have a meatier character than the oil-packed ones. For potato salad, try tossing thick slices of steamed small new potatoes with a little of this dressing and some additional olive oil.

1 large head escarole or curly endive
2 heads Belgian endive
Ice water
DRESSING
2 whole salted anchovies or 3 oil-packed
   anchovy fillets

1 large clove garlic
2 tablespoons red wine vinegar
2 tablespoons fruity extra-virgin olive
   oil, or to taste
Salt and freshly ground black pepper

1. Use only about half of the escarole or curly endive, the pale inner leaves trimmed of their dark green tops (reserve the outer leaves and tops for other dishes). Cut into long thin strips. Repeat with the Belgian endive. Place in ice water and let stand in the refrigerator 2 hours.

2. Bone whole anchovies by opening each one up like a book and lifting out the spine and other bones in one piece. Trim away the tail and any fins, then rinse under cold running water. For oil-packed anchovies, simply rinse.

3. With a mortar and pestle, or using the rounded handle of a knife and a small bowl, mash the garlic and anchovies to a paste. Blend in the vinegar and let stand 5 minutes.

4. Drain the greens and spin totally dry. Toss the greens with the anchovy mixture, adding olive oil and salt and pepper to taste. Serve immediately.

SWEET-TART SALAD OF APPLES, BASIL AND SORREL

Insalata di Mele, Acetosa ed Erba Cipollina

Serves 4

Angelo Lancellotti, who cooks in his family's Emilia-Romagna restaurant, mingles unexpected flavors in his fresh approach to an antipasto salad—sweet apples and sweet basil with tart sorrel or spinach and chives, all dressed with a little sugar and vinegar. He takes his inspiration from Renaissance cookbooks written by locals, and from his organic farm and herb garden. Open an important dinner with this salad, or have it as supper, with chunks of Parmigiano-Reggiano cheese instead of meat.

➤ *Cook to Cook:* The only trick to this recipe is having all the ingredients ready to go, and slicing the apples no more than about 20 minutes before serving.

3 medium (about 1½ pounds) Braeburn, Fuji, or other sweet crisp apples, peeled and cut into small wedges about 1 inch by ¼ inch

1½ tablespoons white wine vinegar

¼ teaspoon sugar, plus a generous pinch

10 small fresh basil leaves (about 1 inch long)

7 baby spinach or sorrel leaves (about 2 inches long)

Generous ¼ cup finely snipped fresh chives

A large handful of organic spring mix, mesclun, or mixed wild greens

Salt and freshly ground black pepper

1 tablespoon fruity extra-virgin olive oil

1. Place the apple slices in a salad bowl. Toss with 1 tablespoon of the vinegar and the ¼ teaspoon sugar. Stack the basil and spinach or sorrel leaves, roll up tightly like a cigar, and slice into narrow strips. Set aside a few teaspoons of the greens along with a few teaspoons of the snipped chives.

2. Toss the remaining basil, spinach or sorrel, and chives with the apples. Add the salad greens, generous sprinklings of salt and pepper, the olive oil, the remaining ½ tablespoon vinegar, and the generous pinch of sugar. Toss to combine. Taste for seasoning. Sprinkle with the reserved herbs and serve.

BRESCIA GARLIC BREAD AND GREEN BEAN SALAD
Insalata Bresciana di Fagiolini

Serves 4

Toast up some country bread, rub it with garlic, tear it into bite-sized pieces, toss them with chunks of tomato and pieces of green beans and you have a salad from the farm country around the town of Brescia, in northern Italy's Lombardy region. Even though this is a farmhouse dish, there's an underlying elegance that's typical of Brescia's cooking. Although now families have the salad at the beginning of the meal, I serve it as a main course the way farmers did a generation ago—with cheese, like Taleggio or a fresh goat cheese. In autumn, the salad is good over wedges of hot pan-browned polenta (see page 36).

1 large clove garlic, split
1 pound green beans, trimmed and cut into 2-inch lengths
3 quarts boiling salted water
Salt
3 ¹/₂-inch-thick slices coarse-grain bread, toasted and still warm

2 medium-sized delicious ripe tomatoes, cut into 1-inch chunks
2 tablespoons extra-virgin olive oil
1 tablespoon red wine vinegar
Freshly ground black pepper

1. Rub a serving bowl with half the garlic, and reserve the other half.

2. Drop the beans into the boiling water and boil, uncovered, 5 minutes. Taste the beans; when they are tender and beginning to lose their crispness, drain. Sprinkle with salt and turn into the bowl.

3. Rub the warm toast with the reserved garlic and tear into irregular bite-sized pieces. Add to the bowl along with the tomatoes. Gently toss with the olive oil and vinegar. Season to taste with salt and pepper. Serve at room temperature.

Antipasti / Light Meals

SHEPHERD'S SALAD
Insalata del Pastore

Serves 6 to 8 as an antipasto, 4 to 6 as a main dish

Tart and mild greens, thin slices of salami, plump beans and strips of nutty-tasting hill cheese, all seasoned with a warm dressing of rosemary and sage, make this old-time salad more a meal than an antipasto. Shepherds improvise dishes like this in the high summer pastures of the Apennine Mountains. From northern to southern Italy, shepherds still take their flocks to high mountain pastures for summer grazing, traveling only with what can be packed on the back of a small donkey—minimal clothing, tools for cheese making and food that keeps—salami, garlic, onions, vinegar and oil. Greens for salad are gathered on the mountainsides.

➤ *Cook to Cook:* Organic salad mixes are perfect here—or a combination of small dandelion leaves, lamb's-quarters and arugula. Our own American sheep cheeses could be used if you cannot find Italy's ricotta salata, Pecorino di Norcia, Italico, Lago Monate Pecorino, Toscanello or Fiore Sardo.

Wine Suggestion: A fresh young red like Cavalchina Bardolino

DRESSING

3 tablespoons extra-virgin olive oil
1 thin slice mild coppa, soppressata, or hard salami, cut into thin strips
1/2 medium to large red onion, cut into 1/2-inch dice
A 4-inch branch fresh rosemary
6 large fresh sage leaves
4 large cloves garlic, minced
Pinch of hot red pepper flakes
1/2 cup red wine vinegar, or more as needed
2 cups chicken broth (preferably Mother's Broth, page 196)
Salt and freshly ground black pepper

SALAD

1 medium red onion, sliced into thin rings
Ice water
1 large head Bibb lettuce
1/2 large head romaine lettuce
3 to 4 cups mixed wild greens or 1 small head curly endive
2 small inner stalks celery with leaves, cut on the diagonal into thin slices
1 small fennel bulb, cut into thin strips
6 thin slices mild coppa, soppressata, or hard salami, cut into thin strips
1/4 pound Italian or American sheep cheese (see Cook to Cook), cut into strips
2 cups cooked cannellini, borlotti, or organic pinto beans (a 15-ounce can of beans can be used)
Salt and freshly ground black pepper

1. Heat the oil in a 1-quart saucepan over medium-high heat. Add the salami, onion, rosemary, and sage and sauté until the onion colors. Add the garlic and red pepper and stir for a few seconds, then add the vinegar. Boil 4 minutes. Stir in 1 cup of the stock and boil down to nothing. Add the rest and boil 2 minutes, or until the flavors blend and deepen. Taste for balance and season with salt and pepper. Cover the pan and set aside until needed, or up to 2 hours.

2. Meanwhile, immerse the onion in ice water and refrigerate about 45 minutes. Drain.

3. Wash and thoroughly dry the greens, setting aside any bruised or coarse leaves for other dishes. Arrange the greens on a large platter. Scatter the celery over the salad and tuck clusters of the fennel strips into it. If necessary, the salad can be covered and chilled up to 2 hours.

4. Shortly before serving, cluster the salami strips into seven to nine bundles, tucking them in here and there in the salad. Do the same with the drained onions and with the cheese strips. Nest large spoonfuls of the beans in several of the lettuce leaves. Sprinkle the salad lightly with salt and pepper, and set it out.

5. Bring the dressing to a boil. Taste for seasoning again, this time checking if it needs a tablespoon or so of vinegar. Present it in a deep bowl, and spoon it over the salad just before serving.

A Lombardy shepherd with his donkey and flock.

47   *Antipasti / Light Meals*

GRILLED CHICKEN PIECES IN SICILIAN MINT SAUCE

Pollo in Salsa Siciliana

Serves 4; doubles easily

Chunks of chicken pick up the snap of vinegar-marinated onion, fresh mint, garlic and oregano. This old Sicilian dish, nearly a warm salad, seems like a modern idea. Long ago, Palermo fishermen grilled their catch and served it in this tart mint sauce. The technique spread inland, where cooks paired the sauce with chicken, especially grilled or sautéed breasts. Serve the chicken hot or at room temperature.

➤ **Cook to Cook:** Tuna or bass could replace the chicken. Cook the fish only until firm and opaque at its center.

Wine Suggestion: A Sicilian white Etna Bianco or Bianco Alcamo

CHICKEN

4 large boned and skinned chicken
    breasts (totaling 1 to 1 1/2 pounds), cut
    crosswise into 1/2-inch-wide strips (if
    possible, hormone- and antibiotic-free)
1 tablespoon extra-virgin olive oil
Shredded zest of 1 medium lemon
1/2 teaspoon dried oregano
1/8 teaspoon freshly ground black pepper
Salt

MINT SAUCE

1/4 medium red onion, minced
1 clove garlic, minced
Generous pinch of sugar
3 tablespoons white or red wine vinegar
Salt and freshly ground black pepper
1 tablespoon extra-virgin olive oil
1/4 tightly packed cup fresh mint leaves,
    finely chopped

1. Toss the chicken with the oil, lemon zest, oregano, and pepper. Marinate in the refrigerator 1 to 6 hours.

2. About 30 minutes before cooking, stir together the minced onion, garlic, sugar, vinegar, and salt and pepper to taste in a small bowl. Let stand 20 minutes, then whisk in the oil.

3. About 15 minutes before serving, heat a heavy gridded skillet, a griddle, or a 12-inch sauté pan over medium-high heat. Sauté the chicken, sprinkling it with salt. Turn the pieces as they pick up color and immediately reduce the heat to medium-low. Continue cooking about 4 minutes, stirring occasionally, or until the chicken is barely firm when pressed; be sure there is no sign of raw meat. Transfer it to a serving platter.

4. Stir 3 tablespoons of the fresh mint into the sauce. Taste for seasoning, then spoon over the chicken. Sprinkle the remaining mint over the dish just before serving.

CRUSTY POTATOES WITH WILTED ARUGULA

Patate con Rucola

Serves 4

Dishes like this mark the beginning of the potato harvest in the Puglia region of southern Italy, where small, sweet new potatoes are dug from kitchen gardens in May and June. Slices of new potato are browned in a skillet. At the last moment, leaves of arugula are wilted in the pan, then they are served with a dash of vinegar as an antipasto or accompaniment to a platter of cheeses and bread. Farm cooks pair them with wild arugula, which tastes peppery and bright. Here we can use young cultivated arugula, or tiny dandelion leaves. Try Yellow Finn potatoes or small red-skins.

Wine Suggestion: A young Valpolicella Classico like Brigaldara

1 1/2 pounds small Yellow Finn or red-skinned potatoes
Robust extra-virgin olive oil
8 large cloves garlic, cut into 1/2-inch dice
2 tablespoons water

Salt and freshly ground black pepper
1 cup finely chopped young arugula or baby dandelion greens
1/4 medium onion, minced
1/3 cup white wine vinegar

1. Start potatoes in cold water to cover. Simmer until tender enough to be pierced with a knife but not falling apart. Drain and cool. Slice the potatoes about 1/2 inch thick. Lightly film the bottom of a 12-inch sauté pan with olive oil. Add the garlic and water and warm over medium-high heat, then turn the heat to low, cover, and cook 20 minutes, or until garlic is soft but not browned. Remove the garlic with a slotted spoon and reserve.

2. Turn the heat to high and, standing back so as not to get spattered, add the potatoes, sprinkle with salt and pepper, and turn gently to coat with oil. Then spread out in a single layer and sauté until golden brown on the bottom. Turn and take to golden brown on the other side. Add the greens and onion and cook over medium-high heat 1 to 2 minutes, turning frequently. The greens should wilt and begin to crisp. (You could also hold back 1/2 cup of the chopped greens, folding them into the finished dish off the heat.)

3. Quickly add the vinegar and scrape up the glaze at the bottom of the pan, taking no more than about 30 seconds. Immediately turn out of the pan onto a serving plate. Sprinkle with the reserved garlic, taste for seasoning, and serve at room temperature.

WARM CRUSHED POTATOES WITH ANCHOVIES

Patate Schiacciate con Acciughe

Serves 4 to 6

This is so simple to make and such a good supper on its own—buttery, sweet-tasting new potatoes set off by rich, salty anchovies. My friend Nicla brings her own gentle innovations to the country dishes of her area of the Lombardy region, which lies between Lake Garda and Mantova. She and her husband, Sergio, own La Dispensa, a specialty food shop, wine bar and restaurant, in the castle town of Castellaro. This dish, her creation and one of the easiest imaginable, uses local potatoes that taste similar to our Yellow Finns and young red-skinned potatoes.

For anchovy lovers, serve the potatoes as Nicla does with the whole fillets on the side. For those who aren't as enthusiastic about them, chop the anchovies and blend them into the potatoes.

➣ *Cook to Cook:* Salted anchovies taste meatier than oil-packed ones. You can find them in some Italian groceries and specialty food stores. To use them, rinse away their salt coating, trim off the heads and fins and open each anchovy up like a book. Bone by lifting out the tail and with it, the entire spinal column. For milder flavor, soak in cold water up to 15 minutes (for this recipe I suggest a 5-minute soak). Oil-packed anchovies need only rinsing under cold running water.

Wine Suggestion: A Valpolicella Classico Superiore like Il Vegro or
Cavalchina's Santa Lucia Bardolino Superiore

3 pounds sweet, buttery-tasting
potatoes (such as Yellow Finns or
young red-skins)
Water
4 to 6 whole salted anchovies or 8 to 12
oil-packed anchovy fillets

2 tablespoons unsalted butter
(optional)
Salt and freshly ground black pepper
2 tightly packed tablespoons fresh
Italian parsley leaves, chopped
Fruity extra-virgin olive oil

1. Start potatoes in cold water to cover. Simmer until tender enough to be pierced with a knife but not falling apart. Drain.

2. While the potatoes cook, clean salted anchovies by rinsing them under cold water, then trimming away the fins, opening each like a book, and removing the bones

by grasping the tail and lifting out the entire skeleton. For milder flavor, soak the salted anchovies in cold water 5 minutes. Simply rinse oil-packed anchovies.

3. While the potatoes are still hot, peel them and place in a bowl. Crush with a fork as you go. Add the butter, if desired, seasoning the potatoes to taste with salt and pepper. Keep warm.

4. Present the dish by mounding about ⅔ cup of the hot potatoes in the center of each individual salad plate. Sprinkle with the parsley and arrange 2 anchovy fillets beside each mound. Pass the olive oil separately, encouraging everyone to blend a spoonful or two into the potatoes, and suggest they eat the potatoes with small pieces of anchovy. Or, chop the anchovies and blend them with the hot potatoes before serving.

Keeping Potatoes "Sweet"

Thin-skinned waxy potatoes like Yellow Finns, Desirees, Red Bliss, German fingerlings, and others keep their characteristic sweetness when stored in a cool cupboard or in the refrigerator. Store them in plastic bags, punctured in several places to allow for air circulation, for up to 2 weeks.

MUSHROOMS STUFFED WITH RADICCHIO AND ASIAGO

Funghi Farciti con Radicchio e Asiago

Serves 6 to 8 as an antipasto, 4 as a light meal

The stuffing for these mushrooms brings home the idea of what grows together goes together. Radicchio and Asiago cheese come from neighboring areas in the Veneto region. Families there forage for wild porcini every year, preserving them by lacing slices on strings and drying them. Local cream binds the stuffing and sweetens the radicchio. Eat these mushrooms the way farmers do in the Veneto—with polenta for supper.

➤ *Cook to Cook:* Radicchio can be bitter. Before purchasing, discreetly taste a little from an outside leaf. If it's bitter, substitute curly endive or frisée.

Wine Suggestion: A sparkling white Zardetto Prosecco di Conegliano

TOPPING

1 tablespoon extra-virgin olive oil
³/₄ cup fresh bread crumbs (preferably from unsweetened whole-grain bread)
1 clove garlic, minced
Salt and freshly ground black pepper

FILLING

¹/₂ ounce dried porcini mushrooms
Hot water
1 tablespoon fruity extra-virgin olive oil
A 6-inch branch fresh rosemary
5 large fresh sage leaves, coarsely chopped
Salt and freshly ground black pepper

¹/₂ medium onion, minced
1 cup chopped radicchio leaves (about ¹/₄ medium head)
1 large (about 6 ounces) portobello mushroom cap, cut into ¹/₄-inch dice
1 large clove garlic, minced
¹/₂ cup dry white wine
¹/₄ cup heavy whipping cream
²/₃ cup shredded young Italian Asiago cheese or ¹/₂ cup shredded domestic Asiago
1 pound fresh mushroom caps, about 1¹/₂ inches in diameter, stems removed and cleaned
Salt and freshly ground black pepper

1. In a medium skillet, toss together the oil, bread crumbs, and garlic over medium heat, stirring until golden. Turn into a bowl, season with salt and pepper, and set aside.

2. Rid the porcini of sand by quickly stirring into a bowl of cold water, pausing for a second, and lifting them out. Repeat two more times, checking for grit. Soak 20 minutes in hot water to cover.

3. Meanwhile, heat the oil in a large skillet over medium-high heat. Sauté the rosemary and sage 30 seconds, sprinkling with salt and pepper. Stir in the onion and radicchio and cook 2 minutes, then add the portobello. Sauté 4 to 5 minutes over high heat.

4. Line a strainer with a paper towel. While the onion cooks, lift the porcini out of the liquid, squeezing dry. Reserve the liquid. Finely chop the porcini. Stir them, along with the garlic, into the pan and sauté 1 minute. Add the wine and cook down to nothing, scraping up the glaze from the bottom of the pan. Pour the reserved mushroom liquid through the strainer into the pan. Boil down to nothing, then stir in 2 tablespoons of the cream and cook 10 seconds. Remove from the heat and taste for seasoning. Let cool.

5. Preheat the oven to 350°F. Oil a 9-inch square baking pan. Combine the porcini mixture with the cheese. Season the mushroom caps with salt and pepper. Stuff them, mounding the filling high. Place the mushrooms in the baking pan, drizzle the remaining 2 tablespoons cream over them, and sprinkle with the toasted bread crumbs. Bake 25 minutes or until the filling bubbles. Serve hot or warm.

PORTOBELLO "STEAKS" WITH HOLY OIL

Portobello alla Griglia

Serves 6 as an antipasto, 2 to 4 as a main dish

When country women find big, meaty-tasting mushrooms, they grill the caps whole until they're browned and crusty, just like steak. Adelina Norcia, who farms in Sicily, brushes her mushrooms with her "holy oil" before she places them on the wood-fired grill that stands outside the kitchen door of her farmhouse. Crisped and spicy, the mushrooms are infused with Adelina's holy trinity of garlic, oregano and chile, all pureed in olive oil from the trees on her property. She serves them like meat, with a salad and bread. Try them the same way, and cook them on top of the stove when outdoor grilling isn't possible.

➤ *Cook to Cook:* Once you've made "holy oil," use it right away. Keeping it more than a day, even in the refrigerator, could encourage the growth of harmful bacteria. Since everything whirls together in seconds in a processor or blender, making the oil ahead is of no benefit.

Wine Suggestion: A Sicilian red Cerasuolo di Vittoria, Agrigento Rosso or Corvo

HOLY OIL
2 large cloves garlic
1/2 teaspoon dried oregano
Generous 1/4 teaspoon crushed dried hot chile (such as anchos, New Mexican string chiles, or Italian peperoncini) or hot pepper flakes

1/2 cup fruity extra-virgin olive oil

1 pound portobello mushrooms
Salt and freshly ground black pepper

1. In a blender, puree together the garlic, oregano, chile, and oil. If possible, let mellow an hour or so at room temperature.

2. Remove the mushroom stems and save for another use. Clean the caps with a damp cloth and trim away any bruised or tough areas. Arrange the caps on a platter and season on both sides with the "holy oil." Marinate at room temperature 15 minutes to a couple of hours.

3. Prepare a hot grill outdoors, or heat a griddle, gridded skillet, or sauté pan. Grill the mushrooms, turning to brown on all sides, or sauté over medium-high heat until browned on all sides. Move the mushrooms away from the hottest coals, or reduce the heat to medium-low, and cook 4 minutes longer, or until tender when pressed. Season with salt and pepper. Serve hot or at room temperature. For an antipasto, quarter the caps; serve whole for a main dish.

ROASTED ROMAN ARTICHOKES
Carciofi alla Matticella

Serves 6

Few artichoke preparations are easier or better. In the Roman countryside, cooks chop together garlic, mint, parsley, coppa and pancetta and stuff the blend between the artichokes' leaves. The artichokes are then baked in true Roman style, with bastings of white wine and olive oil, and yield a sauce as good as meat gravy. Eat these before a light main course, or make a meal of a single big artichoke. Have lots of bread to soak up the sauce.

➤ *Cook to Cook:* The artichokes can be made a day ahead and refrigerated overnight, but serve them warm or at room temperature.

Wine Suggestion: A modest, fresh white like Frascati Superiore

7 large cloves garlic	4 thin slices pancetta
½ tightly packed cup fresh Italian parsley leaves	Salt and freshly ground black pepper
½ tightly packed cup fresh mint leaves (peppermint if possible)	6 large artichokes
	2 lemons, halved
8 thin slices hot coppa or soppressata	About ⅔ cup extra-virgin olive oil
	2 cups dry white wine

1. Mince together the garlic, herbs, coppa, and pancetta. Season to taste with salt and pepper.

2. Trim off the top third of the artichokes. With scissors, snip off the top third of the remaining outer leaves. Rub all cut surfaces with lemon as you go. Pull open the centers of the artichokes and, using a sharp small grapefruit spoon or teaspoon, scoop out the fuzzy choke. Rinse the artichokes.

3. Preheat the oven to 375°F. Oil a 2-quart shallow baking dish large enough to hold the artichokes snugly in a single layer. Divide half the filling among the artichokes, placing about 1 tablespoon of filling into each of the centers and tucking another tablespoon here and there between the leaves of each one.

4. Arrange the artichokes on their sides in the baking dish. Sprinkle with the remaining filling and drizzle generously with the olive oil. Pour in the wine. Sprinkle with salt and pepper. Cover the dish with foil and bake, basting occasionally with the pan juices, 1 hour, or until the artichokes are easily pierced with a knife. Cool in the dish and let mellow at room temperature 2 to 3 hours before serving.

5. Serve the artichokes with the pan juices poured over them.

MOZZARELLA BUNDLES
Fagottini di Mozzarella

Serves 4

In Puglia, I watched a cheese maker's wife wind strips of pancetta around bite-sized pieces of the mozzarella her husband made in the back room. "They don't last an hour," she laughed. "The women buy them up, take them home and cook them for a few moments in a hot pan for their lunch." That's exactly what I ate for lunch at the trattoria around the corner. The pancetta crisped in spots and was juicy in others. Under it, the mozzarella was a moment away from melting, yet still tasted fresh and milky.

These cook in minutes. They're exceptional on their own, but try them, too, hot from the pan on top of a green salad (page 299). Try cooking them a minute or two on the grill over medium hot coals until the pancetta is blistered.

➤ *Cook to Cook:* Use the freshest mozzarella you can find. Buy only the type packed in liquid, not the "low-moisture" kind wrapped in plastic. You can assemble the bundles 6 to 7 hours ahead. Keep them cold and cook them off just before serving.

Wine Suggestion: Quintarelli's Secco Ca' del Merlo Bianco Veronese

1/3 pound fresh mozzarella (not the low-moisture type)
5 very thin slices pancetta

2 teaspoons extra-virgin olive oil
Freshly ground black pepper

1. Cut the cheese into 10 stubby sticks about 2 inches by 3/4 inch. Unroll the coiled pancetta slices and cut crosswise in half. Tightly wrap each slice around a cheese stick. If the pancetta threatens to unwind, secure it with a toothpick. Chill at least 20 minutes before cooking.

2. Heat the oil in a 10-inch sauté pan (a nonstick pan is best) over medium-high heat. Add the cheese bundles and quickly sear about 10 seconds per side, sprinkling with pepper. The pancetta should be seared but not browned; at most, the cheese should be softened very slightly. (If grilling, prepare a hot fire and quickly grill a few seconds per side; watch for the cheese softening.)

3. Immediately transfer the bundles to a warmed platter.

ELIMINATING THE MIDDLEMAN

Mimmo Nadile kneads and braids his mozzarella in the tile-lined room behind his cheese shop, La Nuova Casearia. The store is on a side street of Martina Franca, the gracious old town on a hill above Puglia's Itria Valley. His wife winds each bite-sized mozzarella braid in pancetta and sells them from the store's glass case. Fresh and young cheeses, and fresh-churned butter are their specialties—ricotta, cacioricotta, formaggio fresco, burrata, scamorza and mozzarella. The last two are kneaded into fanciful shapes— the scamorza is drier, salted and aged; the mozzarella is kept tender and sweet in baths of water or heavy cream.

Everything is made in the back room, a white tile and stainless steel space—except for the old-fashioned wooden tub on a bench in front of Mimmo. It is filled with steaming water. Dry crumbs of fresh cheese curd go into it. With a wooden bat, Mimmo stirs for a few moments, then he lifts out a wad of the softened curd. This will become mozzarella or scamorza. He works the curd like taffy, stretching it up and down, in and out of the water as it starts falling away in thick strands (*filato* in Italian, from *filare,* to spin or draw out). Finally it is "right." With rapid twists, he shapes the curd into braids, balls, and knots that go into cold water and later, maybe, cream.

Mimmo and his wife moved into town from their farm eleven years ago, deciding to open their own shop instead of selling their cheese wholesale from the country. "Sure, there's more profit, but also we know our customers now, and the cheese is better, fresher when they buy it. You know the saying with us mozzarella makers, 'Mozzarella has twenty-four attributes, and it loses one each hour.'"

PASTA

Pasta, like so much else in Italy, defies generalities. In Palermo, Sicily, a plate of spaghetti, made of just flour and water, can be so stiff that twirling it on a fork is a contest of submission. Far to the north, in Bologna, the capital of the Emilia-Romagna region, ribbon-shaped tagliatelle, made of flour and egg, are as supple as satin. While it is true the northerners usually like their pasta more cooked than southerners, it is also true that Italy is a country of exceptions. Every cook and manufacturer brings his beliefs, traditions and individual personalities to his pasta. Take the central Italian region of Marche, where pasta is usually served far more tender than in the deep south. There, Carlo Latini, who manufactures the highly regarded Latini-brand dried pasta, insists the only way to cook and serve his pasta is like that dish in Palermo—almost as stiff as a helicopter blade.

Pasta size, whether dried or fresh, is never consistent. This is why when we mix, let's say, one brand of dried spaghetti with another, they never cook evenly. Any two linguines aren't the same thickness. In Italy, there is no defining diameter for dried vermicelli, nor is there a nationwide rule for the width of a fettuccine noodle. In the deep south, the heel of the Italian boot, is the region of Puglia, where prime high-protein, or what is called "hard," wheat grows. There pasta shapes are more robust than elsewhere. Even spaghetti made in Puglia is thicker. The region's trademark pasta, orecchiette, or little ears, was never meant to even hint at delicacy. When you eat a plate of pasta in Puglia, you feel as though you've had a complete meal.

Come to understand pasta, and you can begin to understand Italy. Imagine yourself being Italian. Then know that the kind of pasta you have, the way you cook it, how you sauce it and the way you eat it has always revealed where you are in Italy, your place on the local economic and social scales, the time of year and even the day of the week.

For instance, the fortress farms (*masserie*) of Puglia haven't changed much over the past several hundred years—at least in terms of what you can see as you travel through the countryside. The farm's main house is always painted white. It sits in the center of a walled courtyard and is several stories high. Years ago the *padrone,* or farmer/landowner, always lived on the upper floors, safer from marauders, farther away from unappealing aromas of animals in the barnyard and the noise of the courtyard. Then, as now, at his table, Sunday dinner was a plate of hollow *maccheroni* sauced with meat ragù, served after an antipasto of vegetable dishes and before the meat, maybe pot-roasted lamb with braised chicory and roasted potatoes. Until very recently, on the floor below, on the table of his *contadini,* or farm workers, a bowl of thick orecchiette pasta with tomatoes from the garden was all of Sunday dinner. Class and affluence determined the kind of pasta on the table and how it was sauced.

As for the time of year: If you are Neapolitan and it is Carnival time, you will be eating lasagne. A day of harvesting grapes in Catania, Sicily, will end with a bowl of pasta cloaked in a sauce the color of garnets—a syrup of the boiled-down juice of just-pressed wine grapes spiced up with pepper and cinnamon.

Celebrating spring almost anywhere in Italy will have you eating artichokes with some kind of pasta. If you sit down to Christmas dinner in the Puglia town of Lecce, sweet Christmas Orzo in Swallow's Milk will appear on the table as a first course.

In addition to class and occasion, the kinds of wheat used to make pasta helped shape regional and personal tastes for firm or tender noodles. With their modest amounts of protein, northern Italian wheats (known as "soft" wheats) mill into softer flours that produce pastas that are velvety and best eaten fresh. Try to dry these pastas for storing for a long time and they become brittle, breaking easily. Whether fresh or dried, they cook to a softer consistency with some bite, but not as chewy as dried pasta made with high-protein flour. High-protein, or hard, wheats flourish in southern Italy. When milled into flour and worked with water, these wheats yield a pasta that dries well in the hot climate and is sturdy enough for long storage with little breakage. Today, much of the hard wheat for Italy's commercial pasta is imported from the United States and Canada, but the southern Italian preference for hard wheat pasta was originally shaped by what grew there.

When cooked, this hard wheat pasta is naturally chewier than its northern counterpart. And southern Italy's taste for firm, less-cooked pasta may be because its wheats lent themselves so gracefully to this style. It could be, too, that firm pasta is filling and more satiating than tender noodles. In a world where many people were hungry, filling food that satisfied was vital.

Yet, as I said, pasta defies pigeonholing. Ettore Guatelli grew up on a farm in the Parma hill country of northern Italy's Emilia-Romagna region, which is famous for its fresh homemade flour and egg pasta. He's the son of a sharecropper. During one of my visits, Guatelli, who is in his seventies, reminisced about the Christmas dinners of his childhood.

"Our Christmas treat was store-bought Neapolitan pasta made of flour and water, dry, in a box, and my mother would make her soffritto with butter, not salt pork." Surprising. The people of Emilia-Romagna boast about their hand-rolled pasta of flour and eggs. It is high art there.

"Did your family like a box of store-bought spaghetti better than your mother's homemade tagliatelle?" I asked, assuming wheat from their fields went onto their table.

"That was a special, rare treat," he explained. "You see, most of our wheat was sold. We didn't eat pasta very much; we lived on polenta. Besides, that store-bought pasta was much better to us than homemade. It was foreign and exotic—a real Christmas gift."

(I was reminded of how as a child I longed for the snow-white squishiness of store-bought white bread. I felt that having to eat my mother's homemade bread with its hard crust and gold flecks of whole wheat was just a cross I had to bear until I was old enough to be independent and do better.)

Until the nineteenth century, eating pasta in Italy was the option of the middle and upper classes. It didn't become the peasants' mainstay until the early 1800s, when transport, political and taxing changes made the south's industrially produced pasta cheaper, and wheat for homemade pasta more affordable. Northern peasants continued eating polenta. Their wheat, as Guatelli remembers, went to market. It was sold to bread and pastry makers, and to those who could afford it for pasta making at home.

After Italy's recovery from World War II, pasta became affordable to most, but it wasn't always a first choice. In the mountain areas of Italy's northern regions, farmers lived on a variety of starchy foods. Each area had its specialty, from polenta, bread dumplings and buckwheat porridge to risotto and rice dishes. The occasional dish of pasta was for a change of pace. Over time, however, pasta permeated even those mountains. It was always the second choice among the older generation, but became first with the young people.

These days, fast-cooking dried or fresh pasta is viewed as convenient, modern and healthy. Even those raised in homes where pasta was never eaten now eat it often in local trattorie, embracing pasta with all the enthusiasm we have for it in America.

In the recipes of this chapter, we experience pasta as Italy's country cooks do. Traveling from the far north of the Alto Adige down into the deep south of Puglia and Sicily, I realized that pasta as it is made in country homes is the food that captures the Italian spirit of improvisation and art in everyday life better than any other. I've seen a farm cook in Umbria make a lively tasting spring sauce from a handful of wild chives she picked in a field next to the house, then chopped with garlic, pine nuts and onion. She didn't even cook the sauce—all she did was toss it with hot pasta.

In the countryside, pasta is eaten as fast and simple weeknight suppers or as the food of celebration. Sunday dinner on southern Italian farms almost always opens with a casserole of *maccheroni* baked with meat ragù and cheese. Shepherds who live in the mountains of Lazio make Bucatini alla Amatriciana over fires outdoors when they take their sheep to mountain meadows for grazing. When Lazio farmers go to the woods to make charcoal, they make Spaghetti alla Carbonara. Country weddings in Calabria and Sicily often show off a stunning timbale of pasta in a decorated, glazed crust. Parties bring baked dishes like handkerchiefs of pasta folded over a filling of wild mushrooms.

Approach these recipes as the country women who inspired them do. Cook with your imagination. Let your hunger, not just a written recipe, drive what you put into the pot. Pasta in Italy's countryside is highly personal; it expresses heritage, geographic origins, personality and individual taste. And it is becoming the same here in America—a statement of the mood of the moment as well as a tribute to our zest for living, whether we are Italian or not.

A GUIDE TO PASTA
THE ART OF BUYING, COOKING, SAUCING AND ENJOYING PASTA

Buying Pasta

The Question of Fresh Versus Dried   Setting pasta snobbery aside, fresh and dried pastas are not better or worse than each other, only different. The pasta's quality is far more important than whether it is fresh or dried. Pasta should taste good on its own. Some pastas, depending upon their style and where they come from, are springy and lively and taste substantial, like the long rods of bucatini in central Italy's Bucatini all' Amatriciana (page 144). Others are supple and light, like the ribbons of tagliatelle with ragù (page 92) from Emilia-Romagna. Good pasta, whether fresh or dried, is never gummy, slack or leaden.

Store-bought fresh pasta often doesn't come up to those standards and is a study in mediocrity. Certainly creditable commercially made fresh pastas do exist. Only trying what's available in your area will reveal them, but know that you, with your own hands, can make superb fresh pasta—see page 69. When I have the time, I love to treat family and friends to homemade lasagne, fettuccine or ravioli. Yet the way my life is these days (and probably yours too), a stock of dried pasta in the cupboard is what keeps us fed and happy.

Finding the Best Dried Pasta   Imported Italian pastas frequently offer higher quality than their American counterparts. In many cases, Italian pasta manufacturers use superior flours, as well as superior mixing and drying techniques. Forget any boxed dried pastas that instruct you to rinse after cooking. They're made of wheats with low-grade proteins, which produce starchy and slack pasta instead of being springy and resilient. These pastas are dried quickly and cheaply so they cook to a gummy consistency. All this adds up to pasta no one should put in his or her mouth.

The hallmarks of high-quality dried pasta are a roughened surface that holds sauce the same way pebbly textured hand-rolled pasta does. Extruding pasta through expensive bronze instead of cheaper Teflon dies creates that rough finish. When cooked, premium pasta tastes lively and resilient, because it's kneaded and stretched more than lesser pastas and is made of flours with quality proteins that can be lengthened and worked like this. Slow drying yields the best consistency after cooking. All these methods and attributes are associated with small-scale artisan producers. Boutique artisan-made pastas are chic in Italy at the moment, but not all are created equal.

Brands to Look For   Good artisan pastas include Dallari, Rustichella, Michele Portoghese, Cav. Giuseppe Cocco, Settaro, Latini, Mamma Angelica, Spinosi, Gianfranco Zaccagni and the sturdy Pugliese-style Benedetto Cavalieri. For less money but sound, dependable pasta, look for Barilla, De Cecco, Delverde, Geraldo and Nola and La Molisana. New Italian pastas are constantly appearing in the market. Taste and see what you think.

I wish I could heartily recommend American brands as well, but I've not found one yet that equals or surpasses any of the ones mentioned above. Store boxed pastas in a cool dry area up to one year.

Cooking Pasta

The Formula   For every pound of dried or fresh pasta, use six quarts of boiling salted water. For filled or extra-large pastas like lasagne, count on seven or eight quarts per pound.

How Much Salt in the Pasta Water?   Pasta isn't solely a vehicle for sauce. It has a wheaten flavor of its own, and salt brings it out. How much salt in the pasta water? Sicilian farmer and skilled cook Adelina Norcia explains with the logic of a woman who's cooked pasta all her life, "Salt your pasta water before the pasta goes in, whenever you think of it. Taste for salt. Think you're tasting soup. Could you eat this pasta water and not find it oversalted or undersalted?" Two to three tablespoons salt per six quarts water is usually right.

How to Cook Pasta   Drop the pasta into fiercely boiling water. Cook it fast. Stir and stir and stir. Rely on tasting, not package instructions, for judging doneness. Look for a tiny white point at the heart of the noodle. Sample for firm texture, yet no taste of raw flour. Once the pasta is close to done, but a little firmer than you'd like, drain it in a large colander. Count on the residual heat to finish the cooking. Never rinse pasta unless it's destined for baking, as in lasagne or stuffed pastas.

Some Italian cooks drain the pasta even earlier, then finish cooking the pasta by tossing it with the sauce in the pasta pot over moderate heat. They say this "marries" sauce and pasta better. I have one cardinal rule: Overcooked pasta is thrown out, never eaten.

Oil in the Water?   Oil never keeps pasta from sticking; boiling in plenty of water does. Oil and water don't mix, and oil doesn't coat the pasta. Puglia olive oil producer and gifted cook Rosalba Ciannamea claims, "When you press your own oil, you don't waste it in pasta water. You save it for more important work, like seasoning the pasta at the table. It can taste better than cheese."

Saucing Pasta

Which Sauce for Which Pasta?   It's said pasta comes in more than three hundred shapes. Whatever the number, one thing is certain: each shape welcomes many sauces. Experiment with these suggestions in mind:

The bolder, richer or chunkier the sauce (pages 84, 124 and 138) the larger or more convoluted the pasta—like fusilli, cavatappi, strozzapreti, ziti, lumache, maniche and shells.

Nubby ragùs (page 92) are perfect for ribbons of fettuccine and tagliatelle, as well as modest-sized hollow pastas like penne, ditali, sedani, pater nostri, gramigna, zita and cup shapes like small shells.

Brothy light sauces or finely chopped fresh-tasting ones (pages 128, 76 and 122) are best with fine string pastas like vermicelli, spaghettini and capellini.

Chunky but not necessarily rich sauces (pages 82, 86 and 132) go with spaghetti, hollow maccheroni, hollow rods of perciatelli or bucatini, or the dimpled discs of orecchiette.

Respecting Tradition, or What Evolves Together Goes Together   In partnering pasta with sauces, consider the Italian concept of "*si sposa*," or "it marries," meaning foods that share the same local heritage and traditions are best eaten together. For many Italians, violating local tradition is like violating their own personal identify. Italy's home cooks improvise constantly with pasta, but rarely do they stray from their heritage when it comes to traditional dishes.

Never would Puglia's chewy discs of orecchiette pasta appear a thousand miles to the north in Lombardy sauced with cream and butter. Saucing Rome's fettuccine with Genoa's pesto is not just sacrilege to Italians; for them, they simply do not taste right together. Pesto deserves the local long strands of square-cut trenette, or at least linguine.

Fettuccine and tagliatelle are two pastas we Americans see as identical, yet Italians know they come from two different worlds. Tagliatelle is of the north, especially the Emilia-Romagna region. Its classic partner is the sauce of Emilia-Romagna's capital city, Bologna—Ragù Bolognese. Fettuccine is of central and southern Italy, especially Rome, where it's sauced with fish or butter and cheese. And some purists insist fettuccine is lighter than tagliatelle.

Spur of the Moment Saucing   With all that said, let's face it: No food is more of a vehicle for spur of the moment ideas and appetites than pasta—which is why we love it. What constitutes a sauce can be as uncomplicated as olive oil and a few torn leaves of fresh herbs, or butter and cheese, or a fast vegetable sauté moistened with a little of the pasta's cooking water or some tomatoes hand-crushed and mixed with anchovies and capers.

Using Pasta Water in Sauces   Small quantities of pasta water, with its starch and salt, are sometimes stirred into sauces, like sautés, that produce only a little liquid on their own. Lately I have noticed Italian cooks using this technique to lengthen sauces much more often. The pasta water seems to be taking the place of generous amounts of oil or fat used in these kinds of sauces in the past. Several recipes in this chapter illustrate the technique.

New and Old Ways of Blending Pasta and Sauce

We rarely consider that the method used to mix pasta and sauce might affect how the final dish tastes. It'll come as no surprise to learn that Italian cooks rarely agree on how to sauce their pastas, and certain regions have methods that are distinctively their own. For us outlanders, these variables give us all the more ways of enjoying pasta.

- Try this favorite Neapolitan trick for a totally different taste and texture: In recipes of sauced pasta sprinkled with grated cheese before or after serving, toss the hot pasta first with the cheese, then with the sauce.
- For authentic Puglia-style pasta and tomato sauce, shave fresh and salty cacioricotta cheese (or substitute ricotta salata) into the sauce before adding the pasta.
- Serve pasta with pesto the way it's eaten in its home region of Liguria. Cooks there don't thoroughly drain their pastas for pesto. The pasta water clinging to the noodles brings just the right consistency to the pesto.
- Marry pasta and sauce more intensely by undercooking the pasta slightly (so the white point at the center of the pasta is larger than usual) and tossing it with the sauce for several minutes over moderate heat.
- Carry this idea even further for a one-pot supper by learning from old farmhouse recipes where cooks stirred raw dried pasta into sautéed vegetables and herbs, then added water and/or wine to the pasta as it cooked. All the liquid absorbed by the pasta as it cooks is packed with flavor.

Serving Pasta

Keep pasta hot and easy to twirl on forks by serving it in warmed bowls, not on flat plates. Heat the bowls in a 180° to 200°F oven about 10 minutes. Pasta is best eaten on its own as a first course or main dish. It's far too complex to be a side dish. Italian farming families frequently ate pasta as a one-dish meal.

Cooking Pasta Ahead

Baked pasta dishes can be assembled ahead. Sauced pasta must be boiled and eaten immediately. Like a soufflé, pasta waits for no one. Then again, much of the reason for pasta's popularity is how fast it cooks.

Leftovers

Leftovers are favorite farmhouse breakfasts and suppers. Pasta is sautéed into a crispy pancake, or reheated with a little water in a saucepan. Pasta omelettes are a treat. Stir eggs into leftover pasta, no matter how it was sauced, and sauté or bake slowly in a wide shallow pan until crisp on both sides and heated through.

HOMEMADE PASTA

Pasta Casalinga

Makes the equivalent of 1 pound dried pasta; enough for a
single recipe of ravioli, lasagne or other filled pasta

Nothing is more associated with Italy's country cooks than homemade pasta. Every woman has her favorite recipe. This is mine—a style of pasta made all over Italy, an easy dough so supple and forgiving a friend says it practically rolls itself. Please use a rolling pin rather than a pasta machine. Only hand rolling creates the pebbly texture so prized in every Italian kitchen because as sauce collects in its tiny pits and crevices, the pasta and sauce bind together. Yes, it would be all the more authentic if you owned an Italian *matterello,* a long narrow pin smoothed and trained to the hand by women who have made pasta all their lives, but any heavy rolling pin will do.

Softer than most, this dough becomes extraordinarily light when cooked. Made with water and egg, not just egg, it is strong and elastic, especially good for filled pastas as well as ribbon pastas like fettuccine and sheets of lasagne. For richer pasta, eliminate the water and add two more eggs.

➤ *Cook to Cook:* To protect filled pastas from becoming gummy, keep them on porous surfaces, spacing the pieces so air can circulate around them. Cake racks and towel-covered flat baskets work well. Depending upon their fillings, they may refrigerate or freeze well. Each recipe gives specific suggestions.

Hang other cuts on racks or spread on flat baskets. Fresh pasta can be made hours ahead—certainly in the morning for the evening. Unfilled pastas dry well. Don't refrigerate or freeze them.

2³/₄ cups (about 14 ounces) unbleached all-purpose flour (preferably organic), plus extra for kneading

3 large eggs
¹/₂ cup warm water

1. *If working by hand,* make a mountain of the 2³/₄ cups of the flour in the center of a work surface. Hollow out a well in the middle. Have a pasta scraper handy. Blend the eggs and water in a bowl, turning them into the well. Using a fork, gradually start incorporating shallow scrapings of the flour from the walls of the well into the liquid. As you work in more and more flour, the well's sides may collapse. No fear—stop any liquids from running off with the pastry scraper, using it to incorporate the last bits of flour into the dough. It will look hopelessly rough and messy. Don't worry. Just start kneading.

After about 3 minutes, the dough should be slightly sticky and elastic. If it's very sticky, lightly dust the surface with a couple of teaspoons of flour. Continue kneading 10 minutes or until the dough has become satiny, elastic, and alive in your hands. If it becomes too sticky again while kneading, work in more flour a little at a time. Lightly wrap the dough in plastic and let it relax at room temperature 30 minutes to 4 hours.

If using a food processor, have the eggs and water cold to protect the dough from overheating. Combine the liquids by processing with the steel blade for a few seconds. Add about $1^1/_2$ cups of the flour. Pulse no more than 5 seconds. Add all but $^1/_4$ cup of the flour, pulsing 5 seconds more. If the dough is very sticky, pull it apart into several pieces, sprinkle with 1 tablespoon flour, and pulse again. The dough should be smooth and slightly sticky. Sprinkle a work surface with the remaining $^1/_4$ cup flour and knead 5 minutes. Wrap the dough and let rest as directed above.

2. *To roll out the pasta:* Cut the dough into quarters. Roll it out a quarter at a time, keeping the rest wrapped. Very lightly flour the work surface (no more than $1^1/_2$ teaspoons). Shape the dough into a ball. Roll out into a circle by stretching as well as pressing down with the rolling pin: Stretch by rolling the dough a quarter of the way up on the pin and gently pushing the pin away from you. Turn the disc a quarter turn and repeat, then do twice more. Keep rolling and stretching until pasta is thin enough to see the color of your hand, or this print, through it. For filled pasta, use the rolled-out dough immediately. For other shapes, spread it out on a flat surface and dry about 20 minutes, until leathery in texture, turning it several times for even drying. Cut as desired.

A SELECTION OF PASTA CUTS

For the following shapes, roll up pasta like a jelly roll and cut with a sharp knife:

Fettuccine: $^1/_8$- to $^1/_4$-inch-wide strips

Tagliatelle: $^3/_8$-inch-wide strips

Tagliarini: $^1/_6$-inch-wide strips

Maltagliati: 1-inch wedges cut at an angle into irregular triangles

Pappardelle: $^1/_2$- to $^3/_4$-inch-wide strips

Trenette: usually rolled and cut with a special grooved rolling pin, but can be simulated by cutting dough that's been rolled about $^1/_8$ inch thick into $^1/_8$-inch-wide strips

Cut the following shapes from flat sheets:

Lasagne: 4 by 8-inch rectangles

Cannelloni: 4-inch squares

Tacconi: $1^3/_4$-inch squares

RECIPES WHERE FRESH PASTA IS ESPECIALLY FINE

Mamma Ida Lancellotti rolling out her pasta in the kitchen of
Ristorante Lancellotti, in Soliera (Emilia-Romagna).

LINGUINE WITH PISTACHIO-ALMOND PESTO

Linguine con Pesto di Pistacchi e Mandorle

Serves 8 as a first course, 4 to 6 as a main dish

Crushed almonds, garlic, pistachio and mint—this is a sauce like no other. Friends are always surprised by first the fragrance and then the ingredients of this pesto. The fact that it comes together in minutes, calls for no cooking and tastes like nothing we've known makes it one of my favorite celebration pastas. The sauce is a member of a family of pestos found in Sicily, where cooks crush almonds and other nuts with herbs, garlic and tomato. Tasting the most famous of these won me over; it was Trapani's almond pesto. But in re-creating it at home, I realized our almonds lack the fragrance of Sicily's. No surprise really—almond trees seem to grow in every Sicilian's back garden and the nuts taste as though someone's infused them with almond essence. Then I discovered this pesto from the island of Lipari, off Sicily's northeastern coast. With its pistachios, pine nuts, mint, garlic and tomato, along with almonds, this is everything a nut pesto should be.

Wine Suggestion: A round, full Sicilian white like Planeta La Secreta Bianco

A scant ¹/₂ cup unblanched whole almonds, toasted

A scant ¹/₂ cup shelled salted pistachio nuts, toasted

¹/₃ cup pine nuts, toasted

1 large clove garlic

Pinch of hot red pepper flakes

2¹/₂ to 3¹/₂ tablespoons fruity extra-virgin olive oil, or more to taste

40 large mint leaves (a blend of spearmint and peppermint if possible)

Salt and freshly ground black pepper

1 pound linguine, spaghetti, bucatini, or other string pasta

6 quarts boiling salted water

1¹/₃ pint baskets (1 pound) flavorful cherry tomatoes, quartered

1. Mix the cooled toasted nuts. Coarsely chop about one quarter of them and set aside.

2. In a mortar (a processor is second choice), pound (or grind) the garlic to a paste with the hot pepper and 2 to 3 tablespoons of the olive oil. Work in the remain-

ing whole nuts and a little more than half the mint leaves until the mixture looks like very coarse meal, with pieces of nuts at about $1/8$ inch. Season to taste with salt and pepper. Tear up the remaining mint leaves.

3. Cook the pasta in fiercely boiling water, stirring often, until tender yet firm to the bite. As the pasta cooks, gently blend the pesto, tomatoes, and $1/2$ tablespoon of the oil in a deep pasta bowl.

4. Skim off $1/2$ to $3/4$ cup of the pasta water just before draining, and drain the pasta in a colander. Add the pasta water to the bowl. Add the sauce, pasta, chopped nuts, and salt and pepper to taste and toss. Then toss in the reserved torn mint. Taste for seasoning, adding extra oil, mint, salt, and/or pepper if needed. Serve hot or warm. No cheese is used here.

GETTING THE PASTA RIGHT FOR POP

Mamma would wait on the balcony of our family apartment. As soon as she spotted my father, my brother and myself coming around the corner at the bottom of the hill, she gave the signal to our cook to drop the pasta into the pot of boiling water," recalls journalist Gaetono Afeltra of his childhood in the Amalfi of the 1930s.

Knowing the precise timing of cooking pasta for dinner is the special province of the family matriarch. Too soon, and the pasta comes to the table barely warm, its sauce congealed. Too late, and the meal is ruined by bad tempers and impatience. Italian food historian Massimo Alberini writes in his book *Maccheroni e Spaghetti* that in southern Italy, in the days before telephones, husbands sent their wives messages via runners from their offices: "I'm leaving now, start the pasta."

"My mother would then take over in the kitchen," Afeltra remembers. "She never left the pot, tasting and retasting the pasta until the raw white of the pasta disappeared except for a tiny white dot at its center that she saw when she bit into the strand of spaghetti." This is *"il punto bianco,"* "the white point," the key in southern Italy to that instant when pasta is just right. The moment must be seized, the pasta drained immediately. Family contentment pivots on that tiny white point at the heart of the pasta.

Pasta

THE KING OF PESTOS

Trenette al Pesto

Serves 6 to 8 as a first course, 3 to 4 as a main dish

If you want to experience pesto as it's eaten in the land where pesto is king, the city of Genoa and all over the Liguria region, buy your basil at the nursery, not the supermarket, or mail-order seeds for the type grown in Liguria (Sweet Genovese, *Genovese profumitissima*) and plant a few pots on the windowsill. Young basil is a key to reproducing the lush pestos of Liguria in America. Use leaves picked from infant plants no taller than six inches, and instead of our usual two to three cups of basil leaves per recipe, you'll need only two thirds of a cup.

Ligurians cook a sliced potato and a seasonal vegetable right with their pasta and sauce everything with the pesto—broccoli flowerettes, green beans, fava beans, even peas. And they add a little pasta water to the pesto to bring the sauce to just the right creamy consistency.

➤ *Cook to Cook:* Surprisingly, after tasting the basil leaves used by Ligurian cooks and young leaves from standard sweet basil plants (*Ocimum basilicum*) in my garden, I didn't find a dramatic difference. Olive oil and cheeses do make a great difference in your pesto. Use a buttery, gentle-tasting Ligurian oil like Roi, Rainieri, or Ardoino, and seek out the cheeses in the recipe. Trenette is a square-cut string pasta. You can substitute linguine or spaghetti.

Wine Suggestion: Liguria's white Vermentino or a fruity Verona white like Secco Ca' del Merlo Bianco Veronese by Quintarelli, Giuseppe

1 large clove garlic, any green center removed

1/8 teaspoon salt, plus more to taste

2/3 tightly packed cup fresh young basil leaves

2 heaping tablespoons pine nuts

1/4 cup grated Fiore Sardo sheep cheese or domestic Fontinella

Scant 1/2 cup freshly grated Parmigiano-Reggiano cheese

6 to 8 tablespoons extra-virgin olive oil (Ligurian preferred—Roi, Ardoino, or Rainieri brand)

1 medium red-skinned potato, peeled and thinly sliced

6 quarts boiling salted water

3/4 pound trenette, linguine, or spaghetti

1 1/2 cups broccoli flowerettes

Freshly ground black pepper

1. In a mortar and pestle, puree the garlic with the salt. Or, with the motor running, add the garlic and salt to a food processor and puree. Gradually add the basil and then the pine nuts, crushing or processing everything into a rough paste. Add the cheeses and then finally enough oil to bring the pesto to the consistency of heavy cream. Turn it into a pasta bowl.

2. Drop the potato into the boiling water and boil 5 minutes. Add the pasta and broccoli and cook until the pasta is tender but still firm to the bite. Take out $1/3$ cup pasta water and stir it into the pesto. Drain the pasta in a colander and immediately toss it with the pesto. Taste for seasoning and serve hot.

CHOPPED CHIVE "PESTO" ON PERCIATELLI

Perciatelli con Pesto Primaverile

Serves 8 as a first course, 4 to 6 as a main dish

I watched a cook on a horse farm in Umbria make this sauce on her cutting board with wild chives she picked just outside the back door. With a mezzaluna (two-handled, half-moon-shaped knife) she minced the long green spears with other herbs, pine nuts and garlic and then tossed the pesto with hot pasta. Pure serendipity was coming home from Umbria in mid-May to find my own chives taking over the garden. Mincing everything may not follow traditional pesto technique, which calls for crushing in a mortar, but I like the idea of this fast sauce made on a cutting board and the fun of biting into bits of chive and red onion. And, the sauce tastes like spring.

Wine Suggestion: An Umbrian white like Lungarotti's Torre di Giano or Castello della Sala's Cervaro della Sala

$\frac{1}{8}$ teaspoon salt, or more to taste

2 large cloves garlic

1 tightly packed cup coarsely chopped fresh chives

3 tightly packed tablespoons fresh basil leaves

1 tightly packed tablespoon fresh spearmint leaves

$\frac{1}{2}$ medium red onion, halved

$\frac{1}{3}$ cup pine nuts

2 tablespoons plus 2 teaspoons extra-virgin olive oil

Freshly ground black pepper

1 pound perciatelli or other long narrow hollow pasta

6 quarts salted boiling water

1 cup (4 ounces) freshly grated medium-aged sheep cheese (such as Pecorino dell'Umbria, Pecorino Toscano, American artisan-made sheep cheese, or domestic Fontinella)

1. Make a little pile of the salt on a chopping board. Crush the garlic into it with the side of a large knife and finely chop. Add the herbs and half the onion and chop until minced very fine. Add the pine nuts and coarsely chop. Blend in 2 tablespoons of the oil right on the board, seasoning to taste.

2. Finely chop the remaining onion. In a large skillet, heat the remaining 2 teaspoons oil, add the onion, and sauté to soften it.

3. Meanwhile, cook the pasta in fiercely boiling water, stirring often, until tender but still firm to the bite. Drain the pasta in a colander.

4. Scrape up the chopped mixture from the cutting board into the sauté pan. Warm over medium heat only a few seconds to let the flavors blossom—do not cook. Add the pasta off the heat, tossing with the pesto and the cheese. Taste for seasoning and serve hot.

GEMELLI WITH ROASTED PEPPERS AND GREENS

Gemelli con Peperoni Arrostiti

Serves 6 to 8 as a first course, 4 as a main dish

Instead of being sautéed, this country sauce is roasted. As everything roasts together, the peppers and greens play on each other's strong suits. The peppers become sweeter and more interesting because of the greens' deep brown, tart flavors. Everything tastes even better if you roast the sauce five or six hours before serving. Keep it lightly covered at room temperature, then reheat while you cook the pasta.

Wine Suggestion: A Valtellina red like Sfursat by Nino Negri or a light-bodied California Zinfandel

1 tablespoon plus about 2 teaspoons high-quality commercial balsamic vinegar

2 oil-packed anchovy fillets, rinsed

1/2 lightly packed cup fresh basil leaves

Leaves from a 4-inch branch fresh marjoram

1 lightly packed tablespoon fresh mint leaves

2 1/2 tablespoons extra-virgin olive oil

4 to 5 sweet red peppers, cored, seeded, and cut into 1 1/2-inch pieces

1 1/2 medium red onions, cut into 1 1/2-inch wedges

3 large cloves garlic, minced

A generous handful of mixed organic greens or mesclun or washed and dried curly endive, coarsely chopped

1 heaping tablespoon drained vinegar-packed capers

Generous pinch of hot red pepper flakes

Salt and freshly ground black pepper

1 pound stubby pasta, such as gemelli, cavatappi, penne, sedani, or fusilli

6 quarts boiling salted water

1. About 40 minutes before cooking the sauce, slip a large shallow baking pan (a half-sheet pan or jelly-roll pan works perfectly) onto the oven's middle rack. Preheat to 450°F.

2. In a small bowl, combine the 1 tablespoon balsamic vinegar and the anchovies. Set aside. Coarsely chop the herbs.

3. In a large bowl, toss the herbs with 1 1/2 tablespoons of the oil, the peppers, onions, garlic, greens, capers, hot pepper, and salt and pepper to taste. Let stand about 30 minutes.

4. Shortly before cooking, toss the anchovy mixture with the peppers. Drizzle the remaining 1 tablespoon oil onto the hot baking pan. Spread out the pepper mixture, blending it with the oil, and roast about 45 minutes, turning frequently with a metal spatula. Encourage browning and crisping by keeping everything spread out in the pan, and roast until greens are wilted, dark, and beginning to crisp and the peppers are wrinkled but still have a little body. Taste for seasoning. (You can keep the roasted vegetables at room temperature about 6 hours. Reheat 15 minutes in a 350°F oven.)

5. Drop the pasta into the boiling water and cook, stirring often, until just tender to the bite. Drain in a colander and toss with the roasted vegetables and the remaining 2 teaspoons balsamic vinegar. Turn into a heated bowl and serve warm.

SIRACUSA MARKET PASTA

Pasta alla Moda del Mercato di Siracusa

Serves 6 to 8 as a first course, 4 as a main dish

A pasta inspired by the black olives that farmwives marinate and sell at the morning market in the Sicilian port town of Siracusa. They toss the olives with fresh basil, shreds of orange zest, oregano, garlic and hot pepper. One woman told me she did the same thing with pasta, adding fresh tomato too. I tried the idea and found it was a spicy, fragrant pasta quite different from anything I'd tasted. She said you could add a little fresh sheep cheese or mozzarella to tame down the strong flavors—she was right.

➤ **Cook to Cook:** Cooks shopping in the Siracusa market were buying bunches of tiny-leafed basil that we know as Spicy Globe basil. These bushy little plants have an appealing citrus-pepper scent. Find them in nurseries and farmers' markets in summer. If not to be had, use regular fresh sweet basil.

Wine Suggestion: A fresh, flinty white Etna Bianco Superiore or a Corvo Rosso

Fruity extra-virgin olive oil
8 large cloves garlic, cut into 1/2-inch dice
1/2 medium red onion, cut into 1/4-inch dice
Salt and freshly ground black pepper
Shredded zest of 1 large orange
1/2 teaspoon dried oregano
1/2 teaspoon crushed dried medium-hot chile (ancho or peperoncini)
1 pound bucatini or spaghetti
6 quarts boiling salted water

1 loosely packed cup fresh basil leaves, chopped (preferably Spicy Globe or Greek Bush variety)
16 herbed or oil-cured black olives, pitted and coarsely chopped
1 pint basket (3/4 pound) delicious cherry tomatoes, quartered
1 1/2 cups (6 ounces) crumbled fresh Italian or domestic sheep cheese or diced mozzarella packed in liquid (optional)

1. Coat the bottom of a 12-inch sauté pan with a sheer film of oil. Sauté the garlic over low heat until soft but no more than pale blond. Remove with a slotted spoon and reserve.

2. Turn up heat to medium-high. Sauté onion to pale gold, seasoning with salt and pepper. Stir in the orange zest and cook 30 seconds to a minute. Blend in the oregano and chile, cooking 10 seconds. (At this point, you can set the sauté aside, covered, up to 3 hours. Reheat before proceeding.)

3. Cook the pasta in fiercely boiling water, stirring often, until tender yet firm to the bite. Remove 1 cup of the pasta water before draining pasta in a colander.

4. Just before serving the pasta, stir the reserved pasta water into the sauté pan along with the reserved garlic, cooking 30 seconds. Add the pasta, basil, and olives, tossing to coat. Stir in the tomatoes, taste for seasoning, and turn into a warm bowl. Sprinkle with the cheese if desired. Serve hot or at room temperature.

TAGLIARINI WITH FRESH ARTICHOKES, PARMIGIANO AND LEMON

Tagliarini con Carciofi, Parmigiano e Limone

Serves 6 to 8 as a first course, 4 as a main dish

Artichokes are combined with two of Italy's most fabulous foods, prosciutto di Parma and Parmigiano-Reggiano cheese, in a light supper pasta. This pasta evolved from an artichoke and Parmigiano salad I ate in the Parma hills years ago. Cook the artichokes ahead. At the last minute, toss them with their lemony dressing, the hot pasta, shreds of Parma ham and shavings of Parmigiano-Reggiano cheese.

ARTICHOKES
Juice of 1 large lemon
3 cups water
4 to 5 large artichokes
1 cup white wine vinegar
6 quarts boiling salted water

DRESSING
1/8 teaspoon salt, or more to taste
1 large clove garlic
Juice of 1/2 large lemon
1 to 2 teaspoons red wine vinegar

5 tablespoons robust extra-virgin olive oil
Freshly ground black pepper

1 pound tagliarini, spaghetti, or
    linguine
6 quarts boiling salted water
2 ounces thinly sliced prosciutto di Parma,
    sliced into strips 1/4 inch by 2 inches
3 ounces Parmigiano-Reggiano cheese,
    shaved into long furls with a
    vegetable peeler
Salt and freshly ground black pepper

1. In a medium bowl, combine the lemon juice and 3 cups water. One at a time, break off all the leaves around the base of each artichoke until you come to the pale green ones at its center. Cut away the stem with a knife. Peel away all the dark green leaf stubs from the sides and bottom of the artichoke until the part that remains is pale green—this is the artichoke bottom. Now cut off the leaves and, with a spoon, scoop out the hairy choke. Rinse and put into the lemon water.

2. Have the boiling salted water over high heat. Add the vinegar and artichokes to the boiling water. Cook 3 to 4 minutes, so the artichokes are barely tender. They should still be quite firm when pierced with a knife. Drain and rinse under cold water. (Hold at room temperature up to 6 hours, or refrigerate up to 2 days in a sealed plastic bag.)

3. Make a little pile of the salt on a chopping board. Crush the garlic into it with the side of a large knife and finely chop.

4. In a pasta serving bowl, mix together the lemon juice, garlic, and 1 teaspoon vinegar. Let stand about 10 minutes (while you cut the prosciutto and shave the cheese). Slice the artichoke bottoms into strips about $1/8$ inch thick. Blend the olive oil into the dressing and add salt and pepper to taste.

5. Cook the pasta in fiercely boiling water until just tender yet firm. When you put the pasta on to cook, blend the artichoke bottoms into the dressing, along with the prosciutto. Taste for seasoning and vinegar, adding the second teaspoon if necessary.

6. Drain the pasta and toss with the artichokes and the cheese, tasting again for seasoning. Serve hot or warm.

SEAFOOD SAUTÉ WITH STUBBY PASTA

Pasta col Pesce

Serves 6 to 8 as a first course, 4 as a main dish

Do you eat fresh tuna with pasta?" I asked the fishmonger in Siracusa's morning market. Taking center stage behind his display of fish, the vaudeville act began. He called to the crowd, "Do we eat pasta with tuna?" With shoppers cheering him on, he sang out the source for each ingredient in this recipe: "The beautiful Teresa's olives," gesturing to the olive stall and Teresa, who wouldn't see seventy again; "Marcello's zucchini!"—a broad wink; "Sylvia's pine nuts! She cracks them between her knees"; and "Mozzarella no older than the memory of your last kiss."

Tuna and swordfish are the steaks of Sicily. Cut tuna up and toss in a hot pan with diced zucchini, black olives, red onions, currants and herbs and you have a sauce made in the time it takes to cook the pasta. In Siracusa, this pasta dish is served in an unusual way for Italy—with diced mozzarella. Many Italians are adamant about fish and cheese never occupying the same bowl, but they do here. And mozzarella's fresh milkiness is just what the sauté needs.

➤ *Cook to Cook:* Look for mozzarella packed in liquid, rather than dry and wrapped in plastic. Taste for sweet milk with a hint of sourness and a creamy center. If you can't find a good one, leave it out.

Wine Suggestion: A white Planeta La Secreta Bianco
or Regaleali Bianco

1 pound ditali or other short hollow pasta

6 quarts boiling salted water

Extra-virgin olive oil

1 large clove garlic, lightly crushed

1 medium stalk celery with leaves, finely diced

2 medium zucchini, finely diced

1 medium red onion, finely diced

2/3 cup herbed black olives, pitted and finely chopped

Salt and freshly ground black pepper

1 pound tuna steaks, trimmed of skin and cut into 1/2-inch cubes

1/4 cup toasted pine nuts

1/4 cup currants, soaked in hot water for 15 minutes and drained

1 tablespoon tomato paste

1 cup (about 4 ounces) diced fresh mozzarella (optional)

2 tightly packed tablespoons fresh mint leaves (preferably peppermint), chopped

1. First chop and measure all the ingredients. Cook the pasta in fiercely boiling water, stirring often, until tender yet firm to the bite. Remove and reserve 1 cup of the pasta water and drain the pasta in a colander.

2. While the pasta cooks, make the sauce by filming the bottom of a 12-inch sauté pan (not nonstick) with olive oil and heat over medium-high. Spear the garlic with a fork and rub it over the bottom of the pan until it's pale blond. Discard the garlic. Add the vegetables, olives, and a little salt and pepper and cook, stirring, until the onions turn pale gold, about 3 minutes.

3. Add the tuna, pine nuts, and currants and stir 2 minutes, seasoning with salt and pepper. Stir the tomato paste into the reserved pasta water, add to the pan, blend well, and simmer 30 seconds to 1 minute, or until the fish is cooked through.

4. Turn the hot pasta into a heated bowl. Gently mix in the fish with its sauce, seasoning to taste. Fold in the cheese, if desired. Sprinkle with the mint and serve.

Siracusa fishmonger-vaudevillian (right) with his friend.

Pasta

SPAGHETTINI WITH SHRIMP, CHICKPEAS AND YOUNG GREENS

Spaghettini con Gamberetti e Ceci

Serves 6 to 8 as a first course, 3 to 4 as a main dish

A little olive oil, a hot pan, a handful of greens from the garden or market, chunks of fresh shrimp and some chickpeas and chiles, and you have a supper pasta in about ten minutes. This sort of seafood pasta is found in homes up and down Italy's coasts. Of course, once the dish is set before you, your hostess, who is also the cook, will explain all the little touches that make it solely hers. Chickpeas and seafood is a combination I always associated with Tuscany's seaside resorts until I tasted this spicy version of the pairing in the Marche region's coast town of Pesaro.

➤ *Cook to Cook:* Take care with chiles. If too hot, they will overwhelm the dish. Use any medium-hot chile. Red ones, like hot Italian frying peppers or red jalapeño, give good color accent to the dish. Chop and measure everything before beginning the recipe. Cook the pasta, reserve 1/2 cup of its water, drain it, and immediately finish the sauce.

Wine Suggestion: A flowery, nutty white Verdicchio dei Castelli di Jesi from makers Garofoli, San Michele or Sartarelli

1/2 medium red onion
1 Italian frying pepper or sweet red pepper
2 fresh red medium-hot chiles, stemmed and seeded (such as hot Italian frying peppers, cherry peppers, peperoncini, or red jalapeños)
4 plump black olives (Sicilian or Kalamata), pitted
1 pound spaghetti
6 quarts boiling salted water
2 to 3 tablespoons fruity extra-virgin olive oil

1 15-ounce can chickpeas, rinsed and drained
Salt and freshly ground black pepper
4 tightly packed cups (1/2 pound) mixed organic salad greens, young dandelion greens, or curly endive leaves, coarsely chopped
3 large cloves garlic, minced
1 1/2 pounds jumbo shrimp, shelled, deveined, and cut crosswise into thirds
1 cup snipped fresh chives or thinly sliced scallion tops

1. Chop together the onion, pepper, chiles, and olives into $^1/_2$- to $^1/_4$-inch pieces. Set aside.

2. Cook the pasta in fiercely boiling water, stirring often, until tender yet firm to the bite. Remove and reserve $^1/_2$ cup of the pasta water and drain the pasta in a colander.

3. While the pasta boils, heat the oil in a 12-inch sauté pan over medium-high heat. Add the onion mixture and chickpeas, sprinkling generously with salt and pepper, and sauté 3 to 5 minutes, or until the onions are gold at their edges.

4. Stir in half the greens and garlic and cook about 10 seconds, or until the greens barely soften. Stir in the shrimp. Cook a few minutes, to barely firm; the greens should be wilted. Blend in the reserved pasta water, scraping up the glaze from the bottom of pan. Cook 30 seconds, or until the shrimp are firm but juicy.

5. Immediately add the pasta, the remaining greens, and the chives to the pan, toss, and taste for seasoning. Turn into a warmed bowl and serve.

THE FIRST PASTA MACHINE

Long before today's automatic pasta machine was even a glimmer in an inventor's eye, Italians figured out a way of not having to hand-make every piece of pasta they ate. Households all over Italy had a contraption called a *torchio*. Many still do. The torchio is the home version of the machine that eventually built southern Italy's commercial dried pasta industry. It looks like a meat grinder, but it extrudes pasta. People bolt it to their tabletops just the way our grandmothers did their meat grinders to make sausage. You turn a wheel at the top of the torchio that presses a disc down onto the pasta dough in the chamber below, forcing the dough through holes in a pierced disc, or die, that sits at the bottom of the chamber. Pasta is extruded from the disc into a dish set on the floor beneath the torchio. Little round holes in the die make long thin strings of spaghetti; other dies have different cuts for hollow maccheroni, squiggly "priest stranglers," or cavatappi, or wide ribbons of fettuccine. I've seen torchios everywhere from country life museums all over Italy to farm kitchens in Sicily, Puglia, Umbria and Tuscany. It was and is a "pasta machine" to save women time. Convenience and saving effort are not new concepts.

Pasta

FRIDAY NIGHT SPAGHETTI WITH TUNA AND BLACK OLIVES

Spaghetti del Venerdì Sera

Serves 6 to 8 as a first course, 4 as a main dish

Tuna never tasted so good. Tossed with spaghetti in a sauce of crunchy onion, black olives, garlic and parsley, canned tuna is the essence of sound home cooking. In the hands of country cooks from Sicily to the Veneto, these few ingredients from the cupboard turn into a magical meatless sauce for pasta in almost no time—a Friday night dinner or quick supper after a movie.

➤ *Cook to Cook:* A generous amount of pasta water plays three roles in this sauce. A little added to the garlic sauté helps to finish cooking the garlic while protecting it from burning. A little more added later dilutes the tomato paste and anchovy mixture, actually turning the sauté into a sauce. Finally, once the tuna is in the pan, a few more tablespoons of pasta water assure that the sauce will cloak the spaghetti, not remain dried up on the bottom of the sauté pan.

Wine Suggestion: A crisp white Frascati Superiore like Fontana Candida Santa Teresa, Conte Zandotti or Casale Marchese

2 large cloves garlic
2 tightly packed tablespoons fresh
  Italian parsley leaves
1/8 teaspoon salt, plus more to taste
1 pound spaghetti
6 quarts boiling salted water
2 tablespoons extra-virgin olive oil
1 medium red onion, cut into 1/4-inch
  dice
2 oil-packed anchovy fillets, rinsed and
  chopped

1 tablespoon tomato paste
1 6-ounce can tuna packed in olive oil,
  lightly drained
Freshly ground black pepper
1/3 cup oil-cured black olives, pitted
  and coarsely chopped
1 tablespoon vinegar-packed capers,
  drained

1. Chop the garlic and parsley with the salt in a food processor. Or mound the salt in a small pile near the edge of a cutting board. Crush the garlic into it with the side of a knife blade. Add the parsley and chop everything fine.

2. Drop the spaghetti into fiercely boiling water and cook until it's a little firmer than you'd like it. Quickly measure out about 1¼ cups of the pasta water and set aside. Drain the spaghetti in a colander.

3. As the pasta cooks, heat the oil in a 12-inch sauté pan over medium-high heat. Stir in the garlic-parsley mixture and half the onion. Sauté until the onion is beginning to soften, about 3 minutes. Don't brown the garlic. Blend in ¼ cup of the reserved pasta water and cook to nothing. Stir in the anchovies and tomato paste, along with about ⅓ cup more of the reserved pasta water. Continue stirring over medium heat 1 minute. Blend in the tuna, seasoning with salt and pepper to taste. Cook another minute, adding a little pasta water if there's no moisture in the pan. Remove from the heat.

4. If the sauce has dried up, stir in enough pasta water to moisten the bottom of the pan. Toss in the drained pasta, the remaining red onion, the olives, and capers. Toss over medium heat a few minutes to thoroughly cloak the spaghetti with sauce. Taste for seasoning and serve hot. No cheese is needed for this dish.

SPAGHETTI ALLA CARBONARA

Serves 6 to 8 as a first course, 4 as a main dish

This dish comes straight from the farms of central Italy, especially the mountains separating Lazio and Abruzzo. Pasta alla Carbonara, or "pasta of the charcoal maker," is Italian bacon and eggs—a country dish of cured pork cooked brown and crisp, tossed with hot pasta, eggs and sheep cheese and finished with lots of black pepper. Cooks from the mountains are indignant when they hear about recipes calling for adding cream to Carbonara. They say it must be the idea of city cooks or ignorant food writers. It has no place in the dish. Keep the pasta simple with pancetta, or even bacon, standing in for the cured pork jowl used in Italy, called *guanciale*. Put aside concerns about fat for one meal and relish old-style Italian cooking. Taste the true Carbonara.

Wine Suggestion: A soft, medium-bodied red like the Abruzzo region's Montepulciano Cerasuolo

2 teaspoons extra-virgin olive oil
6 1/8-inch-thick slices lean pancetta or
    thick-cut bacon, cut into 1/4-inch
    pieces
1 cup (4 ounces) freshly grated
    Pecorino Romano cheese

4 large eggs
Salt and freshly ground black pepper
1 pound spaghetti
6 quarts boiling salted water

1. Heat the oil and pancetta in a 12-inch sauté pan over medium heat, cooking until the pancetta is crisp. Take care not to burn the glaze that appears. It should be brown and cover the bottom of the pan. Cover and set aside.

2. In a bowl, beat 2 teaspoons of the cheese into the eggs, along with a little salt and pepper.

3. Cook the pasta in fiercely boiling water, stirring often, until tender yet slightly undercooked. Just before draining, remove 1/4 cup of the pasta water and add it to the pancetta. Drain the pasta in a colander.

4. Reheat the pancetta over medium heat, scraping up the brown glaze. Add the pasta to the pan, tossing to blend. Mix in the eggs and keep mixing until they're firm and clinging to the pasta. Taste for salt and season generously with pepper. Turn into a warmed bowl and serve immediately. Give the pasta its final seasoning at the table by passing the rest of the Pecorino Romano.

THE CHARCOAL MAKER

The charcoal maker (*il carbonaio*) is a country artisan, usually a farmer making extra money by producing and selling charcoal. He'll work with friends or an assistant, going into the woods and living in a primitive hut until the work is done. They'll work continuously for about three days, with little sleep. They carry the pasta, cheese and pork for this dish in knapsacks to the site and buy eggs at a nearby farm.

Charcoal making is a dying craft. The blacksmiths, coopers and machine shops that once used charcoal are rare today, but *carbonai* still supply restaurants throughout Italy with charcoal for grilling. How they make charcoal hasn't changed in centuries.

Deep in the forest, the men clear a circle nine or so yards in diameter down to bare dirt. They fashion a narrow chimney in the center of the circle by driving three or four tall cut saplings into the ground, spacing them about a foot apart. Logs are stacked upright around the chimney in tight rows until they form a huge mound. The mound is completely covered with sod and weeds, creating what is called *l'uova di legna*, the egg of wood. The chimney of saplings keeps the mound's center hollow and open at the top. The *carbonaio* lights his fire around the mound's base so the hollow chimney draws the fire inward.

The fire burns for three days, demanding constant tending. Lacking much oxygen, the wood burns into charcoal. Carbonai talk of the biting smoke when winds turn unexpectedly, of struggling to keep fires alive in the rain, of sleeping barely at all during the three-day burn. Finally the work is done. The branches of charred wood are loaded into carts to haul to customers and to sell at the Saturday market.

TAGLIATELLE WITH CHICKEN RAGU AND ASPARAGUS

Tagliatelle alla Campagnola

Serves 6 as a first course, 3 to 4 as a main dish

In making this chicken ragù, you could simmer the chunks of browned meat and vegetables in just broth. But adding milk to the broth transforms the sauce. The chicken becomes meltingly tender and the flavors soften and mellow. Partner the ragù with fresh asparagus and good tagliatelle as described below, or layer it with leaves of lasagne and Parmigiano cheese for a different kind of baked pasta.

Emilia-Romagna cook Ida Lancellotti and her son, Angelo, inspired this recipe. The Lancellottis were farmers before they went into the restaurant business. Angelo continues working their land, growing organic vegetables and herbs. He follows his own drummer in the kitchen, while his mother and father still prepare the great traditional dishes of their area. Emilia-Romagna is ragù country. Angelo takes family recipes and makes them his own. We can do the same thing in our kitchens. Serve this pasta as a light supper dish, replacing the asparagus with other vegetables as they come into season—peas, then green beans, followed by broccoli and, finally, thin-cut cabbage.

➤ *Cook to Cook:* Using a deep saucepan instead of a shallow skillet slows down the browning of the chicken and vegetables because the moisture evaporates more slowly in it. This technique mellows the sauce. Do take your time and cook the chicken until it's a rich golden brown.

Wine Suggestion: A lush white Chardonnay like La Palazza's Il Tornese from Romagna or a Piedmont Arneis by Ceretto

½ medium carrot
½ celery stalk
½ red onion
2 thin slices cacciatora or other good-quality salami
1 tightly packed teaspoon fresh Italian parsley leaves
2 tablespoons fruity extra-virgin olive oil
1 bay leaf

1 boned and skinned chicken breast (about 5 ounces), cut into ¼-inch dice
2 boned chicken thighs (about 5 ounces), cut into ¼-inch dice
½ cup dry red wine
1 tablespoon tomato paste
Generous pinch of freshly grated nutmeg

¾ cup milk
¾ cup Mother's Broth (page 196) or
    canned low-sodium chicken broth
Salt and freshly ground black pepper
½ pound pencil-slim asparagus,
    trimmed of tough stems

¾ pound dried tagliatelle or fettuccine
    or 1 recipe Homemade Pasta (page
    69), cut into tagliatelle or fettuccine
6 quarts boiling salted water
1 cup (4 ounces) freshly grated
    Parmigiano-Reggiano cheese

1. Mince together the vegetables, salami, and parsley into tiny pieces. Heat the oil in a 4-quart saucepan over medium-high heat. Stir in the vegetable mixture and the bay leaf. Sauté until the vegetables are pale gold, about 7 to 8 minutes. Add the chicken, reduce the heat to medium, and stir until browned, about 10 minutes.

2. Stir in the wine and tomato paste, reduce the heat, and simmer, uncovered, until the wine is evaporated. Add the nutmeg, milk, and broth. Cover tightly and simmer very gently 30 minutes. The chicken should be tender and the sauce rich and deeply flavored. If necessary, intensify the flavors by simmering a few minutes uncovered. Season to taste.

3. Meanwhile, put the asparagus in a metal basket, set it in a large pot with 1 inch boiling water, cover, and steam about 2 minutes; it should be firm and under-done. Remove and slice on an angle into ½-inch pieces, separating the tips. Set the asparagus aside.

4. Cook the pasta in fiercely boiling water, stirring often, until tender yet firm to the bite. Drain in a colander.

5. Toss the pasta with the sauce and asparagus pieces, reserving the tips. Turn into a hot serving bowl, fold in the cheese, and scatter the asparagus tips over the top. Serve hot.

A FAMILY KEEPS ALIVE THE TRADITIONS OF ARTISANSHIP

A sign outside the door says Ristorante Lancellotti is closed on Sunday. Inside, the family has been in the kitchen since eight cooking a typical farmhouse breakfast of years ago—from the days when the Lancellotis were solely farmers. We are in the country town of Soliera, in the Emilia-Romagna region, and food, even breakfast food, is taken very seriously here.

Eleven of us are doffing aprons, opening bottles of homemade wine, setting out jugs of water and putting in place the last of the big platters piled with the puffy discs of fried bread called *gnocco fritto*. We make room for bowls of fruit conserve and plates of prosciutto, salami and coppa. Most everything on the table was made by the people sitting down to eat it—the Lancellottis and their friends from nearby farms.

Chairs scrape as we pull up to the long table. The entire Lancellotti family is here. Matriarch Mamma Ida at the center of the table is probably sixty—sturdy and strong-looking. She's scanning the table, making sure everything is as it should be. Thanks to an adoring Italian press, Italians would have to be living under a rock not to have heard of her fabulous handmade pasta. Next to her, husband Camillo, in his usual shirt and tie, looks more like a banker than the farmer he once was. They call him *Il Primario*, "Mr. First." He's head of the family and king of first courses. His specialties are the traditional sauces to dress his wife's pastas, the first courses that are the pride of Emilia-Romagna's cooking.

Seated among the friends are their three grown sons. As is typical of family restaurants and farm operations everywhere, each son has focused on a skill needed for the business.

Francesco keeps the wine cellar and the balsamic vinegar attic, and he runs the dining room with brother Emilio, who is also the historical researcher and collector of local country lore. His research into Italy's culinary history feeds older brother Angelo's imagination. Italy's food writers have dubbed him the farmer cook—he brings new dishes to the menu inspired by running the family's organic farm and his herb garden. This is more a Renaissance wonderland of every sort of culinary and medicinal herb than a little patch of plants for the kitchen. Angelo's wife, Zdena, is his partner in the kitchen.

Our mutual friend Marco Costanzini, of Modena's consortium of traditional balsamic vinegar makers, has brought his new wife, Anna, to breakfast. And he's brought a gift—his mother's fruit conserve, made with fruits from her orchard cooked in grape syrup from her vineyard. Farm breakfasts are no novelty to Marco.

Between bits of salami and sips of wine, the Lancellottis talk about being part of a net-work of small-scale or artisan food producers, restaurateurs and scholars. They share con-cerns I've heard from other people in the food business in Italy. New laws from the European Union require changes in food production methods. Most follow large-scale

Angelo Lancellotti in
his herb garden.

industrial models. The Lancellottis and their colleagues insist the key to Italy's culinary and cultural identity is small-scale artisan production. Everyone's talking back and forth across the table. "Food here is an expression of local values," grunts one of the men.

Camillo's opinion is that the politicians don't understand or care. "Italy isn't about factory food. No offense, but we are not America." I stay quiet. "Here, even city people go to the country each year to buy their wine from the man who raises the grapes, their salami from the farmer who kills the pigs—not from a big factory! These artisans have good businesses. Now the laws say they have to change or lose them. Even if they want to follow the new rules, many can't afford it."

What they understand the new laws to mean is that if you sell the foods you produce directly to the people who eat them, you can go on making them the way you always have. But if they have to pass through the hands of another person, like a distributor, a shop or a restaurant before getting to the consumer, they must follow the new laws.

Down the table, the salami maker, who's debating over complying with the laws, thinks with these changed methods he'll earn less money than he used to for his salami. The quality will go down. "Look," he says, "they tell me I have to put in new tiled walls and floors. Fine. Except my salami tastes the way it does because of the microorganisms, the good bacteria, on my walls and floors. They ripen it in a special way. Don't misunderstand. We're clean. You have to be. But new walls and floors will kill the salami."

Emilio adds, "A man in the Piedmont who makes some of the best air-dried beef you'll ever taste is closing up. Too much is lost. For him, it isn't worth it. Look, he has enough money to do this. Don't forget that. Not everyone does." No solutions are reached. We lean back in our chairs. Someone philosophizes about how nothing ever stays the same and says the subject will not end until the new laws change.

Mamma Ida reminisces about the changes from when she was a girl on the farm to now. Camillo explains to me that how you ate in a farm family depended upon how much time and help the women had for the kitchen garden and for cooking. When there were sisters and a mother who loved the garden, you ate well. When there were only boys, often you didn't. The boys point out that Mamma never needed help from any daughters.

PASTA OF THE GRAPE HARVEST

Pasta della Vendemmia

Serves 6 to 8 as a first course; doubles easily

Tart, sweet and piquant, this pasta is made during the grape harvest in Catania on Sicily's eastern coast. It's sauced with a spicy sweet syrup of the boiled-down juice from fresh-pressed wine grapes, called *vin cotto*, or cooked wine. An ancient sugar substitute, vin cotto was made all over the Mediterranean by farmers who couldn't afford expensive sugar. Even now, when sugar is cheap, Sicilian farmers still make vin cotto because, as one woman said, "Sugar sweetens; vin cotto flavors." When they celebrate bringing in the grapes, they toss the garnet-colored syrup with pasta and sometimes sprinkle the dish with green pistachios. The pasta has an enchanting quality—it tastes new and fresh, yet a little mysterious, perhaps because it possesses such an ancient lineage.

➤ *Cook to Cook:* Store Vin Cotto in the refrigerator up to 5 days or freeze it up to 6 months. Drizzle over fresh fruit, ice cream, meat and poultry, or simmer it into pan sauces. In Italy, it has seasoned and sauced savory and sweet dishes for centuries.

Wine Suggestion: A Sicilian red Rapitala Rosso or a dry, grapy Lambrusco di Sorbara

5 pounds flavorful red grapes (organic wine grapes are ideal—Zinfandel, Cabernet Sauvignon, Pinot Noir, or Sangiovese)

1½ cups dry red wine

1 generous teaspoon anise seeds, crushed

⅛ teaspoon ground cinnamon

2 whole cloves

Shredded zest of 1 large orange

Generous pinch of salt, or more to taste

¼ teaspoon freshly ground black pepper, or more to taste

¾ pound spaghettini or thin linguine

6 quarts boiling salted water

¾ cup shelled salted pistachios, coarsely chopped

About ¾ pound high-quality ricotta (optional)

1. Stem and wash the grapes well. Finely chop in a food processor. Turn into a 12-inch skillet along with the wine, spices, orange zest, salt, and pepper.

2. Bring to a boil and cook, uncovered, 20 minutes, or until reduced by about half. With a wooden spatula, scrape down the sides of the pan and stir often. Cool.

3. Strain the grapes, pressing down on the skins to extract as much juice as possible. The mixture should coat a spoon and measure $2^1/2$ to 3 cups; if necessary, reduce another 10 minutes. Pour the strained syrup back into the skillet. Taste for seasoning and spice balance.

4. Cook the pasta in fiercely boiling water, stirring often, until tender yet firm to the bite. Drain in a colander.

5. Toss the pasta with the sauce and $1/2$ cup of the pistachios until coated. Mound in warmed pasta bowls, top each serving with a dollop of ricotta if desired, and sprinkle with the remaining $1/4$ cup pistachios. Serve hot.

**Wine grapes for Vin Cotto in the Palermo market
labeled "nostrale," meaning "ours," or local.**

LITTLE HANDKERCHIEFS WITH PORTOBELLO MUSHROOMS

Fazzoletti coi Funghi

Serves 8 as a first course, 4 to 6 as a main dish

Baked in a sauce of broth, tomato and a little cream, this mushroom-stuffed pasta is much lighter than versions napped in rich ragù and béchamel. The dish was lunch on a May afternoon on the guest farm of Black Elk, one of Italy's oldest organic farming cooperatives. Set on a slope in Marche's hilly farm country, Black Elk's small factory processes flours, grains, pasta sauces and jams from foods grown within sight of its windows. At the guest farm up the hill, the cooperative's farmwomen take turns in the kitchen, treating the work as a lark, a break in the rhythm of farm life.

They showed me why the baked dish is called "little handkerchiefs." They cut Black Elk's boxed lasagne noodles in half, spoon filling in their centers and flip over the other half to enclose it—like loosely wrapping a handkerchief around something to cover it. It's such an easy method you could use with most lasagne or ravioli fillings. The effect is lighter and more interesting than the usual lasagne.

➤ *Cook to Cook:* Wedges of portobello mushrooms replace the fresh porcini so plentiful in the Marche. Use fresh porcini if you are lucky enough to have them.

Wine Suggestion: A medium-bodied red from Umbria or Marche by Castello della Sala, Lungarotti or Le Terrazze

2½ tablespoons extra-virgin olive oil

¾ pound portobello mushrooms with stems, cut into ½-inch chunks

¼ pound salami (such as soppressata, Toscano, cacciatori, or Genoa), cut into ⅛ by 1-inch strips

2 large cloves garlic, minced

2 tightly packed tablespoons fresh Italian parsley leaves, minced

1 medium onion, cut vertically into thin shards

1 cup Mother's Broth (page 196) or canned low-sodium chicken broth

3 large delicious tomatoes, cut into ½-inch dice, or 1 14-ounce can whole tomatoes, drained and chopped

Salt and freshly ground black pepper

½ pound dried lasagne pasta or ½ recipe Homemade Pasta (page 69), cut into lasagne noodles

6 quarts boiling salted water

½ cup freshly grated Parmigiano-Reggiano cheese

¼ cup heavy cream

1. Heat 2 tablespoons of the oil in a 12-inch skillet over medium-high heat. Quickly brown the mushrooms and half the salami, stirring often and blending in half the garlic toward the end of cooking. The mushrooms should be crisp and dark brown. Remove from the pan and reserve. Clean the skillet.

2. Heat the remaining $1/2$ tablespoon oil in the pan, at medium high. Add the parsley, onion, and the remaining salami and brown the onion and salami, stirring in the remaining garlic near the end of cooking. Add $1/2$ cup of the broth and reduce to nothing. Add the remaining broth and reduce again. Blend in the tomatoes and toss over high heat a few minutes. Season to taste and set aside.

3. Preheat the oven to 375°F. Oil a 9 by 13-inch baking dish. Cook the pasta in fiercely boiling water, stirring often, until tender yet firm to the bite. Drain in a colander.

4. Cut the noodles crosswise in half. Place 2 tablespoons of the mushroom mixture on one end of each noodle and fold the pasta over the filling. Arrange in a single layer in the baking dish. Nap with the tomato sauce. Cover the pan with foil and bake until hot, about 30 minutes. Sprinkle the Parmigiano-Reggiano and cream over the rolls just before removing from the oven. Serve hot.

ARTICHOKE WEDDING TIMBALE

Timballo Matrimoniale

Serves 8 to 12 as a main dish

After seeing the movie *Big Night,* with its showstopping pasta pie, or timbale, a friend asked me to come up with a meatless version of the dish for her daughter's wedding. This is the result: A golden crust encloses corkscrews of fusilli pasta sauced with chunks of artichokes, peas and béchamel. I add the pasta in two layers, separating them with a spicy mix of pine nuts and onion, and finish the last layer with garlicky tomato sauce before putting the top crust in place.

This is the kind of pasta extravaganza Italy's old nobility showed off on its banquet tables. Over the centuries, recipes like this one filtered down to landowners, farmers and peasants. These families always saved them for celebrating great occasions, and after the impossibly baroque Tortellini Pie in *The Splendid Table,* I couldn't resist another version here.

I believe dishes like this are worth the work. When I knock myself out cooking something elaborate, I want my guests to stand and cheer. With this stunning timbale, they do.

➤ *Cook to Cook:* Do all the components ahead of time, then assemble and bake the timbale before serving. At southern Italian feasts, timbales like this one are first courses. For us, they're main dishes. With a dish this important, serve only a simple antipasto like Sweet-Tart Salad of Apples, Basil and Sorrel (page 44), and have Iced Summer Peaches (page 372) or Figs in Honeyed Wine (page 374) for dessert.

Wine Suggestion: A Veneto Ripasso di Valpolicella by
St. Stefano, Quintarelli, or Spinosa

PASTRY (MAKE 30 MINUTES TO 3 DAYS AHEAD)

4 cups (1 1/4 pounds) unbleached all-purpose flour (preferably organic)

1 1/4 teaspoons salt

1/4 cup sugar

3 sticks (12 ounces) cold unsalted butter, cut into chunks

2 large eggs, beaten

9 to 10 tablespoons cold dry white wine or water

ARTICHOKES (MAKE 1 TO 2 DAYS AHEAD)

3 large lemons, halved

10 large artichokes

1 cup white wine vinegar

6 quarts boiling salted water

Salt and freshly ground black pepper

BECHAMEL SAUCE (MAKE 2 DAYS AHEAD)

5 tablespoons butter

1 medium onion, coarsely chopped

1 tablespoon black peppercorns, crushed

4 whole cloves, cracked

3 large bay leaves, broken

3 large cloves garlic, crushed

4 1/2 tablespoons all-purpose unbleached flour (preferably organic)

4 1/2 cups milk

1/4 cup heavy cream

1 teaspoon fresh thyme leaves

TOMATO SAUCE (MAKE 1 DAY AHEAD)

2 tablespoons olive oil

12 fresh basil leaves, torn

1 large clove garlic, minced

1 14-ounce can whole tomatoes, drained

Salt and freshly ground black pepper

PINE NUT CONDIMENT (MAKE DAY OF BAKING)

About 1/8 teaspoon salt

1 medium clove garlic

About 1/8 teaspoon freshly ground black pepper

Generous pinch of hot red pepper flakes

1 1/2 to 2 tablespoons fresh lemon juice

1/2 medium onion, cut into 1/4-inch dice

2 tightly packed tablespoons fresh basil leaves, coarsely chopped

3/4 cup pine nuts, toasted

1 generous tablespoon currants

ASSEMBLY AND GLAZE

2 tablespoons hot water

Generous pinch of saffron threads

2 large egg yolks

3/4 pound fusilli

6 quarts boiling salted water

1 1/4 cups (5 ounces) freshly grated Parmigiano-Reggiano cheese

3/4 cup (3 ounces) shredded Sini Fulvi Pastore, Pecorino Toscano, or domestic young sheep cheese or Fontinella

1 cup frozen tiny peas, defrosted

Salt and freshly ground black pepper

1. **For the pastry,** combine the dry ingredients in a food processor or large bowl. Cut in the butter with rapid pulses of the processor, or with your fingertips, until the butter is the size of peas. Add the eggs and 9 tablespoons of the cold liquid. Pulse or toss with a fork only until the dough starts to gather in clumps. Add up to 1 tablespoon more liquid if it seems dry. Gather into a ball, wrap, and chill 30 minutes to 3 days.

2. **For the artichokes,** squeeze the lemons into a bowl holding 2 quarts of water. One at a time, break off all the leaves around the base of each artichoke until you come to the pale green ones at its center. With a sharp knife, cut away the stem. With the knife, peel away all the dark green leaf stubs from the sides and bottom of the artichoke until the part that remains is pale green—this is the artichoke bottom.

Now cut off the top two thirds of the artichoke and, with a spoon, scoop out the hairy choke. Rinse each artichoke bottom and put into the lemon water.

Add the vinegar and artichokes to the boiling water. Cook over high heat 3 to 4 minutes, until the artichokes are barely tender—they should be quite crisp when pierced with a knife. Drain and rinse under cold water. Cut each artichoke into 6 pieces. Hold at room temperature up to 6 hours, or refrigerate up to 2 days in a sealed plastic bag.

3. **For the béchamel,** set a 4-quart saucepan over medium-high heat. Add the butter, onion, pepper, cloves, bay, and garlic and sauté and stir 4 minutes, or until very aromatic. Blend in the flour and cook, stirring, 3 minutes, or until frothy. Gradually stir in the milk until smooth and keep stirring until it boils. Lower the heat so the sauce simmers and cook, uncovered, 8 minutes, or until the sauce is thick enough to coat a spoon and has no raw flour taste. Season to taste.

Pour through a fine strainer into a bowl, stirring and pressing on the ingredients to extract every bit of flavor. Stir in the cream and thyme. Lay a sheet of plastic wrap on the surface of the sauce. Cool, cover, and refrigerate up to 2 days. Bring to room temperature before assembling the timbale.

4. **For the tomato sauce,** in a 10-inch skillet, heat the oil over medium-high heat. Stir in the basil and garlic. Cook no more than a minute, then stir in the tomatoes, breaking them up with your hands as you add them. Stir over high heat until thick, about 3 minutes. Season to taste. Cover and set aside for a few hours, or cool and refrigerate up to 1 day.

5. **For the pine nut condiment,** mound the salt in a small pile on a cutting board, crush the garlic clove into it, and mince it fine. Place in a medium bowl along with the black and red pepper, lemon juice, and onion. Let stand at room temperature until shortly before assembling the timbale.

6. When ready to assemble the timbale, stir the basil, pine nuts, and currants into the onion–lemon juice mixture. Taste for seasoning. Keep at room temperature.

7. **To assemble and bake,** butter a 10- to 11-inch springform pan. Roll out two thirds of the dough on a floured surface to a 16- to 17-inch circle. Fit it into the pan, trimming the edges to a 1½-inch overhang. Reserve the scraps. Roll out the rest of the dough into a 15-inch circle. Place on a baking sheet. Chill both doughs for 30 minutes.

8. Set the oven rack in the lowest position. Preheat the oven to 400°F. Stir the hot water and saffron together in a small bowl. Beat in the yolks. Season the artichokes with salt and pepper.

9. Cook the pasta in fiercely boiling water until it is slightly firmer than usual. Drain in a colander. Turn it back into the pasta pot and add the béchamel, artichokes, cheeses, and peas. Fold together and taste for seasoning.

10. Spread half the pasta in the bottom of the pastry-lined pan. Top with the pine nut mixture. Add the rest of the pasta and top it with the tomato sauce.

11. Brush the overhanging rim of the pastry with the egg yolk mixture. Set the dough round on the pie. Press together the edges. Form a thick upstanding rim by rolling the edges toward the center of the pie. Crimp or flute the crust all around. Brush the rim and top of the pie with the egg yolk mixture. Decorate the top of the crust with the reserved pastry scraps, using them to make star-shaped cutouts, or crisscross thin strips of pastry in a lattice pattern. Brush again with the egg.

12. Set the pie on a baking sheet. Bake 45 minutes. Lower the heat to 350°F and bake another 25 minutes, or until the crust is a rich deep golden brown. Remove from the oven. Let cool 10 to 15 minutes.

13. **To unmold,** set the pie on a large can and, with an oven mitt, release the springform. Place the pie on a plate and decorate with clusters of Champagne grapes if desired. Cut in wedges to serve.

LITTLE PARCELS OF SWEET SQUASH

Caramelle di Zucca

Makes about 48 parcels, serving 6 to 8

These are filled pasta with a difference—sweet, savory and mysterious. Detecting their subtleties becomes a dinner game—is the sweet from almonds, candied fruits or anise? Is that black pepper or the spicy mustard fruits of Cremona? Imagine all this against a backdrop of velvety yam and sweet winter squash. One friend claims the filling all by itself is sublime tossed with pasta. But this is a dish straight from the medieval court of Mantua, interpreted and reinterpreted by the Lombardy region's cooks for centuries and served for Christmas.

This version is from Nicla Zarattini, who cooks at La Dispensa, in the country town of Castellaro, south of Lake Garda. La Dispensa is Nicla and her husband's, Sergio's, tiny food and wine shop, where they sell Nicla's dishes to take home and serve them in the second-floor dining room. She calls the pastas *caramelle,* or bonbons. They imitate Italy's cellophane-wrapped hard candies with their two twisted ends. Instead of cellophane, pasta forms the little packages.

➤ *Cook to Cook:* The filling can be moistened with broth and tossed with pasta, or used to fill tartlet shells. Prepare the filling up to a day ahead and store in the refrigerator. This is the Mantua version of sweet squash-filled pasta. In my first book, *The Splendid Table,* I gave the Ferrara recipe—austere by comparison: squash, cheese and spice. Ferrara and Mantua are practically neighbors across the Po River. Their two Renaissance courts had much in common, but their cooks never agreed about squash fillings.

Wine Suggestion: A rich, berry-tasting red like Franciacorta Rosso
by Cola or Ricci Curbastro

FILLING

$1/2$ large ($1^1/2$ pounds) seeded butternut squash or sweet pumpkin

1 medium yam

1 small to medium onion, minced

A 4-inch branch fresh rosemary

2 teaspoons unsalted butter

1 generous tablespoon currants, soaked in hot water to cover with 1 teaspoon anise-flavored liqueur (optional) and drained

$1/3$ cup blanched almonds, toasted and ground

2 tablespoons minced mostarda di Cremona (Italian candied fruits in spiced syrup sold in jars in specialty food stores)

$1/8$ teaspoon freshly ground black pepper

1 cup (4 ounces) freshly grated
   Parmigiano-Reggiano cheese
Salt
Freshly grated nutmeg

1 recipe Homemade Pasta (page 69)
SAGE BUTTER SAUCE
10 fresh sage leaves
4 tablespoons unsalted butter

$1/2$ cup Mother's Broth (page 196) or
   canned low-sodium chicken broth
Salt and freshly ground black pepper
8 quarts boiling salted water
$2/3$ cup freshly grated Parmigiano-
   Reggiano cheese

1. Preheat the oven to 375°F. Cover a baking sheet with foil and lightly oil it. Turn the squash cut side down on the foil and place the whole yam next to it. Roast about 1 hour, or until easily pierced with a knife. Cool.

2. Split the yam and scoop out the flesh of the yam and squash. Puree in a food processor. Turn into a bowl.

3. In a small skillet, sauté the onion and rosemary in the butter until golden. Discard the rosemary. Add the onions, currants, almonds, candied fruits, pepper, and cheese to the squash mixture. Blend, tasting for seasoning. Finish with salt and freshly grated nutmeg to taste.

4. Following the directions on page 70, roll out a quarter of the dough at a time to sheer enough that you can see the color of your hand, or the print from this page, through it. With a sharp knife, cut into rectangles 2 inches by 3 inches.

5. Mound about 1 to $1^{1}/2$ teaspoons of filling down the center of each piece, forming a small log about $1^{1}/2$ inches long. Moisten the edges of the pasta with water and carefully pinch closed over the filling into a secure seal. Twist the ends to look like hard candy wrappers, pinching to seal. Arrange on porous surfaces—cake racks or towel-covered flat baskets—without touching. Do not cover—they need to dry a bit. Refrigerate until about 20 minutes before cooking. (These hold well for 24 hours in the refrigerator; they do not freeze well.)

6. Sauté the sage leaves in the butter in a small saucepan over medium-high heat 2 minutes, or until crisp. Lift out the leaves and reserve. Add the stock to the pan and boil 1 minute. Season to taste and remove from the heat. Reheat the sauce when the pasta is ready for serving.

7. Slip the pasta into the boiling water and cook about 3 minutes. Test by snipping off a corner of one "bonbon" to see if it is tender but still has some "bite," or firmness. Drain gently in a colander.

8. Layer the pasta parcels in a heated deep bowl, spooning a little of the reheated sage butter over each layer. Scatter the sage leaves and cheese onto the pasta before serving hot.

Pasta

PASTA MEETS THE TOMATO

Destiny in a Bowl

I must begin this chapter with a confession: There is nothing, absolutely nothing that pleasures me more than a bowl of pasta and tomato sauce. When I want to reach out with all my love to my husband, a dish of pasta and tomatoes is almost always in my hands. When I am worn out and the world isn't such a nice place to be in, I make tomato sauce and pasta. When time is short but dear friends must be fed with joy and not pressure, I make pasta with tomato sauce. Never are any two of these pastas alike, because for me, this is the food of instinct. I cook listening to something beyond a recipe—the tomatoes always seem to tell me what kind of sauce they want to be this time. Pasta and tomatoes restores me. I believe every tomato sauce tastes like a new experience. And I believe the tomato and tomato sauces with pasta have never been given their due. This chapter is a beginning.

In the years of exploring Italy's countryside, I cannot think of a farmhouse or country home I have visited where I did not see tomatoes preserved in some way or another. I remember September in my Tuscan cousin Edda's kitchen, and a year's worth of bright scarlet tomato sauce cooling in canning jars on the old marble counter. In Umbria, I watched from afar as a woman simmered her garden's tomatoes in a huge battered pot set on a brazier outdoors, under a tree. Next to her on a table, bottles and jars were lined up waiting for the tomato puree. Elizabetta Del Monaco, a farmwoman who, with her brother, runs one of Puglia's oldest pottery businesses, hangs branches of whole small tomatoes in the cool grotto that is also their workshop. The tomatoes will winter there, shriveling slightly, their flavors intensifying with each passing week. Nine hundred miles to the north, farmwomen in Romagna twist small tomatoes from their stems, thread them on strings and hang them like garlands across the mantles of their homes.

Everyone I met reminisced about putting up tomatoes—drying them or boiling them, making paste or hanging the whole fruit on its branches in cool pantries. No other single food has become so much a part of Italy's country cooking. The tomato grows everywhere, from the Alps of the Alto Adige at Austria's border to Sicily in the middle of the Mediterranean Sea.

Tomatoes flavor countless foods—pizza, polenta, rice, beans, meats, seafood and all kinds of vegetables. But at every table, in every home, no matter what else I was offered, eventually a bowl of pasta with some kind of tomato sauce was set down before me. Even in places like Lombardy's high mountain valleys near the Swiss border, where the tomato was a latecomer and pasta was not part of the local tradition, the two were served.

Pasta twirls on the fork, wonderfully messy, chewy, wheaten, lively. Add tomato—bursting with taste, juicy, tart, sweet, meaty—and the whole becomes greater than its parts. Far more than just good eating, the coupling of pasta and tomatoes is enormously satisfying. Scientifically, the carbohydrates in wheat and tomatoes stimulate the production of serotonin—our body's "feel-good" chemical. But I believe, beyond science in a realm of the subconscious, we respond to the genius of perfect simplicity in two foods meant for each other but kept apart until relatively recently by an accident of botany. Wheat of the Mediterranean and tomatoes from the Americas belie the idea of what grows together goes together. These two ancient foods came together from two ancient worlds separated by an ocean. In their joining, identified a nation. To the world in this century, a plate of pasta with a tomato sauce is Italy.

Since the ancient Carthaginians first sold wheat to the Romans, it has been Italy's most valuable grain both in the marketplace and in the kitchen. Yet in over three thousand years, no single food had brought to pasta and bread what the tomato did. Although tomatoes arrived in Italy in the 1500s from the Americas via Spain, their pairing with pasta did not become popular for three centuries. Instead, tomatoes immediately stirred controversy. Vivid, exotic and new, they were grist for debate among botanists over how edible, nourishing or deadly they might be. They remained a curiosity of the wealthy, eventually eaten stuffed, sautéed, stewed or as salad. Early tomato sauces were for meat. The first written recipe of tomato sauce for pasta did not appear until 1839, published by Ippolito Cavalcanti, the Duke of Buonvicino, in his cookbook, *Cucina Teòrico-Pratica (Cooking Theory and Practice)*.

Tomatoes gradually moved from the tables of the wealthy to the gardens of middle and lower classes. Many other foods had traveled this path, yet nothing took over kitchens like the tomato in nineteenth-century Italy. Why? After two centuries of cultivation, tomatoes had probably come to taste better, and they've always been easy to grow. A year's worth grew in the garden patch a landowner usually allotted to his sharecroppers to feed their families. Except for what they raised on this piece of ground, everything else they harvested had to be shared with the landowner. Farmwomen discovered how delicious tomatoes are on their own and also learned they stretched a little meat into good-tasting, plentiful sauces. Tomatoes brought unique sumptuousness to minestrone, bean or bread dishes, almost anything made with polenta and stews of fish or meat. No other single, easily had ingredient—except salt—married flavors as the tomato did.

By the mid-1800s, the fragrance of cooking tomatoes meant summer in the countryside. In farmyards and back gardens, cauldrons of tomatoes simmered over outdoor fires as families put up bushels and bushels for winter. Although few country people probably thought of vitamins back then, they knew tomatoes made them feel good and made their food taste better.

Countless tomato sauces for pasta evolved in a matter of decades, not centuries. Nearly every savory food successfully joined tomatoes in the sauce pot. Tomatoes and pasta had their detractors, who called them commonplace, the result of tasteless cooking and overindulgence. Few Italians paid much attention.

Pasta traveled north and west into Europe long before the tomato's acceptance, yet not until tomato sauces joined pasta in foreign parts did its popularity climb. Pasta and tomatoes were the siren's song, drawing foreigners into Italian restaurants. Once there, they learned to love other things Italian. Interestingly, initially most of them had tomato too—pizza, Chicken Cacciatora, Steak Pizzaiola and the Parmigiano family of eggplant, veal and poultry. Today, no city in Europe—and in much of the world beyond—is without an eating place serving spaghetti with some kind of tomato sauce. This pair is the foreigner's talisman of Italy. And for most Italians, pasta with tomato is the talisman of family and home.

As my collection of pasta and tomato recipes grew, I realized every Italian cook I met had at least several favorites. Tomato sauce is a sauce for every man. Anyone can afford a tomato. Anyone can make a good tomato sauce with what's on hand, and most country cooks do. Tomato sauces require no stocks or fancy ingredients. Yet for their incredible variety—I saw at least two hundred recipes in my travels—no one had codified tomato sauces. As I mulled over the tomato and its sauces, a structure revealed itself. There is logic to the tomato sauce. With its "Guide to Tomato Sauce," this chapter gives us the keys to understanding the four fundamental types of tomato sauces. We learn how Italian farmwomen call out different aspects of tomato character by selecting one seasoning over another.

As my notes on tomato sauces piled up, so did notes on tomato lore, especially on country ways of preserving tomatoes. "Rites of Red" tell the stories of tomato traditions on Italy's farms.

With what is old, there is also something new. We have a new tomato culture in America. Taste is back. We have an explosion of kinds of tomatoes that even a few years ago were only available if you grew them yourself. Today you can go to a good market in tomato season and have your pick of all kinds of really good tomatoes. Now we can have a guide to tasting tomatoes (see page 113). A tomato is not a single flavor experience anymore. There are at least three distinctly different taste profiles in the tomato world today. So why not learn how to identify them and use them in sauces? Most Italian farm cooks always grow and mix several kinds of tomatoes in their pasta dishes.

My cousin Edda's Uncooked Tomato Sauce for Fusilli (page 122) illustrates the easiest way to eat tomatoes with pasta and it has all the hints we need to blend tomatoes if an assortment is available. It is part of a small set of recipes that are a lesson illustrating how method rather than ingredients yields dramatic differences in a dish. Just changing the pot you cook in can give you a new tomato sauce for supper. Every recipe in this chapter offers a technique you can apply elsewhere. For instance, Spiced Cauliflower with Ziti (page 138) illustrates how tomatoes bolster other vegetables. Use the same method with any number of vegetables. You will see how a tomato sauce with meat means Sundays and family (page 146), and how it can be not-so-subtle weapon of mothers-in-law with penchants for control (page 145). Tomatoes and pasta have stories to tell.

A Guide to Tomato Sauces

This deep exploration of all the possibilities tomatoes and tomato sauces present may seem excessive to some. Yet my goal is to open up new realms of pleasure and invention, not overwhelm. Consider this an invitation into a world of taste possibilities you may not have known existed. Between this guide to sauces and to the new tomatoes we can find much more easily these days, you'll see how with no extra work you can now possess a sorcerer's cache of flavoring secrets. It's all waiting in the tomato.

Italian women claim there is nothing to making a good tomato sauce. They are right, and they are wrong. In years of watching and talking with cooks throughout Italy, I have discovered that extraordinary tomato sauce is about the small touches, sometimes unconscious ones.

Sicilian farmer Adelina Norcia brings a vibrance to her sauce by flicking a few seeds of hot pepper into the sauté for a barely detectable tingle under the other flavors. Tuscan cook Sylvia Martignoli makes a leaner sauce than she used to by starting pancetta in a cold pan, to cook out more of its fat. She says the browned bits of meat have more flavor and with them in the sauce, she doesn't need as much fat. Puglia restaurant owner Dora Ricci deepens the taste of her sauce by sautéing her whole small tomatoes in a hot, hot pan with onions and herbs, then pureeing them in a food mill. On an olive estate an hour's drive from Dora Ricci, Rosalba Ciannamea silkens her sauce with her own home-pressed extra-virgin olive oil at the end of cooking.

What follows is a guide to tomatoes and tomato sauces that brings together all the secrets shared by country cooks I've met throughout Italy, and all the information I have gathered in years of being obsessed with tomatoes. I love tomatoes. Although my tomato dementia embraces a passion for just about every use of the fruit, nothing for me is as utterly extraordinary as pasta and tomatoes. Clearly this is why the tomato was placed on earth.

Tomatoes are a sauce just as they come from the vine. All the elements are there in a good tomato—the meaty lusciousness, the right play of acid and sweet and nuances that keep them from being one-dimensional and boring. No other savory food can so easily become so many different sauces by merely pairing it with different ingredients, or changing its method of cooking. This is why tomato sauces are so popular in Italy and America. And if you think there is solely a single tomato sauce with a few variations, think again. This guide and the recipes following it are about the genius and the diversity of the tomato.

TOMATO BASICS

Finding, Tasting and
Using Fresh Tomatoes

Taste Before Buying   "Vine-ripened" is no assurance of good taste. Seek varieties bred for flavor, not shipping. Happily, we are in the throes of a tomato revolution. Many new varieties are appearing in the market, with more heirloom seeds being rediscovered as I write. Organic growers are leading the way, offering a range of exciting varieties with enormous individuality and taste.

Shop at farmers' markets, co-ops, roadside stands and specialty stores. Ask to taste before buying. If asking isn't possible, buy a single tomato and bite into it just as you would a piece of fruit. This is the only way of knowing if the tomato is any good. I have learned the hard way that, unlike most fruits, how a tomato smells gives no hint at its taste. And, if you have the space and inclination, try growing your own tomatoes. (See page 396 for mail-order sources.)

Think of Each Variety of Tomato as an Individual Seasoning   In summer, we now have the luxury of picking and choosing our tomatoes. They fit into three flavor profiles that can be combined to create exciting sauces: The trio is mellow, high-contrast and sweet. Remember, acid in a tomato is like salt in cooking—it is essential to bring out all the other flavors.

> First is the mellow, suave tomato—rich and round-flavored, with acidity and sweetness in soft, equal balance. This is our most familiar tomato taste and the one that has been the foundation of fresh sauces in the past. Examples: Brandywine, Rutgers, beefsteak and Zebra.

> Second is the high-contrast, brash-tasting tomato, with dramatic peaks and valleys of high-sugar and high-acid flavors. These bring panache to sauces made with either mellow or sweet tomatoes or both. Examples: cherry tomatoes, Sweet 100s, Sun Gold, "cocktail" tomatoes, Red Currant, Green Grape and Early Cascade.

> Third is the low-acid, sweet tomato. These are sweet with little or no acid for contrast. For my taste, they are too noncommittal, too nice, too sweet. Use them with restraint, as they can flatten tastes. Examples: These are usually orange, yellow, or white; specific varieties include Taxi Cab and White Wonder.

> Plum tomatoes are frequently tasteless. Exceptions are heirlooms and plum tomatoes bred for flavor, not shipping, like Polish Paste, Oxheart and Cornucopia. Certainly use any plum tomato tasting really delicious. Just remember, the Roma is probably the most overrated tomato in America.

Store Tomatoes Outside the Refrigerator   Cold kills flavor. At 40°F (the temperature of most refrigerators), tomatoes turn hard and taste dull. Keep them at room temperature, in a basket for air circulation. To ripen, cover lightly with newspaper to trap the fruit's natural ethylene gases that will speed the process. Keep ripening tomatoes away from direct sunlight and turn them each day. If you start out with a good-tasting but underripe tomato, you'll have a decent-tasting one ripened off the vine—not quite the equal of vine-ripening, but at the end of the season, these are still a pleasure to eat. At their peak, tomatoes should give a little when squeezed but not be soft.

To Peel and Seed, or Not to Peel and Seed?   Over three hundred elements create the taste of a tomato. The gel that surrounds the seeds contains a significant amount of them. Italian cooks have always known this. Traditional sauce recipes often call for the entire tomato—seeds, peel and flesh—to be cooked and then passed through a food mill. Personal preference and a sauce's tradition dictate whether or not to peel and seed.

For instance, Tomato Sauce Mellowed by Simmering (page 128) exemplifies the tradition of cooking the entire tomato, then passing the sauce through a food mill to separate out peels and seeds. In contrast, when Neapolitans call one of their favorite simple tomato sauces *filetto di pomodoro* (literally fillets of tomato), they have peeled and thoroughly seeded the tomatoes, leaving only the meat of the fruit. In Tuscany, I met one farmhouse cook who was scandalized by the sight of unpeeled tomatoes in a raw tomato sauce, while her neighbor was convinced diced fresh tomatoes uncompromised by the heat needed to skin them are essential to the sauce's goodness. Obviously, the directive here is do what feels best for your own tastes.

Do Peel and Seeds Turn a Sauce Bitter?   Find the answer in this test: I made the same fresh tomato sauce in two batches with excellent-tasting fruit, cooking them side by side. They simmered over medium-low heat, uncovered, in two identical three-quart saucepans. The sauce of peeled, seeded tomatoes tasted bitter, overcooked and metallic, while the sauce made of whole tomatoes was vibrant and appealingly fresh. The same logic applies to canned tomatoes.

Obviously, if a raw tomato's skin tastes bitter, it should be peeled away before cooking. Sometimes Italian cooks seed tomatoes to eliminate liquid in a sauce so it will thicken faster, keeping a fresher tomato taste. Some cooks love the meatiness of peeled, seeded tomatoes, whether fresh or canned. The decision to seed and/or peel rests with us cooks. Know it is not absolutely necessary.

How to Peel and Seed Tomatoes   Since brief heating usually flattens the tomato's flavors, when I want to seed and peel tomatoes for a raw sauce, or have a meaty puree, I just cut them in half and rub them skin side out against the side of a grater with big holes. Do this in a shallow bowl.

If bigger chunks of tomato are needed for a cooked sauce, sear the skin over a stove burner until it puckers. Cool, cut in half, slip off the skin and squeeze out the seeds.

All Canned Tomatoes Are Not Alike

Let's start with origins. Surprisingly, the much-touted imported Italian San Marzano tomatoes often disappoint when tasted against canned American examples. Then again, I wonder how many are actually the true San Marzano grown in the rich volcanic soil of the Naples area. It is difficult to tell.

Quality Brands of Domestic Canned Tomatoes   Whole tomatoes packed in tomato juice by Hunt's, Contadina and the organic Muir Glen. Red Pack brand's whole tomatoes "in tomato puree" are excellent. Their whole tomatoes "in thick puree" tend to taste metallic in cooking because there seems to be low-quality tomato paste used to thicken the puree.

Quality Brands of Imported Canned Tomatoes   Cirio, La Valle, Tutto Rosso and Asti.

Types of Canned Tomatoes

➤ ***Whole Canned Tomatoes***   Whole tomatoes are my first choice because many brands of pureed, crushed or ground tomatoes, though convenient, are thickened with low-grade tomato paste, which brings a metallic flavor to dishes. I use "plum" tomatoes and "whole" tomatoes interchangeably. When crushed tomatoes are needed, I just break them up with my hands as they go into the pot.

➤ ***The Liquid in the Can***   Check labels. Ideally, whole tomatoes are packed in tomato juice with or without basil leaves. (Maybe I've missed it, but I have never detected any basil flavor from these leaves.) Drain away the liquid when you want less tomato taste or want to thicken a sauce quickly. Short cooking time protects the simple bright taste of barely cooked canned tomatoes. Keep the liquid for sauces where quantity, more tomato flavor or longer cooking is desired. Slightly longer cooking usually deepens and enriches the flavors of canned tomatoes.

➤ ***Chopped or Diced Tomatoes***   A gift to the cook made by Hunt's, Muir Glen and Contadina, as well as other packers. These are time-savers with sound, pure tomato taste unsullied by paste or puree. Usually there's some tomato juice added and that is all.

➤ ***Ground Tomatoes***   Trust your own taste. Compare what is available in your supermarket by tasting different brands straight from the can before you make a sauce with them.

About Tomato Paste

Tomato paste is concentrated tomato made in two steps. Tomatoes are cooked down and the peels and seeds removed, then they are cooked again until thick and finally dehydrated to a paste consistency. Years ago, the puree was spread in shallow containers and the sun did the work of extracting enough moisture to end up with a paste. Today commercial tomato paste is made in ovens.

Tomato paste can enhance flavors in a tomato sauce, but it should not become a main ingredient. Stirring a spoonful of paste into thin-tasting sauces enriches and deepens them, whether they are made from canned or fresh tomatoes.

Sautéing a generous tablespoon of tomato paste into a sauce's foundation sauté (the *soffritto*) for a full minute or two develops a meaty quality where no meat is used, as in Friday Night Spaghetti with Tuna and Black Olives (page 88). But be cautious. Too much paste deadens a sauce.

Selecting a Paste   Good paste tastes of intense tomato with a clean, pleasing finish. Bitter or metallic aftertastes indicate poor quality and such pastes can ruin a dish.

Pastes in Tubes   Usually imported from Italy, these pastes can have fine flavor. Though expensive, tubes keep better than cans, a possible savings in the long run. Store opened tubes in the refrigerator, tightly sealed, up to three weeks. Discard any leftover paste with an off smell and extremely dark color. Suggested brands: Mutti and Pagani.

Canned Tomato Paste   Reliable domestic canned pastes include Muir Glen, Hunt's, Contadina and Red Pack.

Keeping Canned Tomato Paste   Freeze unused canned tomato paste by dolloping teaspoonfuls about 1 inch apart onto a sheet of waxed paper or foil set on a large plate. Freeze until solid. Peel the dollops of paste away from the paper and drop them into heavy-duty plastic bags. Seal and store up to six months. These can be used without defrosting.

Other Tomato Enrichments

Roasted Tomatoes   These lend sweeter lusher notes to sauces than do pastes. They are also a wonderful saucing on their own. See the recipes on pages 27 and 29.

Sun-Dried Tomatoes   A little goes a long way. These bring salt and a concentrated, almost dried-apricot quality to sauces. Italian cooks use only a few, first soaking them, then chopping the tomatoes into the sauce. They rarely make sauces with only sun-dried tomatoes.

THE ESSENTIALS OF MAKING A TOMATO SAUCE

The Pot

The pot, its size and its shape will influence the taste and texture of a sauce. In shallow wide skillets or sauté pans, sauces cook faster and taste brighter. In deep saucepans, moisture evaporates more slowly and sauces cook longer, tending to taste mellower, more evolved and complex. Tasting is the only way of knowing when a sauce is ready. Look upon recipes as guides, but let your palate be the final judge.

Building Flavors

Tomato sauces begin one of two ways. One method begins with a sautéed base called a *soffritto*. The other method has all the ingredients simmering together with no preliminary sauté. Both are delicious, yet they have important differences.

Building a Sauce with a Sauté, or Soffritto Understanding a soffritto is to be free to create when you cook. I want you to understand that the method of sautéing a soffritto, whether fast, slow or in-between, can shape the taste and character of your tomato sauce. With this information, the soffritto becomes your own tool to use in building whatever kind of tomato sauces you wish to make. A soffritto is the flavor base of a sauce. It is made by sautéing chopped vegetables, herbs and/or cured meats in oil, butter or pork fat. A soffritto can be as simple as garlic and parsley, as complex as carrot, celery, onion, chile and herbs.

Here is how to use the soffritto in creating distinctive tomato sauces. Obviously, ingredients shape a sauce too, but the base sauté builds its foundation.

For Bold Sauces Brown the soffritto fast over medium-high to high heat before you add the tomatoes. This produces big, meaty-brown flavors. A Sauce of Sautéed Tomatoes and Seasonings (page 126) is a dramatic example of this method.

For Gentle, Sweeter Sauces Sauté the soffritto very slowly, beginning with medium heat for a few moments, then cooking over medium-low until its ingredients are limp but not colored. For even deeper, sweeter character, once the soffritto is limp, raise the heat and sauté it to golden brown, as in A Sauce of Uncooked Tomatoes and a Sauté (page 124).

For Sauces with Both Bold and Gentle Notes—Between the Two Extremes   Sauté the soffritto to golden brown over medium heat. Try Penne with Sicilian Shepherd's Sauce (page 136) to experience this technique in all its glory.

Building Flavors Without a Sauté

This method always surprises people because of how effortless it is and yet how very good the resulting sauces taste. Instead of sautéing the soffritto, put whatever soffritto ingredients you want to use in a saucepan along with the fat you'd usually use for the sauté and the tomatoes. Simmer everything together, uncovered, about 25 minutes, or until the sauce is thick. (Some Italian women warm the garlic and/or herbs in the fat for a few moments before adding everything else, but the results are essentially the same.) These sauces show how a single change in method gives you a tomato sauce tasting much subtler and mellower. See what I mean by making Tomato Sauce Mellowed by Simmering (page 128). Another intriguing aspect of these sauces is how a single sauce will go from elegant to big and bold depending on whether you strain it, puree it or spoon it over pasta straight from the pot. Here is what I mean:

The "Passed" Sauce (Sugo Passato)   This is the smoothest, most restrained style of sauce without a sauté. You pass the sauce through a food mill to eliminate everything that isn't crushable, like seeds, peel, and other solid ingredients. "Passing" lends a sauce elegance by turning it satiny-smooth. Use passed sauces over most pastas, from ones as fine as angel hair to modestly thick shapes like small penne, as well as in lasagne, on pizza and anywhere a smooth sauce is needed.

The Pureed Sauce   The same sauce tastes bolder and more substantial when you puree it in a blender or food processor to a fine cut instead of passing it through a food mill. Fresh tomatoes might be peeled for this style of sauce if you think the peels are too thick to taste good once they are broken down into tiny pieces.

Serve this style with medium to bold pasta shapes, from spaghetti to penne and rigatoni to fusilli. As with the passed sauces, pureed sauces are a secret weapon when it comes to layering lasagne, saucing pizza, moistening polenta or cooking into a risotto as part of its liquid.

The Untouched Sauce The biggest flavors come from simmered sauces served straight from the pot. Just be sure to chop the ingredients into small pieces. The untouched sauce marries with everything from linguine and spaghetti to the bolder cavatappi, ziti, snails and shells.

Improvising: The Next Stage

This is where tomato sauces really become fun. Once you understand how seasonings work, you can quickly conjure up any style of sauce you want, from classic tomato-basil to a wildly luscious tumble of flavors that make the tomato seem like the newest thing you've ever eaten. Here's how:

> Think of the tomato's dominant tastes and character, whether using fresh tomatoes, canned tomatoes or a mix of both. These are sweetness, tartness, saltiness and the substantial meat-like quality shared by most types of tomato. All of these elements can be subtly played upon by different seasonings.

> Call out sweet by slowly cooking the soffritto. Use soft-flavored herbs (basil, chives and mint), sweet peppers or liqueur-like artisan-made balsamic vinegar. Finish the sauce once it's tossed with pasta with fresh creamy cheeses like ricotta to bring out the softest, sweetest tastes of tomato, as in Penne with Sicilian Shepherd's Sauce (page 136).

> Heighten the tart dimensions of the tomato with wine, citrus zests, capers or red or white wine vinegars. The Puglia Streetwalker (page 132) shows off this idea deliciously, as does Spiced Cauliflower with Ziti (page 138).

> Bring out the tomato's salty flavors with anchovies, olives, capers, cured meats, sausage (try Sausage, Peppers and Shells, page 142) or cheeses like Parmigiano-Reggiano, cacioricotta, Asiago, Fiore Sardo, Fontinella, Dry Jack and the like.

> Open up the tomato's suave richness and meaty quality by first browning the soffritto quickly and then cooking the tomatoes with any one or a blend of the following: cured meats, fresh meat or poultry (see Sunday Ragù, page 146), soaked anchovies, sun-dried tomatoes, olives, onions, garlic, black pepper and/or strong herbs (like sage, rosemary, bay, thyme,

oregano and savory). A Sauce of Sautéed Tomatoes and Seasonings (page 126) and Bucatini all' Amatriciana (page 144) also show off this approach.

➤ Stirring a little butter or olive oil into a tomato sauce just before serving rounds out, silkens and lifts it.

Cooking

Tomatoes do overcook. They can become bitter and lose that lush quality we find so appealing.

Sauces Made with Fresh Tomatoes   Either leave fresh tomatoes raw or cook them until they have broken down and thickened. Between these two extremes, most tomatoes turn flat-tasting.

Sauces Made with Canned Tomatoes   Taste as you cook for the moment when the sauce is at its brightest or flavors are at their mellowest. At this moment, stop cooking.

Reheating   Since some tomato sauces are ruined by overcooking, always reheat to hot, but take care not to continue cooking the sauce.

Storing

➤ Raw sauces do not hold more than a few hours. Keep them out of the refrigerator because, as with fresh tomatoes, cold kills flavor.

➤ Most cooked sauces are at their best freshly cooked but will keep, covered in the refrigerator, up to five days.

➤ Freeze cooked sauces containing generous amounts of olive oil no more than one month. After that, the oil can take on a fishy taste.

➤ Freeze all other cooked sauces up to five months in airtight containers.

➤ Thaw frozen sauces in the refrigerator and reheat them over a gentle flame, stirring often. Be careful not to overcook.

Four Tomato Sauce Techniques

In these four recipes, tomato sauces with similar ingredients (garlic, basil, olive oil, perhaps onion) are varied dramatically by different cooking techniques. First try these sauces as written to understand how method, not solely ingredients, builds flavors, giving each sauce a different character. Then play with the seasonings and enjoy experimenting.

TOMATO SAUCE I

Uncooked Tomato Sauce for Fusilli

Serves 6 to 8 as a first course, 4 to 6 as a main dish

With this recipe, the only thing you have to cook is the pasta. My cousin Edda makes it all summer long. This is the freshest, purest-tasting recipe I have found for a sauce of raw tomatoes and uncooked seasonings. You rub a bowl with garlic, dice up ripe tomatoes, leaving their skin and seeds intact, tear a few leaves of fresh herbs over the tomatoes, twirl in a thread of olive oil and finish with salt and pepper. Nothing could be easier, or taste better. In some country houses, you might find capers and oregano in the bowl, or hot pepper and crushed garlic, or mint or even celery leaves. Everything in this dish is about what the country cook has on hand.

➤ **Cook to Cook:** Exceptionally good tomatoes and olive oil you want to eat with a spoon are the only requirements for this recipe. Try a variety of tomatoes if possible—the punchy little Sweet 100's or Sun Golds, mellow beefsteaks and maybe one or two sweet yellow or orange ones. Tear the basil with your hands, rather than chopping with a knife. You enjoy more of its fragrance this way.

I discovered a trick for making pasta with raw tomato sauces taste lustier. Slightly undercook the pasta. Drain it. Spoon the juices that raw sauces always throw off into the empty pasta pot. Set it over medium-low heat, add the pasta and toss until the juices are absorbed, then add the pasta to the sauce. Pasta and raw tomato sauce is served at room temperature, never chilled.

Wine Suggestion: A simple Tuscan red like
Monte Antico or Santa Cristina's Chianti

1 clove garlic, split

2½ to 3 pounds richly flavored tomatoes (if possible, one third cherry type, one third mellow-tasting, and one third low-acid), unpeeled, unseeded, cut into ¼-inch dice

1½ tightly packed tablespoons fresh basil leaves or other favorite herb, torn

3 to 4 tablespoons fruity extra-virgin olive oil

Salt and freshly ground black pepper

1 pound penne, fusilli, linguine, or spaghetti

6 quarts boiling salted water

½ to 1 cup freshly grated aged Pecorino Romano cheese or domestic Fontinella (optional)

1. Vigorously rub a pasta serving bowl with the garlic. Add the tomatoes, basil, oil, and salt and pepper to taste. Let stand at room temperature while you cook the pasta, or up to several hours.

2. Cook the pasta in fiercely boiling water, stirring often, until tender yet firm to the bite. Drain in a colander and turn it into the pasta bowl, tossing all the ingredients together. Taste for seasoning and serve. If you like, pass cheese at the table.

TOMATO SAUCE II
A Sauce of Uncooked Tomatoes and a Sauté for Spaghetti

Serves 6 to 8 as a first course, 4 as a main dish

For this sauce, you sauté onions, garlic and herbs and toss them with fresh uncooked tomatoes. Why the sauté? Slow-cooked onion plays on the tomatoes' sweet rich nature, garlic on their mellowness and depth. Basil is simply the happiest seasoning to happen to a tomato. With different types of tomatoes readily available in summer, we can mix sharp, mellow and bold varieties as do Italian cooks who select a range of tomatoes from the garden. Cherry tomatoes, a beefsteak type, and low-acid orange, yellow or white tomatoes essentially do the trick. See page 113 for more specific ideas. Certainly canned tomatoes stand in beautifully when fresh ones are out of season (see Cook to Cook).

➤ *Cook to Cook:* Add ¼ teaspoon of oregano to the sauté along with the basil and you have Marinara Sauce.

Using Canned Tomatoes: This recipe gives you the basic tomato sauce technique for cooking tomatoes into a sautéed flavor base, or soffritto. When fresh tomatoes are out of season, use a 28-ounce can and a 14-ounce can of whole tomatoes, undrained, breaking them up with your hands as they go into the skillet. Simmer them, uncovered, over high heat about 8 minutes, stirring often, until the sauce is thick.

Wine Suggestion: A red Veneto Merlot or an Aquileia Refosco from Friuli

1 to 1½ tablespoons robust extra-virgin olive oil

2 medium onions, finely chopped

Salt and freshly ground black pepper

2 large cloves garlic, minced

½ tightly packed cup fresh basil leaves, chopped

Pinch of hot red pepper flakes (optional)

1 pound spaghetti or other favorite string pasta

6 quarts boiling salted water

3 pounds delicious tomatoes (if possible, a blend of cherry, big globes, and low-acid, as explained on page 113), cored and cut into ½-inch dice, but left unpeeled and unseeded

About 1½ cups freshly grated Parmigiano-Reggiano cheese (optional)

1. Heat the oil in a 12-inch skillet over medium-high heat. Stir in the onions and salt and pepper to taste. Cover and cook over low heat 30 minutes, stirring occasionally and checking for sticking. The onions should be clear, limp, and sweet-tasting.

2. Uncover the pan, raise the heat to medium-high, and sauté the onions to pale gold, stirring frequently. Stir in the garlic, basil, and red pepper if using. Cook 1 minute. Cover and set aside.

3. Cook the pasta in fiercely boiling water, stirring often, until tender yet firm to the bite. Drain in a colander.

4. Quickly rewarm the onion mixture, tossing with the hot pasta in the pan. Finally toss in the tomatoes. Season to taste. Turn into a heated bowl and serve hot. The cheese is totally optional. When tomatoes are sensational, it gets in their way.

VARIATIONS
Try these flavorings alone or in combination, tasting as you go.

➤ 2 rinsed anchovy fillets, sautéed into the onions until they dissolve

➤ 3 slices soppressata, minced and cooked with the onions

➤ Shredded zest of 1/2 large orange, added with the garlic and basil

➤ 8 fresh Italian parsley leaves, chopped and added with the garlic and basil

➤ 1/4 teaspoon dried oregano, added with the garlic and basil

➤ 1 tablespoon capers, stirred into the sauce just before serving

➤ 2 tablespoons *each* minced celery and carrot, sautéed with the onions

➤ 2 tablespoons dry white or red wine, stirred in with the garlic and basil

TOMATO SAUCE III
A Sauce of Sautéed Tomatoes and Seasonings for Fettuccine

Serves 6 as a first course, 3 as a main dish

Sautéeing tomatoes along with browned onions and herbs comes close to caramelizing them. With this technique, you have a tomato nectar so concentrated it tastes like a demi-glace sauce. While it's superb on pasta, a little brings salvation to so many dishes—fish, meats, risotto and polenta. Stir in a tablespoon or two to enrich pan sauces and soups.

Dora Ricci makes this sauce at the restaurant she and her husband, Angelo, have in the Pugliese village of Ceglie Messapico. The secret of her sauce is the small oval "winter tomatoes," as they are called in Puglia, that she cuts each summer, vine and all, and hangs through winter. Rather than drying, these tomatoes shrivel slightly, becoming incredibly intense. The fast sauté of our ripe cherry tomatoes along with some larger mellow ones in this recipe comes close to replicating Dora's oval tomatoes.

➤ *Cook to Cook:* Make the sauce ahead. It keeps covered in the refrigerator up to 4 days. Canned tomatoes don't work in this sauce. But since it freezes well, consider making enough in late summer for several months. Don't shrink from taking the onions to rich golden brown, then cooking down the tomatoes fast until they become really thick. Use a food mill, not a blender.

Wine Suggestion: A young Barbera d'Asti

3 tablespoons extra-virgin olive oil
1/2 medium onion, minced fine
A 3-inch branch fresh rosemary
3 large fresh basil leaves, each torn into
   several pieces
Salt and freshly ground black pepper
1 large clove garlic, minced
1 1/2 pounds (about 4 medium) rich-
   flavored tomatoes, cored and

chopped, but left unpeeled and
   unseeded
1 pint basket (3/4 pound) good-tasting
   cherry tomatoes, halved
1/4 teaspoon sugar
3/4 pound fettuccine, fedellini,
   spaghetti, or tagliatelle
6 quarts boiling salted water

1. Heat the oil in a 12-inch skillet over medium-high heat. Add the onion, rosemary, basil, a light sprinkling of salt, and several grinds of black pepper. Sauté the onions to golden brown, stirring with a wooden spatula.

2. Stir in the garlic, tomatoes, and sugar. Bring to a boil over high heat, stirring often and scraping down the glaze forming on the sides of the pan. Watch for signs of burning. Cook about 8 to 10 minutes, or until the wooden spatula leaves a wide trail when run along the bottom of the skillet. Take the pan off the heat, cover, and let stand 15 minutes.

3. Cook the pasta in fiercely boiling water, stirring often, until tender yet firm to the bite.

4. As the pasta cooks, pass the sauce through a food mill set over a bowl, getting every bit of pulp possible. Taste for salt and pepper.

5. Drain the pasta in a colander. Toss with the sauce and serve immediately.

RITES OF RED: PUTTING UP THE SALSA

From Sicily to the Veneto, summer on Italian farms means putting up homemade tomato puree, called *sugo* or *salsa* in Italian. Every farmer I've met has reminisced about childhood memories of vats of tomatoes cooking over outdoor fires, and of all the children in the family taking turns stirring as the fruit spit up red jets of hot juice. Nothing has changed. "It's the fires of hell for a week," says Rosalba Ciannamea of her farm in Puglia. "You don't want to be here when we're making salsa."

The puree is put up in sterilized bottles. Years ago, they were usually wine bottles that rotated through kitchen life, sterilized again and again, never thrown away. One year they held wine, the next year vinegar and, finally, puree. Men capped them with old corks. When corks were too expensive, they carved wooden plugs. Whether wood or cork, they were secured to the bottles with string, first wound around the cork, then looped around the bottle's neck and tied.

The women sterilized bottles of puree in tubs of water simmering over outdoor braziers, or in cooling bread ovens. Old photos of farmhouse interiors show bottles of puree crowding pantry shelves and lining moldings over doorways and windows, anywhere and everywhere a bottle could sit away from light. An old woman I met in Lazio told me her recipe for salsa and explained, "We needed at least one bottle of salsa for every dinner after summer was over—fall, winter and spring."

Pasta Meets the Tomato

TOMATO SAUCE IV

Tomato Sauce Mellowed by Simmering for Maccheroni

Serves 6 to 8 as a first course, 4 to 6 as a main dish

This requires the least work of all the cooked tomato sauces. With this technique, everything—tomatoes, olive oil and seasonings—goes into the pot more or less at once, usually with no presauté, and simmers until thick. Instead of the distinctively layered tastes of sauté-based sauces, the simmered sauce is softer, more tomatoey and mellow.

Every summer, in country kitchens and city apartments, this and similar sauces are put up in jars or frozen, ready for all kinds of dishes from pasta and pizza to pot roast, soup and polenta. Its seasonings and the proportions of ingredients vary from house to house, but the technique rarely changes.

A farmwoman I met at a weekly market in Umbria insisted that before adding the tomatoes you must warm all the seasonings in the oil for just one minute, never longer. Her version is so good, I haven't fiddled with her technique.

➤ *Cook to Cook:* Italian cooks make this sauce with unpeeled fresh tomatoes or canned ones, passing it through a food mill once it's cooked. My preference is for a more rustic juicy sauce with bits of tomato, so I roughly chop it in a blender or food processor. Only if the fresh tomatoes' peels are tough or bitter do I peel them. This is a matter of personal choice.

Wine Suggestion: A Sangiovese di Romagna or a Chianti Classico, not Riserva

5 large cloves garlic, coarsely chopped
12 large fresh basil leaves, torn
1/4 medium onion, coarsely chopped
1/8 teaspoon *each* salt and freshly ground black pepper
1/4 cup fruity extra-virgin olive oil
3 1/2 pounds mixed ripe delicious tomatoes, cored and possibly peeled (do not seed), or 2 28-ounce cans whole tomatoes, drained

1 pound modest-sized maccheroni, such as gemelli, strozzapretti, casareccia, zita, or penne, or substantial string pastas, such as perciatelli, spaghetti, linguine, or bucatini
6 quarts boiling salted water
1 1/2 to 2 cups (6 to 8 ounces) freshly grated Parmigiano-Reggiano cheese (optional)

1. In a 4-quart saucepan, combine the garlic, basil, onion, salt and pepper, and oil. Heat over medium-high heat 1 minute, no more. Add the tomatoes, breaking them up with your hands as they go into the pan. Bring to a lively bubble, uncovered,

and cook 30 minutes, or until the sauce is thick and reduced by half. Stir often, watching for sticking or scorching. Remove the pan from the heat, cover, and let stand 15 minutes.

2. Pass the sauce through a food mill or chop it in a blender or food processor until in small pieces. If desired, the sauce can be cooled and refrigerated up to 2 days, or frozen up to 3 months.

3. Cook the pasta in fiercely boiling water, stirring often, until tender yet firm to the bite. Drain, toss with the reheated sauce, and serve immediately. Grated cheese is an option.

RITES OF RED: THE TOMATO AND SEASONS OF MEMORY

Puglia writer Antonio Maglio remembers that childhood summers on his family's farm on Puglia's Salentino Peninsula were about tomato paste and the women of the family. "A rite of our long hot summer was putting up the tomato paste, *la conserva*. Big round ceramic platters spread with red tomato puree were set out in the courtyard to bake in the sun until it was concentrated into paste. Once the paste turned from scarlet to cordovan, my mother and aunts packed it into crocks. They sealed each one with a layer of olive oil and a few basil leaves, then covered the top with stiff paper and tied it down with string.

"We all picked tomatoes in the hot fields. My mother boiled them down in big pots. To drain away the excess liquid, she and my aunts stretched big square white cloths between four chairs, tying each corner of the cloth to the back of a chair. Then they poured the tomatoes into the cloths to drain. Finally, all the children took turns hand-cranking the old machine that separated seeds and skins from the tomato's meat.

"The sun's heat baked strength into our tomato paste that no industrial oven ever gives. The women hung branches of bay leaves over the platters. My mother said they worked spells. In fact, the bay discouraged insects, but far more important, she knew bay leaves guarded against malicious spirits that spoil the tomato paste, or use it to enter a home and possess those who eat it."

Pasta Meets the Tomato

GREEN TOMATO SAUCE FOR MIDSUMMER'S EVE

Pasta di San Giovanni

Serves 6 to 8 as a first course, 4 as a main dish

Green tomatoes, lemon, garlic and creamy ricotta are uncommon saucing for pasta. Yet in Puglia, all the rhythms are in place for this dish to be eaten on San Giovanni's Day, June 24, Italy's midsummer's eve. Last year's little green tomatoes, hung up on their branches under shady porches the previous fall, practically snap with zingy acid and fruit. Lemons are easily had. New garlic is ready for pulling in every kitchen garden, and fresh ricotta is in its prime—milky and sweet, tasting better than cream. Elizabetta Del Monaco makes her pasta for her family every San Giovanni. Elizabetta, an art teacher and farmer, and her brothers own the oldest pottery of Grottaglie, the ceramic center of southern Puglia. I've found that lemon zest and juice bring our green tomatoes close to the one Elizabetta hangs each year and uses in this pasta. Celebrate San Giovanni as if you were in Italy; outside under a full moon, with bowls full of pasta. Enjoy the dish again and again through summer and fall as tomatoes go in and out of season.

➤ *Cook to Cook:* **A Red Tomato Version**—Pugliese cooks also use small red tomatoes hung through winter in this recipe. Instead, try our good-tasting cherry tomatoes (like Sweet 100's or Sun Golds), or big tomatoes, left unpeeled and chopped up, and double the amount of lemon juice.

Wine Suggestion: A white Roero Arneis like Ceretto's

2 tablespoons fruity extra-virgin olive oil

10 large cloves garlic, cut into ¹/₂-inch dice

1 tablespoon water

Salt and freshly ground black pepper

3 medium green tomatoes, cored, but left unpeeled and unseeded and cut into ¹/₄-inch dice

Juice of ¹/₂ lemon

¹/₂ medium red onion, minced

1 pound stubby pasta, such as casareccia, gemelli, or ribbed small penne

6 quarts boiling salted water

Shredded zest of 1 medium lemon

Pinch of hot red pepper flakes

¹/₂ cup thinly sliced fresh chives or scallion tops

1 cup (8 ounces) high-quality sheep's or cow's milk ricotta

1. In a 12-inch skillet, combine the olive oil, garlic, water, and generous sprinklings of salt and black pepper. Cover and cook over low heat 15 minutes, or until garlic is very soft and barely blond, stirring often. With a slotted spoon, remove the garlic and reserve.

2. Sprinkle the tomatoes with the lemon juice and set aside. Set the skillet over high heat and cook the onion for 1 minute. Remove from the heat and set aside. Cook the pasta in fiercely boiling water, stirring often until slightly underdone. Drain in a colander.

3. Quickly reheat the skillet. Add the lemon zest, hot pepper, and one third of the tomatoes and sear, tossing, no more than 1 minute. Blend in the pasta, reserved garlic, and the remaining tomatoes, with their liquid. Toss to heat through, tasting for salt and an assertive tingle of black pepper. Add the chives or scallions and cheese, blend for a second or two, and turn into a warmed serving bowl. Serve right away.

THE DEW OF MIDSUMMER'S EVE

In Italy, the eve of San Giovanni is a night more for spirits than saints, a time when witches and fairies dance in the moonlight as the earth tilts on its axis. Summer solstice, the shortest night of the year, brings the feast of St. John the Baptist to city and country. Technically the solstice is June 21, but for Italians it is June 24, the feast of San Giovanni and a remnant of the old Julian calendar.

I was with my friend Paola Bini, a woman whose cordial reserve hides great warmth. We were finishing dinner at Villa Gaidello, her guest farm outside Modena, sipping the last of our dinner wine, listening to the crickets, drifting easily in and out of conversation. Suddenly she jumped up. "How could I forget?!" she said. "It's San Giovanni. We must gather the dew." It was close to midnight, yet she collected the farmwomen who were washing the last of the dinner dishes and, almost dancing, led us all out into the meadow. Years dropped away as we played in the damp grass, rubbing the dew over our faces, arms and legs as the women had done in childhood.

"Our whole family used to bring out blankets and sit up almost until dawn, romping, looking at the stars, collecting dew. If you're looking for a husband, the dew brings him to you. The dew even makes you feel younger. San Giovanni is a night of mischief and magic." Standing in the moonlight, my face wet with dew, who was I to argue?

THE PUGLIA STREETWALKER

Pasta Puttanesca Pugliese

Serves 6 to 8 as a first course, 4 to 6 as a main dish

Vibrant and spicy, this is Puglia's uncooked version of Puttanesca, streetwalker's pasta. Every time I mix together this sauce of fresh tomatoes, garlic, olives, herbs, capers, cheese and chiles, I imagine the same story: A Puglia farmer makes his once-in-a-lifetime trip across the Italian peninsula to Naples, like our cowboys going to the big city. There he tastes Naples' Pasta of the Streetwalker. He goes home and tells his wife about the dish, but probably not where he ate it. She starts making it, but can't resist adding the Puglia touch of wild arugula. This is my picturesque way of saying if you love Puttanesca, you'll love this pasta. It's an example of how pungent ingredients like olives and capers, raw onion and chiles can call out each facet of the tomato's complicated flavors. By the way, note how a little tomato paste deepens the character of an uncooked sauce.

➤ *Cook to Cook:* The sauce can wait several hours, lightly covered, at room temperature. Do not refrigerate it.

Wild arugula (also called wall rocket; botanically, *Diplotaxis muralis*) has small, fleshy leaves and tastes peppery, clean and sharp, quite different from the more familiar cultivated arugula, which can become medicinal and bitter when it's too mature. Substitute either young arugula or the inner leaves of curly endive or mesclun.

Wine Suggestion: A red Copertino, Rosso del Salento
or Salice Salentino from Puglia

About 4 cups ice cubes

1/2 medium onion, thinly sliced

1 tightly packed tablespoon fresh basil leaves

1 tightly packed teaspoon *each* fresh marjoram and Italian parsley leaves

1 clove garlic

Generous pinch of hot red pepper flakes

1/4 teaspoon salt

2 oil-packed anchovy fillets, rinsed (optional)

1/3 cup Puglia, Liguria, or Niçoise black olives, pitted and coarsely chopped

About 3 pounds richly flavored tomatoes, unpeeled, cut into 1/2-inch dice

1 teaspoon red wine vinegar

1/2 cup crumbled Pecorino Ricotta Salata from Puglia, Cacio Romano, ricotta salata from Sicily, or domestic Vella Dry Jack or Fontinella

2 tablespoons fruity extra-virgin olive oil

1 tablespoon tomato paste
Freshly ground black pepper (optional)
3/4 pound orecchiette pasta
6 quarts boiling salted water

1/3 tightly packed cup wild arugula
(wall rocket), or young arugula,
mesclun, or tender curly endive
leaves, coarsely chopped

1. Put half the ice cubes in a medium bowl, add the onion, and top with the rest of the cubes. Cover with cold water. Refrigerate 20 to 30 minutes. Drain. (Chilling the onion in ice water renders it crisp and mild.)

2. Mince together the herbs, garlic, and hot pepper with the salt. Turn into a big serving bowl. Add the anchovies, olives, tomatoes, vinegar, cheese, and oil and blend in the tomato paste. Taste for seasoning, adding a little freshly ground black pepper if needed.

3. Cook the pasta in fiercely boiling water, stirring often, until there is no raw flour taste. Orecchiette cook to a chewier consistency than most pastas. Drain in a colander.

4. Put the pasta pot back over medium-high heat. Spoon most of the sauce's liquid into the pot. Stir in the drained pasta and cook a few minutes, or until the liquid is absorbed. Turn the pasta into the sauce and add the drained onion and fresh greens. Taste for seasoning, toss, and serve.

RITES OF RED: HANGING WINTER TOMATOES

I practically reeled at my first taste of Puglia's little oval tomatoes. Once I broke through the tough skin, the tomato tasted so lavish it could have been a sauce—brilliant flashes of sweet and tart with bursts of ripe fruit in each bite. I was at a farm stand in southern Puglia. The woman there explained that these tomatoes are cut in late summer and hung on their branches in pantries or outdoors under shady porches, where they shrivel slightly but do not dry. They are used just like fresh tomatoes all through Puglia's mild winter, when garden tomatoes are not to be had. And there's no work to them—no canning, no expensive jars and no tedious drying in fitful weather. Even the tomato's seed packets call them *"Pomodori d'Inverno"* (tomatoes of winter), and though it's hard to imagine, their flavors become even more intense as they hang from late summer until the following spring.

Most of the tomatoes treated this way are shaped like small eggs with pointed blossom ends. Dora Ricci, who cooks in the restaurant she and her husband run outside the country town of Ceglie Messapico, gave me my first taste of a wintered-over red tomato—it was even punchier and more luscious than the fresh one I'd tasted the year before. Across Puglia, in the pottery town of Grottaglia, Elizabetta Del Monaco introduced me to green tomatoes treated the same way—cut while still green on the branch and hung all winter. They don't turn red, but instead go from tasting simply like green tomatoes to tasting of lemon and herbs and black pepper—more complex and interesting.

Puglia's farmers don't hold the patent on this method of holding tomatoes through winter. People all over Italy do it.

Cooking with these tomatoes is even easier than with fresh—the intense flavor is already in place. Dora Ricci cooks them quickly in a hot skillet to sauce pasta and meats (see page 126). Elizabetta Del Monaco dices her green winter tomatoes and barely cooks them before dressing her Green Tomato Sauce for Midsummer's Eve (page 130). Country women all over Italy season broths, stews and pot roasts with a few winter tomatoes.

Hang your own fresh tomatoes through the winter. You need a dry, airy place that remains above freezing, ideally between 45° and 60°F. Delicious small tomatoes are the other requirement. Think about Red Currants, Sweet 100's, Sun Golds, Early Cascades or Principessa Borgheses. Cut the vines, being sure the tomatoes are firmly attached to stems. Hang them so plenty of air circulates around the tomatoes. Space them out on several nails rather than having them hang in a single tight bunch. Turn the branches twice a week for maximum exposure to the air. Twist off tomatoes as you need them.

GOING TO THE SHEPHERD

Adelina Norcia is behind the wheel of her little Fiat. Sitting beside her, I am still groggy. Adelina and her husband, Alceste, farm a small piece of land outside the city of Siracusa, in eastern Sicily. They originally treated the farm as a country getaway. When Alceste retired, they moved to the farm and started taking in guests, growing citrus fruits and tending olive trees older than several generations of their families. It is 5 A.M. on Sunday morning and Adelina is driving me to the farm of shepherds Pietro and Stefano. She says we must see them make ricotta. Fine, only why can't ricotta be made at a civilized hour?

When Adelina was a child, Sunday mornings meant "going to the shepherd." Her father took her to see the magic of milk turning into ricotta. Now she goes when she needs ricotta and to reminisce. We arrive just in time to see the ricotta made.

In a corner of a small stone hut, the brothers lift a copper cauldron half their height filled with whey and sheep's milk onto a big truck tire. A fire burns in its center, directly on the dirt floor. Surprisingly, I don't smell burning rubber, only wood smoke. Across the room, a ten-pound pecorino cheese drains in a basket. It's the whey from this cheese that is in the cauldron. Forty quarts of milk went into that pecorino. The milk was separated into solid curds and liquid whey by a piece of suckling lamb's intestine the size of a pea. I've watched sheep being milked. They hate standing still, and their udders are one tenth the size of a cow's, so they give less milk for a lot more effort. Making sheep cheese is no picnic.

The milky-looking whey heats fast, separating into a clear greenish liquid and white flecks of curd. Pietro makes the sign of the cross in the liquid. A few moments later, he and his brother begin checking the curd constantly as it evolves from tiny white specks to big splotches and finally clusters together into what looks like ruffled white carnations. Without either a thermometer or timer, they know the exact moment it's ready. With slotted ladles, they quickly strain the curds into baskets for draining. If cooked longer, the curds, now tender and creamy, would turn hard and grainy, like some of the ricotta we find in American supermarkets.

The brothers ladle mounds of hot ricotta into our bowls. The cheese tastes innocent, almost sweet and a little wild. The wonder of it—milk, leftover liquid from another cheese, heat and merely a few generations of craft. Stefano brings us a bowl of his second breakfast—thick hollow pasta in his own tomato sauce finished with the hot fresh ricotta. Now his cheese has become lusty.

Pasta Meets the Tomato

PENNE WITH SICILIAN SHEPHERD'S SAUCE

Penne dei Pastori Siciliani

Serves 6 to 8 as a first course, 4 as a main dish

Shepherds in Sicily offered me this dish —a spicy tomato sauce over chewy pasta, transformed by ricotta—after making ricotta at dawn. For them, it was a second breakfast; for me, it has become a favorite supper in a bowl. Pasta, tomato and cheese is one of the most irresistible of all combinations, but in this dish, ricotta makes everything sing. It must be the sweetest, creamiest you can find. If you don't have a good one, leave out the ricotta, finishing the pasta with a generous handful of shredded Asiago cheese. Quite a different dish, but you won't be disappointed.

➤ *Cook to Cook:* Here's an excellent example of sautéing a soffritto over medium heat to build both bold and gentle qualities into a tomato sauce. Protect the soffritto from burning by lowering the heat if it seems to be cooking too fast. Sauté it to golden, stirring frequently but letting some bits stick to the pan; they will build a crusty glaze. The sauce's depth and resonance lies in this glaze. Once it's swept into the other ingredients when the tomatoes are added, it opens up all the other flavors.

Wine Suggestion: A Sicilian red like Regaleali Rosso, Etna Rosso or Corvo Rosso

Top third of 3 large celery stalks with leaves

1 medium carrot

10 large fresh sage leaves

1 tightly packed teaspoon fresh Italian parsley leaves

2 tablespoons robust extra-virgin olive oil

1 1/8-inch-thick slice salami (such as soppressata or Genoa), coarsely chopped

2 medium onions, cut into 1/2-inch dice

Salt and freshly ground black pepper

2 large cloves garlic, minced

Generous pinch to 1/4 teaspoon hot red pepper flakes (to taste)

3/4 cup dry red wine

1 tablespoon tomato paste

1 28-ounce and 1 14-ounce can whole tomatoes, both thoroughly drained

1 pound penne rigate or bucatini

6 quarts boiling salted water

1 pound creamy whole-milk ricotta (sheep's milk, if possible)

1. · Mince together the celery and carrot, adding the herbs toward the end to chop only coarsely. Heat the oil in a 12-inch skillet over medium-high heat. Add the salami and cook to release a little of its fat, then stir in the minced celery blend, the onions, a little salt, and a generous amount of black pepper. Turn the heat down to medium and sauté to golden brown.

2. Stir in the garlic and hot pepper, cooking a few moments. Add the wine and slowly simmer down to nothing, scraping up the brown bits at the bottom of the pan. Stir in the tomato paste and cook 1 minute. Add the tomatoes, crushing them with your hands as they go into the pan. Cook, uncovered, at a lively bubble (turn the heat up if necessary), stirring and scraping down the sides of the pan with a spatula. Cook 10 minutes, or until thick. Taste for seasoning, cover, and remove from the heat.

3. Meanwhile, cook the pasta in fiercely boiling water, stirring often, until slightly underdone. Drain in a colander.

4. To marry the pasta and sauce, add the pasta to the sauce and toss together over medium heat 2 to 3 minutes, tasting for hot pepper and salt. Spread about a third of the pasta in a heated serving bowl and daub with a third of the ricotta. Layer in more pasta and ricotta, then the remaining pasta, finishing with a few spoonfuls of ricotta. Serve hot.

SPICED CAULIFLOWER WITH ZITI

Ziti con Cavolfiore Piccante

Serves 6 to 8 as a first course, 4 as a main dish

In this dish, cauliflower chunks are browned and slowly cooked with spices and tomato into a sauce for hollow ziti pasta. Typical of Sicilian cooks' talent for mixing the sweet with the piquant, clove and cinnamon season the cauliflower, along with anchovy and vinegar, which cook into the dish until they're only pleasing base notes. Tomatoes perform their usual magic, bringing everything into harmony.

➤ ***Cook to Cook:*** **Instead of cauliflower, try about 1 1/2 pounds green beans (cut into one-inch lengths) in this dish, or 2 generous heads of escarole that have been rinsed, thoroughly dried, and torn into bite-sized pieces. Both cook just as the cauliflower does.**

Wine Suggestion: A red Corvo

1 large head cauliflower, cut into
   1 1/2-inch flowerettes
6 quarts boiling salted water
Extra-virgin olive oil
1 medium onion, finely chopped
Salt and freshly ground black pepper
Generous pinch of hot red pepper
   flakes
Generous pinch *each* ground cloves
   and cinnamon
1/4 tightly packed cup mixed fresh basil
   and Italian parsley leaves, chopped

2 large cloves garlic, minced
4 oil-packed anchovy fillets, rinsed
3 tablespoons red wine vinegar
1 pound ziti
1 14-ounce can whole tomatoes,
   drained and finely chopped
1/4 pound ricotta salata cheese, shaved
   into long furls
1/3 cup pine nuts, toasted

1. Drop the cauliflower into the boiling water and cook 1 minute. Scoop out with a slotted spoon and drain. Keep the water boiling.

2. Film the bottom of a 12-inch sauté pan (not nonstick) with olive oil and heat over medium-high heat. Sauté the cauliflower 2 minutes. Stir in the onion, sprinkle with salt and pepper, and stir frequently until the cauliflower is golden brown. Stir in the hot red

pepper, spices, herbs, garlic, anchovies, and vinegar, cooking about 1 minute. Remove from the heat.

3. Cook the pasta in fiercely boiling water, stirring often, until tender yet firm to the bite. Remove and reserve 2/3 cup of the pasta water, and drain the pasta in a colander.

4. Place the sauté pan over medium-high heat, blend in the reserved pasta water, and scrape up the brown glaze on the bottom of the pan. Stir in the tomatoes and boil 3 minutes, or until the cauliflower is crisp tender. Reduce the heat to medium-low and add the pasta, tossing to blend. Season to taste with salt and a generous amount of black pepper. Fold in the cheese and serve hot, sprinkled with the pine nuts.

BROKEN BRIDEGROOMS WITH ROASTED TOMATOES
Ziti con Pomodori Arrostiti

Serves 6 to 8 as a first course, 4 as a main dish

This quick dish tastes bold and **important with its big plump pieces of roasted tomato and a unique pasta, one of the few times I've ever seen pasta purposely broken in Italy. The hollow tubes called *ziti* translate as "bridegrooms" for obvious reasons. Ziti the length of spaghetti are impossible to eat without breaking. So home cooks take them down to manageable lengths. Broken bridegrooms.**

Wine Suggestion: A red Barbera d'Alba or d'Asti

3/4 pound ziti lunghi (long hollow tubes of pasta about 1/2 inch in diameter), broken into 2- to 3-inch lengths
6 quarts boiling salted water

1 recipe Oven-Roasted Canned Tomatoes (page 29)
Salt and freshly ground black pepper
1/2 to 1 cup whole-milk ricotta

Cook the pasta in fiercely boiling water, stirring often, until a little firmer than you'd like it. Drain in a colander. Toss the pasta with the tomatoes, seasoning to taste. Serve hot, dolloped with the fresh ricotta.

ZITA WITH TOMATOES, CAPOCOLLO AND DICED MOZZARELLA

Zita con Pomodori, Capocollo e Mozzarella

Serves 6 to 8 as a first course, 4 as a main dish

In this dish, tubes of pasta are sauced with tomatoes, browned bits of pancetta and capocollo, garlic, basil and big chunks of milky mozzarella. Country cooks know the secret of getting a stunning amount of flavor from a little meat and a lot of tomatoes. Their trick is using cured meats—salami, pancetta, prosciutto or the capocollo some people call poor man's prosciutto. In this recipe you simply brown the meats in olive oil, sauté in lots of garlic and basil, add part of the tomatoes and cook the sauce down fast. Then add the extra touch—near the very end of cooking, you stir in some drained canned diced tomatoes. They give the sauce a juicy, meaty finish. Toss with the pasta and mozzarella and serve it in a deep bowl.

➤ ***Cook to Cook:*** Zita are narrow hollow tubes 2¹/₂ to 3 inches long and between ¹/₄ and ¹/₂ inch in diameter. De Cecco is one producer. You could substitute sedani or penne, but I like zita's distinctive length.

Wine Suggestion: A Puglia red Copertino or Salice Salentino

Extra-virgin olive oil

2 to 3 ¹/₄-inch-thick slices (4 ounces) high-quality hot capocollo, coppa, or soppressata, cut into generous ¹/₄-inch dice

3 to 4 ¹/₄-inch-thick slices (6 to 8 ounces) pancetta, cut into generous ¹/₄-inch dice

¹/₈ to ¹/₄ teaspoon freshly ground black pepper

1 tightly packed tablespoon fresh Italian parsley leaves, chopped

5 large cloves garlic, chopped

¹/₂ tightly packed cup fresh basil leaves, chopped

2 28-ounce cans whole tomatoes, thoroughly drained

Salt

1 14-ounce can diced tomatoes, drained

1 pound zita, sedani, or small penne

6 quarts boiling salted water

14 to 16 ounces fresh mozzarella, cut into generous ¹/₂-inch dice

1. Film the bottom of a 12-inch sauté pan with olive oil and heat over medium heat. Add the capocollo, pancetta, and pepper and cook until lightly browned, adding the parsley toward the end. Raise the heat to medium-high. Stir in the garlic and basil, sautéing until fragrant, about 30 seconds to 1 minute.

2. Add the 2 28-ounce cans of tomatoes, crushing them with your hands, and boil, uncovered, about 8 minutes, or until thick. Season with salt and assertive black pepper. Stir in the diced tomatoes and cook just 1 minute. Remove from the heat and cover the pan. (The sauce can wait about an hour at room temperature. It can also be refrigerated in a covered container up to 2 days; reheat before proceeding.)

3. Cook the pasta in fiercely boiling water until a little less done than you'd like it. Drain immediately.

4. Toss the pasta with the sauce over medium heat a few minutes. Fold in the mozzarella and turn into a warmed serving bowl. Serve hot.

Farm tomatoes in a Sicilian village market.

SAUSAGE, PEPPERS AND SHELLS
Conchiglie con Salsiccia e Peperoni
Serves 8 as a first course, 4 as a main dish

The shells hold bits of this sauce with its chunks of tomato, peppers and sausage. What sets these sausage and peppers apart is how the sausage is cooked. It simmers in red wine, then the wine is boiled down to an essence which finally is blended into the sautéed vegetables and sausage. Serve the pasta as a one-dish supper with tumblers of red wine and a coarse-grain bread.

In the days when wedding feasts were cooked by neighbors and the reception filled every room in the house, this pasta was wedding food in the mountain homes north of Rome. The sausages were always homemade and the tomatoes and peppers had probably been put up by the mother and grandmothers of the bride. Now the same dish opens many a Sunday dinner, or is cooked up by working couples for a weeknight supper.

Wine Suggestion: A Chianti Classico Villa Cafaggio or Chianti Rufina
Nipozzano Riserva by Marchesi de Frescobaldi

1 pound sweet Italian sausage
3 cups dry red wine
Water
$1/2$ medium red onion
$1/2$ medium stalk celery with leaves
2 tablespoons extra-virgin olive oil
1 large sweet red pepper, cut into
   $1/4$-inch dice
1 dried medium-hot chile (such as
   ancho, California, or peperoncino)

Salt and freshly ground black pepper
1 large clove garlic, minced
4 large fresh basil leaves, torn
$1/2$ teaspoon dried oregano
1 14-ounce can whole tomatoes
1 pound medium-sized shell pasta or
   tacconi (see page 70)
6 quarts boiling salted water

1. Prick the sausages all over with a fork. Lightly brown in a 12-inch skillet over medium-high heat, then add the wine and enough water to barely cover. Simmer gently, partially covered, 20 minutes, or until a thermometer inserted in the center of a sausage reads 160°F.

2. Remove the sausages and set aside to cool, then cut into $1/2$-inch dice. Skim the fat from the pan liquid. Boil the liquid down by three quarters, scraping down the sides of the pan. Turn into a bowl and set aside. Clean the pan.

3. Mince together the onion and celery. Set the skillet over medium-high heat, add the oil, and sauté the minced vegetables, sweet pepper, and chile until the onions are lightly browned. Add salt and pepper to taste. Stir in the garlic and basil, cooking for a few seconds. Add the oregano, the reduced sausage liquid, and the tomatoes with their juices, crushing them as they go into the pan. Cook, uncovered, at a lively bubble 5 minutes. Blend in the sausage, cover, turn the heat down to medium-low, and simmer another 5 minutes. (The sauce can be set aside, covered, 30 to 40 minutes, or refrigerated overnight.)

4. Cook the pasta in fiercely boiling water, stirring often, until tender yet firm to the bite. Scoop out and reserve 1 cup of the pasta water and drain the pasta in a colander.

5. Meanwhile, remove the chile from the sauce and reheat the sauce if necessary. "Lengthen" the sauce by stirring in the reserved pasta water and simmering a few minutes. Taste for seasoning.

6. Toss the sauce with the hot pasta and serve immediately. No cheese is needed with this dish.

BUCATINI ALL' AMATRICIANA

Serves 6 to 8 as a first course, 4 to 6 as a main dish

Amatriciana is probably the most famous pasta of central Italy. Nubs of onion, pancetta, tomato and piquant Romano cheese cling to strands of bucatini. Amatriciana began in the mountains between Rome and Abruzzo, around the town of Amatrice. This recipe is the best one I've tasted. It involves a special technique that began in the days when tomatoes first entered Amatriciana sauce. Only a few were used, and they practically browned in the sauté. The secret to this recipe is sautéing part of the tomatoes and onions with pancetta until they're flecked with gold. They caramelize, changing the whole dish. Once the sauté is done, you add the rest of the tomato and onion and finish the sauce with ten minutes of simmering.

Wine Suggestion: A big red Montepulciano d'Abruzzo by Masciarelli

3 tablespoons extra-virgin olive oil
8 thin slices (4 ounces) pancetta, finely chopped
1 28-ounce can whole tomatoes
1 medium onion, cut into 1/4-inch dice
Scant 1/8 teaspoon hot red pepper flakes
Scant 1/4 teaspoon freshly ground black pepper
Salt
1 pound bucatini or spaghetti
6 quarts boiling salted water
3/4 to 1 cup freshly grated Pecorino Romano cheese

1. Heat the oil in a 12-inch skillet over medium heat. Cook the pancetta 5 minutes, or until crisp. Remove with a slotted spoon and reserve.

2. Lift about half the tomatoes from the can, poking each with your finger to drain the seeds and juice back into the can, and add to the pan, along with half the onions and the red and black pepper. Sauté, stirring often, over high heat 5 minutes, or until the onions are golden and the tomatoes are thickened and taste very rich.

3. Stir in the rest of the tomatoes with their juices, the remaining onions, and the reserved pancetta. Adjust the heat so the sauce simmers gently. Cover and cook 10 minutes. Taste for seasoning. Turn off the heat and cover the pan while you cook the pasta.

4. Cook the pasta in the fiercely boiling water, stirring often, until tender yet firm to the bite. Drain in a colander.

5. Toss the pasta with the sauce over medium-low heat. Turn into a heated bowl and serve hot, passing the cheese separately.

PASTA ALLA GRICIA

Double the amount of pancetta and eliminate the tomatoes and onions. Increase the cheese to 1½ cups. Toss the pasta with the browned pancetta and red and black pepper. Turn into a bowl and toss with the cheese.

Il Sugo, the Sauce

In Italian dictionaries, *sugo* is defined as juice, sauce or gravy. But for Italian families, *sugo* is one of those words with meanings never found in a dictionary. In Italian homes, especially in the south, *il sugo* is always sauce or "gravy" for pasta. Never is it *a* sauce (*un* sugo), meaning one of many. Always it is *the* sauce (*il* sugo). When an Italian says, "Mamma is making sauce or gravy," no explanation is needed about which sauce. Mamma must be cooking the family's own gravy, a formula barely altered over generations, usually a lavish-tasting meat and tomato ragù.

Il sugo with pasta is home, family and all the safety and security of tradition. *Il sugo* is Sunday dinner with generations of family crowded around the table. *Il sugo* is Christmas, Easter, christenings, weddings, birthdays, homecomings and funerals.

Years may go into perfecting *il sugo*, with each change commented on at the table by wary husbands and children. Tampering with *il sugo* is tricky business. Many a new wife knows the intimidation of attempting to duplicate the sauce of her husband's mother. And many a mother-in-law "helps" by sending her *sugo* to the newlyweds each week—a gift and a reminder of the order of things.

BAKED MACCHERONI WITH SUNDAY RAGU

Maccheroni al Forno

Serves 8 to 10 as a full-course meal, 6 to 8 as two separate meals

Forget fashion and trends, this is the home cooking that has been Sunday dinner to generations of southern Italian families. When Mamma finally emerges from the kitchen with the steaming casserole of baked maccheroni, the most important meal of the week has finally begun.

Two meals from one pot—could we ask any more from a recipe? No! Follow southern Italian tradition—make a ragù by braising generous pieces of meat in tomato-wine sauce. End up with a sumptuous old-style casserole of baked maccheroni in ragù studded with pockets of creamy ricotta and mozzarella. The meat becomes one of the most memorable pot roasts you'll ever eat.

➤ **Cook to Cook:** Although Italian families eat the pasta first and the meats as a second course, we can turn this single recipe into two separate meals. Serve the pasta as a main dish, then, a day later, have a dinner of meats, sliced and served with reheated sauce, salad and vegetables. Nothing is better than sandwiches of the leftovers. Dip rolls into a little rewarmed sauce, then stuff them with sliced meat. For the best flavor and easy defatting, cook the ragù a day or two ahead. Take care to not overcook the meats in rewarming.

Wine Suggestion: A rich red like Montepulciano d'Abruzzo
by Masciarelli, Illuminati or Edoardo Valentini

RAGU AND BRAISED MEATS

3/4 tightly packed cup fresh Italian
   parsley leaves
3/4 tightly packed cup fresh basil leaves
5 large cloves garlic
Shredded zest of 1 large lemon
1/4 teaspoon hot red pepper flakes
1/4 teaspoon freshly ground black
   pepper
1 teaspoon salt

2 1/2 to 3 pounds pork butt
2 pounds turkey breast with skin and
   bone
2 large lamb shanks
2 tablespoons extra-virgin olive oil
1 pound sweet or hot Italian sausage,
   sliced 1/2 inch thick
4 medium red onions, minced
2 cups dry white wine
3 28-ounce cans whole tomatoes

BAKED MACCHERONI
1 pound ziti, orecchiette, rigatoni, or
   any big hollow ribbed pasta, boiled
   to barely tender and drained
Reserved sausage and sauce from the
   braised meats

½ pound fresh mozzarella, 6 ounces
   cut into ¼-inch cubes, 2 ounces
   thinly sliced
1 pound, 6 ounces (2 ½ to 3 cups)
   high-quality whole-milk ricotta

1. Mince together the herbs, garlic, and lemon zest. Blend with the red and black pepper and salt. Make 8 deep slits about 1 inch wide in each of the meats except the sausage. Stuff the slits with three quarters of the herb mixture.

2. In a 12-inch sauté pan, heat the oil over medium-high heat. In 2 or 3 batches, leisurely brown the meats and sausage on all sides to a deep rich golden brown, lowering the heat to medium as necessary so as not to burn the brown glaze developing on the bottom of the pan. Place the browned meats in a heavy 8-quart pot.

3. In the same sauté pan, cook the onions to golden, adjusting heat to prevent the glaze from burning. Stir in the remaining herb mixture, cooking 1 minute. Blend in the wine, simmering over medium heat while scraping up all the glaze from the bottom and sides of the pan. Reduce the wine by about half. Stir in the tomatoes with their juice, breaking them up with your hands as you add them. Bring to a boil.

4. Turn the sauce into the pot with the meats and adjust the seasoning with salt and pepper. Partially cover and simmer for 1½ to 2 hours, or until the meats are barely tender. Take care not to overcook. Taste for seasoning. Cool, cover, and refrigerate overnight.

5. Remove the layer of fat that has formed on top of the ragù before reheating. Slowly warm the meats, covered, over medium heat, about 20 minutes. Lift the meats except the sausage onto a platter, moistening them with 3 cups of sauce. Reserve the sausages and the remaining sauce to dress Sunday Baked Maccheroni.

BAKED MACCHERONI WITH SUNDAY RAGU

1. Preheat the oven to 375°F. Oil a shallow 2½-quart baking dish. Warm the braising sauce. Slice the sausage ¼ inch thick. Blend back into the sauce. Set aside 1½ cups of sauce. Toss the freshly cooked pasta with the remaining sauce. Blend in the cubed mozzarella.

2. Cover the bottom of the baking dish with half the pasta. Top with all of the ricotta. Pile the rest of the pasta onto the ricotta, prodding it into place. Top with the reserved sauce. Cover with foil. Bake 35 minutes, or until heated through.

3. Uncover, spread the sliced mozzarella over pasta, and bake another 10 minutes, or until the cheese begins to melt. It should not brown. Let rest 5 minutes and serve.

NONNA'S HOME-STYLE LASAGNE

Lasagne della Nonna

Serves 10 as a first course, 6 to 8 as a main dish

Mention lasagne to most southern Italians and their eyes glaze over with memories of Nonna, madonna-like in her goodness, working under a shining halo, stretching golden sheets of pasta sheer enough to read a newspaper through. Only *her* hands could fashion the perfect lasagne. Nearly as many versions of lasagne exist as there are nonnas. Each signaled an occasion. Lasagne was not everyday food. In Emilia-Romagna, it marked the birth of a girl. In Puglia's city of Bari, lasagne rounded out Christmas reveling, appearing on December 26, the Feast of San Stefano. Special company and weddings brought lasagne to the table in Marche. An old saying, "swimming in lasagne," means to be in the money.

This meatless lasagne may adhere to the rules of Lent's stern denial in fact, but in spirit and flavor it is rebellious opulence. Meltingly creamy ricotta, a tomato sauce so fine you'll want to eat it with a spoon, herbs and pasta—all utterly satiating. Leftovers will not last long. Even a boxed, thick lasagne pasta won't compromise this dish.

➤ **Cook to Cook:** Find sweet, creamy ricotta in Italian groceries, cheese shops, specialty food stores and some supermarkets. This tomato sauce holds well in the refrigerator up to 3 days.

Wine Suggestion: A southern Italian red like Corvo, Montepulciano Cerasuolo or Cannonau

TOMATO SAUCE

1 recipe Tomato Sauce IV (page 128)

OR

3 tightly packed tablespoons *each* fresh basil and Italian parsley leaves

1 teaspoon fresh oregano leaves

2 medium onions, coarsely chopped

2 tablespoons fruity extra-virgin olive oil

2 large cloves garlic, minced

1 pint basket ($^3/_4$ pound) flavorful cherry tomatoes, halved

1 28-ounce can whole tomatoes

$^1/_2$ cup water

Pinch of sugar

Salt and freshly ground black pepper

$^1/_8$ teaspoon hot red pepper flakes

1 cup (4 ounces) freshly grated Parmigiano-Reggiano cheese

1 3/4 to 2 pounds high-quality, creamy
   ricotta cheese
1/2 pound fresh mozzarella cheese,
   shredded
8 scallions, trimmed of root ends
2 tightly packed tablespoons fresh basil
   leaves
1 tightly packed tablespoon fresh
   Italian parsley leaves
1 teaspoon fresh oregano leaves

2 cloves garlic
Salt and freshly ground black pepper
1 medium large onion, cut vertically
   into strips about 1/4 inch wide
Extra-virgin olive oil
1 pound dried lasagne pasta (or 1 recipe
   Homemade Pasta, page 69, cut into
   lasagne noodles)
6 quarts boiling salted water

1. If using Tomato Sauce IV, bring to room temperature. Or, prepare the tomato sauce by mincing together the herbs and chopped onions. Heat the oil in a 12-inch skillet over medium-high heat. Sauté the onions and herbs to golden brown. Add the garlic and cook a few seconds, then stir in the cherry tomatoes and the canned ones with their juices, crushing them with your hands as they go into the pan. Boil, uncovered, over high heat until thick, stirring often. Add the water and cook a few moments more. Stir in the sugar and season with salt and black pepper to taste and the red pepper flakes. Cool briefly, then pass the sauce through a food mill or puree in a processor or blender. Cover and set aside.

2. Holding back 2 tablespoons of the Parmigiano, blend the cheeses in a bowl. Mince together the scallions, basil, parsley, oregano, and garlic. Stir into the cheeses, seasoning to taste with salt and pepper.

3. Toss the onion strips with a little olive oil, salt, and pepper. Heat a sauté pan over high and sauté the onion until brown but still crisp. Turn out of the pan.

4. Cook the pasta in fiercely boiling water, stirring often, until barely al dente (it should be underdone); drain in a colander. Hold in a bowl of cold water.

5. Preheat the oven to 350°F. Oil a shallow 2 1/2-quart baking dish. Drain the pasta and pat dry. Moisten the bottom of the dish with sauce. Cover with a single layer of pasta. Daub with one quarter of the cheese mixture and one quarter of the browned onions. Moisten with one sixth of the remaining sauce. Top with a layer of pasta and continue layering, topping the fifth layer of pasta with the remaining sauce. Cover lightly with foil.

6. Bake 40 minutes, or until heated through. Sprinkle with the reserved 2 tablespoons cheese. Let rest 10 minutes in the turned-off oven with its door open, then serve.

RICE, GRAINS AND BEANS

rains and beans, along with vegetables, have been the soul of Italy's country cooking since before the Roman Empire. You'll see in these recipes collected from home cooks all over Italy how grains and beans satiated appetites and took to all kinds of flavorings. Ancient Mediterranean peoples believed focusing their diets on these foods, amending them with only modest amounts of meat, was essential to being civilized and in harmony with nature. Now, several thousand years later, we're told eating this way is good for our health and for the earth's ecology. Every country in the world probably has a version of the adage "What is old is new again." Italy certainly does. It's the key to its cooking.

Ancient Romans imported rice from Greece not for eating, but for medicinal uses. By the fifteenth century, however, Italian farmers were growing rice in the southern region of Campania, and possibly up north near Milan. Rice had become food. Today, most of Italy eats risotto, but it is definitely a dish of the north, tied to the rice fields of Piemonte, Lombardy, the Veneto and parts of Emilia-Romagna. Making a risotto brings the whole body into play. You can't help swaying with the rhythm of stirring together rice and broth. Risotto becomes itself right under your hands, as the oval grains swell, taking in the bubbling broth and seasonings. It nearly surpasses pasta as a vehicle of flavor, turning unexpected ingredients into a meal. Farmwomen say risotto welcomes just about anything from the pantry or garden. True, except for one hallowed rice dish—the inviolate classic, Risotto alla Milanese.

Those Romans of long ago in fact ate another grain, an ancient wheat called farro. They ate farro as a whole grain and ground it into flour for bread. In modern Italy, farro's a tradition of farming families in the central regions of Tuscany, Umbria, Marche and Lazio, and you'll find it used farther south too. Simplest Farro (page 160) shows how to turn farro into main dishes, salads, snacks and even dessert. Farro Risotto (page 163) deliciously reunites chickpeas with farro—a pairing that's been going on since long before the Roman Empire was dreamt of.

Eating wheat is a southern Italian tradition. Each year, on December 13, bowls of boiled whole wheat kernels are dressed with honey and ricotta, or a sweet syrup of grapes and spice, to mark the annual planting of the wheat and the feast of Santa Lucia. For me the dish, called Cuccia, is a delicious brunch, breakfast or dessert. In the heel of the Italian boot, the region called Puglia, country people eat wheat another way. Women pound the kernels to loosen their outer skin, boil the grain and then dress it just as we do pasta. My favorite is wheat with lamb ragù, eaten by farmers on Fat Tuesday. Try it for winter suppers.

Southern Italian wheat farmers grind their flinty durum wheat into a sandy golden flour called semolina. While most semolina goes into pasta and bread, gnocchi of this sunny flour are easy to make and wonderfully good eating—a farmhouse dish for Sunday dinners, buffet tables and one-dish suppers.

The porridges of crushed grains Italy's country people had been eating since before the Romans paved the way for polenta of cornmeal when it arrived from the Americas in the 1500s. Over the next three hundred years, polenta became a quintessential staple—central and northern Italy's single most important food for both peasants and landowners. Both relished the cooked cornmeal, but for different reasons. "Cheater's Gold," on page 171, relates polenta's story and its tragic flaw. Sweet Squash with Crisp Polenta (page 176) and Ettore Guatelli's Soffritto with Tomatoes for Polenta (page 178) are two farmhouse classics from polenta country.

Beans hold a special place in Italy's country cooking. Practically every region possesses beans it sees as its exclusive property. Bean dishes satisfy the way meat does. Just try a bowl of Tuscan Mountain Supper (page 186) and see what I mean. What polenta was for the peasants in northern Italy, fava beans were for southerners. Fava bean puree has all the versatility of polenta and tastes like mashed potatoes. It used to be eaten every day by farmworkers. Now Pugliese eat the puree because they enjoy it, no matter how rich, poor or in between they may be.

Whenever country cooks showed me a dish, or reminisced about a recipe, their cooking advice ended the same way: "Take what you have and use your imagination—be free!" Yet, too, there was always this proviso: ". . . but I should tell you my mother always did it this way." These recipes are how mother did it, or her daughter, or her son or how I was inspired by the same influences—country traditions and the land. I hope you take as much pleasure in them as I have.

FARMWOMAN'S RISOTTO
Risotto alla Contadina
Serves 6 to 9 as a first course, 4 as a main dish

Tomatoes, herbs, browned pancetta and bits of vegetable all bring their goodness to this risotto. It's practically a garden in a pot—typical country home cooking. And it's a good model for using whatever you have on hand to improvise your own risotto. Vary the herbs. Instead of stock, use half red wine and half water. Try some cabbage or cooked beans along with the vegetables. Eliminate the meat if you'd like. Remember, too, in twenty minutes risotto can be dinner.

Wine Suggestion: A Rosso di Montalcino or Rosso Cònero

Top halves of 2 celery stalks with leaves
1 medium carrot
1 medium red onion
Leaves from 5 sprigs fresh Italian
    parsley
6 large fresh sage leaves or whole dried
    leaves
3 1/8-inch-thick slices pancetta or good-
    quality salami, coarsely chopped
2 tablespoons extra-virgin olive oil
2 bay leaves
4 sprigs fresh thyme or a generous
    1/4 teaspoon dried thyme
A 4-inch sprig fresh rosemary

Salt and freshly ground black pepper
About 8 cups Mother's Broth (page 196),
    Hearty Vegetable Broth (page 198),
    or water
2 cups Italian Carnaroli rice or Arborio
3/4 cup dry white wine
1/2 cup Tomato Sauce IV (page 128) or
    drained canned tomatoes
About 1/2 cup freshly grated
    Parmigiano-Reggiano cheese (if
    unavailable, use good Grana Padano
    or domestic Asiago)
1 tablespoon unsalted butter (optional)

1. Mince together the vegetables, parsley, sage, and pancetta or salami. Heat the oil in a 5- to 6-quart deep heavy pot over medium heat. Sauté the minced blend with the bay, thyme, and rosemary until golden, not dark brown, seasoning with salt and pepper. Meanwhile, bring the broth or water to a gentle simmer.

2. Blend the rice into the vegetables and cook, stirring frequently, 3 minutes, or until it looks chalky and a white dot is clearly visible in the center of each grain. Stir in the wine, cooking until it has been absorbed. Add the tomato sauce or tomatoes, crushing them with your hands, stirring until no longer soupy.

3. Begin adding the broth a cup at a time, simmering and stirring until each addition has been absorbed by the rice. After about 6 cups, add the broth in 1/2-cup portions and start tasting the rice. It should be tender but still a little firm, never mushy. Risotto is creamy without being soupy.

4. When the rice is a little firmer than you'd like, remove the pot from the heat. Remove the bay leaves and herb sprigs. Fold in the cheese and the optional butter. Taste and season with salt and pepper. Let the risotto rest a moment to meld the flavors, then spoon into heated soup dishes and serve immediately.

Which Rice for Risotto?

Medium-grain rice makes risotto risotto. Because it contains a starch called amylopectin, medium-grain rice cooks to a creamy consistency while its grains keep a pleasing firmness to the bite. That juxtaposition of creaminess and bite, and its method of cooking, define risotto. Overcooked, mushy risotto is thrown out, never eaten.

The amylose starch in the long-grain rices we use here in America produces fluffy, separate grains when cooked—a good rice for pilafs, but not for risotto.

Here are my favorite medium-grain imported Italian rices for risotto, in order of preference:

➤ Carnaroli

➤ Arborio (the easiest to find)

➤ Vialone Nano

➤ Baldo, Corallo and Roma

When it's impossible to find any of these, try domestic organic medium-grain rice, sold in many markets. It's not as fragrant or as dense a grain as the Italian rices, but it makes respectable risotto.

In any case, buy organically grown rice if possible. Check the labels on Italian rices for *"biologici"* or *"biologica,"* meaning organic. *"Senza uso di diserbanti e concimi chimici"* translates as "grown without harmful herbicides and fertilizers," an expression sometimes used by packagers. See page 394 for rice mail-order sources.

Store rice in a sealed container up to 1 year in a cool dark place.

RISOTTO IN THE STYLE OF MILAN

Risotto alla Milanese

Serves 8 as a first course, 4 to 5 as a main dish

The color of a gold coin, Risotto alla Milanese is the jewel in the crown of Milan and Lombardy's cooking. The most famous risotto of Italy, this dish is a prime example of sound ingredients and consummate skill. The way it is made and the ingredients used are inviolate, practically a religion. Risotto alla Milanese tolerates few variations. Once you taste it, you'll understand why. This is one of the best dishes of all northern Italy.

➤ **Cook to Cook:** Risotto alla Milanese deserves homemade poultry broth. Use saffron threads, as powdered saffron may be adulterated.

Marrow is the creamy substance found in the hollow center of round leg bones of all large animals. I prefer my risotto without marrow, but do try it to see what you think. Marrow bones are found in most supermarkets and at butcher shops.

Wine Suggestion: A red Ripasso di Valpolicella by St. Stefano

3 to 4 tablespoons unsalted butter
Marrow from 3 fresh veal or beef
  marrow bones, chopped (optional)
1 small to medium onion, minced
  very fine
Salt and freshly ground black pepper
2 heaping cups (1 pound) Italian
  Arborio rice

About 9 cups Mother's Broth
  (page 196)
3 generous pinches saffron threads
1/2 cup dry white wine
1 1/2 cups freshly grated Parmigiano-
  Reggiano cheese

1. In a deep 5- to 6-quart heavy pot, melt 2 to 3 tablespoons of the butter and the optional marrow over medium-low heat. Sauté the onion with a little salt and pepper until soft and clear. Raise the heat to medium and stir in the rice. Cook about 3 minutes, stirring frequently, until it looks chalky and a white dot is clearly visible in the center of each grain.

2. Meanwhile, bring the broth to a gentle simmer. Remove 1/2 cup and blend with the saffron; set aside.

3. Stir the wine into the risotto, cooking until it is all absorbed. Begin adding the broth a cup at a time, simmering and stirring until each addition has been absorbed by the rice before adding the next cup. After about 7 cups, add the saffron-flavored stock and continue adding the broth in 1/2-cup portions. Begin tasting the risotto. When

ready, the rice should be close to tender, but with a little more firmness to the bite than you'd like, and have a slightly loose, creamy consistency (it will finish cooking and absorb a little more broth in the next step). Never cook it to mush. Season to taste.

4. Off the heat, fold in the remaining 1 tablespoon butter and 1 cup of the cheese. Let the risotto rest for a few moments, then serve in heated soup dishes, passing the remaining cheese separately.

A TRUE RISOTTO ALLA MILANESE?

Every day, Enrico Rastelli and his colleagues lunch at the trattoria around the corner from their office in the center of Milan. Everyone has their own table—the famous sportswriter and his wife, the man alone with his newspaper, the two architects, Enrico and his friends. Each day they greet each other: "Hello, Signor Engineer of Electronics," "Good day, Signor Architect." The mood is cordial, but no one intrudes upon the others' tables.

No menus appear. The waiter explains the daily specials, already knowing the sportswriter's wife doesn't like black pepper and the man with the newspaper must have his soup before deciding on anything else. More private club than public dining room, trattorie are extensions of home, where the familiar is prized over new.

I ask Enrico, a native of Milan, to define Risotto alla Milanese. "Butter, a little onion, rice only from Vercelli [about fifty miles from Milan], white wine—a good one you like to drink," he explains. "Only threads of saffron, never powder, the broth of a fat hen—never bouillon cubes—Parmigiano, and give it a rest before serving." Those at the next table have become quiet; they are listening. To be polite, Enrico asks, "What do you think, eh?"

"Signor Engineer of Electronics, you are absolutely right," replies the man with soup. "But my wife, also a Milanese like you, would use a little fat of our Milanese cervellata sausage with the butter." At the table on the other side conversation stops. Enrico raises an eyebrow. "Well," the architect leans in, "my mother, whose family has been here since before the Sforzas [a famous Renaissance family], always adds a corner of a bouillon cube to the broth for flavor." The sportswriter chimes in, "Come on, what kind of Milanese are you? Beef marrow has to be part of it! The rice will never be right without it. It won't have the right . . ." He rubs his thumb and forefinger together, indicating the feel of it.

At each table, knives and forks are put down. Meat is getting cold. Opinions fly, backed by the authority of grandmothers, historians, mothers, family sages. The communal chord has been struck, the gauntlet laid down, family, honor and a true Risotto alla Milanese are at stake. It is as though civilization itself warrants defending . . . and perhaps it does.

Rice, Grains and Beans

▼ ▼ ▼ ▼ ▼ ▼ ▼ ▼ ▼ ▼

RISOTTO WITH SEA SCALLOPS AND BALSAMIC VINEGAR

Risotto ai Pèttini con Aceto Balsamico

Serves 6 to 8 as a first course, 3 to 4 as a main dish

Sweet scallops, tart greens and lush, woodsy balsamic vinegar—what could be better in a risotto? I first tasted this nearly twenty-five years ago in the back room of a tiny country bar on the flat Po River plain that stretches between the cities of Ferrara and Modena, just north of the Adriatic Sea. A teenage girl served the three tables while her mother cooked in the kitchen behind a curtained doorway. When we talked later, the mother explained that the scallops came from the sea that morning and her daughter had picked the greens from their garden. But her pride was the vinegar. She took me upstairs to see the rows of old wood barrels in her vinegar attic. I've never made it back for a visit, but I prepare this risotto whenever scallops look good in the market. Pistachios are my addition, a favorite garnish at the Renaissance banquets served in Ferrara four hundred years ago.

➤ *Cook to Cook:* Balsamic vinegars fall into two categories: liqueur-like, expensive artisan-made vinegars and sharper commercial balsamic vinegars that range in quality from excellent to inedible. For information, see page 383.

For perfect tenderness, the sea scallops, so easily overdone, cook in the risotto's residual heat just before serving.

Wine Suggestion: A soft, lush white like La Palazza's Il Tornese or Secco Ca' del Merlo by Quintarelli, Giuseppe

2 tablespoons fruity extra-virgin olive oil
1 medium onion, finely chopped
A 6-inch branch fresh rosemary
Salt and freshly ground black pepper
About 8 cups Mother's Broth (page 196) or Hearty Vegetable Broth (page 198)
2 large handfuls (1/2 pound) tiny dandelion leaves or mixed organic greens, coarsely chopped
2 cups Italian Arborio or Roma rice

1 large clove garlic, minced
1/3 cup dry white wine
1 pound sea scallops, rinsed and halved
1/2 cup finely snipped fresh chives
1/3 cup shelled salted pistachios, coarsely chopped
About 3 tablespoons high-quality commercial balsamic vinegar

1. Heat the oil in a deep 5- to 6-quart pot over medium heat. Stir in the onion, rosemary, and salt and pepper. Cover and cook over medium-low heat 10 minutes, or until the onion is soft and clear. Meanwhile, bring the broth to a gentle simmer.

2. Uncover the pot, remove the rosemary, and raise the heat to medium-high. Stir in the greens and sauté 2 minutes to wilt. Blend in the rice and cook, stirring frequently, 3 minutes, or until it looks chalky and a white dot is clearly visible in the center of each grain. Add the garlic.

3. Stir in the wine and 1 cup of the hot broth. Keep at a simmer and cook until the liquid is absorbed. Continue adding the broth 1 cup at a time, stirring until each addition has been absorbed by the rice. After about 6 cups, add the broth in 1/2-cup portions and begin tasting the risotto. It should be close to tender, with a little more firmness to the bite than you'd like.

4. Adjust the seasonings and stir in the scallops. Remove from the heat and let stand, uncovered, 3 to 4 minutes, or until the scallops are barely firm. Fold in the chives and pistachios. Serve immediately, sprinkling each serving with a little balsamic vinegar. No cheese is used in this risotto.

SIMPLEST FARRO

Farro Semplice

Makes 4 cups, serving 4 to 8

Farro looks like large grains of wheat and has subtle flavors of hazelnuts and sweet barley. It takes to almost as many saucings as pasta. Most farm cooks boil farro this way to use in any dish they like. It's the best method for tasting the grain's pure flavor. Once boiled, it should be tender but retain a pleasing firmness at its center. Eat farro hot or at room temperature, with a twirl of olive oil, a few torn leaves of herbs and grinds of black pepper, as a first course, a main dish or a side dish. Then prepare any of the variations described below.

➤ *Cook to Cook:* Always check the package directions before cooking farro. Depending upon their origins, some farros may need presoaking. Farro doubles in volume when it cooks. It keeps in the refrigerator, covered, 3 or 4 days. Make it ahead for last-minute additions to soups, salads and stews.

2 cups (12 ounces) whole-grain Italian farro (*Triticum dicoccum*)	Salt
	Freshly ground black pepper
6 cups water	

1. Rinse the farro in a strainer under cold running water. Combine in a 4-quart saucepan with the water, salted to taste. Bring to a very gentle simmer, cover, and cook 30 to 45 minutes, or until tender. Taste for doneness.

2. Drain the farro in a sieve. Eat hot or at room temperature, adding salt and pepper to taste.

TURNING SIMPLEST FARRO INTO OTHER DISHES

Antipasto of Farro   Toss farro with a small amount of minced red onion and olive oil and wine vinegar to taste. Let stand at room temperature 30 minutes to 1 hour. Just before serving, fold in coarsely chopped fresh Italian parsley and basil to taste. Diced tomato and peppers, stemmed greens, and/or cold poached seafood could go into the antipasto as well.

Farro Salad   Dress as described above with onion, oil, vinegar, and herbs. Blend in diced raw fennel, diced sweet red pepper, and capers to taste.

Farro and Bean Salad   Add 2 cups rinsed and drained canned borlotti or pinto beans to the Farro Salad or Antipasto of Farro.

Shepherd's Farro   Toss warm farro (rewarm over medium heat in a covered saucepan with a little water, stirring often) with a little good-tasting olive oil. Rub a serving bowl with garlic. Turn the farro into the bowl along with chopped scallions, young ramps, or chives, salt, and freshly ground black pepper to taste. Blend in shredded young sheep cheese to taste (Pecorino Toscano, Cacio Romano, Pecorino Sardo, Sini Fulvi Pastore, or domestic Fontinella).

Farro with Sautéed Mushrooms   Brown together thickly sliced portobello or wild mushrooms and chopped onion in olive oil. Add a small amount of white wine and deglaze the pan. Season to taste and toss with the warm farro.

Sweet Farro, Mountain-Style   Toss room-temperature farro with fresh ricotta and honey to taste. Finish with a sprinkling of cinnamon. Mountain farmers used to make meals of chestnut-flour polenta eaten this way. They say farro is just as good.

Farro with Vin Cotto   Stir Vin Cotto (page 96), spiced wine syrup, into room-temperature farro. Top with fresh ricotta and serve as a first course or dessert.

Farro with Pasta Sauce   Replace the pasta with farro in the four tomato sauces on pages 122 to 128, Spaghettini with Shrimp, Chickpeas and Young Greens (page 86), or Gemelli with Roasted Peppers and Greens (page 78).

Other Dishes   Stir cooked farro into roasted vegetables (page 286), green salads (pages 299 to 300), beans (pages 182 to 186), or light soups and broths (pages 193 to 216).

FARRO IN PROSPERO'S SHOP

Antica Bottega di Prospero is Lucca's oldest seed and grain shop. The place is dim and cave-like, with barrels of dried beans and sacks of seeds and grain. In the back, a large room with farmers' tools has a floor display announcing seed hybrids new in the 1950s. All over Italy, shops like this sell everything dried—birdseed, dried beans, grains and seeds for the garden, field or pot.

The elderly woman behind the counter does not chat until you buy. She withholds her encyclopedic knowledge of local agriculture and cooking, gauging how much to reveal by the size of your purchase. My five-pound bag of farro releases a deluge of information. Obviously this is the grain of her region and one she loves.

"This is the best farro in Italy," she announces. "It's grown in the Garfagnana mountains and hills, on narrow terraces that can drain properly. Farro is strong—it doesn't need chemicals like pesticides. You do not soak it before cooking. Ours is better than Umbria's because on their low plain, it's too wet. The farro becomes hard. Theirs needs soaking or cracking before cooking."

Looking out at the street, then turning back to me as though reminded by something she has just seen, she remarks, "Roman soldiers carried a sack of farro tied to their belts as they marched. Wealthy Romans always ate a focaccia of farro flour at weddings. You see how important it was?" Her look says it all—an outlander can never grasp farro's importance, but she gives it another try. "Some people carry three grains of farro in a sack under their clothes. It protects them from bad luck." She raises an eyebrow. "I don't argue with these things." My time is up. She dismisses me with a nod and turns away.

Farro became a small obsession for me. I learned that it is one of a trio of ancient grains (spelt, einkorn and farro) that are the ancestors of all our modern wheats. In English, farro is *emmer*; botanically, it's *Triticum dicoccum*. In the Marche region, farro is cooked in a broth of sausage and pork bones. In the Umbria region, when a baby is born, neighbors bring farro porridge to strengthen the nursing mother.

All through central Italy, farro figures in all kinds of dishes. Deep in the south, in southern Puglia, women bake farro flour into bagel-shaped breads that their husbands take to the fields for lunch. But back up north in Lucca, when I related all my discoveries to my Tuscan cousin Francesca, our family's designated best cook, she waved away all these foreign ways with a sweep of her hand and pronounced, "Farro is always with beans! *Basta* (enough)!" The lady at the shop of Prospero said she's right.

FARRO RISOTTO WITH CHICKPEAS, ORANGE AND SAGE

Risotto di Farro

Serves 6 to 8 as a first course, 4 as a main dish

I believe chickpeas and farro were meant for each other. This unusual Tuscan-inspired takeoff on risotto illustrates my point. Sautéing farro with chickpeas, onion and sage releases all the grain's nut-like qualities. Tart orange zest counters the sweetness farro and chickpeas share in common. Sage is the savory note. Tuscans are crazy about sage. They lavish it on bean and grain dishes.

Farro and chickpeas mingling so beautifully is no accident. They were being cultivated together in northern Syria nearly ten thousand years ago and came to Italy not long afterward.

A nice bonus of this recipe is that you can cook farro risotto several hours ahead. Treat rice the same way, and it turns mushy. You can reheat this dish, just take care not to overcook it.

➤ **Cook to Cook:** Because farro from different areas of Italy cooks at varying rates, this recipe has a range of liquid and cooking times. Since cooking farro with acids and fats takes longer than in water, a brief presoak helps things along.

Wine Suggestion: A Tuscan red Carmignano by Artimino,
Tenuta Cantagallo or Il Poggiolo

1 1/2 cups (9 ounces) whole-grain Italian farro (*Triticum dicoccum*)

Hot water

2 tablespoons fruity extra-virgin olive oil

1 medium to large onion, finely chopped

15 to 16 large fresh sage leaves, torn into small pieces

A 4-inch branch fresh rosemary

1/2 teaspoon fennel seeds, crushed

Salt and freshly ground black pepper

1 15-ounce can chickpeas, rinsed and drained

8 to 10 cups Hearty Vegetable Broth (page 198), Mother's Broth (page 196), or canned low-sodium chicken broth

Shredded zest of 1 large orange

2 large cloves garlic, minced

1/2 cup dry white wine

1/2 cup freshly grated Parmigiano-Reggiano cheese

1 tightly packed tablespoon fresh Italian parsley leaves, chopped

Rice, Grains and Beans

1. Place the farro in a bowl and cover with very hot water. Soak at room temperature while you prepare the other ingredients.

2. In a heavy 5- to 6-quart pot, heat the oil over medium-high heat. Stir in the onion, sage, rosemary, fennel seeds, and salt (if using canned broth, eliminate the salt) and pepper to taste. Cover and turn the heat to low. Cook 15 minutes, or until the onions are soft and clear. Uncover, raise the heat to medium-high, and sauté the onions to rich golden brown, taking care not to burn the glaze at the bottom of the pan. About halfway through browning, stir in half the chickpeas.

3. Meanwhile, bring the broth to a gentle simmer.

4. Drain the farro. Blend half the orange zest, all the garlic, and the farro into the onions. Stir 1 minute. Cooking takes about an hour for Garfagnana farro, possibly longer for farro from other areas: Add 1 cup of the broth and cook, uncovered, at a lively simmer until it has been absorbed. Stir frequently. Keep adding the broth $1/2$ cup at a time, stirring until it is absorbed. Add salt and pepper to taste as dish cooks. When the farro is nearly tender, blend in the remaining chickpeas. Stir in the wine and the remaining orange zest and cook until the wine has been absorbed. Sample the farro for tenderness with some firmness and no raw taste. Its cleft will have opened up, revealing more of its white interior. If it is still too firm, add another $1/4$ cup or more stock and simmer until the consistency is creamy and the grain is done. Remove the rosemary sprig.

5. Remove the pot from the heat, fold in the cheese, and let rest, uncovered, 5 minutes. Taste for seasoning. Serve hot, sprinkled with the parsley.

Buying Farro and Substitutions

You can find farro in some Italian groceries and specialty food shops. I like the Rustichella brand, which gives the grain's botanical name on its label, *Triticum dicoccum*. Rustichella's importers claim that their farro comes from the Garfagnana, although nothing is stated on the package. It does not need soaking, and it cooks in about 40 minutes. Use farro in dishes where rice, barley or wheat is called for.

Store farro well sealed in the freezer up to 1 year. Whole-grain farro keeps several months in an open bowl in a cool, airy part of the house.

WHEAT

Again and again, farmers told me that in times past, wheat was like gold—their ancestors' most valuable crop, especially in the south. Everyone there still marks the December planting of wheat with bowls of Cuccia—cooked wheat kernels dressed with sweet things, maybe honey, ricotta, spices or chocolate—and it is always eaten on Santa Lucia's Day, December 13. Cuccia is a good-luck charm. Southern Italian farmers plant wheat in December, at the time of the winter solstice, the year's darkest days. It ripens for harvest in June at the summer solstice, the year's brightest and most fertile time. Cycles are never ignored in the country, especially not one this meaningful. After planting their wheat, farmers have always sealed their faith in a good crop by eating bowls of Cuccia from last year's harvest.

In the Puglia region, I tasted yet another wheat tradition—pounded wheat, done by farmwomen. Rosalba Ciannamea, who raises olives and wheat near Brindisi, insists the old strain of wheat growing in her fields makes the best pounded wheat (called *grano pestato,* or *cranu stumpatu* in local dialect). I heard the same about other wheats from other farmers— everyone has his or her favorite. The wheat in Rosalba's fields has sprays of long black whiskers sprouting from golden kernels at the head of long stiff stalks. Dramatic. She bundles sheaves of it to decorate mantles and tables. For *grano pestato,* Rosalba soaks the kernels overnight. After draining, she pounds them in a deep stone mortar until the grains release their beige skin (called the pellicule) and are soft and white, but still whole. She dries the wheat and stores it. For eating, she boils the grain until creamy-tender and dresses it like pasta or serves it as salad or in soups. When I first had it at her table, I was surprised by how delicate it was. Without its pellicule, her wheat had little of the grainy-earthy taste I associate with the grain. It was more like eating fragrant basmati rice.

The tradition of pounding wheat began thousands of years ago. Ancient cooks were probably ridding their wheat of its indigestible coarse outer coverings. What intrigues me is that the process is still done today in the same way.

PUGLIA LAMB RAGU WITH WHEAT

Ragù Pugliese

Serves 6 as a one-dish supper

Imagine a ragù of sausage, lamb and tomatoes served not over pasta, but over cooked wheat kernels that taste nutty and sweet. Saucing cooked wheat kernels the way we do pasta is new to us, but Puglia's country people have been doing it for generations. Make the ragù and wheat a one-dish supper for friends. Tell them its story—this used to be eaten on Fat Tuesday, the last fling for Puglia farmers before the forty days of Lenten fasting began. Everyone in the countryside feasted on this day—even the poorest field worker ate meat, though it may have been a bit of lamb and sausage in a lot of tomato sauce. Try the ragù, too, on Puglia's orecchiette pasta.

Wine Suggestion: A Puglia red Copertino or Castel del Monte Rosso

1 cup (about 6 ounces) hard wheat kernels (wheat berries)
3 quarts boiling salted water
1 tablespoon olive oil
1/2 pound bulk sweet Italian sausage meat
1/2 pound boneless lamb shoulder or leg, diced into 1/4-inch cubes
1 medium onion, minced
Salt and freshly ground black pepper

1 large clove garlic, minced
1/4 tightly packed cup fresh basil leaves, minced
1/2 cup dry white wine
1 cup Mother's Broth (page 196) or canned low-sodium chicken broth
1 14-ounce can whole tomatoes
1/4 cup crumbled young sheep cheese or shredded domestic Fontinella

1. Cook the wheat kernels in the boiling water until very tender, about 1 hour and 15 minutes. Drain and set aside.

2. Meanwhile, in a 3 1/2- to 4-quart saucepan (not nonstick), heat the oil over medium heat. Stir in the meats. Cook 15 minutes, or until crusty brown, stirring often. Lift the meats out with a slotted spoon and reserve. Pour off all but about 3 tablespoons of the fat.

3. Add the onion to the pan, sprinkle it with salt and pepper, and sauté over medium to medium-low heat 5 minutes, taking care not to burn the glaze at the bottom of the pan. When the onions are softened, stir in the garlic, basil, meats, and wine. Cook, uncovered, over medium heat until all the liquid is gone. Add 1/2 cup of

the broth and simmer it down to nothing. Add the tomatoes, crushing them with your fingers as they go into the pot. Simmer 3 minutes to thicken slightly.

4. Add the remaining ½ cup broth and enough water to barely cover the meat. Slowly simmer, covered, 45 minutes. Uncover and cook 10 minutes, or until the flavors are rich and mellow; the sauce should be only slightly soupy. Stir in the wheat berries and cook another 10 minutes. Taste for seasoning. Blend in the cheese and serve hot in bowls.

Buying and Keeping Wheat

Buy the freshest organic whole wheat kernels possible in natural food stores, supermarkets and specialty food shops with a lively turnover. If both hard and soft wheats are available, go for the hard wheats. Pounded wheat like Puglia's *grano pestato* is sometimes found in shops selling Greek foods. It looks like white wheat kernels. Store whole wheat kernels sealed in a cool dark place up to 1 year. Store pounded wheat in the refrigerator up to 3 months.

GOLDEN GNOCCHI

Gnocchi di Semolino

Serves 6 as a first course, 4 as a main dish

The easiest of all Italy's gnocchi, these golden circles of semolina can be waiting in the refrigerator, ready to bake, for a quick weeknight supper. Creamy and sensuous at their centers, with crisp browned edges, the gnocchi are laced with scallions and Parmigiano-Reggiano cheese. Add their topping of goat cheese only at the last moment so it turns barely creamy from the heat. That's the adamant instruction from their creator, Emma Martini, who, with her husband, makes goat cheese and takes in guests at their farm, Le Frise, in the mountains of northern Lombardy. Emma encourages improvising—season them with a favorite herb, or add a quarter cup of cooked spinach. "Semolina gnocchi are not new, nor particularly chic," she tells me. "They've been around forever." When you taste them, you'll know why.

➤ *Cook to Cook:* For crisp, almost crunchy gnocchi, spread them farther apart, using two baking dishes instead of one. For a center that is creamy and sensuous, prepare the gnocchi as described below. Buy semolina in specialty food stores. Look for packages labeled "semolina, made from durum wheat."

Wine Suggestion: A red Merlot from the Veneto or Lombardy

1 quart milk

1½ cups (½ pound) semolina (ground durum wheat flour with a sandy texture)

3 tablespoons unsalted butter

3 to 4 scallions, thinly sliced

¾ cup (3 ounces) freshly grated Parmigiano-Reggiano cheese

Salt

2 large egg yolks

⅓ cup Mother's Broth (page 196), Hearty Vegetable Broth (page 198), or canned low-sodium chicken broth

Freshly ground black pepper

2 to 3 ounces creamy fresh goat cheese

1. Bring the milk to a simmer in a heavy 6- to 8-quart pot. Whisk in the semolina, whisking until it's free of lumps. Simmer gently 20 minutes, or until very thick and with no raw flour taste, stirring frequently to keep the mixture smooth. Remove from the heat.

2. Beat in 2 tablespoons of the butter, the scallions, Parmigiano-Reggiano cheese, salt to taste, and the yolks. Run a baking sheet under cold running water. Turn the hot semolina mixture onto the sheet and shape it with two spatulas into 2 or 3 long cylin-

ders about 2 inches in diameter. Cool several hours. (At this point, you can wrap it and refrigerate overnight.)

3. Preheat the oven to 375°F. Butter a 9 x 13-inch shallow baking dish. Slice the semolina cylinders into ¼-inch rounds and overlap in the dish. (At this point, the gnocchi can be covered and refrigerated for baking the next day.)

4. In a small saucepan, simmer the remaining 1 tablespoon butter with the broth a few seconds. Pour over the gnocchi and dust lightly with salt and pepper. Bake 25 to 35 minutes, or until golden and slightly crispy on top. Dot with the goat cheese and heat another minute. Serve hot.

Le Frise farm.

Rice, Grains and Beans

WHEAT BERRIES WITH RICOTTA AND HONEY

Cuccía

Serves 4 to 6

All over southern Italy, this dish is lunch, dinner or a snack. Here in America, it's a terrific dish for brunch or dessert. Who can resist the fresh warm tastes of whole wheat kernels with honey and ricotta? You can cook the wheat a day ahead and keep it in the refrigerator. Have Cuccía the way you'd eat it in an Italian farmhouse—served at room temperature in small bowls with soupspoons.

Wine Suggestion: A sweet Moscato Passito di Pantelleria

1 cup (5 ounces) hard wheat kernels
   (wheat berries)
Water
$1/2$ teaspoon salt
$1 1/2$ cups high-quality, creamy ricotta

Honey to taste
$1/2$ cup currants or raisins
Generous pinch of ground cinnamon
   (optional)

1. Soak the wheat in cold water to cover overnight in the refrigerator.

2. Drain and place in a 3-quart saucepan along with the salt and enough water to cover by 2 to 3 inches. Cook at a slow simmer, partially covered, about 1 hour, or until tender. The kernels will open up slightly.

3. Drain the wheat and combine it with the ricotta. Blend in honey to taste and the currants or raisins. Turn into a deep serving bowl and dust with cinnamon, if desired. Serve warm or at room temperature in small bowls.

VARIATIONS

Cuccía with Vin Cotto   Instead of ricotta, stir in $1 1/2$ cups vin cotto (page 96) spiced wine syrup.

Cuccía with Chocolate   Some Italians like warm Cuccía with ricotta, honey, and shaved semisweet chocolate to taste. They add, too, 1 to 2 tablespoons chopped candied orange rind.

POLENTA: CHEATER'S GOLD

It was like a round golden sun in the center of the table, mounded on the board, steaming, waiting for my grandmother to slice it by pulling the string taut and sawing it into the mound. Everything tasted good with polenta, even polenta alone. We ate it day and night, all the time. Polenta consoled us, it filled up all of us. No one in the Veneto is without polenta memories." Although Veneto food authority Giuseppe Maffioli said this in the 1970s, it could have come from almost anyone in northern or central Italy. Until several decades ago, polenta was a mainstay of the diet there.

The word *polenta* means a porridge made from any ground grain, but it is commonly used to name a porridge cooked from ground cornmeal. Corn and polenta are now almost synonymous in Italy.

Corn was a godsend in Italy when it arrived from the Americas via Spain. By the early nineteenth century, it had changed the way land was worked, the way farmhouses were built and the way people who lived from the land ate. Corn answered the landowner's prayer for a cheap, filling food that his sharecroppers and workers would like. It saved his profitable crops, like wheat, for the market instead of the workers' bread. The marvels didn't stop there. Its yield surpassed every other grain of the age—plant a single kernel of corn and get back two hundred and fifty kernels at harvest time.

Corn plants worked triple time: Cobs, stalks and leaves fed farm animals and fertilized fields. Leaves filled family mattresses too. At one extreme, families ate only polenta, perhaps with a little pork fat or vegetable; at the other, polenta sopped up rich ragùs and was mounded high next to meats. Either way, polenta left everyone full and satiated. Except for its tragic flaw.

"We called polenta cheater's gold," one farmer told me, "beautiful to look at on the table, so warm, so good. We thought it made us strong, but it made us weak and sick." Corn narrowed peasant diets, nudging away the variety of grains and beans they'd eaten for centuries.

Polenta lacks niacin and certain amino acids that exist in corn but aren't released when it's merely ground and boiled. So pellagra, the often-fatal disease of amino-acid-and-niacin deficiency, struck those who ate only polenta, without niacin-rich foods like beans. Sadly, Italy never adopted Central America's simple corn technology, which released the grain's niacin and amino acids by treating it with slaked lime.

Polenta's appeal fell sharply when the prosperity after World War II all but banished it from peasants' tables. About twenty years ago, though, polenta's popularity returned with affectionate, if myopic, nostalgia for the simple country life of long ago. The taste of corn worked its spell. Today, all over central and northern Italy, every weekend in October brings polenta festivals. The children of peasant polenta eaters celebrate autumn with the first polenta of the new corn.

Rice, Grains and Beans

COOKING EFFORTLESS POLENTA

One cup cornmeal yields about 4 cups polenta,
enough for 4 to 6 people

Cooks in the Veneto, Friuli and Lombardy, who know polenta better than any other Italians, insist cornmeal needs an hour or more of cooking to come to full tenderness and flavor, and to lose any trace of bitterness. Unless you like harsh, raw cornmeal mush, please ignore any recipe recommending cooking polenta fifteen to twenty minutes.

Tedious stirring and traditional polenta aren't synonymous. This double boiler method is nearly effortless. Italian cooks often make a big batch of polenta, eat some fresh and store the rest in the refrigerator for later grilling, baking or sautéing.

The Double Boiler Method

The double boiler technique consists of pouring boiling water into a bowl, whisking in the polenta and salt, setting the bowl over a pot of simmering water, covering it and cooking 1 1/2 to 2 hours. Stir the polenta occasionally, and it's done. Here is the basic formula and method for a polenta that stands in high mounds and cools to a firm and sliceable consistency. For creamier polenta, increase the liquid by about one third.

FORMULA

3 parts liquid (water, broth, milk and
water, or buttermilk and water) to
1 part cornmeal, and salt to taste

1. Have handy an 8-quart stainless steel bowl and a whisk. Bring the amount of liquid needed for cooking the polenta to a boil. Meanwhile, fill a 6-quart pot one-third full with water. Bring to a lively simmer. Pour the boiling measured liquid into the bowl. Whisk it into a whirlpool while slowly pouring in the cornmeal, vigorously whisking away all lumps.

2. Cover the bowl tightly with foil and set it over the simmering water. Cook 1 1/2 hours. During the first 20 minutes, stir the polenta several times. Then stir only every 20 or 30 minutes, tasting for salt. Replenish the simmering water as necessary. Taste the polenta for bitterness and tenderness, cooking up to another 30 minutes if necessary. If serving the polenta soft, it can be held over hot water for up to 3 hours. Or spread the polenta on an oiled shallow pan or in a loaf pan, cool, cover, and refrigerate up to 5 days.

DISHES FOR POLENTA

BUYING CORNMEAL FOR POLENTA

All over northern and central Italy, deep unlined copper polenta pots pass from mother to daughter and even from father to son, keeping alive the ritual of making polenta. Even today, after generations of polenta eating, the whole family comes to the kitchen to watch the shower of cornmeal go into the pot, to inhale its fragrance, to help stir and, finally, to bring the bright golden mound to the table.

Eat it fresh from the pot, or make polenta ahead and bake it, fry it or grill it later. Polenta tastes good with everything. But each dish begins with cooking cornmeal into polenta. The quality of the cornmeal determines everything. "Bake with flour ground two weeks ago, make polenta with cornmeal ground two hours ago," counsels an old saying from Tuscany.

➤ **Fresh ground corn** blossoms into delicious polenta. Freshness is more vital than whether it is imported or not, or how coarse or fine the meal is ground. Little difference exists between Italian and American cornmeals. Since there is no way of knowing when cornmeal was ground, buy where turnover is lively—mills, co-ops or markets. Sample until you find a cornmeal tasting of good corn, with no rancid or bitter aftertaste. Cornmeal freezes well, so stock up if your source isn't convenient. Avoid any tasteless commercial varieties. A personal favorite of mine is the coarse-ground flaky polenta meal from Giusto's in California (see mail-order sources, page 394).

➤ **Organic cornmeal** is a good choice for ecological reasons. Also, many organic farmers in Italy and America are turning back to older, tastier corn strains.

➤ **Stone-ground corn** with its germ intact makes a hearty polenta, typical of old-style farmhouse eating. Again, freshness is vital, as the fragile germ quickly turns rancid.

➤ **Fine or coarse grinds** are dictated by a dish's origins and family taste. For instance, Treviso, near Venice, likes cornmeal silken and sometimes white. Lombardy's Bergamo and Brescia areas prefer a coarse-to-very-coarse grind.

➤ **Instant polenta** lacks corn flavor. Far better to use prepared polenta in a tube. It is an acceptable stand-in when you're in a hurry. Avoid those with flavorings. Serve it very hot, or it will taste like wax.

Attilio Brino, an organic corn farmer in the Veneto, holding ears of corn.

POLENTA WITH CHEESE AND BALSAMIC VINEGAR

Polenta al Formaggio e Aceto Balsamico

Serves 6 to 8 as a side dish

Stirring Parmigiano-Reggiano cheese into hot polenta releases such fragrance. Sprinkle a little balsamic vinegar over the polenta the way they do in Reggio and Modena for a fine side dish. Have the polenta with stews, roasts like Harvest Capon (page 228), pasta sauces and bean dishes. Grill slices of the leftovers and cut them into bite-sized pieces to serve with drinks. Experiment with other cheeses in the polenta like Gorgonzola, Pecorino di Pienza and Montasio.

5^1/2 cups water, Hearty Vegetable Broth (page 198) or Mother's Broth (page 196)

1^3/4 cups coarse-ground cornmeal (preferably organic)

1 teaspoon salt, or to taste

About ^{1}/2 cup balsamic vinegar

1 to 1^1/2 cups (4 to 6 ounces) freshly grated Parmigiano-Reggiano cheese

3 tablespoons unsalted butter (optional)

1. Bring the water or broth to a boil and pour it into a large stainless steel bowl. Whisk in the cornmeal, whisking until smooth. Season with the salt.

2. Cover the bowl with foil and seal the edges. Set the bowl over a 6-quart pot one-third full of water bubbling at a lively simmer. Cook 1^1/2 hours, stirring every 20 minutes or so, and replenishing the simmering water as needed. Taste the polenta. If there's a slight bitter edge or the grain seems too hard, re-cover and cook up to another 30 minutes. Taste for seasoning. (The polenta can be kept hot over hot water up to an hour before serving.)

3. Have the balsamic vinegar in a small pitcher. Reserve a tablespoon of the cheese for garnishing the polenta. Just before serving, fold a cup of the remaining cheese and the butter (if using) into the polenta. Taste for more cheese.

4. Mound the hot polenta on a cutting board. Sprinkle with the reserved cheese. Take it to the table and slice it with a taut string or spoon it out. Invite everyone to season their polenta with the vinegar. Store leftover polenta tightly wrapped in the refrigerator up to 3 days.

SWEET SQUASH WITH CRISP POLENTA
Zucca con Polenta

Serves 4 to 6 as a one-dish meal

In farmhouses in the hills of Emilia-Romagna, women used to sauté sweet squash with onion and tomato and serve it over wedges of polenta. Do not be timid about browning the onion and searing the squash until it is speckled with gold. Their flavors deepen with the browning, turning what is usually a side dish into a one-dish dinner.

Wine Suggestion: A Lombardy red like Oltrepó Pavese Barbera
or Franciacorta Rosso

POLENTA (MAKE UP TO 5 DAYS AHEAD)
5½ cups Hearty Vegetable Broth
 (page 198), Mother's Broth
 (page 196), or water
1¾ cups coarse-ground cornmeal
 (organic if possible)
1 teaspoon salt, or to taste
Extra-virgin olive oil
Freshly ground black pepper

SQUASH (MAKE UP TO 1 HOUR AHEAD)
2 tablespoons extra-virgin olive oil
1 ⅛-inch-thick slice lean pancetta,
 finely chopped

4 medium onions, cut into thin slivers
6 large fresh sage leaves
¼ tightly packed cup fresh Italian
 parsley leaves, chopped
Salt and freshly ground black pepper
1¾ pounds butternut squash, peeled,
 seeded, and cut into sticks about
 ½ inch thick by 2 inches long
5 whole canned tomatoes, drained
½ cup water
2 tablespoons red wine vinegar

1. **To make the polenta:** Bring the broth or water to a boil and pour it into a large stainless steel bowl. Whisk in the cornmeal, whisking until smooth. Season with the salt.

2. Cover the bowl with foil and seal the edges. Set the bowl over a 6-quart pot one-third full of water bubbling at a lively simmer. Cook 1½ hours, stirring every 20 minutes or so, and replenishing the simmering water as needed. Taste the polenta. If there's a slight bitter edge or the grain seems too hard, re-cover and cook up to another 30 minutes. Remove from the heat.

3. Taste the polenta for seasoning. Pack it into an oiled 9 by 5-inch (1½-quart) loaf pan. Cool, cover, and refrigerate.

4. Once the squash is ready, keep it warm while you cut the polenta into $1/2$-inch-thick slices, rub each one lightly with olive oil, and season with salt and pepper. Sear in a sauté pan or on a hot grill to crisp and heat through.

1. **To make the squash:** In a 12-inch sauté pan, heat the oil and pancetta over medium-high heat. Sauté the onions with the sage and half of the parsley until softened. Sprinkle with salt and pepper. Stir in the squash and cook until speckled with gold on all sides, stirring frequently.

2. Add the tomatoes, crushing them with your hands as they go into the pan; turn the heat down to medium-low, cover, and cook until the squash is tender, about 12 minutes. Blend in the water and 1 tablespoon of the vinegar, scraping up the brown glaze in the bottom of the pan. Simmer 30 seconds.

3. Serve the squash next to the polenta slices, sprinkling it with the remaining parsley and vinegar.

VARIATION

Serve the squash over soft freshly cooked polenta by turning the hot polenta onto a board and setting it out with the squash. A little butter and cheese is usually spread over the polenta to keep it moist. Use a strong thread to cut slices of polenta for serving. Invite everyone to help themselves.

Rice, Grains and Beans

ETTORE GUATELLI'S SOFFRITTO WITH TOMATOES FOR POLENTA AND PASTA

Soffritto Guatelli

Serves 6 to 8 as a main dish

This is a farmhouse classic—an old-time breakfast that women took to the fields—slices of golden polenta layered with chunky red tomato sauce. For us, the dish is a crowd pleaser for buffets and suppers.

Ettore Guatelli says everything can be done ahead, and once you've sautéed the vegetables, the sauce cooks in only five minutes. Guatelli still lives on the farm where he was born over seventy years ago, in the Parma hills of northern Italy. He recalls that around nine o'clock in the morning, his mother used to bring the polenta to the fields where everyone had been working since before dawn. Today, Ettore and his brothers make soffritto and polenta for the midday meal, or supper.

➤ *Cook to Cook:* Cook the tomato sauce and polenta up to 3 days ahead. Store, covered, in the refrigerator.

Make a fine soup with a cupful of leftover sauce, about 3 cups of chopped vegetables and water to cover. Simmer until the vegetables turn tender.

Wine Suggestion: A Chianti by Castello di Volpaia, Tenuta Fontodi or Badia a Coltibuono

1 1/2 medium onions
1 1/2 medium stalks celery
1 1/2 medium carrots
1 tablespoon extra-virgin olive oil
4 1/8-inch-thick slices lean pancetta, finely chopped
1/2 cup water
2 1/2 cups Tomato Sauce II made with cooked tomatoes (page 124)

Polenta (page 172), made with 1 1/4 cups cornmeal and 3 3/4 cups water, cooled and sliced a generous 1/4 inch thick
2 tablespoons freshly grated Parmigiano-Reggiano cheese (optional)

1. For the soffritto, mince together the vegetables to about 1/8- to 1/4-inch pieces. Heat the olive oil in a 12-inch skillet (not nonstick) over medium-high heat. Stir in the pancetta, turn the heat down to medium, and sauté until pale gold, about 5 minutes. Add the vegetables. Cook over medium heat to a rich golden brown, about 8 minutes, taking care not to burn the glaze in the bottom of the pan. Add the water. Simmer down to nothing while scraping up the glaze. Remove from the heat.

2. Puree the tomato sauce in a blender or food processor. Pour into the soffritto and simmer over medium-high heat, uncovered, 5 minutes, to thicken slightly. (The sauce can be held, covered, at room temperature about an hour.)

3. In a preheated 400°F oven, heat the polenta through. In a shallow serving bowl, make a layer of 2 or 3 slices of polenta and top with generous spoonfuls of the sauce. Alternate layers of polenta and sauce, finishing with sauce. If desired, top with the Parmigiano-Reggiano cheese. Serve hot.

POLENTA WITH BEANS IN SOFFRITTO

Stir 2 cups cooked cranberry beans (see page 185), borlotti, pinto, or chickpeas into the soffritto along with the tomato sauce. (The beans can be canned. Rinse and drain them first.)

HONEYMOONERS AND CORN HUSK MATTRESSES

Lucca photographer Alcide Tossi was warming up for the story he was about to tell. "They were as green as new corn, just married, all soap and water—their first time in a real town. They came for me to take their wedding photos, and always asked if they could leave their bags until the afternoon train for Viareggio, while they saw Lucca. Usually this would be the only trip those farmers ever took—their three-day honeymoon at the sea, in Viareggio. They went around Lucca with eyes like saucers, seeing the elegant shops, so many things for sale, the cafés, the way people dressed, the afternoon *passeggiata*, our beautiful walls. And they saw the real mattresses.

"You want to know about farm life in the Garfagnana? Garfagnana is polenta country—and those corn husk mattresses. That's how people in the Garfagnana slept for their whole lives—on big sacks of scratchy cloth stuffed with dried corn leaves. Those mattresses were lumpy, had bugs. Sleeping on them was like being in Purgatory. Money for a real mattress was a dream—no one had money then.

"Sometimes those kids didn't come back to my shop until just before closing. The Viareggio train was long gone. No, they hadn't forgotten the time. They'd seen the mattresses in the store down the street—the ones so clean and soft-looking, so inviting. They'd traded their trip of a lifetime for the mattress."

Rice, Grains and Beans

BEANS AND THE SECRET OF GOOD CROPS

It's no accident that farmers all over Italy have always eaten bean dishes. Remember "Jack and the Bean Stalk"? Beans might well have seemed magical to farmers long ago. They grew easily. They tasted good. With little effort, they went from plant to pot. They were excellent animal feed. And when the whole bean plants, or solely the stalks and leaves, were plowed back into the soil, they became free fertilizer. Organic farmers still do this. They say beans keep the land rich. In much of Italy, old farm records of crop rotations show that people raised crops of beans in a field before planting it with their money crop of wheat. Favas and most other beans fertilize soil naturally, giving back exactly what most grains take away—nitrogen.

"Favas planted before wheat bring miracles" is an old southern Italian saying. What polenta was for country people in northern and central Italy, the fava was for peasants in the south, except favas are more nutritious. They called favas the meat and wheat of the peasants. Favas and other beans possess powers corn does not. They make the soil rich.

Fava beans have a special place in Puglia. If wheat is the heart of the region's cooking, the fava is its soul. As one Pugliese puts it, "This was the food of our poor that everyone still loves to eat. No one will give up their fava puree."

Cooking fava puree is a ritual in Puglia. It begins with soaked beans, a wooden spoon and a tall, vase-shaped terra-cotta pot. It probably hasn't changed for at least a thousand years. The pot sits directly on the hearth, braced between two crossed logs. Embers banked up around it heat the pot. The favas simmer in water. The wooden spoon stays in the pot, a reminder to occasionally stir the beans until they're a smooth pale green cream. An unequivocal "Never!" meets any suggestion of pureeing favas in a food processor or blender. Pugliese country cooks insist that if done right the beans puree themselves, falling apart in cooking. They're right. Given a tall terra-cotta vase first soaked in water overnight and a fireplace, cooking favas the old way is culinary adventure. But even Puglia cooking teacher Paola Pettrini claims favas cook beautifully on the stove in a saucepan.

Buying and Keeping Dried Beans

This is a selection of Italy's most frequently used dried beans. For times when imports aren't available, I've included American substitutions. Find beans in natural food stores, Mediterranean groceries and specialty food shops. I prefer organic beans for ecological reasons and their occasionally superior flavor. Buy plump, unbroken beans with no signs of withering. They should smell fresh. Store dried beans sealed in a cool dark place up to 1 year.

➤ **Bianchi di Spagna (Spanish whites)** White and shaped like oversized limas, these beans are also called *corona* or *bianco grande* in Italian, and *soisson* in French. They taste especially meaty. Do not buy Greek gigante beans, as they taste grassy.

   American Substitute Domestic cannellini or Christmas beans.

➤ Borlotti The most popular member of an entire family of small kidney-shaped speckled beans (*Lamon, stregoni, scritti* and *saluggia*). Colors range from ivory dappled with light red to beige freckled with deep maroon. The flavor is meaty without pronounced earthiness.

   American Substitute Organic pinto beans.

➤ Cannellini Small white kidney-shaped beans with a delicate skin and sweet, creamy meat.

   American Substitute Organic cannellini are being raised in the western United States. Find them in natural food stores. Or use Anasazi or pinto beans.

➤ **Ceci** These are chickpeas. Muted gold, small, round and grooved, these are the least "beany" of beans—sweet and meaty. I haven't found a marked difference between imported and domestic dried chickpeas. Organic chickpeas are often tastier.

➤ **Favas** Lima bean–shaped pale green to creamy-white beans. Buy dried favas that have been skinned. Favas have a sweet, round flavor that always reminds me of the best mashed potatoes.

   American Substitute None.

Just-harvested fava beans in Puglia.

Rice, Grains and Beans

FAVA PUREE, PUGLIA-STYLE
Purè di Fave

Serves 6 as a first course or side dish, 4 as a main dish

Fava beans taste like a cross between a green bean and a new potato. A bowlful of pureed fava beans seasoned with olive oil and pepper is like eating very good mashed potatoes. Have favas Puglia farmhouse–style and make a party of it. Set a bowl of the hot puree in the center of the table. Surround it with little plates of vegetables like the ones in the recipe. Everything is done ahead—the fava puree is served hot but all its accompaniments are at room temperature—an easy way of entertaining.

➤ **Cook to Cook:** The puree can be kept hot up to 1½ hours in a covered bowl set over simmering water. Or make it a day ahead and reheat in a saucepan.

Wine Suggestion: A fresh Puglia rosé like Rosata del Salento or Rosa del Golfo

1 pound peeled, dried fava beans (from Italy, Greece, or the Middle East)
Water
2 medium-sized (generous ½ pound) Yellow Finn or red-skinned potatoes, peeled and thinly sliced

1 to 2 teaspoons salt
Fruity extra-virgin olive oil (optional)
Freshly ground black pepper (optional)

1. In a 4-quart saucepan, cover the favas with cold water and bring to a boil. Take off the heat and let stand about an hour. Drain and rinse; return to the rinsed-out pan.

2. Add the potatoes and enough water to barely cover the favas. Set the saucepan over low heat and simmer very gently, uncovered, about 1¼ to 1½ hours, or until the favas are tender and falling apart. Stir often. After 45 minutes, add 1 teaspoon salt. Stir in a little water only if the beans threaten to stick. They should be so tender that stirring breaks them up. When they are tender, cook away any excess liquid so the favas are not soupy.

3. With a wooden spoon, stir the beans into a puree, then taste for salt. They need not be perfectly smooth. Hand-mashed favas are a badge of honor for Pugliese cooks. The occasional lump will not ruin the dish.

4. Mound the hot favas on plates and enjoy just as they are instead of potatoes. The Pugliese shape a little crater into the mound with the back of a spoon, pour in a little olive oil, grind a little pepper over it, and then stir it all together.

SERVING SUGGESTIONS

Serve fava puree with any of these raw vegetables: arugula, mesclun (spring salad mix), curly endive, or sliced cucumbers, radishes, tomatoes, scallions, or peppers.

Accompany Fava Puree with any of these cooked dishes:

➤ Whole Pan-Roasted Peppers (see page 184)

➤ Sautéed Greens (see page 184)

➤ Melting Tuscan Kale (page 277)

➤ Grilled Lettuces (page 303)

HIRE MY MAN!

Puglia country women believed cooking dried fava beans "in their coats," that is, with their skins on, gave them special powers. These beans were eaten every day by farmworkers' families. According to Puglia lore, favas with their coats on made the men stronger in the fields and in the marriage bed. That conviction carried right into the town's main square, where the men were hired each evening to work the following day. Women would shout out, "Hey, Mr. Boss, hire my man! Hire my husband! Tonight I feed him favas with their coats on."

Whole Pan-Roasted Peppers

Serves 4 to 6

These quick peppers are traditional with a dinner of fava puree. The peppers retain their shape but will be cooked through. Try them as antipasti.

Extra-virgin olive oil
5 to 6 mild Italian frying peppers or
   sweet red peppers

Salt and freshly ground black
   pepper

   Film a large sauté pan with olive oil, set over medium-low heat, and sauté the whole peppers, rotating gently, until cooked through but not overly soft. They should be tender and their skins just a little puckery. Sprinkle with salt as they cook. Finish them with black pepper and serve whole, warm or at room temperature.

Sautéed Greens

Serves 4 to 6

Pugliese home cooks often wilt greens ahead of time, drain and dry, ready for a quick last-minute sauté. This traditional accompaniment to fava puree is also a side dish for roasted or grilled chicken, pork or lamb.

2 pounds curly endive, escarole,
   Catalonia chicory, or dandelion
   greens
6 quarts boiling salted water

Extra-virgin olive oil
1 to 2 cloves garlic, slivered
Salt and freshly ground black
   pepper

   Drop the greens into the boiling water. Boil about 3 minutes uncovered. Drain and thoroughly dry. Film a sauté pan with olive oil and set over medium heat. Stir in the garlic and quickly add the greens, sautéing until heated through. Season with salt and pepper to taste.

FRESH CRANBERRY BEANS

Borlotti Bolliti

Serves 6 to 8 as a side dish, antipasto or supper

Every September, my cousin Edda goes to Lucca's wholesale market for fresh cranberry beans. She buys them by the crate. Over the next week, Edda makes sure no hands are idle. Everyone who passes through the kitchen or the patio is put to work shelling: twenty-something son Mimmo in his soccer jersey; cousin Francesca, telling Edda the beans can't ever be cooked with black pepper; and daughter Antonella, bribed by Edda baby-sitting her toddler son, Michèle. Fresh cranberry beans are shiny and plump to bursting. Once cooked, they taste almost like peas—sweet but more grown-up. Edda's trick in keeping the beans' maroon-and-cream colors is to not stir them while they cook.

Edda serves the beans at room temperature, inviting everyone to dress their own beans the way they like them—with a little olive oil and maybe vinegar. Leftovers become salads and Tuscany's classic beans braised in tomato sauce (page 186). For fresh beans throughout winter, Edda simply freezes shelled raw cranberry beans in plastic bags.

➤ *Cook to Cook:* Cook any fresh or dried bean this way, presoaking dried ones 2 hours, and adjusting simmering time as needed. Find fresh cranberry beans in farmers' markets, supermarkets and specialty stores August through October. For best flavor, buy beans in their pods that are shiny and plump, with no signs of withering or deterioration. One pound unshelled beans yields 1 cup shelled.

Save bean cooking liquid for Tuscan Crazy Water (page 200); it can be frozen up to 3 months.

12 large fresh sage leaves, torn	Salt
3 large cloves garlic, crushed	Extra-virgin olive oil
3 to 4 pounds cranberry beans in the pods, shelled	Freshly ground black pepper

1. Fill a 6-quart pot two-thirds full of water. Add the sage and garlic and bring to a boil. Add the beans and 2 teaspoons salt. Simmer, partially covered, until the beans are barely tender, 15 to 20 minutes. Remove from the heat and leave covered about 20 minutes, or until the beans finish cooking and are tender but not too soft. Take care not to let them sit too long. You don't want their skins to split.

2. Serve the beans hot or at room temperature, accompanied by good olive oil, salt, and pepper.

TUSCAN MOUNTAIN SUPPER

Fagioli all'Uccelletto e Insalata

Serves 4; doubles easily

Outside, a wild October night of rain and wind; inside, a table before the fire and this Tuscan Mountain Supper—hot, plump beans flecked with tomato and herbs, and their perfect foil, a cool salad of tart escarole and red onion. I took a little of each on my fork and tasted pure heaven. This meal's secret lies in extremes—the salad must be prickly and tart, the beans luscious and slow-cooked in their tomato sauce to meld all their seasonings. These are Tuscany's famous Beans in the Style of Wild Birds, as they served at the old coaching inn Il Casone, practically at the top of the Apennine Mountains in Lucca province.

➤ ***Cook to Cook:*** The beans benefit from being made ahead. Cooked fresh cranberry beans are the first choice, followed by cooked dried American organic pinto beans. Even canned pinto beans, rinsed and drained, are good here.

Wine Suggestion: A simple Tuscan red like Monte Antico
from Santa Lucia or a Montecarlo

1 medium onion
¼ tightly packed cup fresh Italian
   parsley leaves
4 large fresh sage leaves
2 tablespoons extra-virgin olive oil
Salt and freshly ground black pepper
2 large cloves garlic, minced
4 canned whole tomatoes, with ¼ cup
   of their liquid

1 tablespoon tomato paste
2 cups cooked beans (see Cook to Cook
   and page 185)
1 to 2 cups reserved bean cooking
   liquid or water
Salad of Tart Greens and Red Onion
   (page 299)

1. Finely chop together the onion, parsley, and sage leaves. Heat the oil in a 10- to 12-inch sauté pan over medium heat. Sauté the onion mixture until golden, sprinkling with salt and pepper. Stir in the garlic, cooking another minute. Blend in the tomatoes, their liquid, and the tomato paste. Sauté 10 minutes to deepen the flavors.

2. Gently fold in the cooked beans and sauté a few minutes. Stir in I cup of the liquid, taste for seasoning, and bring to a slow simmer. Cover and cook over medium-low heat 30 minutes, checking for burning and adding a little more liquid if needed. The beans should absorb the other flavors, but not be falling apart. Serve hot with the salad. The beans and salad are eaten together.

A HOTEL IN THE CLOUDS

Riccardo Rigoli runs the dining room of his family's old coaching inn, Hotel Il Casone. I've come in October, between seasons. No one else is staying at the hotel, but local hill farmers and chestnut gatherers come to dine. The inn sits on a wide ledge almost at the top of the Apennine Mountains. On this side of their peaks is Tuscany's Garfagnana Valley, on the other side is the Emilia-Romagna region. It's the top of the world up here. I can look down at clouds covering the valley. Almost as a reminder of how country life changes more slowly in the mountains than on the plains, from Il Casone's front door I can see on the next ridge the important folklife museum of the Garfagnana, Il Museo Etnografico di San Pellegrino in Alpe. It's the reason I came here. At least that's what I thought when I planned the trip.

Riccardo's in his late twenties. At first he's shy, maybe feeling awkward with an American. But each night we talk a little more. Gradually, Riccardo tells me if I want to taste real homemade bread, I must go to the girl at the red house halfway down the mountain. He sends me to a gifted cook who runs a shop I'd probably not find on my own. He explains how to spot farmers' bread ovens, which at first look like storage buildings. He talks about people who know how to find the best chestnuts and wild mushrooms, and never reveal where except to their children.

Each night before I come down to dinner, Riccardo moves my napkin and bottle of wine, which are held from one dinner to the next, to another table closer to the dining room's prime location, just in front of the fire. Finally I'm given that place of rank. It is the same night the local teenage soccer team comes for a victory dinner.

As they sing and thump the table at the other end of the room, I occupy myself with a new book by a local photographer on the country people of the Garfagnana. Riccardo peeks over my shoulder at a picture, apologizing for intruding, but explaining, "I know him—he taught me to hunt mushrooms. Excuse me, signora, but that photo there is the old uncle of this boy," gesturing to one of the soccer players. One by one the youngsters come over. I expect blasé reactions. But no, we leaf through the book together.

"Look, it's your sister, Carla," they nudge each other. "That's my aunt, who still collects nettles. Hey, you know, you tasted her nettle gnocchi?" "There's the man who always finds the biggest chestnuts." The teenagers begin telling me stories about their families—fathers who make cheese, grandmothers who make "ice cream" by pouring sweet grape syrup over glasses packed with the first snow—and about the gnomes old-timers say soured the milk or tricked the farmer if he wasn't good to them. And I sit back to listen and learn.

Rice, Grains and Beans

SOUP

I have seen everything you can imagine, and some things you might not, go into soup in the country. One story from Puglia relates how on nights when the catch was sparse, shrewd fishermen's wives substituted imagination and whimsy for the absent fish. They'd gather seashells and stones at the beach and simmer them with what was on hand—usually some tomatoes and garlic, and something piquant like chiles and vinegar. Once the broth "tasted good," they ladled it over toasted bread and finished the soup with a little olive oil. When the child asked Mamma where were the fish in the soup, she'd explain, "Ah, but this is soup of the fish that swam away."

I've always made soup, but in watching Italian women cook, I came to appreciate even more how soup is the most forgiving of foods. Country women's lives have always been filled with farmwork, tending children and, often, running a business outside their homes. They don't have time for fussing with lots of last-minute dishes, especially for the evening meal, which is when soup is served more often than not. In these recipes from their kitchens, you will see how almost every soup is better for being made ahead. And when one ingredient isn't handy, be assured another can be used. Several cook in short time, like one of my favorites, Marche Wedding Soup (page 193). If you do want to fill the house with wonderful fragrances from a pot simmering away on a back burner, try Mother's Broth (page 196). With its turkey wings, tomatoes and whole heads of garlic, the broth accepts a whole range of ingredients for a week's worth of suppers.

Homemade soups may seem to be catchalls, but thought and craft govern the selection of each ingredient. For example, minestrones similar to the ones on pages 208 and 210 might clear the end-of-summer garden, or use up what will no longer hold in the refrigerator, but they are never haphazard.

I learned from country cooks that you can make soup using any one of several different approaches. The first technique is the simplest of all. Flavor a simmering broth with almost any ingredient you fancy—shreds of vegetables and/or herbs, bits of salami or a spoonful of Parmigiano-Reggiano cheese. If the broth is Hearty Vegetable Broth (page 198), or Mother's Broth, all the better. Both can be prepared ahead and frozen. For Italian families, cooking pasta in broth, especially filled pasta, equates with Sunday dinner and Christmas, particularly in the north. In the old spa town of Brisighella, south of Bologna in Emilia-Romagna, a country chef served me Farmhouse Sunday Soup (page 194) with the easiest filled pasta I've ever encountered. He claims it's a specialty of local farmers and unheard of even ten miles away.

Broth isn't always purposely made. Sometimes it's the by-product of another cooking process. Cooking dried beans with garlic and sage gives up a broth so admired by frugal Tuscan farmers, they eat it on its own. Well, not entirely on its own—Tuscany's beloved garlic toast goes into the bowl first. Coarse bread, first toasted, rubbed with garlic and moistened with olive oil, lines the soup bowl. Ladle in hot bean broth, then finish the soup with shreds of pecorino cheese, black pepper and a twirl of oil, and you will probably be as amazed as I was by how good it tastes (see Tuscan Crazy Water, page 200). Chickpea Soup for All Souls' Day (page 214) is another example of the deliciousness of bean broth. Chickpeas are sweet to begin with. Scent their broth with rosemary and garlic, and you get one of those effortless soups you'll love.

Farmhouse cooks never throw away the rind of Parmigiano-Reggiano cheese even when every last shred of cheese has been grated away. Parmigiano rind is pure gold in the kitchen. On page 201, read how country women perform seasoning miracles with it in nearly any soup.

In a second technique for making soup, you create a robust foundation of flavor with the sauté of aromatic ingredients called soffritto, then cook everything in water or broth. Sautéing builds up deeper flavors, giving the soup more complexity. Add almost any ingredient to the pot afterward, but always balance mild and aggressive flavors. You can create soups with distinctly different styles with this technique—bright-tasting Vicenza Sweet Pea Soup (page 216); the sort of "rough-and-ready" Marble Cutter's Soup (page 204), with its tomato sauce, rugged country bread and peppery olive oil; mellow Minestrone (page 210); and Supper Soup of Sweet Squash, Farro and Beans (page 218). For bolder, more "up front" character, play with adding the sauté in the middle or at the end of cooking the soup.

A third approach to making soup has no sauté at all. You put everything in the pot and simmer until the flavors melt into each other. Do this in water or broth. I usually mix one part mild-tasting ingredients like beans, squashes, potatoes and mild greens with one part aromatic ones—onion, carrot, celery, Parmigiano-Reggiano cheese rind, tomato (another great lifter of flavors). Be sparing with earthy-tasting foods like turnips, rutabaga and black-eyed peas. Accent your soups with flavorings such as herbs, peppers, spices, cured pork, wine or vinegar, tasting as you go.

Almost all soups benefit from the family of final seasonings beloved by Italian cooks. You could stir these in at the table, or just before you take the soup off the stove. The classic I can't rave about enough, because it's good in any soup, is spoonfuls of freshly grated Parmigiano-Reggiano. Another is pesto (page 74)—wonderful in minestrone and bean soups. Try drizzles of olive oil and freshly ground black pepper, or blend a favorite herb with a little shredded citrus rind, garlic and olive oil. Taste. Experiment. Trust yourself.

At the heart of each of these ways of making soup is the importance of never wasting anything. Saying that farm cooks use every crust of bread, every bean, every leaf might communicate a sense of desperation. Just the opposite is true. The best country cooks understand scarcity *and* abundance. Give a good cook a few salami slices, an onion, some tomatoes and a piece of stale bread and see how a pot full of water becomes dinner. We can do the same thing. These soups are not about stinting, but about going all out, finding bold flavors by nurturing all the taste we can from what the land gives us each season. Taste as you cook these recipes, deciding what pleases you. Trust your instincts. The best Italian cooks I know rely on their own taste and no one else's. Your soup should always be your soup. When in doubt, remember how forgiving soup can be.

These recipes begin with brothy soups and move on to soups with sautés. If you're trying to eat lower on the food chain, with less meat and more vegetables, grains and dried beans, these soups are a good place to begin. Consider them a gift from Italy's country cooks, who have been feeding their families this way for a long, long time.

Antipasto plate:
Signora Bimbi's
Peppers (*page 26*),
Seared Broccoli
with Lemon (*page 284*)
and Portobello
"Steaks" with
Holy Oil (*page 54*)

Sicilian Farmer's Bruschetta *(page 34)*

2

Linguine with Pistachio-Almond Pesto (*page 72*)

Seafood Sauté with Stubby
Pasta (*page 84*)

4

Spaghettini with Shrimp, Chickpeas and Young Greens (*page 86*)

5

Zita with Tomatoes, Capocollo and Diced Mozzarella (*page 140*)

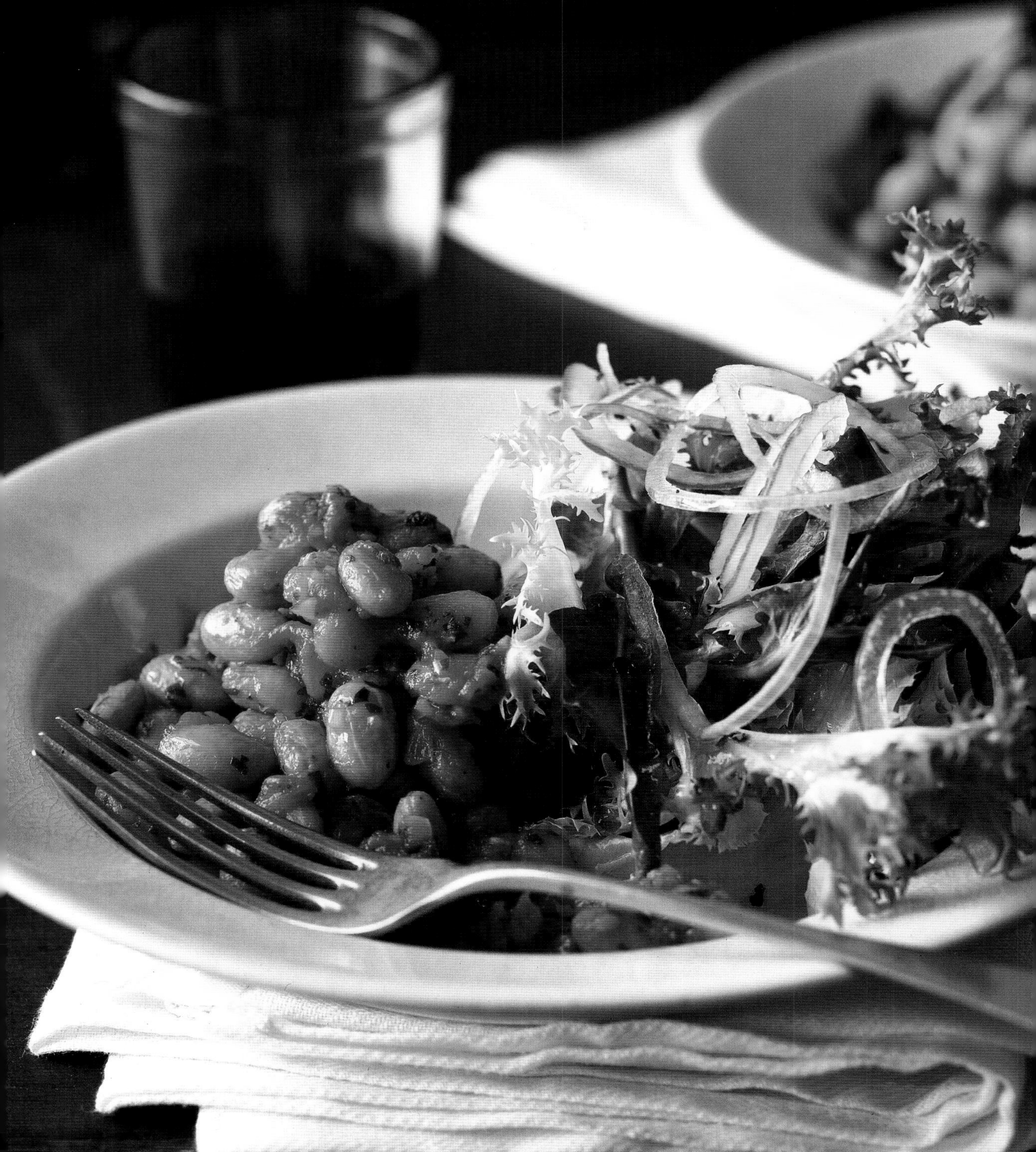

Tuscan Mountain Supper *(page 186)*

**Balsamico Roast Chicken
and Potatoes** (*page 224*)

**Braised Pork with
Three Peppers** *(page 240)*
with Polenta *(page 172)*

Leg of Lamb Glazed with Balsamic
and Red Wine (*page 256*)

Trout Marinated with Sweet Onions *(page 264)*

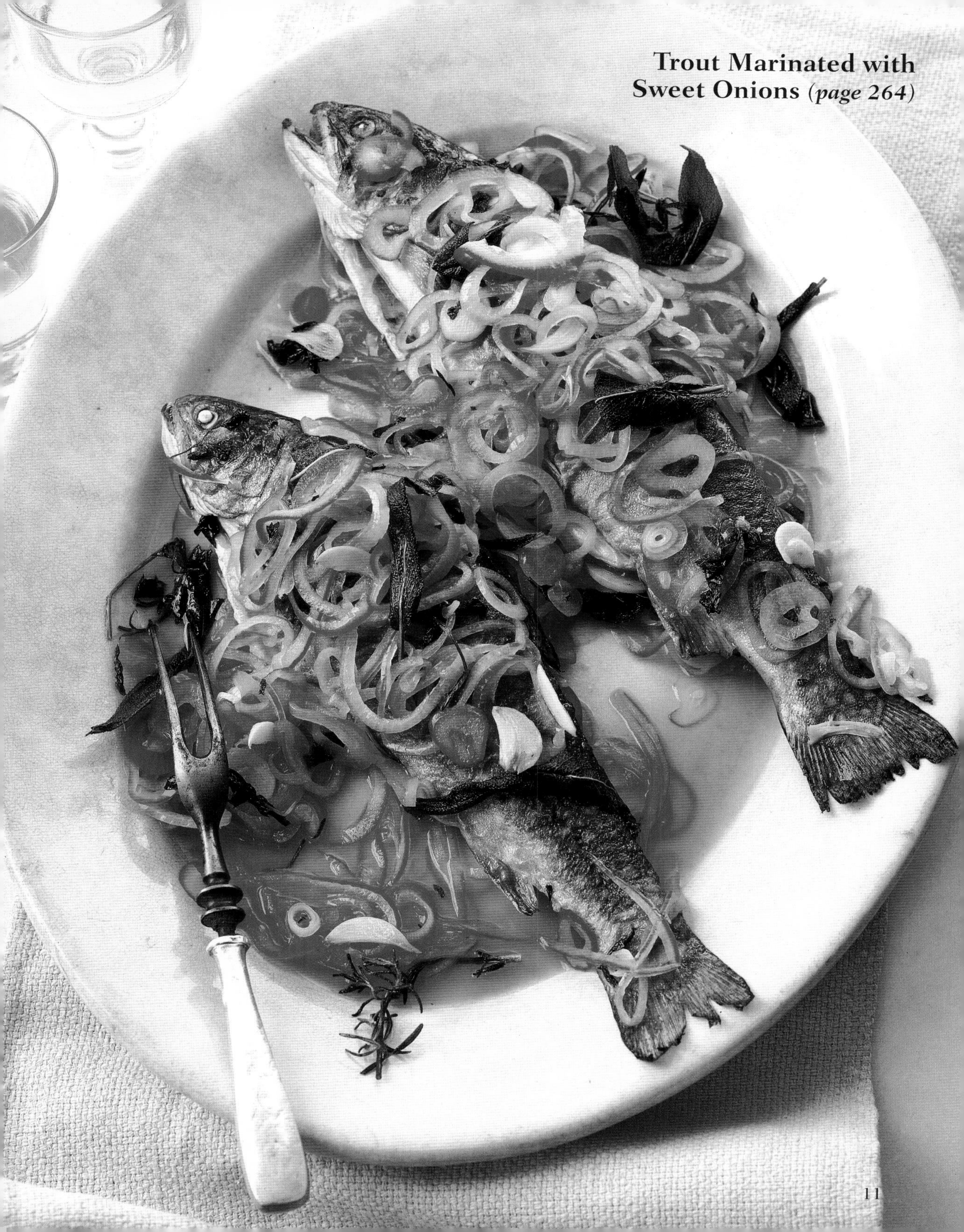

Early Autumn Vegetable Roast *(page 286)*

Potato "Gatto" (*page 296*)

14

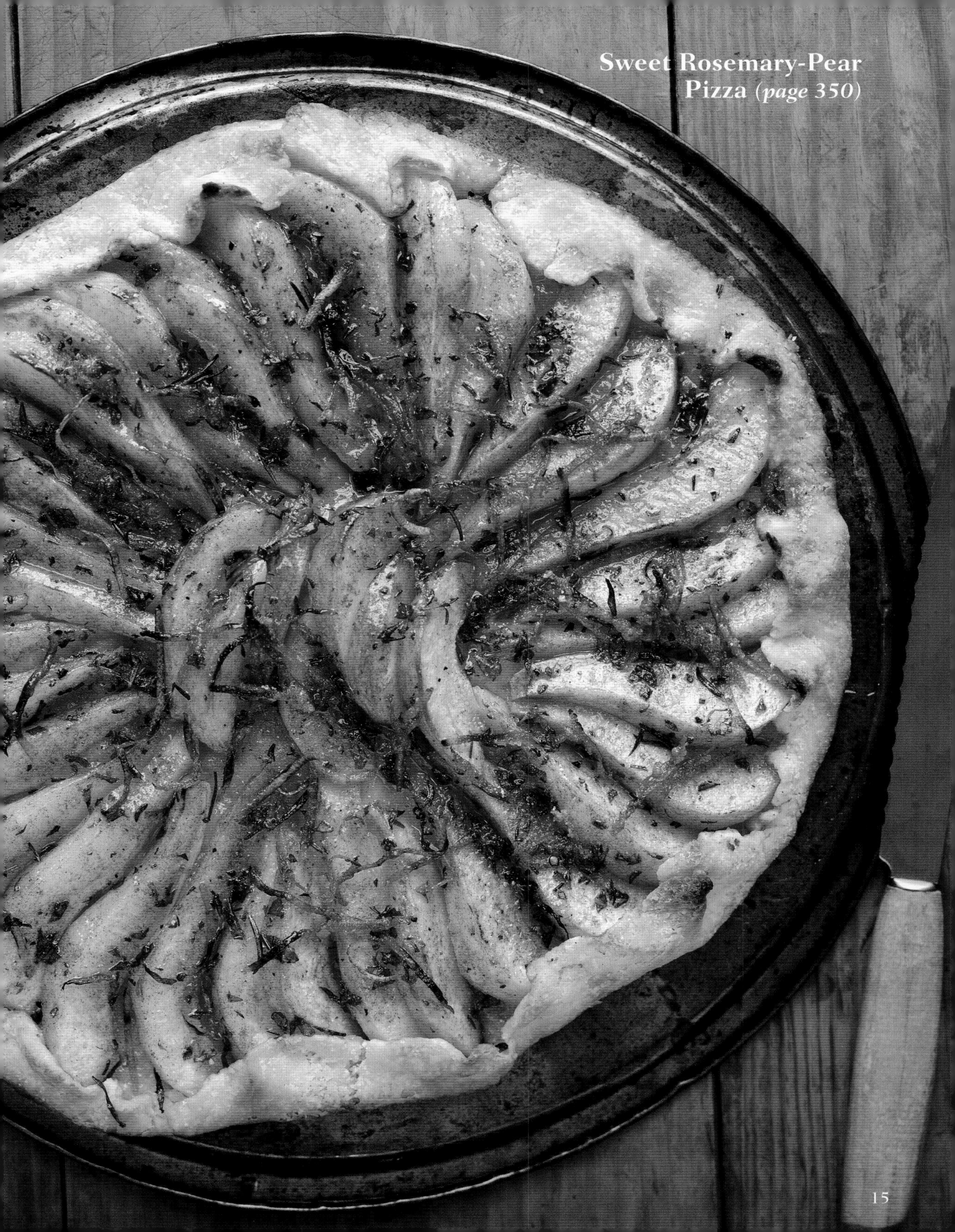

Sweet Rosemary-Pear Pizza *(page 350)*

Chocolate Polenta Pudding Cake (*page 360*)

16

MARCHE WEDDING SOUP

Stracciosa in Brodo

Serves 6 to 8

Lacing hot broth with a blend of Parmigiano-Reggiano cheese, egg, lemon zest and spices transforms a pot of good-tasting liquid into an elegant event. The creamy mix firms into threads. The soup is a close relative of Rome's Stracciatella and a favorite opening to wedding feasts in central Italy's Marche region. Eggs and meat broth are old symbols of celebration. Begin almost any meal with the soup, as long as cheese and lemon are not important flavorings in any other dish. I like it, too, as a quick, light lunch or supper, easily cooked up in about ten minutes.

Wine Suggestion: A white Verdicchio dei Castelli di Jesi

10 cups Mother's Broth (page 196) or
    canned low-sodium chicken broth
1/4 cup dry white wine
Salt and freshly ground black pepper
2 large eggs, beaten

2 tablespoons water
1 cup freshly grated Parmigiano-
    Reggiano cheese
Shredded zest of 1/2 large lemon
Pinch of freshly grated nutmeg

1. In a 4-quart saucepan, simmer the broth and wine 5 minutes, partially covered. Season to taste.

2. Meanwhile, in a bowl, blend the eggs, water, cheese, lemon zest, nutmeg, and about 1/8 teaspoon pepper.

3. Take the soup off the heat. With a fork, gently stir in the egg mixture with long slow strokes until it firms into pale shreds floating in the broth. The long strokes lengthen the shreds slightly. This should take 10 to 15 seconds. There will be a moment when the Parmigiano and lemon release their fragrances—enjoy it. Quickly taste the soup for seasoning and serve it while it's still very hot and fragrant.

FARMHOUSE SUNDAY SOUP

Spoja Lorda

Serves 4 to 6

If you're daunted by recipes for filled pastas, this is the one to begin with. Little nuggets of cheese-filled pasta float in hot poultry broth. Buy ready-made fresh pasta sheets, or do your own. Then merely crumble cheese over the sheer sheet of pasta, fold it over, cut it into small pieces and cook it in broth. If a little cheese escapes into the broth, the soup is all the better for it.

This recipe is only made by families in the countryside around the ancient spa town of Brisighella in Romagna. Travel ten miles down the road, and no one has heard of it. Brisighella farmers fill the pasta with their local tomino cheese, often a blend of cow and sheep's milk, or solely sheep, aged several weeks.

➤ *Cook to Cook:* Quite a few cheeses can stand in for Brisighella's tomino. Look for full-flavored eating cheeses like Italy's Italico, Toscanello, Pecorino Toscano, Cacio di Roma, Pecorino Sienese, Sini Fulvi Pastore Sini, Lago Monate Pecorino or aged Asiago. From America, try artisan-made sheep cheeses or domestic Asiago. You could sprinkle the pasta, too, with chopped chives or basil before folding it over.

If buying ready-made fresh pasta, request 1/2 pound of large sheets of egg pasta sheer enough to see print through. If these are unavailable, use lasagne cuts. The dough must be soft and pliable. Keep the pasta soft by wrapping the individual pieces air tight in plastic and refrigerating them. Use within 1 day.

Wine Suggestion: A red Sangiovese di Romagna

PASTA

1 1/2 cups (7.5 ounces) unbleached all-purpose flour (preferably organic)

1 large egg

1/4 cup warm water

OR

1/2 pound high-quality ready-made fresh egg pasta in large sheets or lasagne cuts (see Cook to Cook)

1 large egg, beaten

2 cups (about 8 ounces) shredded cheese (see Cook to Cook)

Scant 1/4 teaspoon salt

Generous 1/8 teaspoon freshly ground black pepper

Freshly grated nutmeg

1/2 cup chopped fresh chives or basil leaves (optional)

THE SOUP

10 cups Mother's Broth (page 196) or canned low-sodium chicken broth

Salt and freshly ground black pepper

1. For homemade pasta (see page 69), blend together the flour, egg, and water to make a semisoft, slightly sticky dough. Knead 10 minutes, or until elastic, satiny, and no longer sticky. Wrap lightly in plastic and let rest about 30 minutes at room temperature. Roll the dough out by hand on a lightly floured surface. Whether using homemade or store-bought pasta, it must be sheer enough to distinguish newspaper print through it. (See rolling out pasta, page 70.) The size of the pasta sheet is not important; its sheerness is.

2. Brush the beaten egg over the dough. Scatter 1 cup of the cheese over half of the pasta. Season with the salt, pepper, and a few gratings of fresh nutmeg and, if you like, sprinkle the chives or basil over the cheese. Fold over the dough to cover the cheese. Seal the sheets together by pressing your rolling pin over the dough.

3. With a scalloped pastry wheel, cut the dough into small irregular pieces about 1/2 inch by 3/4 inch. Pinch their edges together. Spread the pieces on a porous surface like flat baskets or cake racks covered with a cloth, without touching. (You can hold the pasta up to 6 hours at cool room temperature or refrigerate it overnight uncovered or freeze it on a cookie sheet, then turn the pieces into plastic bags. Add to the broth frozen.)

4. About 10 minutes before serving, bring the broth to a boil, seasoning if needed with salt and pepper. Drop in the pasta and boil partially covered. If the pasta is freshly made, it will need 2 to 3 minutes. If kept for several hours or overnight, 5 to 7 minutes may be necessary. Taste for no sense of rawness; the pasta should be pleasantly firm to the bite, never mushy. Serve the soup immediately in hot bowls. Pass the remaining 1 cup cheese at the table.

MOTHER'S BROTH

Brodo di Mamma

Makes about 7 quarts

Whole heads of garlic, juicy tomatoes and overnight simmering are what give this poultry broth its extraordinarily deep and full flavors. Valentino Marcattilii of Ristorante San Domenico in Imola first told me about using turkey wings for broth instead of Italy's more traditional capon. Since wings are neither dark meat nor white, but somewhere in between, the broth they give is substantial, yet subtle. A few tomatoes in the pot are an old Italian trick for giving the liquid its appealing edge. Garlic deepens and enriches, yet leaves no detectable garlicky taste. Long cooking coaxes every bit of flavor and nutrition from the ingredients, an economy honored by so many country cooks.

This is the broth you make to cook the wonderful tortellini from your favorite pasta shop. This is the broth you make for your own homemade pasta. This is the broth you make for your daughter's wedding soup, or for your own birthday. This broth could even seduce a hesitant lover into commitment. And it keeps in the freezer for months—up to six, in fact.

➤ *Cook to Cook:* If possible, use organic vegetables and poultry raised on organic feed without antibiotics and drugs. Freeze some of the broth in ice cube trays (turning out cubes into plastic bags once they are frozen). Each cube equals about 2 tablespoons. Freeze the remainder of the broth in assorted-sized containers for up to 6 months.

5 pounds turkey wings or 5 pounds whole chicken (if possible, hormone- and antibiotic-free)
About 6 quarts cold water
2 large onions (1½ pounds), trimmed of root ends and coarsely chopped (do not peel)
2 medium carrots, coarsely chopped

1 large stalk celery with leaves, coarsely chopped
4 large heads garlic, trimmed of root ends and halved horizontally
2 whole cloves
1 bay leaf, broken
6 canned tomatoes, drained

1. Cut up the turkey wings or chicken, cracking the bones with a cleaver in 2 or 3 places. Place in a 8- to 10-quart stockpot. Add enough cold water to come to within 3 inches of the lip of the pot. Bring the water slowly to a simmer. Skim off all the foam. Add the remaining ingredients, partially cover, and bring to a slow bubble.

2. Simmer 12 to 14 hours, occasionally stirring and skimming off fat. *Do not boil the broth. Keep the liquid bubbling very slowly.* Add boiling water if the broth reduces below the level of the solid ingredients; always keep them covered with about 3 inches of liquid.

3. Strain the broth through a fine sieve. For a clearer broth, strain it by ladling rather than pouring, leaving behind any sediment at the bottom of the pot.

4. Cool the broth as quickly as possible: Set it outside in cold weather, or chill it in several small containers set in bowls of ice. Then refrigerate the broth about 8 hours, or until its fat has hardened. Skim off the hardened fat, and freeze in assorted-sized containers.

MAKING SIMPLE SOUPS WITH MOTHER'S BROTH

"The Cure": Every child in Italy has known the nourishment of a bowl of tiny pasta cooked in homemade broth and finished with grated Parmigiano-Reggiano cheese. It made being sick in bed almost worthwhile. Use any small shape that pleases you.

Brodo con Prosciutto: A dinner party soup of seasoned broth brought to a boil, ladled into bowls and garnished with thin strips of prosciutto di Parma. A few leaves of parsley finish the dish.

Summer Broth with Herbs: Simmer broth and season to taste. Stir into each serving a tablespoon of mixed fresh herbs, coarsely chopped. Pass grated Parmigiano-Reggiano at the table.

Apristomaco **(Tummy Opener):** An old and playful word, meaning a light teaser for awakening appetites. In this case a few thin slices of soaked dried porcini mushrooms, slivers of scallion and basil leaves are floated in hot, seasoned broth.

MOTHER'S BROTH

The mother in this broth's title is mine. For years I'd been gathering broth-making advice from Italian friends, but it didn't all come together until my mother had major surgery. She's Italian and loves to eat. So when she lost all interest in food, we got worried. So did her doctor. She had to eat, he said, an instruction that could throw the Italian army into action. "Make broth," was all I could think. It was like winnowing everything I'd ever learned about stock making. I used only organic ingredients. I simmered the broth a long time to draw out every nutrient and seasoned it with tomatoes and great heads of garlic instead of the salt my mother could no longer use. I made buckets of it and she ate every bit. Her surgery was six years ago. Mom is now eighty-nine and gives dinner parties on a regular basis. We still make the broth. With its track record, why take chances?

Soup

HEARTY VEGETABLE BROTH

Brodo di Verdure

Makes about 3 1/2 quarts

There is nothing weak-kneed about this vegetable broth. Its big flavors hold their own in any dish where poultry or meat stock is usually used. You can make the broth in about two hours. Most of that time is taken up with unattended simmering. Freeze it and see what a good foundation it makes for broth-based soups like Farmhouse Sunday Soup (page 194) and Marche Wedding Soup (page 193). Use it in risottos, pasta sauces and most any vegetable dish. Its depth comes from initially browning the vegetables, a trick discovered by my friend June Favre, who created the broth years ago. She's a gifted Italian cook who's always had a special hand with soups. She used to make a quick supper soup by simmering some pasta and vegetables in the broth, then stirring in fresh herbs at the last minute.

➤ *Cook to Cook:* If possible, use organically raised produce here. The broth keeps up to four days in the refrigerator and six months in the freezer. Freeze some of the broth in ice cube trays (turning out the cubes into a plastic bag once they are frozen). Each cube equals about 2 tablespoons. Freeze the remainder in assorted-sized containers up to 6 months.

2 tablespoons fruity extra-virgin olive oil
2 large carrots, coarsely chopped
2 large stalks celery with leaves, coarsely chopped
4 medium onions, coarsely chopped
1/2 pound fresh mushrooms, cleaned and coarsely chopped
3 large cloves garlic, crushed

1 tablespoon dried basil
2/3 cup dry white wine
6 large romaine lettuce leaves, coarsely chopped
1 large ripe tomato, chopped, or 2 canned plum tomatoes
Pinch of freshly grated nutmeg
About 4 to 5 quarts water

1. Heat the oil in a 12-inch sauté pan or skillet (not nonstick) over medium-high heat. Add the carrots, celery, onions, and mushrooms. Cook, stirring frequently with a wooden spatula, until the onions are golden brown, about 10 minutes. Stir in the garlic and basil and cook a few seconds more. Add the wine and stir, scraping up any brown glaze in the bottom of the pan, until most of the liquid has evaporated. Transfer to an 8-quart stockpot.

2. Add the romaine, tomato (crushing the canned tomatoes as you add them), nutmeg, and enough water to cover by 3 to 4 inches. Bring to a gentle bubble, partially cover, and simmer slowly about 1 1/2 hours.

3. Strain the broth into a large bowl, pressing down on the solids to extract as much flavor as possible. Cool and chill. Skim off any solidified oil from the broth's surface. Refrigerate or freeze until ready to use.

MAKING SIMPLE SOUPS WITH VEGETABLE BROTH

Any of the suggestions for Mother's Broth on page 196 can be done with this broth.

TUSCAN CRAZY WATER

Acqua Pazza

Serves 4 as a first course, 2 as a one-dish meal

This soup is a revelation, merely the liquid of cooking beans that home cooks long ago could not afford to throw away. I am enormously grateful to Tuscan women for introducing me to this new soup with its old lesson—in preparing good food, nothing is wasted and no ingenuity overlooked or taken for granted.

Tuscans love beans, often cooking them with aromatics like sage, onion, carrot or celery. The beans' broth is often called "Crazy Water," no doubt because it's such an improbable soup. I could not believe how luscious it could be. Friends, tasting Crazy Water for the first time, closed their eyes and claimed it tasted like chicken broth.

Delicate and lovely on its own, when served with torn shreds of bruschetta and anointed with olive oil and a light sprinkling of Parmigiano-Reggiano cheese, bean broth is an astoundingly fine soup.

➤ *Cook to Cook:* Superb bean broth comes from several different fresh and dried beans. Select fresh cranberry beans or scarlet runners. For dried, choose cannellini, pinto, borlotti or Lamon. Chickpeas give an excellent broth with a distinctively sweet character. Avoid any dark beans and particularly earthy-tasting ones like black-eyed peas. Use the cooked beans in main and side dishes—soups, stews, salads and the like. Tuscans season them at the table with olive oil, salt, pepper and perhaps vinegar. Keep any leftover bean broth for another dish, covered and refrigerated. The broth holds only 1 day in the refrigerator, but freezes well for 3 months.

BEANS

1 generous cup (¹/2 pound) dried beans, soaked in hot water 1 hour and drained, or 2 generous cups shelled fresh beans (see Cook to Cook)

8 large fresh sage leaves

3 large cloves garlic, crushed

¹/2 medium onion, stuck with 2 whole cloves

Water

1 teaspoon salt

SOUP

2 large slices coarse multigrain bread (¹/2 inch thick)

1 clove garlic, split

Robust, peppery extra-virgin olive oil

Salt and freshly ground black pepper

³/4 cup water

Generous ¹/4 cup freshly grated young sheep cheese or Parmigiano-Reggiano cheese

1. In a 3-quart pot, blend the dried or fresh beans with the sage leaves, garlic, and onion. Add water to cover the beans by 2 inches. For clear bean broth, do not stir from this point on. Bring to a boil, reduce to a simmer, cover, and adjust the heat so the liquid bubbles gently. The beans are ready when they taste tender but still hold their shape; the time can range from 35 minutes for some imported varieties to over an hour for domestic. Add the salt toward the end of cooking. Once they're done, remove the beans from the heat and cool, uncovered, in their liquid. Strain, reserving the liquid.

2. Preheat the broiler. Rub the bread with the garlic, then break it up into small, bite-sized pieces. Lightly brown under the broiler. Drizzle lightly with olive oil, sprinkle with salt and pepper, and divide among four soup dishes.

3. In a saucepan, heat 3¼ cups of the bean broth and the water to a bubble, seasoning to taste with salt and pepper. Ladle over the bread and serve. At the table, season each bowl of soup with a thin thread of olive oil, a little extra pepper, and about a tablespoon of cheese.

VARIATION

A Light Soup: Omit the bread. Lightly rub the interior of the soup dishes with the split garlic clove. Spoon the seasoned hot soup into the bowls. Season with the oil, extra pepper, and the cheese. Finish with a sprinkling of thinly sliced scallion tops.

Never Throw Away a Parmigiano-Reggiano Rind

The rind of this extraordinary cheese is a gift to soups, broths, stews and braisings. It enriches, deepens flavors and gives character in a way unique to Parmigiano-Reggiano cheese. Rather than overpowering other flavors, the cheese seems to enhance them. Use it often. Parmigiano rind is merely hardened cheese, not a coating. As pieces simmer in liquid, the dried rind reconstitutes, turning spongy. A 4- or 5-inch square of rind enriches 4 to 6 quarts of soup or broth. Obviously, use what you have. It's usually easy to remove rind at the end of cooking. But if cooked a very long time, the rind might melt entirely. All the better for the dish.

Refrigerate tightly wrapped Parmigiano rind up to 2 months, or freeze up to 6 months.

HOT-AND-SPICY EGGPLANT SOUP

Zuppa Piccante alle Melanzane

Serves 2 to 4

Fresh mint and chiles give this soup a tingling finishing touch. Eggplant and chickpeas have a natural affinity for each other, one country cooks have known about for a long time. In southern Italy, this soup serves two seasons. In summer, farmers eat it warm or at room temperature. As the weather chills, they puree the chickpeas for a thicker soup and more substantial eating. Chickpeas are the least bean-like of dried beans. Pureeing makes them even sweeter and creamier. The sautéed pieces of eggplant have the effect of juicy croutons in this soup.

➤ **Cook to Cook:** Since eggplants can sometimes be bitter for no apparent reason, I've started using long narrow Japanese or Chinese varieties. They seem consistently mild, and they remind me of eggplants I've tasted in Italy.

The cooked soup can be refrigerated overnight. It will thicken and may need an additional cup or so of water in reheating. Serve it hot, warm or at room temperature.

Wine Suggestion: A round rustic red like
Ceregio Sangiovese di Romagna Superiore

1 1/2 pounds long narrow Japanese eggplants, peeled and cut into 1/4-inch dice

Salt

1 15-ounce can chickpeas, drained and rinsed

2 tablespoons red wine vinegar

Freshly ground black pepper

2 1/2 to 3 1/2 tablespoons extra-virgin olive oil

1 medium onion, cut into 1/4- to 1/2-inch dice

2 tightly packed tablespoons fresh Italian parsley leaves, chopped

6 large fresh basil leaves, chopped

2 large cloves garlic, minced

1/4 cup dry white wine

4 canned whole tomatoes, chopped, with 1/4 cup of their liquid

3 1/2 to 5 cups water

GARNISHES

3 tightly packed tablespoons fresh mint leaves, chopped

2 medium-hot fresh chiles, seeded and cut into tiny dice

1 cup (4 ounces) shredded ricotta salata cheese

1. In a colander, toss the eggplant with about 1 tablespoon salt and let stand 20 to 30 minutes. Meanwhile, in a bowl, marinate the chickpeas in 1 tablespoon of the vinegar and a little salt and pepper 20 minutes.

2. Turn the eggplant onto a towel and squeeze away about half its moisture. Film the bottom of a 12-inch sauté pan with 1 to 2 tablespoons of the olive oil and heat over medium heat. Sauté the eggplant 5 minutes, or until pale gold and tender, seasoning with black pepper. Turn out of the skillet and reserve. Wash the skillet.

3. Set the skillet over high heat and heat the remaining 1½ tablespoons oil. Add the onions and parsley and quickly brown the onions. Reduce the heat to medium, stir in the chickpeas with their marinade, and cook about 3 minutes. Add the basil and garlic and cook another 5 minutes, stirring frequently. Stir in the wine, tomatoes, and tomato liquid, reducing the heat to medium-low. Cook 2 to 3 minutes, uncovered, or until the liquid is rich-tasting and thick.

4. Stir in the eggplant and 3½ cups of water, or enough to make a thick broth. Simmer 15 minutes to blend the flavors. Stir in the remaining 1 tablespoon vinegar and cook another few minutes. Taste for seasoning. In summer, serve the soup at room temperature, garnishing each portion with the mint, chiles, and cheese. In the fall, prepare the variation below.

VARIATION

Autumn Eggplant Soup: Follow the directions through step 3, reserving the sautéed eggplant. Add 3 cups water to the chickpea sauté. Cook 15 minutes. Puree one third of the soup in a blender or food processor, and stir it back into the pan. Then add the eggplant and the remaining 1 tablespoon vinegar. Simmer another 10 minutes. Taste for seasoning. Serve warm with the garnishes.

MARBLE CUTTER'S SOUP

Pancotto al Pomodoro

Serves 6 to 8

Juicy ripe tomatoes, rugged country bread, garlic and Tuscan olive oil make a favorite supper soup of the marble cutters who work the same Carrara quarries where Michelangelo learned his craft. At least that's the story I was told the first time I ate the soup by the woman who ran a roadside trattoria in the mountains near Carrara. I stopped there for lunch because it was the only place to eat I'd seen in a morning of driving tricky mountain roads, and several trucks were parked outside—usually a promising sign in rural Italy.

Her soup tasted like heaven—even better than the tomato-bread soup from farther south in Tuscany called Pappa al Pomodoro. All the flavors are up front in this soup. It's really a gutsy tomato sauce lengthened with water, ladled over coarse peasant bread and drizzled with olive oil. I make it for supper all the time—with canned tomatoes in winter and fresh ones in summer, when we eat the soup at room temperature. The woman in the trattoria said that when she can buy very young sheep cheese from local shepherds, she shreds it and passes bowls of the cheese at the table. American-made sheep cheese is as good, and so is young Asiago. Try the soup with them and see what you think.

2 medium red onions
$1/2$ medium carrot
1 small stalk celery with leaves
4 branches fresh Italian parsley
Robust extra-virgin olive oil
Salt and freshly ground black pepper
3 large cloves garlic, minced
$1/2$ tightly packed cup fresh basil leaves, chopped
2 to 3 pounds delicious ripe tomatoes, peeled and chopped, or 1 28-ounce can and 1 14-ounce can whole tomatoes, both drained

Water
$3/4$ pound (about $3/4$ loaf) rugged country bread of mixed grains (without fat or sweeteners), sliced and left to dry for a day
2 tightly packed tablespoons fresh basil leaves, chopped (optional)
About 6 ounces Pecorino Toscano, Pecorino di Pienza, Toscanello, or young Asiago, shredded (optional)

1. Mince together the onion, carrot, celery, and parsley until very fine. Film the bottom of a 6-quart pot with oil and set over medium heat. Stir in the minced vegetables with a little salt and pepper. Sauté to a rich golden brown, about 8 minutes. Blend in the garlic and basil and cook another minute. Add the tomatoes, crushing canned tomatoes with your hands as you add them. Boil 10 minutes, or until thick and flavorful.

2. Stir in 6 cups water, or a ladleful for each diner. Simmer 10 minutes, uncovered, or until soup is only slightly reduced. Taste for seasoning.

3. Just before serving, break up the bread into bite-sized pieces and add it to the soup, or place the bread in the soup bowls. Ladle the soup into the bowls and serve hot. (The soup is also good at room temperature.) Sprinkle each serving with a teaspoon or two of olive oil and a generous amount of black pepper. A little chopped fresh basil is a modern touch, and a very good one. Pass the cheese, if desired.

Farmers meet once a week at the Saturday market in Ostuni, Puglia.

Soup

BARLEY MOUNTAIN SOUP
Zuppa d'Orzo con Salsiccia

Serves 6

This chunky blend of sausage, barley, carrots and potatoes is pure mountain cooking. It comes from the region that used to be Austria's doorway to Italy.

Through the winter, the mountain people of northern Italy's Trentino region rely on this soup, made with barley grown in their fields and meats they cure themselves—sometimes it is a meaty shank of ham, sometimes sausage and sometimes speck, smoked and air-dried leg of pork. When the cut is plentiful, it simmers whole in the soup and is eaten as a second dish. The Trentino's dry, cold mountain air and long winters are ideal for curing everything from veal to mountain goat. Some of the meats are smoked, others merely salted and spiced. To protect against pests, farmwomen hang them with branches of juniper in airy hillside cellars.

Buttermilk gives the soup a delicious tang. Farmers use it instead of part of or all of the water in the soup, since buttermilk is plentiful in Trentino's dairy country. Everyone churns their own butter, and the buttermilk left after churning is cooked into breads, sweets and soups like this one. It curdles slightly in the soup, but tastes fine. The soup tastes even better the second day.

Wine Suggestion: A Trentino or Alto Adige red like
Pinot Nero, Merlot or Cabernet

2 medium onions
2 medium carrots
1/4 tightly packed cup fresh Italian
   parsley leaves
2 large cloves garlic
3 to 4 medium red-skinned potatoes
   (about 1 pound), peeled and thinly
   sliced

1 cup barley (organic if possible)
1/2 pound smoked ham shank or hocks
   or shank of prosciutto
3 3-inch branches fresh rosemary
1 quart buttermilk (optional)
About 4 quarts water
2 tablespoons olive oil
Salt and freshly ground black pepper

1. Finely chop the onions, carrots, parsley, and garlic. Combine the barley, potatoes, and meat in a 6- to 8-quart pot. Add half the onion mixture to the pot with 2 branches of the rosemary. Add the buttermilk if desired. Then add 4 quarts water. Simmer 50 minutes, or until the barley is almost tender.

2. Meanwhile, heat the oil in a 12-inch skillet over medium-high heat. Sauté the rest of the chopped vegetables to a golden brown.

3. Add to the pot and season with salt and pepper. Simmer another 30 to 40 minutes.

4. Remove the meat and bones. Break up meat into small pieces and return them to the pot, along with more water if the soup is as dense as stew. It should be a thick but soupy soup. Strip the leaves from the remaining 1 branch of rosemary and mince. Stir into the pot and simmer another 10 minutes. Adjust the seasonings to taste. Serve hot.

COOL SUMMER MINESTRONE

Minestrone Estivo

Serves 6 to 8

Eat this fresh-tasting soup at room temperature, the way Italian families eat more traditional minestrone in hot weather. Its sauté of diced carrot, zucchini and peas in their pods still has some crunch. Fresh herbs and a little olive oil finish it off. Make the soup just as its creator Rosalba Ciannamea does—it takes almost no time.

Sometimes a dish's connection to the land and the season just sings out. No one has to tell you where it came from, or how deeply it's linked to where you are—you can taste it. I ate this in the midst of the olive grove on a Puglia farm, Il Frantoio. This kind of walled enclave of whitewashed buildings and its acres of olive groves and wheat fields is called a *masseria*, or fortified farm, in Puglia. *Il frantoio* means olive mill. The original mill, even older than the farm's sixteenth-century buildings, still functions today in its cave under the main house. Rosalba Ciannamea and husband, Armando, restored and opened Il Frantoio to guests. On summer evenings, when the white courtyard bakes in the sun, they serve this soup in the old chapel, now the dining room, where thick limestone walls and high arched ceilings keep guests cool. Everything in the bowl is from their land.

➤ *Cook to Cook:* Serve at room temperature, warm or hot. The soup cooks quickly, but do take a few moments to cut everything into tiny dice. It dramatically affects how the soup tastes—you get a little of everything in each spoonful.

Wine Suggestion: A Puglia rosé like Rosato del Salento or Rosa del Golfo

2 tightly packed teaspoons fresh basil leaves

1/4 tightly packed teaspoon fresh marjoram leaves

Leaves of 1 branch fresh thyme

3 scallions, thinly sliced

2 teaspoons fruity extra-virgin olive oil, plus extra for serving

1 medium onion, cut into 1/8-inch dice

2 small carrots, cut into 1/8-inch dice

2 medium zucchini, cut into 1/8-inch dice

1 cup thinly sliced sugar snap peas (about 1/4 pound)

1 basket (3/4 to 1 pound) delicious cherry tomatoes, cut into quarters

Salt and freshly ground black pepper

5 cups Mother's Broth (page 196), Hearty Vegetable Broth (page 198), or canned low-sodium chicken broth

1. Mince together the herbs. Blend with the sliced scallions and set aside.

2. Heat the olive oil in a 4-quart saucepan over high heat. Drop in the onion, carrots, zucchini, peas, and half the tomatoes. Sprinkle with salt and pepper and sauté 3 minutes, or until slightly wilted.

3. Add the broth and boil 5 minutes, or until the vegetables are tender-crisp (do not cover). Stir in a quarter of the herb mixture and remove the soup from the heat. Serve hot, warm, or at room temperature, topping each serving with some of the remaining tomatoes and the herb blend. Twirl a little olive oil over each serving and sprinkle with freshly ground pepper.

The dining room hearth at Il Frantoio farm.

Soup

MINESTRONE
Minestrone della Famiglia

Serves 8 to 10 as a first course, 6 as a main dish

Good minestrone depends upon letting all the vegetables cook long enough to exchange personalities. The formula here is the essence of country soup making: Use what's in season, deepen the soup's character with plenty of onion, sauté some of the vegetables for contrast and don't forget the beans and herbs for flavor and body. Then let heat and time do the work. This recipe evolved over years of gathering ideas from Italian country cooks. It changes with the seasons and my mood, so don't hesitate to play with what's listed below. There is one inviolate ingredient—the Parmigiano-Reggiano rind. My frugal Tuscan grandmother always simmered leftover Parmigiano rind in the soup. With its incomparable flavor, no broth and little additional salt is needed.

My grandfather always ate his minestrone in true farmer style. He placed a toasted slice of coarse whole-grain bread in the bottom of the soup dish, doused it with olive oil, then ladled in the minestrone. Italians season minestrone at the table with olive oil from the omnipresent cruet and black pepper, or stir in pesto or grate Parmigiano-Reggiano into the soup. One elderly aunt committed heresy, at least in the eyes of Tuscan purists—she used both oil and cheese. In my childhood ignorance, I loved it. Now, with adult wisdom I call it overkill, but I love it still.

Wine Suggestion: A Tuscan red Syrah or Carmignano

2 medium red onions, cut into ¹/₂-inch dice

1 medium carrot, cut into ¹/₂-inch dice

1 medium potato, cut into ¹/₂-inch dice

1 medium stalk celery, cut into ¹/₂-inch dice

¹/₄ pound green beans, trimmed and cut into ¹/₂-inch pieces

2 medium zucchini, cut into ¹/₂-inch dice

2 large kale leaves, finely chopped

Rind from ¹/₂ pound or more (2 by 4 by 5 inches) of Parmigiano-Reggiano cheese (optional)

¹/₂ 14-ounce can whole tomatoes, with their liquid

Salt and freshly ground black pepper

Robust extra-virgin olive oil

1 ¹/₈-inch-thick slice pancetta, minced

1 ¹/₈-inch-thick slice good-quality salami, minced

6 large fresh sage leaves

¹/₄ medium Savoy or green cabbage, cut into ¹/₂-inch dice

2 large cloves garlic, minced

¹/₄ tightly packed cup fresh Italian parsley leaves

¼ tightly packed cup fresh basil leaves, chopped

1½ cups cooked borlotti or pinto beans (rinsed and drained if canned), half of them pureed in a food processor

2 large stalks (with leaves) Swiss chard, cut into ½-inch dice

½ cup small pasta (such as ditalini, acini di pepe, meloni, or stelle)

1 cup freshly grated Parmigiano-Reggiano cheese (optional)

FOR GRANDFATHER'S MINESTRONE FOR 8 PEOPLE

8 ½-inch-thick slices rugged whole-grain bread, toasted

About ½ cup robust, peppery Tuscan extra-virgin olive oil

1. Set aside about one third of the onions. In a 6-quart pot, combine the rest of the onions and all the ingredients up to and including the tomatoes. Cover by an inch with water. Season lightly with salt and pepper. Cover and simmer very gently 45 minutes.

2. Meanwhile, film the bottom of a 10-inch skillet lightly with olive oil. Set over medium-high heat. Add the reserved onions, the pancetta, salami, sage leaves, and a handful of the cabbage. Sauté to a rich golden brown. Stir in the garlic, parsley, and basil. Cook another minute.

3. Blend the sauté into the cooked vegetables along with the remaining cabbage, the beans, including their puree, the chard, and water to cover everything by about an inch. Simmer slowly, partially covered, another 45 minutes. Add more water as needed so the soup has the consistency of a watery stew.

4. Season to taste, stir in the pasta, and simmer until tender, about 15 minutes. Serve hot or warm with olive oil, a peppermill, and the cheese passed separately. (Minestrone reheats beautifully and is even better the second day.)

For Grandfather's Minestrone: Lay a slice of toasted bread in each of eight soup bowls. Moisten each slice with about a tablespoon of olive oil and ladle in the minestrone.

VARIATION

Baked Country Minestrone: This turns minestrone into a casserole dish by adding garlic bread to sop up its juices. It tastes like leftover Ribollita. Place leftover minestrone (about 6 cups or so) in a shallow 2-quart baking dish lined with slices of coarse country bread that have been toasted, rubbed with garlic, and brushed with olive oil. Cover and refrigerate. The next day, tuck grated Parmigiano or mild sheep cheese here and there into the minestrone. Film the top with a little olive oil. Bake at 350°F until hot and bubbling, about 40 minutes. Cut into squares and serve hot with extra cheese.

IMPROVISING YOUR OWN MINESTRONE

Free yourself from recipes by understanding how to improvise your own minestrones. Farmhouse cooks do this all the time—it's the essence of day-to-day home cooking. Take the variety of vegetables available, apply a little imagination and create a supper for the family. Anyone can cook this way once the basic principles are laid out.

The Principles
In minestrone, vegetables cook until they are soft. The soup's character can be enriched by sautéing some of the ingredients in one of two different ways. Minestrone is always finished with a final seasoning at the end of cooking, or at the table.

> **The Vegetable Blend:** Simmer together a collection of vegetables with herbs until they almost melt into each other, and you have minestrone. The blend always includes but isn't limited to beans, potato, squash, leafy greens, cabbage of some sort, a generous amount of onion and herbs.

> **Water or Broth:** Frugal country cooks usually don't waste precious stock when a soup's ingredients give up so much flavor on their own, as in minestrone. I agree. Use water. Save the broth for where you can really taste it.

> **How Long to Cook and Cooking Ahead:** Simmer the soup from 45 minutes to 1 1/2 hours—long enough for the flavors to meld. With ever-changing ingredients, taste always tells the tale. Keep tasting and you will know when the soup has reached its peak of flavor. Minestrone is even better the second and third day. Store covered in the refrigerator.

Ways of Adding Depth and Dimension to Minestrone
> **A Sauté for Bold Depth:** Browning some of the vegetables and herbs in a little olive oil makes the minestrone taste richer. Almost anything works—leftover onion, chopped cabbage, the odd carrot, broccoli stems, lettuce leaves, kale or chard, garlic, sage, rosemary, bay leaves and so on. For even richer flavor, include a few ounces of cured meat, like pancetta, coppa or salami. The later in cooking that you add the sauté, the bolder the soup tastes.

➤ **A Sauté for Gentler Character:** Vary the sauté technique for gentler depth. Begin the minestrone by filming the bottom of the soup pot with olive oil and adding the vegetables and herbs. Stew them covered over low heat until everything softens and is releasing its juices—about 30 minutes. Then add the water and simmer the soup.

➤ **Adding Rice or Pasta:** Rice or small pastas like ditalini, semi di meloni, stelle, orzo or broken spaghetti can be cooked into minestrone. Count on about 15 minutes of simmering for the pasta, 30 to 40 minutes for rice.

Tricks for Rescuing Bland Minestrones

➤ A piece of Parmigiano-Reggiano rind in the soup makes the flavors bigger.

➤ Prosciutto skin or salt pork rind give body and richness to the soup.

➤ Tomatoes, even two or three in a big pot, counteract blandness.

➤ A generous pinch of hot red pepper flakes lifts flavors without detectable heat.

➤ Add herbs at two different times. Use some in the beginning of cooking to lay a foundation of tastes. Stir in more in the last 10 or 20 minutes of cooking to brighten and focus flavors. Be generous with fresh herbs, especially mild ones like basil.

The Final Seasoning

Minestrone always gets a final seasoning at the end of cooking, or at the table. A final seasoning is like a cheerleader; it rallies together all the elements of the soup. Some regional cooks have their favorites. Try each of them and see which you like best.

➤ Ligurian cooks stir in pesto (page 74)—a fabulous finish. The soup's heat releases all the fragrance of the uncooked basil, garlic and cheese. I add a chopped up medium-sized fresh tomato too when they're in season. Vary the pesto idea by blending garlic, oil, and cheese with herbs other than basil—for example sage, rosemary, or marjoram.

➤ In Tuscany, Umbria, and Marche, each diner adds a little olive oil and freshly ground black pepper at the table.

➤ Just about everyone likes grated Parmigiano-Reggiano in his or her minestrone at one time or another.

CHICKPEA SOUP FOR ALL SOULS' DAY

Zuppa di Ceci Tutti Santi

Serves 4 to 6

Light and brothy, fragrant with rosemary and garlic, this is a new style of bean soup for most of us. Such a fine broth comes from merely simmering chickpeas with a few herbs and some onion.

For families in the Piedmont, good fortune and protection come from eating this soup on All Souls' Day, November 2, and on its eve, the day of All Saints, when, it is believed, spirits rise from the grave to find their way home. In some parts of the countryside, families set out lanterns to mark paths, guiding their ancestors' souls from the cemetery to their home kitchen, where a window is ritually left ajar for easy entry. Dishes made from the fall harvest wait on the table, like this soup, sweet squash, roasted chestnuts, and a bottle of new wine. But the food should not be lavish, lest it draw attention to wealth. Spirits can become greedy. Families eat close to the fire within the arc of its warmth and light, aware that the evening may bring mischievous as well as loving souls. This is no time for a walk under the stars.

➤ **Cook to Cook:** This is one of the few instances where canned chickpeas cannot stand in for cooking dried ones from scratch. An incomparable broth comes from cooking the dried chickpeas with a few aromatic herbs. It is the soul of the soup. There's no more work; simply allow time for cooking. Prepare the soup up to a day ahead and store it in the refrigerator. Reheat gently and taste for seasoning before serving.

Wine Suggestion: A white Piemontese Arneis by Ceretto or Pio Cesare

2 cups (14 ounces) dried chickpeas, soaked overnight in the refrigerator in water to cover by 2 inches

Cold water

1½ tablespoons fruity extra-virgin olive oil, plus extra for seasoning at the table

1 medium to large (about ¾ pound) onion, minced

2 6-inch branches fresh rosemary

6 large fresh sage leaves

1 large bay leaf

1 large clove garlic, minced

Salt and freshly ground black pepper

About ¼ cup fresh Italian parsley leaves, coarsely chopped

1. Drain the chickpeas, rinse, and turn into a 4-quart pot. Add water to cover by 2 inches. Cover and bring to a slow simmer.

2. Meanwhile, heat the olive oil in a 12-inch sauté pan over medium-high heat. Add the onion, rosemary, sage, and bay. Sauté 5 minutes, or until the onion is a deep golden color. Stir in the garlic, cooking for a few seconds.

3. Stir about ½ cup of the chickpea liquid into the pan, swish it around to pick up any brown bits from the bottom of the pan, and turn everything into the chickpea cooking pot. Simmer 3 hours, or until the chickpeas are tender but not falling apart. Uncover and simmer another 30 minutes, or until the broth is full flavored.

4. Puree two thirds of the mixture in a blender, then stir it back into the pot. Season to taste. Remove the herbs and ladle into heated soup bowls. Twirl a thread of oil over each serving and sprinkle with pepper and a few parsley leaves.

VICENZA SWEET PEA SOUP

Zuppa di Bisi in Tecia

Serves 4 to 6

Spring soups should taste fresh and new, like this quick puree of sweet peas that braise briefly with young onions and pancetta. The method and ingredients are both designed to bring out the young, tender qualities of the peas.

Vicenza cooks have tremendous respect for peas. This stately town not far from Venice has a main street lined with buildings by Renaissance architect Andrea Palladio. Every spring, the sweet peas grown on farms in the nearby Lumignano district are bought up by local cooks at the market before mid-morning. Local women all told me the same story of harvesting peas when they were young. They put half the pods in baskets for the kitchen and market. The other half they opened up and scooped out the peas with their tongues.

I reworked this recipe from one I found in a Vicenza cookbook from the nineteenth century. The writer cautioned against overcooking the peas and losing their sweetness. Tasting from moment to moment is vital. Do as everyone does in Vicenza—before buying, always taste fresh peas for sweetness. Our sugar snap peas hold their sweetness much longer than other types, which is why I suggest them for this soup.

½ pound (4 to 5) small new onions, cut into ½-inch pieces

4 pounds sugar snap peas, shelled (4 cups)

1½ teaspoons fruity extra-virgin olive oil

2 thin slices lean pancetta, minced very fine

Generous pinch of sugar

⅓ tightly packed cup fresh Italian parsley leaves, minced

Salt and freshly ground black pepper

3 cups Hearty Vegetable Broth (page 198) or Mother's Broth (page 196) or canned low-sodium chicken broth

---

1. Drop the onions and peas into a bowl of cold water. Combine the oil and pancetta in a 3-quart saucepan. Cook over medium heat until the pancetta is golden, about 5 minutes. Drain the vegetables and add to the pancetta, with any water clinging to them.

2. Protect the sweetness of the peas by not overcooking them: Add the sugar and cook slowly, partially covered, 8 to 10 minutes, or until the peas are barely tender. Fold in the parsley and salt and pepper to taste and continue cooking, uncovered, until tender.

3. Remove and set aside ⅓ cup of the mixture. Puree the rest with the broth in a blender or food processor. Turn back into the saucepan and quickly bring to a simmer. Stir in the reserved whole peas and season to taste. Serve the soup at once in warmed soup bowls.

THE ITALIAN TUPPERWARE PARTY

Neighborhood women, including my cousin Edda, gather at the farmhouse of Maria Lembi, outside Lucca in Tuscany. The excuse is buying household products sold by the local Stanhom representative, their friend Gina. It's like a Tupperware party in America. In reality, the women have dressed up for a rare evening together. All are of local farming families, now more affluent than their parents were. Maria dresses like a city lady in Gianni Versace knockoffs with done-up blond hair. She's the only one of the old friends who left Lucca. She married a baker and lived for seven years in San Francisco. Now they've come back to the house where she was born. She seems happy and loves to laugh.

Gina, whom everyone has known since childhood, presents each product earnestly to begin with, then laughs along with the teasing and interruptions and hurries through so everyone can settle down with the coffee and cake and catch up. Talk moves fast—children, vacations, the best price for dressmaking, childhood reminiscences. Upon the mention of soup, however, specifically bean and farro soup, the area's specialty, the tone changes. This is their food and their tradition, and not to be taken lightly at all.

Each woman owns the soup in a different way. Julia cooks everything together, stirring a sauté of onion and herbs in last. Edda politely suggests that only those who don't understand bean and farro soup would add the sauté last. Maria's married daughter, Gisella, read in a magazine that a bouillon cube makes it better. Ever gentle with the young ones, the older women ignore her. Quiet Erminia listens for a long time, speaking only when she can stand it no longer. "You're ignoring the *lardo* (salt pork). That's most important of all!" With staccato nods, Antonella says her butcher's own lardo is the only one she'll use. Each woman has her butcher who cures his own salt pork. Never use the industrial lardo from the supermarket. On this they all agree. Erminia is satisfied.

With the soup settled, talk drifts back to Stanhom. The women like the products as much as they like getting together once a month. Gina collects orders and recipes from everyone. We end the night with Maria Lembi's own homemade grappa. As I'm walking to the car, several more of the women, one at a time, whisper to me how they make bean and farro soup.

SUPPER SOUP OF SWEET SQUASH, FARRO AND BEANS

Zuppa di Maria Lembi

Serves 6 to 8

Bean soup with whole-grain farro, the ancient wheat that tastes like barley and hazelnuts, is Tuscan tradition—practically every countrywoman makes it. But Maria Lembi's is perfection. She has a magic hand with this thick soup of vegetables, beans and grain. Somehow hers is mellower and lusher than any other. She confided to me, "The secret is in the sweet squash. It makes it *più gentile*, more civilized, more elegant. Without it, it is just another bean and farro soup." Her advice applies not only in Italy. Our own sweet squashes give the soup wonderful character.

Wine Suggestion: A country red like Rosso di Montepulciano

^{1}/2 cup (3 ounces) whole-grain Italian farro or domestic hard wheat kernels (wheat berries)

Water

BEANS

2 ^{1}/8-inch-thick slices pancetta, minced

2 ^{1}/8-inch-thick slices Toscano or soppressata salami, minced

1 small carrot, cut into ^{1}/4-inch dice

1 small stalk celery with leaves, cut into ^{1}/4-inch dice

1 medium onion, cut into ^{1}/4-inch dice

6 fresh sage leaves, chopped

1 large clove garlic, minced

1^1/4 cups dried borlotti, Lamon, or organic pinto beans, soaked in hot water 1 hour and drained

2 medium red-skinned potatoes, peeled and cut into ^{1}/4-inch dice

^{1}/3 1^1/2-pound butternut squash, peeled, seeded, and diced (about 1^1/2 cups)

Salt

SOFFRITTO

1 tablespoon robust extra-virgin olive oil

2 ^{1}/8-inch-thick slices pancetta, minced

2 ^{1}/8-inch-thick slices Toscano or soppressata salami, minced

1 scant teaspoon dried rosemary

Salt and freshly ground black pepper

1 medium onion, cut into ^{1}/4-inch dice

1 clove garlic, minced

^{3}/4 to 1 cup canned whole tomatoes, with their liquid

Robust extra-virgin olive oil

Freshly ground black pepper

1. Simmer the farro or wheat kernels in water to cover by 2 inches until tender. Farro cooks in 30 to 40 minutes, while wheat takes up to 1½ hours.

2. Meanwhile, sauté the pancetta and salami together in a 6-quart pot over medium-high heat to release some of their fat. Stir in the carrot, celery, half the onion, and sage, sautéing to golden brown. Adjust the heat to keep the vegetables from burning. Stir in the garlic, cooking another minute. Add the drained beans, the potatoes, squash, and water to cover by 2 inches. Partially cover the pot and simmer gently 1 hour, or until the beans are just tender. Add salt to taste. Let the beans stand, off the heat, 10 minutes, then drain, saving their liquid.

3. While the beans cook, make the soffritto by heating the olive oil in a 10-inch skillet over medium heat. Sauté the pancetta and salami 1 minute. Add the rosemary, salt and pepper to taste, and the remaining onion and cook until the onion is golden brown. Blend in the garlic and tomatoes and simmer until thick. Remove from the heat and cover.

4. Puree half the beans with ⅓ cup of the bean liquid in a food processor. In the bean pot combine the puree and the remaining beans, the soffritto, cooked grain, and 4 cups of the bean liquid. Gently simmer, partially covered, 30 minutes. Taste for seasoning. The soup should be the consistency of heavy cream; add more bean liquid if necessary. Serve hot, swirling each serving with a little olive oil and a dash of black pepper.

POULTRY, MEATS AND FISH

When I was growing up, family gatherings usually ended the same way. After the food was cleared away and the dishes done, my grandmother and her cronies would sit around the table to talk over coffee. They'd compare notes on children, the states of health of everyone they knew and always on what they cooked for their families. Meals of the recent past inevitably led to reminiscing about the meals they'd all eaten at their mothers' tables in Italy. They were immigrants. Most were like my grandmother, the children of Tuscan farming families, usually sharecroppers farming for landowners. If not from my grandmother, then from one of the other women, the talking closed always with the nodding, sometimes in shared pride, sometimes in smugness covered by a smile, but always with the phrase, ". . . and now we eat meat every day."

Having meat to eat every day in the Italian countryside of a century ago during my grandmother's girlhood would have meant the salvation of affluence, the safety of not wanting for security—at least in their minds. I don't think I misspeak in saying every one of her cronies prided herself on what she could do with the everyday foods—the polenta, the vegetables, the beans and the pasta. But meat was treated with special care and thought—every bit of goodness was coaxed from it. A hundred years ago, when Italian farmwomen served their families meat as a main dish, it was an occasion. Today their grandchildren and great-grandchildren eat meat more often as everyday food, but the legacy of those old women's recipes is very much a part of family meals.

At the big dinners celebrating each autumn's grape harvest on farms in the Modena and Reggio area of the Emilia-Romagna region, there's usually roast chicken flavored with herbs and chopped pancetta or prosciutto stuffed under the skin—an old trick for bringing more flavor and juiciness to a tough barnyard bird. In the Marche and Umbria regions, farmers' sayings refer to knowing when June had come by the aroma of roasting porcetta in the countryside. Young pig roasted with fennel, garlic and onion still marks the June haying and wheat harvests. Now porcetta is sold at outdoor fairs all over Italy.

One elderly woman in an Umbria market reminisced, "When meat was roasting, life was good." The women usually knew the right blend of seasonings to take that roasted meat from good to extraordinary. They understood that just tucking some herbs and lemon inside a capon or small turkey made a difference in how luscious the meat tastes. At home, I season our Thanksgiving and Christmas turkeys this way. No Italian grandmothers knew Thanksgiving, but they did know how to feed a hungry troop of family and workers after a day in the fields cutting wheat. Capon and turkey were treats of early summer, just like porcetta, as well as the meats of Christmas.

As you go south in Italy, more sheep and goat is eaten than beef and veal. The warmer climates and rougher grazing lands aren't as accommodating to cattle as northern terrains are. One of the best and easiest lamb stews I've ever eaten is a grandmother's recipe from deep in the south—the Puglia region. Olive grower Rosalba Ciannamea warned me not to change one jot of her nonna's dish. "If you do, it won't work." One taste, and you'll see why no one in their right mind would want to. And the recipe introduces us to how Puglia cooks often season meat—adding cheese to a blend of garlic, parsley and maybe tomatoes. You'll want to try it with other meats too.

The pig has been ubiquitous in Italy, just as it has been on farms in much of the world. An animal that was easy to raise except in the hottest climates of the south, pork preserved well and was delicious almost no matter how it was cooked. Outside Rome, farmwomen knew that sweet and hot peppers, vinegar and anchovy cut home-raised pork's fattiness and actually sweetened the chunks of meat they stewed together in big pans over open fires. Sop up the pork's sauce with polenta.

In a Tuscan mountain valley, farmers used to catch trout in their walled fields when the river flooded, fry them, pickle them with vinegar and onions and ship them off to Florence to pay taxes. Today those farmers' descendants make the trout for Friday night suppers. I like their lightness, and that I can make the trout ahead for parties.

Serve the dishes in this chapter in any number of ways—just the way families do today in Italy. For casual meals, have them with good bread, salad and wine. On more elaborate occasions, enjoy them accompanied by vegetables and followed with fresh fruit and cheese for dessert. Celebrate holidays and special occasions by adding a first course before and a salad after. A homemade dessert always makes the meal even more special. Adopt these dishes into your life, eating them as they pleasure you most. That is the spirit of this food in Italy.

BALSAMICO ROAST CHICKEN AND POTATOES

Pollo Arrosto

Serves 4 to 5

True balsamic vinegar comes only from Modena and Reggio, two small neighboring provinces in northern Italy's Emilia-Romagna region. Only here have families been making balsamic vinegar in the attics of their homes for at least a thousand years. The best balsamic vinegars are always family-made. Liqueur-like and luscious enough to sip from a glass, artisan or family-made vinegar is a way of life for these people. You can't go to a special dinner, a wedding or just about any outing without someone sharing their homemade balsamico.

This chicken illustrates what I mean. Herbs and pancetta under the skin help it roast to bronze and crisp. Potatoes brown right along with the chicken, basted in its juices—an example of the one-pan roasted dinner, done so easily by Italian farmwomen. But in the Modena and Reggio countryside, when the chicken is presented, and you, the honored guest, are helped to the best pieces, someone always leans over with a little decanter of old balsamico—thick, lustrous and fragrant. Politely they'll ask, "May I?" as though you'd ever say no. With no stinting, they pour their pride and joy, the result of decades of nurturing, over the chicken and potatoes. Few things in the world ever get to be this good.

If you don't have an artisan-made balsamic vinegar for the chicken, a good commercial one works well (see page 383 for information). Do try this dish—it's one of those easy, one-pan dinners you'll make again and again.

➤ *Cook to Cook:* Roasting pieces of meat and vegetables need plenty of room to brown. A large shallow pan like a half-sheet pan allows the pieces to be spread out, barely touching. Its low sides allow heat to surround the foods, aiding the slow caramelization that creates the flavors we love in roasted dishes. Using dried herbs with fresh ones is a trick to boost flavors.

Wine Suggestion: A Piemontese red Paitin Sori Paitin Dolcetto d'Alba

1/4 medium onion
3 large cloves garlic
1/4 tightly packed cup fresh basil leaves
1/2 teaspoon dried basil
1/4 teaspoon *each* dried oregano and marjoram

4 slices (1 1/2 to 2 ounces) pancetta, chopped
5 tablespoons high-quality commercial balsamic vinegar
1 tablespoon extra-virgin olive oil
Salt and freshly ground black pepper

1 3½- to 4-pound chicken (if possible, hormone- and antibiotic-free)
6 medium Yellow Finn, Yukon Gold, or red-skinned potatoes, scrubbed and cut into 2-inch chunks

½ to 1 cup dry white wine
Parsley or fresh thyme for garnish

1. If time allows, season the chicken ahead and refrigerate it several hours or overnight. Preheat the oven to 400°F when ready to cook the chicken. Mince together, by hand or in a food processor, the onion, garlic, herbs (dried ones could be in here too), and pancetta. Then blend in 2 teaspoons of the balsamico, the oil, and salt and pepper to taste.

2. Cut out the chicken's backbone and open the chicken out flat, skin side up. With your palm, firmly press down the breast area to flatten. Stuff most of the herb mixture under the skin of the thigh, leg, and breast areas. Rub the rest all over the chicken. Place the bird skin side up on a large shallow pan (a broiler pan or jelly-roll or half-sheet pan). Scatter the potatoes around it and sprinkle everything with salt and pepper.

3. Roast 20 minutes, then pour in ½ cup wine. Roast another 70 minutes, or until the thigh reaches about 175°F on an instant-read thermometer. Baste the potatoes and chicken frequently with the pan juices, turning the potatoes often to brown evenly and prevent them from sticking. Add more wine if the pan is dry. Turn over the chicken two thirds of the way through cooking for even browning. If after an hour of roasting, the chicken isn't browning, raise the heat to 500°F to finish cooking. (Or wait until it is done and run it under the broiler 5 minutes to crisp the skin.)

4. Let the chicken rest 5 to 10 minutes at room temperature, then present on a warmed platter along with the potatoes, sprinkling everything with the rest of the balsamic. Garnish with bouquets of parsley or fresh thyme.

BAKING DAY CHICKEN WITH BLACK OLIVES AND RED PEPPERS

Pollo Arrosto al Forno con Olive Nere e Peperoni Rossi

Serves 6 to 8

This whole meal in a roasting pan from Tuscany is actually an oven-cooked version of Chicken Cacciatora, minus the messy stovetop. Big, unstoppable flavors come from roasting chicken pieces in a cloak of garlic, greens and herbs, along with tomato, peppers and meaty black olives that become the meat's sauce. Don't be put off by the long list of ingredients; many of them are gathered together and dispatched in a single chopping session. In central Italy, people use the wide mezzaluna, or arced half-moon knife. They rock the knife into the pile of herbs and vegetables, chopping them together. Flavors meld differently with this method than when each ingredient is chopped individually. The same thing can be accomplished with a good chef's knife. Years ago, on the weekly baking day, this chicken roasted in the descending heat of the farm's wood-fired bread oven after the loaves were baked.

Wine Suggestion: A Chianti Classico by Fattoria di Nozzole, Fattoria di Felsina or Castello di Ama

Leaves from 4 branches fresh Italian parsley

Leaves from a 6-inch branch fresh rosemary

8 large fresh sage leaves

8 large basil leaves

1 small leaf kale (6 inches long, with stem removed) or 3 whole leaves curly endive

8 large cloves garlic

1 medium red onion

1 1/2 tablespoons extra-virgin olive oil

3 1/2 pounds chicken thighs (if possible, hormone- and antibiotic-free), skin removed (or an equal amount of rabbit)

2 medium red sweet peppers, cored, seeded, and cut into 2-inch wedges

2/3 cup oil-cured or Kalamata olives

2 medium delicious ripe tomatoes, coarsely chopped, or 4 whole canned tomatoes, drained

Salt and freshly ground black pepper

1 cup dry white wine

1 1/2 cups Mother's Broth (page 196) or canned low-sodium chicken broth

1 medium lemon, halved

1. The day before cooking, mince together the herbs, kale or endive, garlic, and onion, then blend with the oil. Rub the mixture over the chicken, layering the pieces and seasonings in a deep bowl. Cover and refrigerate overnight.

2. Preheat the oven to 400°F. Spread the chicken in a large shallow pan (a half-sheet or jelly-roll pan, not nonstick). Tuck the peppers among the chicken pieces. Scatter the olives, tomatoes (crushing canned ones with your hands), and any leftover herb mixture over the chicken. Sprinkle with salt and pepper.

3. Roast 30 minutes, then pour $1/2$ cup of the wine over the chicken. Baste with the pan juices. Turn the heat down to 350°F. Roast another 35 to 40 minutes, basting frequently and adding a little water if the juices threaten to burn. Turn the chicken and vegetables for even browning.

4. When the temperature of the chicken reaches 170°F on an instant-read thermometer, add $1/2$ cup of the broth to the pan. Turn the oven to broil and brown the chicken by placing it under the broiler, about 7 inches from heat. Cook about 5 minutes per side. Transfer the chicken and vegetables to a serving platter and keep warm.

5. Set the roasting pan on two burners and add the remaining $1/2$ cup wine. Boil down by two thirds while scraping up the glaze from the pan. Stir in $1/2$ cup of the stock and boil down to almost nothing. Add the rest of the stock and simmer to blend. Taste for seasoning. Pour the sauce over the chicken. Serve hot, squeezing the lemon juice over the dish at the last minute.

Free-range chickens on a Marche farm.

HARVEST CAPON
Cappone della Raccolta
Serves 6 to 8

Capon is the roast beef of the poultry world—unbelievably succulent, roasting as easily as any chicken and when stuffed with lemon, herbs and garlic, a dinner few ever forget.

A century ago, sharecroppers and peasants fantasized about roasting a whole capon for themselves. They would castrate chickens, turning them into capons, and fatten them for the landlord's table and as gifts to the people most important to their family's security—the pharmacist, the priest, the lawyer. Rarely did they eat them themselves, except at Christmas and the wheat harvest in June. This recipe is an old one from the days when everyone went to the fields to harvest wheat. It works just as well with turkey.

Wine Suggestion: Marche's red Rosso Cònero by Moroder or Fattoria Le Terrazze

1 7- to 8-pound capon or turkey (if possible, hormone- and antibiotic-free), trimmed of excess fat
1/2 medium lemon
8 branches fresh basil
8 branches fresh Italian parsley
8 branches fresh thyme
8 branches fresh marjoram

6 large cloves garlic, split
Freshly ground black pepper
Salt
1 cup dry white wine

PAN GRAVY (OPTIONAL)
1/2 cup dry white wine
1 cup Mother's Broth (page 196) or canned low-sodium chicken broth

1. If possible a day ahead, rub the bird inside and out with the lemon half, branches of herbs, and garlic. Slice the lemon, then tuck it inside the cavity along with the garlic and herbs. Sprinkle the capon with pepper. Lightly cover and refrigerate overnight.

2. The next day, preheat the oven to 325°F. Sprinkle the bird with salt. Place breast side down in a shallow pan and roast 15 to 18 minutes to the pound (about 2 hours or so), or until an instant-read thermometer inserted into the thickest part of the thigh reads 170°F. After the first 20 minutes, pour the 1 cup wine over the bird. Baste frequently with the pan juices. During the last 30 minutes of roasting, turn over to brown the breast. Let the bird rest 10 minutes in a warm place before carving.

3. Set the capon or turkey on a heated serving platter. Carve the breast meat into thick slices and divide the thigh meat into 3 or 4 pieces. Defat the pan juices and spoon them over the meat.

Or make a pan gravy. Defat the pan juices. Set the pan over two burners and add the wine. Simmer as you scrape up all the brown bits from the bottom and sides of the pan. When the wine has nearly evaporated, stir in the broth and boil 2 minutes, or until richly flavored. Spoon over capon. Serve hot.

HOW A CAPON BECAME A FATHER

I never appreciated the importance of chickens to a woman's role in farm life until my friend restaurateur Emilio Lancellotti related this story. Emilio lives in a small town in the midst of Emilia-Romagna's farming country, near the city of Modena. Emilio spends his spare time sitting in farm kitchens listening to the stories of the elderly farmers in his area.

He explained how the barnyard and kitchen garden were the family matriarch's (she is called *rezdora* in local dialect) domain, her center of power. A well-run henhouse showed off a woman's skill. Her hens' eggs and plump capons brought money into the family. But, overnight, an illness infecting the chickens could devastate a henhouse, leaving eggs untended, or, even worse, baby chicks without a mother to protect them against predators. An old farmwoman had told Emilio how a wise *rezdora* used to create a new "mother" for orphaned chicks.

She isolated a young capon in a room. Then she got the bird drunk—first feeding it a delicious (to the bird) mix of cornmeal and wine, then only wine. She put the orphaned chicks in the room, and by the time the capon had sobered up, the chicks were attached to him and he to them. A new "father" capon usually protected the chicks like a proverbial mother hen, taking them out into the world literally under his wings. The bonds remained strong even after the chicks were grown. And the *rezdora* proved once again what a wise farmwoman she was.

Poultry, Meats and Fish

▼ ▼ ▼ ▼ ▼ ▼ ▼ ▼ ▼ ▼

WINE-GLAZED CHICKEN

Pollo Glassato Val Camonica

Serves 4

In the Italian Swiss Alps, north and east of Milan in the long Camonica Valley, farm families mark special occasions with this sautéed chicken. It needs only a handful of ingredients and the simplest of techniques. Sautéing chicken slowly while reducing small amounts of wine over it, one after another, builds a sauce where each ingredient—the wine, lemon, sage, garlic and onion—gives up its individual identity to a melding of luscious, layered tastes. In the process, each piece of chicken glazes to the color of polished teak. Hold back on embellishments. Accompany it with steamed or baked new potatoes, and perhaps spring peas or green beans, but nothing more.

➤ ***Cook to Cook:*** One caution: a 12-inch sauté pan is essential to this recipe's success; it will not work with anything smaller. To build the rich glaze, do not cover the chicken at any point while cooking.

Wine Suggestion: A red from Lombardy's Franciacorta area like
Franciacorta Rosso by Villa, Principe Banfi or Ricci-Curbastro

1 3- to 3½-pound chicken (if possible, hormone- and antibiotic-free), cut into 8 pieces	2 tablespoons extra-virgin olive oil
	3 tablespoons minced onion
½ medium lemon	2 large cloves garlic, minced
8 large fresh sage leaves	1¾ cups dry white wine
Salt and freshly ground black pepper	½ cup water

1. Up to 2 hours before cooking, rub the chicken with the lemon, squeezing out the juice as you go, then rub with the sage leaves. Lightly salt and generously pepper the chicken. Pile it on a platter, tucking in the sage leaves here and there, cover, and refrigerate 2 hours.

2. Remove the sage leaves and set aside. Pat the chicken dry. Heat the oil in a 12-inch sauté pan (not nonstick) over medium-high heat. Place the chicken skin side down in the pan, reduce the heat to medium, and brown on the first side, about 10 minutes. Turn and sauté about 5 minutes, then sprinkle with the onion and reserved sage leaves and finish browning on the second side. Keep the breast pieces at the pan's edges to slow their cooking. Remove the pan from the heat and spoon off all but ½ tablespoon of the fat.

3. Allow about 25 minutes for this final step: Set the pan over medium heat, sprinkle the chicken with the garlic, and add $1/2$ cup of the wine to the pan. Cook slowly, uncovered, scraping up the brown glaze and turning the chicken pieces occasionally, until all the liquid has cooked away. Adjust the heat as necessary so the wine simmers gently, taking care not to scorch. Repeat with another $1/2$ cup of wine, then another, spooning the pan juices over the chicken and turning the pieces to keep them moist. Finally, add the remaining $1/4$ cup wine and let it cook away. Blend in the water and cook down only halfway.

The chicken is cooked when there is no sign of pink when the thigh meat is pierced. The sauce should be syrupy and rich-tasting, and barely coat the chicken. Serve hot.

Glazing

You can dramatically intensify the flavors of roasts and sautés, without adding more flavorings or fat, by using a simple process I call "glazing." After years of watching Italian home cooks, I saw that the best ones use a similar technique for enriching and opening up flavors.

Glazing is repeatedly basting food with its own pan juices, and perhaps other liquids—usually wine. Use glazing when roasting and sautéing meats or poultry. With each basting of liquid, another layer of taste is added, intensifying and deepening the flavors.

The recipe for Wine-Glazed Chicken (above) illustrates glazing a sauté beautifully. You'll need a wide shallow pan—a 12-inch sauté pan—and about 25 minutes more cooking once the chicken is browned. Never cover the cooking meat. Once the chicken is browned, tip the pan and spoon off most of the fat. Then pour a little wine over the chicken. Cook over medium to low heat, moistening the chicken pieces by occasionally turning them in the pan juices. Once most of the wine has bubbled away, add a little more, this time spooning up the juices from the pan too. Repeat several times. Each basting builds another layer of richness.

I think you'll be amazed by the difference this technique makes in any recipe—a world away from the tastes we get by simply pouring wine in all at once and simmering the meat or poultry. Try glazing with roast pork, beef and veal.

PORCINI CHICKEN BREASTS

Petto di Pollo ai Porcini

Serves 4

I learn a lot standing in lines in Italian food shops. The little produce store of Sant'Angelo Lodigiano in Lombardy was crowded with women shopping for the midday meal. While waiting my turn at the cash register, I eavesdropped on the never-changing conversations that can be heard from one end of Italy to the other: "What did you eat yesterday?" "What are you making today?" "And tomorrow, what will you eat then?" All of this comes spiced with mini cooking lessons, more regional food information than cookbooks ever reveal, tidbits of gossip and flashes of ego from cooks who are certain their way is the only way.

That day, butter and porcini mushrooms preoccupied two women on my left—one older than the other. It was porcini season in Lombardy, which is dairy country and one of the few places in Italy where people cook with butter. The older woman practically spit out her words, "My doctor says I can't cook the way I used to—with butter. Now it has to be olive oil. Before you know it, we will be Tuscans!"

The younger woman, struggling with intimidation, replied, "My husband has heart trouble, so I had to try oil for cooking. I did sautéed chicken breast with porcini in olive oil and stirred in just a little butter at the end. It isn't bad. Signora, I think even you would like it." While the scowling signora attempted graciousness, I shyly introduced myself and asked for the recipe. This porcini sauce, with its single tablespoon of butter, is one of the best things that could happen to a chicken breast. Try it when time is short.

➤ **Cook to Cook:** If fresh porcini come into your life, use ½ pound, sliced about ¼ inch thick, and sauté them 3 minutes.

Wine Suggestion: A fine Soave Classico Superiore by
Pieropan, Olinto Gini or Graziano Pra

½ ounce (about ½ cup) dried porcini
    mushrooms
1 cup hot water
4 boned and skinned chicken breasts,
    totaling 1 pound (if possible,
    hormone- and antibiotic-free)
1 cup all-purpose flour

1½ tablespoons extra-virgin olive oil
Salt and freshly ground black pepper
2 tablespoons minced onion
½ cup dry red wine
1 tablespoon unsalted butter
3 tablespoons water

1. Rid the mushrooms of grit by dropping them into a bowl of cold water, swishing them around, letting them settle for a few seconds, and then lifting them out. Repeat two more times, working off any grit with your fingers. Then cover the mushrooms with the hot water and soak 20 minutes.

2. Lift the mushrooms out of the liquid and coarsely chop. Reserve the soaking liquid. Line a strainer with a paper towel.

3. Pound the chicken breasts between pieces of plastic wrap to between $1/4$ and $1/2$ inch thick. Dredge in the flour, shaking off the excess.

4. Heat the oil in a 12-inch skillet over medium-high heat. Add the chicken, seasoning with salt and pepper. Cook about 20 seconds on each side before turning the heat down to medium. Sprinkle the breasts with the onion. Cook another minute or so per side, until barely firm when pressed. Remove to a serving platter and keep warm.

5. Increase the heat to medium-high, add the mushrooms, and sauté 10 seconds. Strain $1/2$ cup of the reserved mushroom liquid through the sieve into the skillet. Boil down until almost evaporated. Repeat the process with $1/4$ cup of the wine. Stir in the rest of the wine and simmer down to a sheer film. Stir in the butter and 3 tablespoons water, stirring until the butter is barely melted. Taste for seasoning, then quickly scrape the sauce over the chicken. Serve immediately.

SWEET-SOUR MEATBALLS FOR ST. JOSEPH'S DAY

Polpette di San Giuseppe in Agrodolce

Serves 3 to 4 as a main dish, 6 to 8 as an antipasto

These meatballs are made of chicken and peppery salami, seasoned with cheese, almonds, cinnamon and diced citron and cooked in sweet basil sauce. They used to be made by Rina Durante's grandmother for the Feast of St. Joseph on March 19, in the middle of Lent. That might be why they're sweet and savory—all the missed treats given up for Lent were piled into them. Rina is a restaurant critic in Puglia. She reminisced with me one night about her grandmother's cooking and these meatballs. Later, I discovered other examples of them in Basilicata and Sicily. Always they were for special occasions like Christmas, Easter or St. Joseph's Day. You can cook the meatballs an hour ahead and let them steep in their sauce, then reheat for serving. My husband eats them stone cold, straight from the refrigerator.

Wine Suggestion: A Puglia red Salice Salentino or Rosso del Salento

MEATBALLS

2 large cloves garlic

2 ounces hot capocollo or pepperoni

3/4 pound skinned and boned chicken thighs (4 to 5) (if possible, hormone- and antibiotic-free)

1/2 10-ounce package frozen spinach, defrosted and squeezed dry

1/2 medium onion, coarsely chopped

1/4 teaspoon cinnamon

1/4 teaspoon *each* salt and freshly ground black pepper

1/2 cup fresh bread crumbs

1 tablespoon red wine vinegar

2/3 cup (3 ounces) grated Fontinella cheese

1/2 cup unblanched almonds, toasted and chopped medium-fine

1/3 cup (2.25 ounces) candied citron, minced very fine

1 large egg

SAUCE

Extra-virgin olive oil

1/2 cup dry white wine

6 large fresh basil leaves, chopped

2 teaspoons sugar

2 tablespoons red wine vinegar

1 cup Mother's Broth (page 196), Hearty Vegetable Broth (page 198), or canned low-sodium chicken broth

1. In a food processor or by hand, mince the garlic and capocollo or pepperoni into small pieces. Add the chicken thighs, spinach, onion, cinnamon, salt, and pepper. Chop very fine. Turn everything into a bowl. Mix in the bread crumbs, vinegar, cheese, almonds, citron, and egg, blending until well mixed. Check the seasoning by sautéing a little patty of the mixture until firm, then tasting. Shape into 2-inch balls.

2. Pour a sheer film of oil over the bottom of a 12-inch sauté pan. Heat over medium-high heat. Add the meatballs, turn the heat down to medium, and brown on all sides, turning gently, about 10 minutes. Adjust the heat as necessary so the meatballs don't burn.

3. Tip the pan and spoon off most of the fat. Pour in the wine. Simmer until thick and syrupy. Blend in the basil, sugar, vinegar, and broth. Cover and simmer very gently 15 minutes, or until the meatballs are firm and their centers have reached 170°F on an instant-read thermometer. Turn them once or twice during cooking. Remove the meatballs to a shallow bowl.

4. Boil down the pan juices until thick and rich-tasting. Pour them over the meatballs and serve hot or warm.

SAUTEED QUAIL IN POMEGRANATE SAUCE

Quaglie al Melograno

Serves 4 to 6

Stunning crimson in color, perfect for Christmastime, the pomegranate in this dish is sweet and tart, with the crunch of meaty pine nuts. I couldn't resist combining two recipes from the countryside north of Venice—one is modern herb-marinated quail roasted in pomegranate juice; the other from centuries ago, a sauté of quail with a pomegranate–pine nut sauce. Marinating and then sautéing the quail makes this a quick dish with juicy meat and a fresh-tasting, ruby-colored sauce.

➤ *Cook to Cook:* Find fresh pomegranates in the market from October through December. When they are unavailable, know the Knudsen people bottle a surprisingly good unsweetened juice. Find it and similar pomegranate juices in natural food stores and specialty food shops. The quail cook quickly (in only 10 to 15 minutes), so have everything ready to go into the pan.

Wine Suggestion: A red Cavalchina Santa Lucia Bardolino Superiore

1 tightly packed teaspoon fresh thyme leaves

1 large clove garlic

1/4 medium onion

1 tablespoon extra-virgin olive oil

6 quail (about 6 ounces each), split, cut down the center of the back, and butterflied

Salt and freshly ground black pepper

SAUCE

3 large pomegranates or 1 1/4 cups unsweetened bottled pomegranate juice

Seeds of 1 large pomegranate (see below for how to seed) (optional)

1 1/2 tablespoons extra-virgin olive oil

2 large bay leaves

1 thick slice lean pancetta, finely chopped

Salt and freshly ground black pepper

1/4 cup dry white wine

2 generous pinches of dark brown sugar

2 tablespoons pine nuts, toasted

1/2 tightly packed teaspoon fresh Italian parsley leaves, finely chopped

1. The day before cooking, pound together in a mortar, or mince in a food processor, the thyme, garlic, and onion with the oil. Rub the seasoning over the quail and dust lightly with salt and pepper. Stack the quail one atop the other on a plate, cover, and refrigerate until 30 minutes before cooking.

2. To juice fresh pomegranates, roll them on a counter to soften slightly. Have a bowl handy. Cut a small hole at the top or bottom of each pomegranate and squeeze the fruit over the bowl to release its juices. To seed the fourth pomegranate, cut it vertically into 8 wedges and with a knife tip, pick the seeds away from the white pulp, working over a bowl to catch the juice. Set aside until needed.

3. Heat the oil in a 12-inch sauté pan over medium-high heat. Lay the quail skin side down in the pan, with all their seasonings and the bay leaves. Brown on the first side about 2 minutes. Turn the heat down to medium-low, sprinkle the quail with the pancetta, and cook 3 to 5 minutes until they begin to become firm. Return the heat to medium-high, turn the quail, sprinkle with salt and pepper, and brown about 2 minutes. Finish cooking over medium-low heat, another 3 to 5 minutes. The breasts should be barely firm when pressed; do not overcook. Transfer quail to a platter and keep warm.

4. Turn the heat up to medium-high and stir in the wine, simmering to almost nothing while scraping up the brown glaze from the pan's bottom. Add 1 cup of the pomegranate juice and the sugar. Reduce by half to two thirds. Lower the heat to medium-low and return the quail to the pan, coating with the sauce and sprinkling with the remaining $1/4$ cup juice. Cover and heat through, 3 to 4 minutes. Serve immediately, arranged on a hot platter, napped with the sauce, and sprinkled with the nuts, parsley, and optional pomegranate seeds.

TUSCAN PORK RIBS
Rosticciana
Serves 6 to 8

A specialty of Lucca in northern Tuscany, these are irresistible ribs—moist, meaty and splendidly crusty, embellished only with rosemary, garlic and the indispensable finish of salt.

In the mountains above Lucca, some farmers still carefully raise their own pigs, and their renditions of this Lucchese favorite have special succulence. Up until several decades ago, this dish was a winter treat for country people, celebrating the last excesses of Carnival.

The best ribs I've tasted were in a village hidden in a little gorge between two mountains. They weren't cooked on an open grill in the usual Lucca manner, but in a big wood-fired bread oven. A fire of oak and chestnut logs heated the oven from the back, while the ribs cooked near the oven's mouth on a footed iron grill over a mound of red-hot coals. At home, I miss the wood fire, but I've discovered that oven-roasting the ribs slowly keeps them tender and moist. Ideally, finish them by browning and crisping with a turn on a wood-fired outdoor grill. Finishing under the oven broiler is fine too.

Wine Suggestion: A generous red Carmignano by Il Poggiolo or Fattoria Ambra

4 large cloves garlic

2 tightly packed tablespoons fresh
   rosemary leaves

1 teaspoon extra-virgin olive oil

3$^{1}/_{2}$ pounds country-style pork ribs
   (if possible, hormone- and
   antibiotic-free), 1 to 2 inches thick

About $^{3}/_{4}$ teaspoon salt

Freshly ground black pepper

1. Mince together the garlic and rosemary, then combine with the oil. Rub over the ribs, cover, and refrigerate 12 to 24 hours.

2. Set a rack in the center and preheat the oven to 325°F. Lay aluminum foil over a half-sheet pan, broiler pan, or other large shallow pan. Arrange the ribs about 2 inches apart on the pan. Sprinkle with the salt and a little pepper, turning to season on all sides. Salting generously at this point intensifies the meat's flavors.

3. Roast 30 to 40 minutes. Test with an instant-read thermometer at the thickest part of the meat for a reading of 150° to 155°F, *no more.*

4. Finish cooking either on an outdoor grill or under the broiler: To taste them at their best, it's crucial that the ribs become a rich, crusty brown. Slowly brown them on all sides on a medium-hot grill about 15 minutes, or set 7 to 8 inches from the pre-heated oven broiler and slowly crisp on all sides. Serve hot.

DIVINE PORCELLO

An Old Parma Saying:
*"The pig is like the music of Verdi,
there's nothing left to throw away."*

Farm families affectionately called the pig *"Il Divino Porcello,"* the Divine Little Pig. A pig was nearly as necessary as water for people living on the land, especially when the families had little money. Unlike cows, sheep or goats, a pig needed no grazing land but flourished in a small yard next to the house, getting fat on whatever the family could spare. In return, it gave its all. Once the pig had met its end, each morsel was preserved, helping to support the family through the year. Any part of the pig gave incomparable flavor, whether it was pancetta, cured jowl (called *guanciale*), lard or salami. As cut after cut of cured pork matured, it was either eaten or sold, or possibly used by the farmer to fulfill his contract with his landowner.

A plateful of roasted pork was rare on most farmhouse tables, but the day-to-day dishes of vegetables, polenta, soups and pastas always tasted better for small additions of cured pork. Even where olive oil or butter was made, many families sold them, or handed over the lion's share to a landlord. Il Divino Porcello sustained the family.

BRAISED PORK WITH THREE PEPPERS

Brasato di Maiale ai Tre Peperoni

In the Roman countryside, this is a favorite party dish. Pieces of browned pork braise in a rosemary-garlic sauce with wedges of yellow, red and green peppers—sweet, hot and lusty. It's colorful, simple to do and better for being cooked a day ahead. Farmwomen used to do it on the hearth in big shallow pans. Some families like chicken instead of pork with the peppers. Others use lamb when it's in season. For my taste, this dish is enough for an entire meal, but I love adding polenta to sop up its juices.

Wine Suggestion: Lungarotti's Torgiano Rosso

Extra-virgin olive oil
1 *each* large sweet red and yellow peppers, cored, seeded, and cut into 2-inch pieces
2 large Italian frying peppers (or 1 more sweet red pepper), cored, seeded, and cut into 2-inch pieces
2 to 3 large medium-hot fresh chiles, such as Hungarian wax or Cubanelle, seeded and cut into 2-inch pieces
Salt and freshly ground black pepper
2³/₄ to 3 pounds boned pork shoulder (if possible, hormone- and

antibiotic-free), trimmed of fat and cut into 2-inch chunks
Leaves from 4 6-inch branches fresh rosemary
¹/₂ medium onion
3 large cloves garlic
3 oil-packed anchovy fillets, rinsed
3 bay leaves
¹/₂ cup red wine vinegar
¹/₂ cup water
4 whole canned tomatoes, drained

1. Lightly film a 12-inch skillet (not nonstick) with olive oil. Set over medium-high heat. Add all the peppers with a little salt and pepper. Toss just to lightly sear them, about 2 minutes. Remove them from the pan, leaving the oil behind, and add a little more oil. Once it is hot, add the pork, sprinkle with a little salt and pepper, and brown well on all sides, adjusting the heat so the glaze at the bottom of the pan doesn't burn, about 10 minutes.

2. While the pork browns, chop together the rosemary, onion, garlic, and anchovies into ¹/₄-inch pieces. Once the pork's half-browned, add the bay leaves. After 1 to 2 minutes more blend in the chopped mixture and finish browning the pork over medium heat, stirring to keep the garlic from burning. The onion should be golden brown.

3. Pour in the vinegar. Simmer it down to nothing while scraping up all the glaze from the bottom of the pan. Add the water, tomatoes, and the peppers; adjust the heat so the liquid bubbles slowly, cover, and cook 50 minutes, or until the pork is tender, stirring occasionally. Taste sauce for seasoning. Serve right away with baked or soft polenta, or cool, refrigerate overnight, and reheat to bubbling before serving.

THE LAST MILLER

Riccardo Ricci-Curbastro wanted me to meet the last miller in his part of Italy, the farmland west of Lake Garda in the Lombardy region. He mills Ricci-Curbastro's corn into polenta meal in the village of Soprarocco di Gavardo. Since Ricci-Curbastro goes out of his way to grow an old strain of corn called *Merano,* using only organic methods, I knew he must mean this was the last miller to stone-grind the grain, that is, between slowly turning stones shaped like thick wheels, instead of between the quickly rotating steel rollers used in industrial mills.

The little mill was literally roaring with work. Two pairs of stone grinders stood side by side, large, thick stone wheels on their sides, one set atop the other. The bottom stone stayed still and the top one turned, grinding the corn between the two. A man with white hair was pouring corn kernels into one of the wooden hoppers suspended over the stones with the agility of a teenager. When he climbed down and reached out to shake my hand, it was surprising to realize he was probably in his late seventies. Adolfo Bruschi had known Ricci-Curbastro since he was a baby and used to come to the mill with his father. "But that was just before we had to close down, so I didn't see him again until he was a grown man with a family."

"My father had this mill, and my grandfather and his grandfather. When my father died, my mother had seven of us to feed. So she took it over. She cooked like an angel and the farmers loved her—she was a good miller. We lived well. When she died, I was the miller. But by the 1950s we had no business. Big mills opened. They have steel rollers that grind corn faster and more cheaply than we could. But that system didn't satisfy everyone. When you grind between stones, the corn keeps more flavor and it keeps all its nutrients. Old-timers wanted the old way. After nearly thirty years, I reopened the mill. I thought just the old ones like me would come. But young ones like Riccardo here came too, especially the ones growing the organic corn, the old corns. The business doubles each year now. My son works with me and his little boy loves to be in the mill. It's supporting the family again." I asked him if he ever got tired of eating polenta? "Me? Never! Polenta's in my blood!"

Miller Adolfo Bruschi.

ROASTED PORCETTA

Serves 6 to 8

Porcetta by any other name?
Some say porcetta is suckling pig, while others claim it is weaned young pig.
Then there are recipes in Italian cookbooks for duck, rabbit and even fish "in
porcetta," which add to the puzzle. Porcetta or porchetta is weaned young pig,
usually not more than 120 pounds, sometimes boned and roasted whole and
supposedly originating in the region of Umbria.

What a difference a single letter makes. Suckling pig is porcetto or
porchetto. "In porchetto" means in the style of porcetta; that is, any roasted or
even braised food seasoned with a blend of herbs, possibly spices and pork
flavoring like minced prosciutto, lard, salt pork or pancetta. So, for the purist,
our American porcetta roasts and my recipe for porcetta are actually in porcetta.

Spring haying parties always meant porcetta—a whole young pig complete
with crackling, seasoned with wild fennel and garlic, roasted over a wood fire.
Today, find porcetta at stands at fairs all over Italy, serving up slices of roasted
meat stuffed into crusty rolls—not a bad idea for any leftovers from this roast.
Since whole pigs or small loins of pork with crackling are hard to come by, use
the shoulder or butt roast, which has no crackling, but the succulence from its
generous marbling makes huge difference in this recipe. If you live in California,
you might even find wild fennel growing nearby. If not, a blend of fennel seed,
fresh fennel and orange zest comes surprisingly close. Don't wait for the haying,
make this for Sunday dinner.

3- to 4-pound boneless pork shoulder
   or butt roast (if possible, hormone-
   and antibiotic-free)
$^{1}/_{2}$ teaspoon whole fennel seed
$^{1}/_{4}$ teaspoon dry rosemary
1 small orange
$^{1}/_{3}$ cup finely minced fresh fennel bulb

$^{1}/_{8}$ teaspoon *each* salt and freshly
   ground pepper, plus additional for
   sprinkling on the roast
3 cloves garlic, minced
1 tablespoon dry white wine
1 tablespoon extra-virgin olive oil
$^{2}/_{3}$ cup dry white wine

1. If possible, season the meat a day ahead. Put the fennel seeds and rosemary in
a mortar or small bowl. With a zester, shred the orange zest over them to capture its
oils. Pound everything into a coarse mixture, blending in the fresh fennel, $^{1}/_{8}$ teaspoon
each salt and pepper, garlic, white wine, and olive oil. Cut deep slits in the pork, stuff
with the mixture, and rub a tablespoon or so of it over the meat's surface. With cotton

string, tie the roast into a compact cylinder at 1½-inch intervals. Sprinkle with salt and pepper. Lightly cover and refrigerate overnight.

2. Preheat the oven to 325°F. Set the roast in a 9 by 13-inch shallow pan. Roast 20 minutes, then pour the wine over the meat. Roast 1 hour to 1 hour and 15 minutes more, basting with the pan juices. Add a little water if the juices threaten to burn. The meat's internal temperature should be between 130° and 140°F.

3. Turn the oven up to 500°F and roast another 15 minutes, or until the meat's internal temperature reaches 150°F. Let the roast rest for 10 minutes at room temperature. Serve on a heated platter, carved into thin slices and moistened with the pan juices.

THE PATRON SAINT OF THE PIGLET

In stables all over Italy, I've seen the same thing: Nailed to a post, or hung over the stall of the fattest sow, is a picture of a saint in brown robes. At his feet is always a plump, pink pig peering up at him, usually in dazzled adoration. I learned that this is San Antonio Abate, patron saint of the pig and all farm animals. Everyone has a story of how farmers honor him. On his day, January 17, farmwomen sometimes bake special white bread to feed the animals, and the priest might come to bless the stable. One tale I heard again and again was that on the eve of San Antonio's Day, when everyone is asleep, the saint performs a miracle. All the farm animals speak in Italian to each other. Farm children hide in haylofts waiting to see the miracle. But they always drop off to sleep just before the animals begin talking.

PORK WITH ARTICHOKES, CONTADINA-STYLE

Maiale alla Contadina

Serves 6 to 8

Crisp roasted artichokes and pork studded with bits of garlic, pepperoni and orange zest—what a dish this turned out to be, and I never could find the woman who shared it again to thank her. Her stand was away from the main part of the market. She was an elderly farmwoman selling bundles of fresh herbs, a few flowers and fresh-cut artichokes from a little table. It was spring, near Rome—the time when everyone eats new lamb with artichokes. She insisted that I try roasting pork and artichokes together. "Do this when lamb isn't good—in fall and winter. You'll need to season it with something piquant; pork can be bland. I use my homemade *salame*, hot chile peppers and herbs. Like this," she pointed to the parsley. She swung into a cooking lesson, explaining how the orange zest was another kind of *"piccante,"* how garlic's perfume brought everything together. Then she warned that without basting and keeping everything moist, the recipe wouldn't taste right. I followed her counsel. My reward was a dish we serve again and again, with either lamb or pork.

Wine Suggestion: A big red Montepulciano d'Abruzzo by Camillo Montori or Masciarelli

5 large artichokes
1 large lemon, halved
4 quarts boiling salted water
1/2 medium onion
4 large cloves garlic
1/4 tightly packed cup fresh Italian parsley leaves
6 small thin slices pepperoni
Shredded zest of 1 large orange
Generous pinch of hot red pepper flakes

Salt
1/4 teaspoon freshly ground black pepper
3 pounds boneless pork butt roast (if possible, hormone- and antibiotic-free), trimmed of excess fat and cut with the grain into 4 equal pieces
2/3 cup dry vermouth
1 cup dry white wine
1 cup chicken broth or water

1. Trim away any darkened areas from the stem of each artichoke. Rub the artichoke with the lemon as you work, then peel it. Break off the leaves until you reach the pale green inner ones. Cut away the top third of the artichoke. Quarter what is left vertically. Trim away the fuzzy choke.

2. Drop the artichokes into the boiling water, cook 4 minutes, and drain.

3. Set a large shallow roasting pan on the oven's middle rack to preheat and preheat the oven to 450°F. Mince together the onion, garlic, parsley, pepperoni, and orange zest. Blend with the hot pepper, $1/4$ teaspoon salt, and the black pepper. Make about 12 slits in each piece of pork with a paring knife. Insert half the seasoning mixture. Toss the rest with the meat and artichokes.

4. Spread the artichokes and pork in the hot roasting pan and roast 20 minutes. Pour in the vermouth and $1/2$ cup of the white wine, turning and moistening the pork and artichokes.

5. Lower the heat to 325°F. Roast another 30 minutes, turning occasionally. Add the remaining $1/2$ cup wine. Continue roasting another 30 to 45 minutes, basting frequently, or until the pork reaches an internal temperature of 150°F on an instant-read thermometer. If the pan juices threaten to burn, add a little water to the pan. The artichokes should be browned with crisp edges, and the pork a bit crusty.

6. Remove the meat and artichokes to a bowl and keep warm. Set the roasting pan on two burners atop the stove, pour in the broth or water, and boil down by two thirds while scraping up any brown bits. The pan sauce should taste full and rich. If not, reduce a little longer.

7. Slice the pork about $1/4$ inch thick across the grain. Arrange on a serving dish with the artichokes. Spoon the sauce over the meat along with all the flavorings from the pan, then sprinkle with salt. Serve hot.

▼ ▼ ▼ ▼ ▼ ▼ ▼ ▼ ▼ ▼ ▼

GARLIC-CAPER GRILLED PORK CHOPS

Cotolette di Maiale all'Adelina

Serves 4

On the back terrace of her guest farm, Adelina Norcia grills her specially seasoned pork chops over a wood fire. She rubs thick chops with a mince of her own salt-cured capers, rosemary and garlic from the garden, olive oil from her trees and lots of black pepper, then refrigerates them overnight. Enjoy the chops with Sicilian Sauce. It's a fine marriage.

➤ **Cook to Cook:** Use salt-cured capers if possible. They bring scents of exotic flowers and herbs to the pork, nuances never even hinted at by vinegar-packed capers. Some of the best salted capers come from the island of Pantelleria, between the coasts of Sicily and North Africa. Southern Italian cooks like Adelina cure capers from their own land.

Wine Suggestion: A Sicilian red Cerasuolo di Vittoria or
Merlot from Plaretta Vineyard

3 tablespoons salted capers, soaked 10 minutes in cold water and drained, or capers in vinegar, drained
3 large cloves garlic
1 tightly packed tablespoon fresh rosemary leaves
1 tablespoon fruity extra-virgin olive oil

1/8 to 1/4 teaspoon freshly ground black pepper
4 1-inch-thick rib or loin pork chops (if possible, hormone- and antibiotic-free)
Salt
Sicilian Sauce (page 248)

1. One day before cooking, mince together, in a food processor or by hand, the capers, garlic, and rosemary. Blend in the oil and pepper. Coat both sides of the chops, set on a plate, cover, and refrigerate overnight.

2. The next day, grill the chops on a medium-hot (white ashes covering the charcoal) hardwood charcoal fire or grill indoors using a gridded skillet or a 12-inch regular skillet, lightly filmed with oil, set over medium-high heat. Sprinkle the chops with salt and quickly brown on both sides (don't worry if the seasonings fall away on the grill), then push the chops away from the hottest part of the grill, or lower the burner heat to medium-low. Cook about 4 minutes per side, or until the chops are barely firm when pressed and lightly blushed with pink inside (150°F on an instant-read thermometer). Serve hot, with a large spoonful of the Sicilian Sauce on the side.

THE RETURN OF A NATIVE

Adelina Norcia scandalizes the neighbors when she rides her tractor to work her farm in Sicily. She loves to shock them. "A *signora*, an upper-class woman, does not do such things," she explains. "But I have been riding tractors since I was a child on my father's farm."

Today, Adelina and her husband, Alceste, tend old olive trees, grow lemons and oranges and offer lodging on their small guest farm, Il Limoneto, about twenty minutes outside of Siracusa. Il Limoneto, part of Sicily's Agritourism, or guest farm, movement, was carved from the vast estate of Adelina's father, a part of her inheritance. She and Alceste chose to settle here later in life, drawn away from their house in Siracusa. Sicilian landowners and farm-workers have always lived in towns and traveled to the land. Some workers still commute from town to country on donkeys. Walking one morning down the road from Adelina's, I encountered a farmer on a pale gray donkey. He was so jovial, I couldn't resist asking him about riding a donkey to work. He replied, "You can't talk to a car, and hay is cheaper than gas."

I had arrived at Il Limoneto not sure what to expect and fell in love with the place. Guest rooms open onto a patio lined with fruit trees—you can pick your breakfast as you walk around the building to Adelina's patio on the other side of the house for morning coffee.

Her food is vivid and sure. Everything she prepares is from within the reach of her life and heritage—her own taste memories, her garden and the foods of local artisans. Hours float by in the kitchen as we cook together and talk, for she and Alceste love sharing their enthusiasm for this world. They insist on showing me ricotta made the old way by nearby shepherds. And they explain I cannot possibly understand life here without strolling Siracusa's old port at sunset, eating gelato, with Alceste telling me of his growing up there— the history, the local characters, the stories people have always told.

One morning, they introduce me to their olive trees. It's as though I am meeting family members. Adelina explains some are over a thousand years old, saying, "My father said traders from ancient Greece might have planted them." One tree's huge trunk is split, probably from lightning long ago. Wedged between the two contorted sections is a boulder a couple of feet in diameter that has grown up with the split tree to about a foot off the ground. This is Alceste's favorite. He chuckles. "Look at how Sicilians deal with adversity."

Adelina Norcia with her oldest olive tree.

SICILIAN SAUCE
Salsa Siciliana

Makes about 1 cup, serving 4 to 6

Everything in this sauce is taken to its essence. Sweet, tart, pungent—this is the taste of Sicily for me. Sugar isn't merely added, it is caramelized; vinegar boils down to remind you it began life as wine; onion doesn't just sauté, it browns; tomato's natural sweet-tart flavor becomes succulent fruit. Even the herbs are exceptional—rosemary, oregano and basil with orange. Be sure to fully complete each reduction with the vinegar and tomatoes—this is really more of a thick jam than a sauce. Make a double recipe and keep it in the refrigerator for a week or more. Spread it on grilled lamb or tuna, thick slices of grilled onion or portobello mushrooms (see page 54). Daub it on bruschetta (page 34) and make a slice of bread supper.

1 tablespoon extra-virgin olive oil	1/4 teaspoon dried basil
1/2 medium onion, minced	Shredded zest of 1 large orange
A 1 1/2-inch sprig fresh rosemary	1 large clove garlic, minced
Salt and freshly ground black pepper	1/2 cup red wine vinegar
3 tablespoons sugar	1 generous cup drained canned whole
1/8 teaspoon dried oregano	tomatoes

1. In a 10-inch skillet, heat the oil over medium-high heat. Add the onion, rosemary, and a generous sprinkling of salt and pepper. Sauté until the onion begins to color, then add the sugar. Stir with a wooden spatula as sugar melts and bubbles (taking care not to burn), then finally turns pale amber, while the onions remain light-colored.

2. Immediately add the herbs, zest, and garlic. Standing back to avoid splatters, quickly add the vinegar. Stir and boil down until the vinegar is a glaze, coating the onion and barely covering the bottom of the pan. Continue to scrape down the pan's sides, to bring the developing glaze back into the sauce; watch for burning.

3. Stir in the tomatoes, crushing them with your hands as they go into the pan. Boil, scraping down the sides and stirring, until the sauce is almost sizzling in its own juices. It should be a thick jam that mounds on a spoon. Finish seasoning with a few grinds of black pepper, turn out of the pan, and cool. Serve at room temperature or warm. Store covered in the refrigerator.

Sicilian farmer commuting to his orange groves.

NINTH-NIGHT LAMB

Agnello della Nona Sera

Serves 3 to 4; if doubling, use 2 casseroles

Rosalba Ciannamea waited until the ninth and last night of my stay at her Puglia guest farm to serve this lamb casserole. She said the dish was family food, not elegant enough for guests. Her family loved it—it came from her grandmother who, in turn, learned the recipe from her grandmother. She layers chunks of seasoned lamb with thinly sliced new potatoes in a deep terra-cotta baking dish. If you follow Rosalba's counsel—never stir the casserole, and bake it slowly—you will have a fabulous dinner. Everything is steeped in the soft roasted tastes of garlic, tomato, cheese and parsley. The lamb practically melts, and the potatoes get a little crusty as they absorb all those flavors. When several of my friends tasted the lamb, they voted that its sauce and chunks of meat were made for Puglia's orecchiette pasta. Try it and see. Plan on only a salad with the lamb.

➤ *Cook to Cook:* The lamb bakes in about 2¼ hours. It can then be held at room temperature an hour and reheated. The next day, it tastes even better. Puglia cooks stuff the same seasoning blend into slits in a leg of lamb for roasting, baked fish and even pork roast and breast of turkey. Toss it with hot potatoes, cooked green beans or sautéed broccoli. Yellow Finn potatoes, with their tight waxiness and buttery sweetness, are just like the potatoes dug from Il Frantoio's vegetable gardens. Next best are small red-skins, then Yukon Golds.

**Wine Suggestion: A warm, full Puglia red like Salice Salentino by
Leone De Castris, Conti Zecca or Cosimo Taurino**

⅓ tightly packed cup fresh Italian parsley leaves, plus 1 tightly packed tablespoon Italian parsley leaves, coarsely chopped

6 large cloves garlic

4 large canned plum tomatoes, drained

3 generous tablespoons freshly grated Parmigiano-Reggiano cheese

1 3½-pound bone-in lamb blade (shoulder) roast or 3½ pounds lamb chops, trimmed of all fat, boned, and cut into 1-inch chunks, or 1½ pounds trimmed boneless leg of lamb, cut into 1-inch chunks (if possible, hormone- and antibiotic-free)

Salt and freshly ground black pepper

About 2 tablespoons extra-virgin olive oil

8 to 10 (1 pound) small Yellow Finn, red-skinned, or Yukon Gold potatoes, peeled and sliced into ¹⁄₁₆- to ⅛-inch-thick rounds

About ⅓ cup water

1. Preheat the oven to 300°F. Mince together the 1/3 cup parsley, the garlic, and the drained tomatoes. Blend with the cheese. Or if using a food processor, first grate the cheese and turn it into a medium bowl. With the machine running, drop in the garlic, then the parsley, and finally the tomatoes just to coarsely chop them. Immediately turn off the processor and blend everything with the cheese.

2. Toss one third of the mixture with the lamb, adding salt and pepper to taste. Lightly oil a deep 4 1/2- to 5-quart casserole or pot. (I use a 5-quart enameled cast-iron pot or deep terra-cotta casserole.) Spread 1 tablespoon of the minced blend over the bottom of the pot. Cover with half the potatoes, arranged in an overlapping pattern. Sprinkle the potatoes with salt and pepper, another 2 tablespoons of the minced blend, and about 1 teaspoon olive oil. Top with all the meat and another teaspoon of oil. Overlap the rest of the potatoes on the meat and sprinkle with the remaining herb blend and a tablespoon or so of olive oil. Finish with salt and pepper. Pour the water down the side of the casserole.

3. Bake, uncovered, 45 minutes. Tip the casserole and carefully spoon up the pan juices to baste the potatoes. Turn the heat up to 325°F and continue baking another 1 1/2 hours, basting 2 to 3 times, or until the lamb is tender when pierced. Serve hot, or hold at room temperature up to an hour and reheat at 350°F. Sprinkle with the remaining 1 tablespoon parsley just before taking to the table.

SERVING WITH PASTA

The stew makes an outrageously good sauce. The leftover lamb is so fine reheated on its own, and outstanding tossed with orecchiette pasta. Count on about 1/2 pound orecchiette for a full recipe.

THE LAST SHEPHERDS IN PUGLIA

Rosalba Ciannamea's lamb-and-potato dish isn't solely a family specialty, it's typical of lamb dishes eaten by most Pugliese. In country cooking, the table always follows the land, and Puglia is lamb and goat country.

Puglia is about as far south as you can go on the Italian mainland. It forms the heel of Italy's boot, a long narrow region running along the Adriatic Sea into the Mediterranean. The land swells here and there but rarely rises into anything as dramatic as mountains. In the southern half of the region, where Rosalba has her farm, olive groves, supposedly begun by ancient Greek settlers, cover the land. Between them are meadows for grazing, fields of wheat and vegetable gardens. From the central plateau, called the Murge, north to the town of Foggia, the land is given over almost exclusively to grazing and wheat.

In Puglia and Italy's other southern regions, climate and terrain dictate which meats are eaten. Goats and sheep thrive on Puglia's lean grazing and hot climate; cattle do not. Lamb, goat and poultry are the most popular meats in Puglia, followed by pork, horse and finally beef.

Sheep dominated much of northern Puglia's economy. It was only early in this century that the huge annual migration of shepherds and their flocks from the regions of Abruzzo and Molise to the north finally ended. For two thousand years, every fall, sheep- and goat-herders urged their flocks south to winter in Puglia, specifically in the countryside around the town of Foggia. This famous trek was called *la transumanza*. Even though la transumanza is over, if you stop almost anywhere in Puglia near open land and wait long enough, eventually a shepherd with his flock of sheep and goats will come by, as though stepping through a time warp. Herding remains a viable way of making a living in Puglia and the rest of southern Italy. Most shepherds sell meat and lamb's wool along with the cheeses they make.

Some of the Puglia farmers I met worried over the future of the shepherds, with the changes in cheese-making methods dictated by new laws from the European Union. Evidently, they require expensive changes most of the shepherds cannot afford. Some farmers said the cheese would be more sanitary. Most agreed the shepherds wouldn't make much cheese anymore; they'd concentrate on marketing meat instead.

GRILLED LAMB CHOPS WITH ONION AND OREGANO

Cotolette di Agnello Grigliate

Serves 4 to 6

Pureeing onion with lemon zest, oregano, wine, garlic and olive oil creates such a fine marinade for lamb chops, and other meats for that matter. I was served these in a farmhouse restaurant called La Ruota, outside the Puglia town of Martina Franca. Grill the chops in a sauté pan or on a wood-fired grill. In spring, serve them with Sweet Peas "in Their Jackets" (page 282); in winter, with Margherita's Crushed Buttermilk Potatoes (page 291).

Wine Suggestion: A generous Puglia red like Salice Salentino by Cosimo Taurino, Conti Zecca or Leone De Castris

6 large cloves garlic

1 medium onion, coarsely chopped

1/2 cup plus 2 tablespoons extra-virgin olive oil

Shredded zest of 2 large lemons

Juice of 1 large lemon (about 6 tablespoons)

1/2 cup dry white wine

4 teaspoons dried oregano

1/4 teaspoon *each* salt and freshly ground black pepper

8 to 9 1-inch-thick rib or loin lamb chops (if possible, hormone- and antibiotic-free)

1. Allow 1 1/2 to 2 hours for marinating the lamb: In a food processor or blender, combine the garlic, onion, 1/2 cup of the olive oil, the lemon zest, lemon juice, wine, oregano, and salt and pepper. Process until finely chopped. Combine in a bowl or heavy plastic bag and add the lamb chops, turning to coat the meat. Refrigerate 1 1/2 to 2 hours.

2. To cook, drain the chops but do not wipe off the marinade. Heat the remaining 2 tablespoons olive oil in a 12-inch skillet over medium-high heat. Arrange the chops in the skillet so they barely touch. Use 2 skillets if necessary. Brown quickly on both sides. Turn the heat down to medium-low and cook another 2 minutes per side, or until the chops are barely firm when pressed with your finger. They should be blushed with pink inside. Serve the chops on a heated platter. Serve hot.

ON THE GRILL

Burn real hardwood charcoal until gray ash forms. Grill the chops about 3 minutes per side, or until they're just firm when pressed with your finger.

Poultry, Meats and Fish

LAMB IN CHILE-VINEGAR SAUCE

Agnello Arrabbiato

Serves 4 to 6

Shoulder lamb chops, whole cloves of garlic and hot chile in a vinegar sauce—what a dish! Tasting the lamb for the first time in a little Roman restaurant, I thought the trio of chile, garlic and vinegar practically vibrated off the plate. I discovered that the lamb comes from the hill-country farms between Rome and Naples, where kid is cooked this way too. Evidently cooks there know that pungent seasonings and fearless browning make anything taste good. Enjoy the lamb with a rough country bread for sopping up the sauce and a few boiled new potatoes.

➤ *Cook to Cook:* Italy's stinging little peperoncini chiles can be replaced with Mexico's velvety dried ancho chiles, available in our supermarkets.

The lamb holds well at room temperature up to a half an hour. Or braise it a day ahead, undercooking the meat slightly. Refrigerate and then reheat gently, adding a little water if needed. Stir in the peas while reheating.

Wine Suggestion: A simple red not deeply offended
by the sauce's vinegar, like a Tuscan Monte Antico

Extra-virgin olive oil
2¹/₂ pounds bone-in shoulder or blade
    lamb or kid chops (6 chops) (if
    possible, hormone- and antibiotic-
    free), trimmed of excess fat
Salt and freshly ground black pepper
12 large cloves garlic, peeled, but not
    chopped

³/₄ cup dry red wine
1 dried ancho chile with seeds (seeded
    for milder flavor)
¹/₂ teaspoon dried oregano
³/₄ cup red wine vinegar
³/₄ cup water
1¹/₂ cups shelled fresh sweet peas or
    frozen tiny sweet peas, unthawed

1. Film the bottom of a 12-inch sauté pan (not nonstick) with oil and heat over medium-high heat. Season the chops with salt and a generous amount of black pepper. Brown to crusty on both sides, adjusting the heat as necessary to protect the glaze on the bottom of the pan from burning, about 10 minutes total. Off the heat, spoon away almost all the fat from the pan.

2. Return the pan to the heat, adding the garlic cloves and wine, and cook over medium-low heat, 10 minutes at a slow bubble, uncovered, until the wine has almost

cooked away. Stir in the chile, oregano, and vinegar and simmer the same way, turning the meat occasionally, until the vinegar is syrupy and barely coats the bottom of the pan.

3. Blend in the water, cover, and simmer gently 30 to 45 minutes, tasting a small piece of meat for tenderness after 30 minutes. Stir in a little more water if the pan gets dry. Add fresh peas during the last 8 minutes of cooking and finish uncovered, stir in frozen peas at the end of cooking just to heat through. Overlap the chops on a warm platter, spooning the sauce and peas over them. Serve hot.

A Sicilian shepherd tending his charge.

Poultry, Meats and Fish

LEG OF LAMB GLAZED WITH BALSAMIC AND RED WINE

Cosciotto d'Agnello Arrosto con Aceto Balsamico

Serves 6 to 8

Roasting a whole leg of lamb on a bed of rosemary branches, onion rings and black olives creates an opulent pan sauce, especially when the meat is basted with balsamic vinegar and red wine. This is a leg of lamb for parties and Easter Sunday. Farmhouse celebrations in balsamic vinegar country—the provinces of Reggio and Modena—inspired the recipe. If you have time, season the lamb the night before roasting. Plan, too, for leftovers so you can have the warm lamb and garlicky greens sandwiches described after the recipe.

Wine Suggestion: A full-bodied red Barbera d'Asti or Dolcetto d'Alba

¹/₃ tightly packed cup fresh basil leaves
2 thick slices (2 ounces) lean pancetta
Leaves from a 4-inch branch fresh rosemary, plus 6 whole 6-inch branches fresh rosemary
6 large cloves garlic
1 tablespoon extra-virgin olive oil
1 teaspoon dried basil
¹/₄ teaspoon salt
Generous ¹/₈ teaspoon freshly ground black pepper

¹/₂ cup good-quality commercial balsamic vinegar
1 5- to 7-pound bone-in leg of lamb (if possible, hormone- and antibiotic-free), trimmed of all surface fat
2 medium red onions, cut into 1-inch dice
¹/₃ cup herbed Sicilian black olives or Kalamata olives
2 cups dry red wine
¹/₂ cup water

1. If possible, season the lamb a day ahead and refrigerate it overnight. Mince together the fresh basil, pancetta, the rosemary leaves, and the garlic. Blend in the oil, dried basil, salt, pepper, and 2 tablespoons of the balsamic. Make about 20 deep wide slits all over the lamb and stuff with all but 3 tablespoons of the mixture. Rub the rest over the meat. Lightly cover and refrigerate overnight.

2. Preheat the oven to 350°F. Spread the onions, rosemary branches, and olives in a shallow roasting pan (a half-sheet pan is ideal). Set the lamb on them. Roast 20 minutes. Pour ¹/₄ cup of the balsamic and 1 cup of the wine over the meat. Roast

1 hour, basting often. Add another $1/2$ cup wine. Roast 20 minutes, or until meat reaches 130°F on an instant-read thermometer for medium-rare.

3. Transfer the lamb to an ovenproof platter. Keep warm in the turned-off oven, leaving the door open. Set the roasting pan over two burners. Stir in the remaining 2 tablespoons balsamic. Boil and stir until thick and syrupy. Add the remaining $1/2$ cup wine and boil down by two thirds, then stir in the water. Simmer and stir until the sauce is rich-tasting, about 2 minutes. Discard the rosemary. Keep the sauce warm.

4. Thinly slice the lamb, arranging the pieces around the leg, and moisten with the pan sauce, onions, and olives. Serve hot.

THE LEFTOVERS

Next-Day Open-Faced Supper Sandwiches: Wrap the leftover sliced and sauced lamb in foil. Warm in a 350°F oven. Meanwhile rub slices of store-bought or home-made country bread with garlic. Heat them on a sheet of foil in the oven too.

For 4 people, have about 3 cups mixed organic salad greens, a handful of thinly sliced red onion rings, and some olive oil and vinegar. Mix $1/2$ cup shredded young sheep cheese or Fontinella with $1/2$ cup sour cream.

To serve, toss the greens and onion with a little oil, vinegar, and salt and pepper. Spread half the warm bread slices with the cheese/sour cream mixture. Arrange the warm lamb on these slices. Top with the greens and onion rings. Top with rest of bread and secure with toothpicks.

HOME-STYLE OSSO BUCO

Osso Buco Casereccio

Serves 4 to 6

Rovato is a meat town with the pedigree to prove it. Weekly, since at least the 1500s, this town of Lombardy's plain at the foot of the Italian Alps hosts one of Italy's oldest cattle markets. A chat with a Rovato butcher quickly included comments from the neighborhood women shopping for lunch and the recipe for this local dish of veal shanks. All the goodness of slowly browned meat, wild mushrooms and a pan sauce that invites wiping the plate with chunks of crusty bread comes together in these braised veal shanks. Like most braised meats, the veal gets better with a day's rest after cooking. Blend in the peas and mushrooms when reheating. If small fresh fava beans are available, the women always use them instead of peas.

➤ *Cook to Cook:* If you can find young fresh fava beans, use 1¹/₂ pounds; shell and parboil them in salted water for 1 minute. Slip off their skins and add the favas with the mushrooms.

When selecting mushrooms for this recipe, try portobello, oyster, morel, chanterelle, fresh porcini, and or black trumpets. Avoid Asian mushrooms like the shiitake, enoki, tree fungus, cloud's ear, and Chinese varieties. Their flavors throw off the dish's character.

Wine Suggestion: A red Sfursat from the Valtellina or a Marcarini-Cogno Barolo

¹/₂ ounce (¹/₂ cup) dried porcini mushrooms
Water
Extra-virgin olive oil
¹/₂ to ³/₄ pound mixed fresh mushrooms (see Cook to Cook), cleaned and sliced ¹/₂ inch thick
Salt and freshly ground black pepper
5 to 6 meaty veal shanks (about 4 pounds) (if possible, hormone- and antibiotic-free), cut 1 to 1¹/₄ inch thick, with at least 1 inch of meat surrounding the bone

4 large fresh sage leaves
A 3-inch sprig fresh rosemary
¹/₄ medium onion, minced
1 salted anchovy, rinsed and boned, or 2 oil-packed anchovy fillets, rinsed (see Cook to Cook, page 50)
1 cup dry white wine
1 cup Mother's Broth (page 196) or canned low-sodium chicken broth
¹/₂ pound sugar snap peas, trimmed

1. Rinse the porcini by dropping them into a bowl of cold water, swishing them around, and immediately lifting them out. Repeat three times, loosening the grit with your fingers. Soak 20 minutes in 1 cup hot water.

2. Lift out the mushrooms, reserving the liquid, and coarsely chop. Have handy a strainer lined with a paper towel.

3. Film the bottom of a 12-inch skillet with olive oil and heat over high heat. Quickly brown the fresh mushrooms, seasoning with salt and pepper. Remove from the pan and set aside. Wipe out the pan. Film it again with oil and heat over medium heat. Leisurely brown the veal on all sides, with the herbs and a sprinkling of salt and pepper, about 15 minutes. Add the onion and chopped porcini halfway through the cooking time.

4. Once the meat is browned, stir in the anchovy and $1/2$ cup of the wine, scraping up the brown glaze on the bottom of the pan. Simmer, uncovered, until the pan is almost dry. Strain the mushroom liquid over the meat and add the rest of the wine. Simmer down by two thirds. Blend in the broth, bring to a slow bubble, cover, and cook about $1^{1}/4$ hours, or until the veal is tender. Add water as needed.

5. Stir in the peas and simmer, uncovered, about 10 minutes, or until tender. Gently fold in the mushrooms to heat through. Serve in a warmed shallow serving bowl.

Farm women in a mountain village above Rovato.

LUCCHESE VEAL CHOPS
Cotolette di Vitello alla Lucchese

Serves 4

A little fresh lemon, peppery Tuscan olive oil and coarse salt transform grilled veal chops. All you need to do is grill the chops and finish their seasoning at the table with lemon and oil. As you cut into the chop, its juices, the lemon juice and the olive oil blend into a sauce on the plate.

These chops were grilling over a wood fire on my first night at my cousins Edda and Alcide's farm near Lucca, a Tuscan province and town about forty miles west of Florence. Mistaking the oversized veal chops for beef, I innocently asked if they were the famous Florentine steaks (Bistecca Fiorentina). Unaware then of Italians' sense of local identity, I didn't realize the depth of my misstep. Alcide patiently explained that their food had nothing to do with Florence. This was Lucca cooking. Besides, he was sure Florentines didn't have the good sense to season their meat with lemon and oil.

**Wine Suggestion: A fine-boned Chianti by Fontodi,
La Massa or Fattoria di Felsina**

4 1-inch-thick loin veal chops (about 2 pounds) (if possible, hormone- and antibiotic-free)	Freshly ground black pepper
	Extra-virgin olive oil (preferably a peppery Tuscan oil)
Coarse sea salt (if possible)	1 large lemon, cut into 4 wedges

1. Cook the chops over a hot hardwood charcoal fire or in a gridded pan or a large skillet set over high heat. Sprinkle the chops on both sides with coarse salt and pepper. Grill 1 minute on each side, or pour a sheer film of oil into the pan and cook 1 minute per side.

2. Move the chops to a cooler part of the grill, or turn the stove heat down to medium-low. Turn the chops 2 or 3 times as you cook another 5 minutes, or until the meat has just a little give when you press it. Immediately remove to a serving platter or dinner plates. Drizzle each chop with 1/2 to 2 teaspoons olive oil. Squeeze just enough lemon over each to moisten its surface. Eat hot.

At my cousins' in Tuscany, the olive oil and lemon is on the table and every one dresses his or her own chops. In America, we are shyer about seasoning with olive oil, so I like to do it for friends.

QUEEN OF THE HERD

Italy's only outdoor museum of country life is the Folklife Museum of Dietenheim (Il Museo Etnografico di Dietenheim) north of the city of Brunico, near Italy's border with Austria. In this region, the Alto Adige, farmwomen still wear traditional shirred dirndl skirts covered with an apron, men wear the knee britches called lederhosen and their cows still wear bells with ornately worked collars just like the ones I saw in the museum. Farming couples received these as wedding gifts. On special occasions, the queen of the herd wears the bell, part of the tradition of the *malga*, or cowherd's hut, which was, and still is in some places, an important element of mountain life.

Every spring, village farmers entrust cowherds with their dairy cattle. These men and their families drive the herds to high mountain meadows for grazing all summer. Malgas are the log huts they live and work in.

The museum's director, Professor Hans Griefsmair, grew up in a malga; his father was a cowherd. He told me that every morning, his father and brothers milked the cows, then the children herded them out to pasture and watched them all day while playing and exploring. Finally they drove them back to their stalls for the evening milking. His mother churned the butter and his father made the cheese. The cowherd's prime responsibility, after protecting cows from illness and wild animals, was keeping track of the production from each farmer's cattle. Not an easy task, since farmers loved to dispute what came down from the mountain each autumn.

By early October, it was time for the trip down the mountains with the cows carrying barrels of butter and cheese from the summer's milking. Before their descent, the cowherds chose the queen of the herd. She might be the best milker, or the herd's natural leader. She was impossible to miss. She wore the wedding gift bell. Laced through her horns were garlands of meadow flowers, and on her forehead, a medallion of a local saint. Villagers always had a welcome festival waiting at the bottom of the mountain to celebrate the cows' safe return.

Malga Sonen.

TYROLEAN POT ROAST

Brasato di Manzo

Serves 4 to 6

Spicing pot roast with cumin, coriander, fennel and bay is something I learned in the Italian Tyrol from a cook named Margherita. Like most Italian braised meats, this roast cooks with red wine and vegetables. Its spicing sets it apart. I came upon the dish close to Italy's border with Austria, in the Alto Adige region. I ate it at a *malga*, an institution in this part of Italy. The Alto Adige is like walking onto the set of *The Sound of Music*. The malga is a beloved part of local life and folklore. Malgas are cowherds' huts in the high mountains. Each summer, a cowherd takes the village's cows to graze up in high pastures. He and his family live in the hut, tending the animals and making butter and cheese. Through the years, malgas have also become stopping places for hikers and skiers, serving food and giving shelter. Most of them are reached only on foot.

Margherita's husband is a cowherd. Their log cowherd hut, called Malga Sonen, sits on a high plateau above the village of Castelrotto. Although Margherita cooks the same dishes as everyone else in the area, her food simply tastes better. She insists the difference in her pot roast is marinating the meat overnight in wine, spices and what locals call the "bread herb." This single herb flavors Castelrotto's breads and it tastes like a blend of fennel, celery seed, calamint and tarragon, most of which I've used in this recipe. Make Margherita's pot roast on winter weekends. Margherita serves Buttermilk Potatoes (page 291) with the roast; I sometimes have polenta (page 172) instead.

Wine Suggestion: A Trentino–Alto Adige region red like Alois Lageder's Cabernet Sauvignon, San Leonardo Marchese Carlo Guerrierin Gonzaga or Il Poggione Brunello di Montalcino

MARINADE AND BEEF

1 medium onion

1 medium carrot

1 medium celery stalk with leaves

1/2 teaspoon *each* coriander seeds, cumin seeds, and fennel seeds

1/8 teaspoon celery seeds

2 whole cloves

1 tightly packed tablespoon fresh tarragon leaves, minced, or 1 teaspoon dried tarragon

2 large bay leaves

2 large cloves garlic, coarsely chopped

2 1/2 cups dry red wine

1/4 cup extra-virgin olive oil

1 3- to 3½-pound boneless beef chuck
   roast (about 2 inches thick) (if
   possible, hormone- and antibiotic-
   free), trimmed of excess fat

BRAISING

1½ cups Mother's Broth (page 196) or
   canned low-sodium chicken broth

1 tablespoon tomato paste
4 whole canned tomatoes, drained and
   crushed
2 tablespoons red wine vinegar
Salt and freshly ground black pepper

1. If you have time, marinate the meat overnight. Mince together the onion, carrot, and celery. Set two thirds aside for the braising liquid. Grind the coriander,
cumin, fennel seeds, celery seeds, and cloves in a mortar or coffee grinder. In a bowl
or heavy plastic bag, blend the spices with the remaining minced vegetables, tarragon,
bay leaves, garlic, 1 cup of the wine, and 2 tablespoons of the oil. With cotton string,
tie the beef into a compact bundle. Poke it 10 times with a knife and add it to the
marinade. Refrigerate until ready to cook, preferably overnight.

2. When ready to cook, remove the meat from the marinade and pat it dry. Strain
the marinade, reserving the liquid and solid ingredients separately. Heat the remaining 2 tablespoons oil in a 12-inch skillet over medium-high heat. Brown the meat
until crusty on all sides, about 15 minutes. Place in a deep heavy 5-quart pot.

3. Pour off all but a tablespoon of the fat from the skillet. Add the reserved
minced vegetables and the strained marinade ingredients. Sauté until golden, taking
care not to burn the brown glaze on the pan's bottom.

4. Add ½ cup of the remaining wine and simmer, scraping up the glaze from the
bottom of the pan, until it has evaporated. Blend in ½ cup of the broth and the
tomato paste. Simmer down to nothing. Turn into the casserole and stir in the remaining 1 cup each wine and stock, the marinade liquid, tomatoes, and vinegar. Add
enough water to cover the meat completely.

5. Bring to a gentle simmer, cover, and cook 2 hours, or until the meat is tender
but not falling apart. Check the meat occasionally for sticking, adding enough water
to barely cover if necessary. Taste the cooking liquid for seasoning. Remove from the
heat and cool 1 hour, then cover and refrigerate overnight.

6. To serve, reheat the roast and sauce gently over medium heat until the meat is
heated through. Remove the meat to a platter and keep warm. Skim all the fat from
the sauce. Boil the sauce down until deeply flavored. Puree in a blender or food
processor just until slightly chunky. Taste for seasoning. Thinly slice the beef and present napped with the sauce.

TROUT MARINATED WITH SWEET ONIONS

Trota Marinata

Serves 4 to 6; doubles easily

This is old-time home cooking from a part of Tuscany I find irresistible—the mountains and valleys of the Garfagnana. Sautéed trout marinates with masses of red onion rings, in a sweet-tart vinegar sauce. The fish is eaten at room temperature, and it must be made about a half hour ahead, so there's no last-minute fiddling with the tricky business of cooking fish just right. You'll discover how vinegar actually sweetens sautéed onions when it's cooked down with them, leaving only a quiet, tart edge to the sauce.

For us, this recipe is a new way of cooking fish, but it uses an ancient method of preserving fish still found every day in much of Italy, and especially identified with the Veneto, where it's called *pesce in saor* (fish in sour sauce or vinegar). Fried fish, along with red onions, marinates in vinegar until almost pickled. Refrigeration is not used. The fish is set out in bowls in wine bars, sold ready-made in marketplaces and eaten as a snack, quick lunch or main dish.

➤ *Cook to Cook:* Cooking ahead is essential to this dish, adding to its appeal for entertaining. Be sure to cook the onions as fast as possible to retain their crispness. They're so good you'll want more to pile on bruschetta (page 34), or for tossing with fennel in a salad.

Wine Suggestion: A white Marchesi de Frescobaldi Pomino Bianco

4 large cloves garlic, thinly sliced
10 large fresh sage leaves
4 4-inch sprigs fresh rosemary, broken in half
10 fresh Italian parsley leaves plus a few extra for garnish
Extra-virgin olive oil
3 to 4 medium red onions, sliced into thin rings

Salt and freshly ground black pepper
$1/2$ cup plus 2 tablespoons red wine vinegar
1 pound trout, Arctic char, or sea trout fillets or 4 whole boned trout (about 8 ounces each)

1. Set aside about one eighth of the garlic, 3 of the sage leaves, half the rosemary branches, and about 3 of the parsley leaves. Lightly film a 12-inch skillet with olive oil and heat over high heat. Sauté the onions and the remaining garlic and herbs

1 minute, seasoning with salt and pepper. Stir in ¹/₂ cup of the vinegar. Cook over low heat 2 to 3 minutes, or until the onions have absorbed all but 2 to 3 tablespoons of the vinegar but are still somewhat crisp. Spread the contents of the pan on a platter and cool. Wash and dry the skillet.

2. With tweezers, remove any bones from the fillets if using. Cut them each into 2 or 3 large pieces. Leave whole fish whole. Dust the fish with salt and pepper. Film the skillet with oil and heat over medium-high heat. Sauté the fish with the reserved herbs to pale gold and cooked through, about 30 seconds to 1 minute per side for thin pieces of fillet, 3 minutes per side for thicker ones. Turn the fish with two spatulas to prevent them from breaking. The fish should be firm and opaque at the center, but not flaking.

3. Spread half the onions over the bottom of a shallow dish. Top with the fish. Spoon any onion pan juices over the fish, then sprinkle with the remaining 2 tablespoons vinegar and cover with the remaining onions. Season to taste.

4. Hold the fish at cool room temperature 30 minutes, then serve. You could scatter the dish with several fresh parsley leaves.

A FISH STORY

Fish stories and tall tales know no ethnic boundaries. Enzo Pedreschi grew up on the banks of the Garfagnana's Serchio River to become his village's bread baker. When Enzo saw the mill on the river that ground his flour go to ruin because it was cheaper for people to buy mass-produced flour, he bought the mill and created Mulin Rancone, a restaurant and inn. Over a plate of trout with onions, on a terrace above the river, Enzo told this story:

Long ago, when Florence ruled the Garfagnana, the city demanded impossibly high taxes from the area's farmers. Although it was a poor region, trout grew fat in the Garfagnana's streams and Serchio River. Lacking tax money, farmers fried and pickled trout (just as Enzo's wife did for our lunch). The farmers packed the trout in barrels, and shipped them down to Florence, where the fish were sold off for taxes. But how the fish were caught was the best part. Several times a year, the Serchio floods its narrow valley. Farmers along the river enclosed their small fields with stone walls, which remain there today. Rushing floods filled the field with water and trout. When the water receded, farmers gathered up baskets of trout, ready for pickling and paying taxes.

ADRIATIC GRILLED SHRIMP

Gamberetti dell'Adriatico

Serves 4 to 5

Big plump shrimp are rolled in chopped bits of garlic, parsley and sun-dried tomato, then pan-grilled. On festival and market days, in food stands lining the wharfs of fishing villages along the Adriatic, shrimp prepared this way sizzle on hot iron griddles over wood fires.

Years ago, a fisherman's wife told me she made her shrimp plumper and juicier by soaking them in seawater—her version of brining. Soaking in salted water does the same thing. You could skip the first step of this recipe, but I urge you not to. It takes only twenty minutes—enough time to gather and prepare the other ingredients—and the shrimp really taste better.

Wine Suggestion: A full, crisp Anselmi Soave Capitel Foscarino

1½ pounds jumbo shrimp (8 to 10 per pound), shelled and deveined, with tails left intact

2 tablespoons salt, plus more to taste

4 cups ice water

3 to 4 sun-dried tomatoes (not packed in oil), plumped 10 minutes in hot water and drained

3 large cloves garlic

3 tightly packed tablespoons fresh Italian parsley leaves

⅛ teaspoon hot red pepper flakes

3 tablespoons extra-virgin olive oil

Freshly ground black pepper

1 large lemon, cut into 8 wedges

1. In a bowl, combine the shrimp with the 2 tablespoons salt and the ice water. Refrigerate 20 minutes, but no more. Meanwhile, mince together the tomatoes, garlic, and parsley. Turn into a medium bowl and stir in the hot pepper and 2 tablespoons of the olive oil.

2. Drain, rinse, and pat the shrimp dry. Toss them with the tomato mixture. Keep cold.

3. Film a large skillet or griddle with the remaining 1 tablespoon olive oil and heat over medium heat. Sauté the shrimp, sprinkling with salt and pepper, about 2 to 3 minutes per side, or until pink and just firm. Pile all the seasonings atop the shrimp after you turn them.

4. Turn the shrimp onto a serving platter, along with the seasonings. Serve hot or warm, with the lemon wedges. Squeeze a little lemon over the shrimp just before eating.

SWEET-AND-SOUR SEARED TUNA

Tonno in Agrodolce

Serves 3 to 4

How Sicilians love playing off sweet and tart ingredients with mint! You can taste it all in the lightly caramelized glaze for this tuna. Tuna is the beefsteak of the sea; it stands up to the boldest flavorings. Brown tuna steaks with onion and a little chile, then pick up the brown bits from the pan by swirling in vinegar and sugar and caramelizing them. Pull back their punch just a bit with a little fresh mint, and coat the tuna steaks with this glaze. In Erice, the ancient village that sits atop a cliff on Sicily's northwest coast, they make the dish with swordfish. Overfishing is threatening swordfish supplies. The tuna is no compromise here—I think it's an even better match for the sauce.

Wine Suggestion: A lush red Tuscan Syrah

1 to 2 tablespoons extra-virgin olive oil
1 pound fresh tuna steaks, cut 1 inch thick
1/2 medium red onion, cut into thin slivers

Salt and freshly ground black pepper
Generous pinch of hot red pepper flakes
1 teaspoon sugar
2 tablespoons red wine vinegar
10 fresh mint leaves, coarsely chopped

1. Film the bottom of a 10-inch nonstick skillet with olive oil. Heat over medium-high heat. Cut the tuna into 3 or 4 portions. Sauté the fish with the onion, seasoning with salt and black pepper and the hot red pepper, to light golden brown on both sides.

2. Reduce the heat to medium low. Cover and cook about 8 minutes, until the fish is barely firm when pressed, turning once. Remove the tuna to a warmed platter and keep warm.

3. Set the pan over high heat. Swirl in half the sugar and half the vinegar. Stir about 30 seconds, scraping up the browned bits from the bottom of the pan. When the liquid is syrupy, blend in the rest of the sugar and vinegar and simmer a few seconds. Don't let much of the liquid evaporate. Taste for sweet/tart balance and depth, adding more sugar or vinegar if needed. Simmer another few seconds if necessary. Add the mint and immediately scrape the sauce over the tuna. Serve hot.

CALAMARI MIXED GRILL

Calamari alla Griglia

Serves 3 to 4

These garlicky squid tossed over a hot fire with chiles, peppers and onions cook in seconds. The first time I tasted Calamari Mixed Grill, two teenagers were flipping the squid the way their American counterparts flip burgers at a fast-food joint. They worked at a battered wood-fired grill set up on the sand a few feet from the Adriatic. It stood just outside the family snack stand on Puglia's seashore below San Foca.

On a tiny counter, the boys' mother chopped seasonings—yellow peppers, scarlet chiles, green parsley and purple onion—talking all the while, telling me how much easier it was to cook squid than fish for it. Her fisherman husband had found cooking and selling the catch made a better living with less risk. "Now I don't wring my hands with every storm," she said. "By next year we'll have enough to open a real restaurant."

➤ *Cook to Cook:* Squid cooks to silky and tender in 20 seconds and is such delicate eating. Please set aside any squeamishness about it. Squid is the least "fishy" of seafood and welcomes so many different seasonings. The jalapeños, Hungarian peppers and serranos called for here have the gutsiness and citrus taste of Puglia's chiles.

Wine Suggestion: A fruity Puglia rosé like Rosata del Salento or Rosa del Golfo

1 pound cleaned small squid with tentacles

1 medium-hot fresh chile (such as red or green jalapeño, small Hungarian, or serrano), seeded

5 large cloves garlic

1/4 tightly packed cup fresh Italian parsley leaves

3 tablespoons extra-virgin olive oil

1 medium red onion, cut into 6 wedges

1 large sweet yellow pepper, cored, seeded, and cut into 1-inch-wide strips

Salt and freshly ground black pepper

2 medium lemons, cut into wedges

1. Trim the squid tentacles into 1-inch pieces. Split the squid bodies lengthwise in half and open up like a book. Lightly score the inside of each body with a cross-hatch pattern.

2. Mince together the chile, garlic, and parsley and turn into a medium bowl. Blend in the olive oil. Transfer half the chile mixture to another medium bowl. Toss the

squid with it, cover, and refrigerate 1 hour. Add the onion and yellow pepper to the remaining chile blend. Cover and refrigerate it too.

3. Cook the squid on a griddle over a hardwood charcoal–fired outdoor grill or on the stovetop using a griddle, skillet, or large sauté pan. Before cooking, have everything at hand, including a serving platter. Heat the grill until the coals are covered in white ash, or heat the griddle, skillet, or sauté pan over high heat. Spread the tentacles and squid bodies, with any seasonings clinging to them, cut side down on the grill or in the pan. Cook 10 seconds, sprinkling with salt and pepper. With a spatula, turn and cook another 10 seconds. Immediately remove the squid and its seasonings to a serving platter, squeezing 2 to 3 lemon wedges over it.

4. Reduce the heat to medium and sear the onion and pepper mixture 3 to 5 minutes, or until tender-crisp. Taste for seasoning and arrange with the squid. Serve hot or warm, with the remaining lemon wedges.

CLASSIC POACHED FISH

Pesce in Bianco

Serves 3 to 4; doubles easily

Taste fish the way Italians love it, simply poached and served warm with a little good olive oil and fresh lemon. Its secret is in careful attention to the quality of each element. Buy the freshest fish, then drizzle with olive oil you want to eat from a spoon. Squeeze fresh lemon over the fish and dust with salt and pepper. Dining on poached fish in Italy is to eat "white" or "*in bianco*" (see page 271), an expression with a subtext all its own.

➤ *Cook to Cook:* Fresh fish looks alive; it shines. Fillets and steaks are moist and tight-grained, smelling of the sea (never "fishy"), and they spring back when poked. With whole fish, look for clear, rounded eyes and bright red gills. Vital here, too, is an olive oil that tastes plump with fruit, nuts and perhaps a grace note of bitterness. It could be a peppery Tuscan oil, a fruity Umbrian one or the soft, flowery oil from Liguria. Ideally the oil should be less than a year old. Older is not better in olive oil. See page 389 for specific suggestions.

Wine Suggestion: A rich Friuli white like Vinnaioli Jermann Vintage Tunina

4 cloves garlic, crushed
8 branches fresh Italian parsley, plus additional for garnish
1 teaspoon salt, plus more to taste
Freshly ground black pepper
Water
1 to 1½ pounds firm-fleshed fish fillets or thick-cut steaks (sea bass, cod, sea trout, salmon, trout, char, haddock, halibut, or bluefish) or 2 to 3 pounds whole fish
2 medium lemons, cut into wedges
Extra-virgin olive oil

1. In a 12-inch skillet or sauté pan, combine the garlic, parsley, 1 teaspoon salt, and pepper to taste in water about 2½ inches deep. Bring to a simmer, cover, and cook 5 minutes. Measure the fish for thickness (cooking time depends on thickness).

2. Slip the fish into the water, adjusting the heat so the water shudders but doesn't bubble. Cook 8 to 10 minutes to the inch, or until all but the very center of each piece of fish is opaque. Check by making a small slit in the thickest part of the fish. As each piece is done, use a slotted spatula to lift it onto a heated platter.

3. Garnish the fish with the lemon wedges and parsley branches, and serve immediately. At the table, invite everyone to season the fish with salt, drizzles of olive oil, and freshly squeezed lemon.

EATING WHITE

Eating white," *mangiare in bianco,* in Italy means a diet of bland foods without color to treat an afflicted liver (*male di fegato*) and almost every other illness, real or imagined. Italian livers seem to take an awful beating. Ask a dejected-looking Italian friend what's wrong and the reply is a cold, flu or whatever, plus ". . . Ah, but I have a little liver trouble too." I grew up in an extended Italian family of unhappy livers, especially those of my grandmother's generation. There was real pride in being old enough to complain about your liver. Claiming your need to "eat white" was high art. The statement had to hint at noble suffering without complaint, but never quite reach the martyr state.

While lunching in the Piedmont, arrogant waiters turned into Florence Nightingales when my host, an elderly agricultural minister recovering from surgery, pushed aside the menu, stating courageously, "I cannot eat any of that, I have liver trouble (not surgery trouble!) and must eat white." The parade began. First, a flan of pale vegetables baked in a blend of eggs and cream, then hot broth with Parmigiano, followed by pasta tossed in cream, mushrooms, butter and cheese. Finally, poached fish and steamed potatoes with lemon and olive oil and a vegetable mayonnaise salad. Dessert was denial itself—a pear poached in white wine, with a little custard. My host was restored.

VEGETABLES AND SALADS

In Italian country homes, the vegetables on your plate immediately tell you what time of year it is. Eating with the seasons is the foundation of country cooking. For Italians who make their living from the land, this means living on what the land gives. And new choices are always at hand. For example, just when everyone is tired of early spring's wild greens and fava beans, the first carrots and potatoes are ready for cooking with herbs and wine. A platter of roasted eggplant, green beans, peppers and tomatoes seems to freeze for a moment summer's inevitable passing into autumn. The almost-brash tastes of summer are just going beyond their peak. Roasting is like stop action in a film; it focuses on their boldness.

Each season has its foods to celebrate. We Americans know the glories of spring, summer and fall, but winter is the stepchild, the underestimated season. Italian farmers know differently. Only December's cold brings radicchio to full flavor. Each December, the Veneto region's city of Treviso becomes the radicchio capital of all Italy. People feast on the four different types of red radicchio as though they'll disappear from the earth in the next minute. Anywhere in Italy, you can sit down at a farmhouse table for dinner before the fire and taste how winter potatoes, the entire cabbage family, squashes, fulsome greens and onions all flourish in the cold. Dishes like Roasted Red Onion Wedges, Melting Tuscan Kale and wine-glazed Lake Garda Potatoes show just how we should never underestimate winter.

Most of us don't live from the land, and eating with the seasons can be a puzzle. It is said our food supply is seasonless, but look closely the next time you shop. The story of the seasons is laid out for us. What is local and in season usually costs less (and tastes better) than out-of-season produce shipped in from other climates. Colors tell everything. Notice which colors dominate displays—winter's colors are in the dark-toned leafy greens with accents of orange squashes, brown potatoes, purple cabbages, golden onions and pale fennel. Spring is a haze of soft shades and more green, but rarely any of winter's dark tones. Think bright green pea pods, dandelion greens, new lettuces and the splash of little orange carrots. Summer is a brass band of primary colors—reds, yellows, greens and purples—nothing halfway here. Autumn colors we all know—golds, russet reds, browns and greens darkening to inky tones or silvery ones. If you reach for these color families, you'll eat with the seasons.

I've purposely collected dishes here that blend the familiar with the new—peppers and onions with an interesting twist, a vegetable ragù that is a garden in a pot and a new way with green beans that calls for only three ingredients—the beans, water and salt. These are the vegetables country home cooks make all through the year. Simplicity is always their underlying theme. Let the vegetables taste, don't drown them in embellishments—this was the advice I got over and over again from all the people I learned from. Even one of my all-time favorites—the positively lavish potato *gattó* from near Naples—is pure potato poetry. This sort of mashed potato lasagne has peas and salami folded into the potatoes. It's baked in a casserole with a stuffing of mozzarella. Where another vegetable could be overwhelmed by all these tastes, the potato embraces them.

Ingredients are everything in these dishes. Use the freshest, best-tasting produce you can get your hands on. For me, that always means organic. Although I've not specified "organic" in the vegetable ingredient lists, I urge you to seek out organic vegetables. I am lucky to live in a part of the country where locally raised organic produce is easy to find. I know that's not true everywhere. But foods grown without artificial pesticides and fertilizers come closer in flavor and spirit to the best vegetables I've had in Italy. In talking with farmers there and here, I discovered that to grow fine vegetables organically, the soil must be rich and nurturing. Good soil produces good-tasting vegetables. Organic farming is growing in Italy. Farmers are looking back to how their grandfathers farmed, before chemicals, while discovering new technology to make those growing methods more effective. The great news there and in America is that many of our organic farmers are reintroducing heirloom varieties of vegetables that were prized for their good taste but fell out of favor because they didn't hold up in long-distance shipping. We can find so much more now in our shops and farmers' markets. Yes, fresh vegetables can be as delicious here as they are in Italy.

SIMPLEST-OF-ALL GREEN BEANS

Fagiolini Semplici

Serves 4 to 6

These are the beans I ate one September—night after night on my cousin's farm in Tuscany—beans so good you will want to eat them with your fingers, one by one. I never tired of them. Salt, pepper and olive oil were always on the table to dress the beans. To taste their full sweetness, cook the beans a few moments beyond the tender-crisp stage we've become accustomed to. Salting the water and salting the beans while they're still hot are essential for opening up their flavors. Good olive oil, tasting of fruit and nuts, makes a lovely finish, but the beans are superb without it too. On our family table in Tuscany, they're served at room temperature. I've come to like them this way.

➤ **Cook to Cook:** Of course, the beans must be good to begin with, and garden-fresh are best. But this recipe works with the sturdier beans of winter. When buying green beans, check for freshness by breaking one in half. It should snap and taste flavorful, with a hint of sweetness. Don't buy beans that are dull and flat-tasting, wilted, puckery or limp.

Serve these beans with almost anything. They freshen mellow roasted or braised dishes, foil hot and spicy ones, tone down tart ones and are just right with grilled fish or meat.

3 tablespoons salt, plus more to taste	Freshly ground black pepper
3 quarts boiling water	Fruity extra-virgin olive oil (optional)
1¼ to 1½ pounds green beans, trimmed	

1. Add the 3 tablespoons salt to the boiling water. Taste for appealing saltiness. Drop in the beans and boil uncovered 5 to 10 minutes, until tender but with no hint of mushiness. Timing varies greatly according to the age, size, and freshness of the beans. Taste for doneness and trust your judgment, not the clock. Drain immediately in a colander and turn into a bowl. Most important is to season the hot beans right away with salt and pepper. Then taste again, adding more seasoning if necessary.

2. Serve hot, warm, or at room temperature. For true Italian home-style eating, invite everyone to toss the beans on their plates with a spoonful or two of olive oil. Don't be surprised if most people like the beans just as is.

MELTING TUSCAN KALE

Cavolo Nero Brasato

Serves 2 to 4

Home cooks throughout Italy sauté greens like Tuscan kale (called *cavolo nero*, or black cabbage, in Tuscany) or chard with onion and garlic until they soften and turn silky-tender, practically "melting." Brawnier greens like American kale or broccoli rabe might be parboiled first. Depending on the region or a family's tastes, the cook might add chile to the pan, or a few olives, some citrus zest, one or two anchovies or whatever herbs appeal at the moment. The trick to that melting tenderness is slow sautéing, adding liquid a little at a time to soften and mellow the greens.

➤ *Cook to Cook:* Use organic greens if at all possible. Tuscan kale has long tongue-shaped leaves pocked with a pebbly texture. Their blue green color is so dark it's nearly black. In some markets, it's called *lacinato*, or black kale. Instead of the kale or chard, try wild greens, escarole, curly endive, beet greens, young mustard greens, young turnip greens, Catalonia chicory, spinach or braising mixes. Parboil stronger-flavored greens like kale, collards and broccoli rabe by cooking them in boiling salted water 1 to 2 minutes, draining and then sautéing.

2 tablespoons extra-virgin olive oil
1 medium onion, minced
Salt and freshly ground black pepper
2 cloves garlic, minced
Leaves from ³/₄ to 1 pound Tuscan kale
   or green or red Swiss chard, washed,
dried, and chopped (save stems for
   another use)
About 1¹/₂ cups water

1. Heat the oil in a 12-inch skillet over medium-high heat. Stir in the onion, sprinkling with salt and pepper, and sauté to golden, about 3 minutes. Add the garlic and greens and cook over medium to medium-low heat until wilted.

2. Add ¹/₂ cup water and continue cooking, uncovered, 5 to 10 minutes, or until almost dry. Stir in another ¹/₂ cup water and repeat the process. Add another ¹/₂ cup water, simmering 5 minutes. Taste to see if the greens are very tender. If not, cook a bit longer in a little more liquid. The greens should be moist but not soupy when done. (The greens can be covered and held up to an hour.) Serve warm or hot.

SKILLET CARROTS WITH FRESH SAGE

Carote alla Salvia in Padella

Serves 4 to 6

Sautéing carrots with browning onion and fresh sage, then simmering them in white wine takes them far, far away from the boring overboiled carrots that have given this vegetable its ho-hum image. Sage's flavors of resin and muskiness lend carrots mystery; it makes them taste more grown up. Try this dish with simple foods like roasted poultry or fish, or spoon it over rice. Though it's not at all Italian, I love these carrots over whole wheat couscous—they become a small meal unto themselves.

➤ *Cook to Cook:* This method of cooking carrots encourages variations. One is to heat the oil in the skillet as described below and quickly crisp the sage leaves in it. Set them aside, proceed with the recipe and sprinkle the crackly leaves over the finished carrots.

1 to 2 tablespoons extra-virgin olive oil
1 1/2 pounds carrots, peeled and cut
    diagonally into 1 1/2-inch-long pieces
1/4 medium onion, cut into long thin
    slivers
10 large fresh sage leaves

Salt and freshly ground black pepper
1/2 cup dry white wine
1/2 cup Mother's Broth (page 196) or
    canned low-sodium chicken or
    vegetable broth

1. Heat the oil in a 12-inch skillet over medium-high heat. Sauté the carrots, onion, and sage about 10 minutes to brown the onion. Season with salt and pepper as the vegetables cook. Pour in the wine and broth, adjusting the heat to a gentle simmer. Cover and cook 15 minutes, or until the carrots are tender when pierced with a knife. As they cook, check for scorching, adding a little water if necessary.

2. Before serving, uncover and simmer off any liquid, leaving only enough to cloak the carrots in a moist glaze. Taste for seasoning and serve hot. The carrots also reheat nicely.

MARSALA-BRAISED CARROTS

Substitute 1/4 cup dry Marsala for 1/4 cup of the dry white wine.

HOME-STYLE CAULIFLOWER AND RED ONIONS

Cavolfiore alla Casereccia

Serves 4 to 6

Rarely do we think of cauliflower as a summer vegetable, yet it is in its prime from midsummer into fall. In this dish, chunks of cauliflower are spiced with lots of black pepper and sautéed garlic and onion. Cauliflower's sturdy cabbage quality meets its match with these seasonings and the unexpected finish of fresh basil. This is the kind of dish you often see set on the sideboard in a farmhouse kitchen to rest and mellow before being served as an antipasto or salad. It's best served at room temperature or slightly warm.

Water
1 large cauliflower, cut into large
  flowerettes
Extra-virgin olive oil
2 large cloves garlic, thinly sliced

1 medium to large red onion, sliced
  into thin rings
Salt and freshly ground black pepper
1/4 tightly packed cup fresh basil leaves,
  torn

1. Set a collapsible steamer in a 6-quart pot. Add about 2 inches of water and bring to a boil. Arrange the cauliflower flowerettes on the steamer rack, cover the pot, and cook about 5 minutes, or until the stems resist only a little when pierced with a knife. The cauliflower should be tender-crisp. Transfer to a colander and rinse under cold water to stop the cooking.

2. Film the bottom of a 12-inch skillet with oil and set over medium heat. Sauté the garlic slices to barely blond, then immediately remove with a slotted spoon. Reserve. Turn the heat up to medium-high and sauté the onion 2 minutes, or until beginning to color. Add the cauliflower and salt and pepper to taste. Cook, turning the pieces, 1 to 2 minutes.

3. Mound on a platter and sprinkle with the garlic and a generous amount of black pepper. Let stand at room temperature at least an hour. Scatter the basil over the cauliflower before serving.

▼ ▼ ▼ ▼ ▼ ▼ ▼ ▼ ▼ ▼ ▼

STUFATO—THE GARDEN IN A POT

Stufato di Verdure

Serves 3 to 4

This ragù of vegetables is one of those sublime one-dish meals that for me captures all the nurturing goodness of the Italian food I was raised with. What Ciambotta is to southern Italians, Stufato is to northerners—the concepts are the same. Vegetables, from greens and beans and zucchini to tomatoes and peppers, all cook together, making their own sauce and becoming a lavish vegetable stew. Merely heat a little olive oil in a big shallow pan, stir in whatever is fresh and good at the moment, sear everything, then cover. When vegetables cook in their own juices, their flavors open up and their textures go from crisp to silken. I grew up eating my Tuscan grandmother's Stufato, and when I began visiting farms, I discovered everyone did some version of it.

This easy way of preparing memorable food is natural for Italian women who cook from their gardens. In spring, it might include fava beans, artichokes, leeks and new potatoes; in winter, it can be cabbage, beans, chard, kale, potatoes, carrots and squashes. And always there is onion and garlic.

➤ *Cook to Cook:* Use a heavy pan and don't shy away from taking the initial sauté to a full rich brown to give this dish its full flavor. Then, keeping the heat low, cover the pan tightly with a lid or aluminum foil to hold in juices and steam. Along with, or instead of, olives, season Stufato with any one or a combination of the following: capers, anchovies, hot peppers, herbs, cured pork, wine or vinegar. Cook Stufato several hours ahead and reheat, or eat it at room temperature. Grated cheese or a little extra olive oil drizzled over the top is wonderful. A rough multigrain bread is perfect with Stufato.

Extra-virgin olive oil

1/2 medium onion, thinly sliced

3 large fresh sage leaves

1 tightly packed teaspoon *each* fresh marjoram and basil leaves, chopped

1/2 pound green beans, trimmed and halved

3 small pale inner stalks celery with leaves, coarsely chopped

9 small (2 pounds) zucchini, cut into 1-inch chunks

1 large (1/2 pound) yellow sweet pepper, cored, seeded, and cut into 1-inch dice

6 oil-cured black olives, pitted and minced

2 large cloves garlic, thinly sliced

3 to 4 medium (about 3/4 pound) ripe tomatoes, peeled and chopped (not seeded), or 1 14-ounce can whole tomatoes, completely drained

Salt and freshly ground black pepper

1. Lightly film the bottom of a 12-inch sauté pan (not nonstick) with olive oil. Set over high heat. Add the onion, herbs, beans, celery, zucchini, sweet pepper, and olives, lower the heat to medium, and sauté until the zucchini is golden brown.

2. Stir in the garlic and tomatoes, crushing canned tomatoes with your hands as you go. Sprinkle with salt and pepper. Reduce the heat to medium-low, cover, and cook 55 minutes, or until the vegetables are extremely tender and richly flavored. Adjust the heat to keep the vegetables from scorching, and add a little water if necessary.

3. If the stew seems too liquid, uncover and cook over medium-high heat a few minutes to reduce and concentrate flavors. Taste for seasoning. Serve warm or at room temperature.

A Tuscan farmer selling the makings of stufato from his truck,
on a street corner in Lucca.

Vegetables and Salads

SWEET PEAS "IN THEIR JACKETS"

Piselli in Buccia con Patate Nuove

Serves 4 to 6

In this recipe, spring peas and new potatoes stew in white wine and herbs and are finished with a dollop of butter just before going to the table. The dish comes from a nineteenth-century Trento cookbook written for prosperous farmers and city people. In those days, Trento was a border city, Italy's doorway to the Austro-Hungarian Empire. Farmers in the mountains surrounding the town raised dairy cattle for cheese and butter. They still do. Farmwives marked the brief moment during the mountains' short growing season when peas were in their prime by simmering them and fresh-dug potatoes with home-churned butter in a covered pot. The only changes I've made to the dish are to cut back on the very generous amount of butter and use our sweet sugar snap peas unshelled.

➤ *Cook to Cook:* Handled properly, a little butter offers big flavor. The secret is adding it at the end of cooking and having the butter barely melt to keep its fresh taste.

1 pound sugar snap peas, stems and strings removed	A 3-inch branch fresh rosemary, plus 1 teaspoon minced fresh rosemary
1/2 pound small red-skinned new potatoes, cut into 1/2-inch dice	1 small onion, cut into wedges
Water	1/2 cup dry white wine
3 sprigs fresh Italian parsley	3 tablespoons unsalted butter
	Salt and freshly ground black pepper

1. Crisp the peas and potatoes in a bowl of cold water for about 15 minutes.

2. Lift out the vegetables and, without drying, place them in a 4-quart pot. Add the herb sprigs, onion, wine, 2 tablespoons of the butter, and salt and pepper to taste. Cover, set over medium-low heat, and cook 18 to 20 minutes, or until the peas and potatoes are tender.

3. Uncover and cook off all the liquid. Pull out the rosemary branch and parsley. Add the minced rosemary and let the flavor blossom for a few seconds, then toss with the last tablespoon of butter. Taste for seasoning. Turn into a heated bowl and serve hot.

SPICY SPINACH AND TOMATOES

Spinaci e Pomodori Piccanti

Serves 5 to 6

Desperate for greens after the happy excess of celebrating my Lucca family's grape harvest, I discovered this dish at the lunch bar in back of a pastry shop: tart spinach, hot chiles, sweet tomato and soul-restoring garlic. Lucca's vegetable stands sell fresh-cooked spinach, shaped into loose balls and ready for dressing with local olive oil and vinegar, or a quick sauté. The snack bar went one better, adding fresh tomato and chiles as the spinach sautéed in the olive oil.

➤ *Cook to Cook:* A sure way not to overcook spinach destined for sautéing is to wilt it by pouring boiling water over the leaves and letting them sit 5 minutes, then draining.

3 pounds fresh spinach, trimmed of
    stems and thoroughly washed
About 3 quarts boiling water
2 to 3 tablespoons extra-virgin olive oil
2 large cloves garlic, thinly sliced
2 fresh medium-hot to hot chiles
    (banana peppers or jalapeños),
    seeded and finely chopped

Salt and freshly ground black pepper
2 medium ripe tomatoes, seeded and
    chopped, or 4 canned whole toma-
    toes, drained, seeded, and diced

1. Place the spinach in one or two large bowls and cover with the boiling water. Let sit 5 minutes, or until thoroughly wilted. Drain and refresh with cool water. Squeeze until almost completely dry. Coarsely chop.

2. Heat the oil in a 12-inch skillet over medium heat. Add the garlic and chiles and cook until the garlic is soft but not colored. Add the spinach and sauté, seasoning with salt and pepper, until heated through. Add the tomatoes and cook another 3 minutes, or until the spinach is tender and flavors have come together. Taste for seasoning. Serve hot or warm.

SEARED BROCCOLI WITH LEMON

Broccoli al Limone

Serves 4

Browning broccoli gives it unexpected lustiness. Try the technique for those who can take or leave vegetables. The trick is browning the broccoli fast enough to keep it from overcooking, yet at a moderate rate to build up rich, caramelized flavors. The recipe shows how to keep a balance between the two.

> *Cook to Cook:* A 12-inch sauté pan (not nonstick) with excellent heat conduction is a great help in recipes like this and so many others. Adjust the heat as needed, using the brown glaze on the bottom of the pan as a guide. You don't want it to burn. Though not brilliant emerald green, browned broccoli has its own unique appeal.

You might find what looks like small broccoli in our markets—called "broccoletti," "broccolini" or "baby" broccoli. Its narrow stalks and small heads resemble aggressive-tasting broccoli rabe (sometimes called rapini) without its leaves, but this broccoli is mild and sweet. Do try it in this recipe.

1 large bunch broccoli or "baby" broccoli (about 1¼ pounds)	Shredded zest of 1 large lemon
Water	Salt and freshly ground black pepper
2 tablespoons extra-virgin olive oil	Lemon wedges

1. Trim off 1 inch of the broccoli stalks. Peel the remaining stalks. Split thicker stalks lengthwise into thirds, slender ones in half.

2. Place a collapsible steamer in a 6-quart pot containing about 2 inches of water. Bring to a boil. Crisscross the broccoli stalks in the steamer. Cover the pot and cook 1 to 3 minutes; a stalk should still show some resistance when pierced with a knife. Immediately rinse the broccoli under cold water to stop its cooking. (At this point, you can set the broccoli aside a few hours at room temperature.)

3. Heat the oil in a 12-inch sauté pan (not nonstick) over medium-high heat. Sauté the broccoli until speckled with brown on one side. Adjust the heat to prevent it from burning, and watch the pan bottom for scorching. Sprinkle the broccoli with the lemon zest and salt and pepper, turn the stalks over, and sauté to brown on the second side. Try to keep the stalks whole by turning them with two spatulas. Taste for seasoning. Serve hot or warm, with lemon wedges. The broccoli is even good at room temperature, but do not refrigerate.

ROASTED BUTTERNUT SQUASH WITH BALSAMIC VINEGAR

Zucca al Forno

Serves 6 to 8

If you've never thought of roasted squash as a side dish, try this recipe. Just rub pieces of butternut squash with olive oil, salt and pepper and bake until their flesh is tender and roasted to tawny gold. Serve the squash the way it's eaten in country houses in the part of the Emilia-Romagna region where nearly every family makes its own balsamic vinegar. Small bottles of balsamico are set out on the table, and everyone seasons their squash to taste with the vinegar. Try the squash with grilled lamb chops, roast chicken, pork and simple sautéed fish dishes.

1½ to 2 pounds butternut squash
Extra-virgin olive oil
Salt and freshly ground black pepper
1 tablespoon artisan balsamic vinegar
    (Aceto Balsamico Tradizionale di
Modena or Reggio-Emilio) or 3 to 4 tablespoons high-quality commercial balsamic vinegar

1. Preheat the oven to 400°F. Line a cookie sheet with foil. Cut the squash lengthwise in half. Seed and cut it into 3- to 4-inch squares, with skin intact. Score the flesh with crosshatch cuts about ½ inch deep. Rub all over with olive oil.

2. Set the pieces, skin side down, on the cookie sheet and sprinkle with salt and pepper. Bake 45 minutes, or until easily pierced with knife and lightly browned. Serve hot or at room temperature, sprinkled with the balsamic vinegar.

EARLY AUTUMN VEGETABLE ROAST

Verdure al Forno

Serves 4 to 6

Ⅰf there is one taste I associate with Italian home cooking, it's foods browned until they're crusty in a sauté pan or roasted in an oven. Roasting elevates vegetables to main-dish status. In Italy, every season has its roasted vegetables, and every household its favorite herbs and other mixtures for flavoring them. Though in this recipe the vegetables are on the cusp of summer and autumn, it invites variations through the year. Don't shy away from those you typically wouldn't roast, such as green beans, corn, peas, asparagus, scallions, parsnips, rutabaga and greens. Timidity is roasting's only enemy. Take vegetables all the way to crusty brown. Although this list of ingredients may seem long, it is only a collection of seasonings tossed with a variety of roasting candidates. Play with it as you will.

1 small to medium eggplant, cut into 1- to 1¹/₂-inch wedges

3 small zucchini, cut into 1¹/₂-inch chunks

Salt

2 medium onions, each cut into 4 wedges

2 to 3 medium carrots, cut into 1-inch pieces

4 sun-dried tomatoes (not oil-packed), minced

3 small pattypan squash, cut into large chunks

1 sweet red pepper, cored, seeded, and cut into large chunks

1 large stalk celery with leaves, coarsely chopped

1 large handful green beans, trimmed and cut into thirds

¹/₃ cup oil-cured black olives, pitted

¹/₂ tightly packed cup fresh basil leaves

¹/₄ tightly packed cup fresh marjoram leaves

A 6-inch branch fresh rosemary

4 branches fresh thyme

2¹/₂ tablespoons extra-virgin olive oil

Freshly ground black pepper

3 large cloves garlic, thinly sliced

3 medium ripe, delicious tomatoes, cut into 1-inch chunks

1. Toss the eggplant and zucchini with about 2 teaspoons salt, spread them out between two triple thicknesses of paper towels, place a baking sheet or cutting board on top, and weight with several cans for about 30 minutes.

2. In a large bowl, blend together the remaining ingredients except the garlic and fresh tomatoes with 1½ tablespoons of the olive oil. Let stand at room temperature.

3. After 30 minutes, if possible, add the eggplant and zucchini to the other vegetables. Set a large shallow heavy roasting pan (a half-sheet pan is ideal) on the oven's middle rack. Preheat the oven to 450°F.

4. With oven mitts, remove the hot pan from the oven. Sprinkle with the remaining 1 tablespoon olive oil. Spread the vegetables over the pan and roast 30 minutes, turning occasionally for even browning. Scatter the garlic and tomatoes over the vegetables and continue roasting 15 to 30 minutes longer, turning occasionally, or until the green beans are tender.

5. Turn the vegetables out onto a platter, taste for seasoning, and serve hot or at room temperature. The vegetables could be garnished with sprigs of fresh herbs.

Puglia wheat and olive trees share the same soil.

GUATELLI'S PEPPERS AND ONIONS

Peperoni e Cipolle alla Guatelli

Serves 4 to 6 as a side dish or antipasto, 3 to 4 as a main dish

Sixty years ago, these luscious peppers and onions were a one-dish supper for Ettore Guatelli's family on their hill farm in Emilia-Romagna. Here, vinegar takes an ordinary sauté into a new realm. Instead of the expected vinegary sourness, reducing in vinegar a little at a time lays down layers of flavor. In Guatelli's boyhood, olive oil was a luxury for Emilia farmers whose land produced no olives. His mother devised this reduction to cut back on the oil needed for a sauté, at the same time making a dish from her garden special. Serve the peppers with diced hard-cooked egg, as Ettore Guatelli ate them as a child, or with shavings of Parmigiano-Reggiano cheese.

➤ *Cook to Cook:* Mild and thin-walled, Italian frying peppers, with their elongated shape and pale green color, taste different from sweet bell peppers. They're subtle and crisp, with a sweet citrus quality, while bell peppers are fleshy, with more aggressive herbal and fruit flavors. One is not the ideal substitute for the other. Check farmers' markets and specialty food stores for frying peppers that may be called by other names, like mild banana pepper, Cubanelle, Marconi, or Corno di Toro. If you cannot find them, sweet yellow or red bell peppers are stand-ins. Avoid green bell peppers. Their taste would overwhelm everything else in the dish.

2 tablespoons extra-virgin olive oil

8 (1 pound) small onions, quartered, or 3 medium onions, cut into sixths

4 (about ¾ pound) mild Italian frying peppers or 2 sweet yellow peppers, cored, seeded, and cut into ½- to 1-inch dice

3 (1 pound) sweet red peppers, cored, seeded, and cut into ½- to 1-inch dice

½ to 1 hot Hungarian wax pepper or other hot fresh pepper, seeded and cut into ¼-inch dice

10 large fresh sage leaves

Salt and freshly ground black pepper

2 large cloves garlic, thinly sliced

2 teaspoons tomato paste

½ cup red wine vinegar

¾ cup water

1 large egg, hard-cooked, shelled, and coarsely chopped (optional)

1. Heat the oil in a 12-inch sauté pan (not nonstick) over medium-high heat. Stir in the onions, peppers, and sage leaves. Sprinkle with salt and a generous amount of

pepper. Sauté, stirring frequently, until the onions are golden, about 5 minutes. Add the garlic and sauté 1 minute, then remove the pan from the heat.

2. Stir in the tomato paste, $1/4$ cup of the vinegar, and $1/4$ cup of water. Set over medium heat and bring to a slow bubble. Cover and cook 5 minutes, or until the liquid is almost gone. Add the rest of the vinegar and another $1/4$ cup water, cover, and simmer another 5 minutes. Remove the lid, raise the heat to medium-high, and reduce the pan sauce until thick and syrupy. It should cloak the pan's bottom.

3. Stir in the last $1/4$ cup water. Simmer a few seconds, scraping up the juices from the bottom of the pan. The vegetables should be glazed with the sauce and deeply flavored. Remove from the heat. Taste for seasoning. Serve hot, warm, or at room temperature, sprinkled with the optional chopped egg.

Ettore Guatelli creating souvenirs of
the country life of his childhood.

ROASTED RED ONION WEDGES

Cipolle al Forno

Serves 6 to 8, with leftovers

These generous-sized wedges of red onion roast with wine, tomatoes, olive oil and herbs to become almost a meal unto themselves. I always make enough for leftovers because the onions are such a good lunch the next day with bread and cheese. Every country cook has a collection of favorite onion recipes, since onions grow easily in kitchen gardens and keep well through the winter in root cellars. Pair these onions with grilled and roasted meats or simple seafood dishes. At one farmhouse lunch, my hostess served sections of onions roasted like these along with their pan juices atop a simple risotto—an even better reason to make extra.

6 medium red onions (3$^1/_2$ to 4 pounds), cut into 4 wedges each
3 branches fresh thyme
Leaves from 2 4-inch sprigs fresh rosemary
2 bay leaves, broken
Generous $^1/_2$ teaspoon fennel seeds, ground

2 canned whole tomatoes, drained
About $^1/_3$ cup dry red wine
About $^1/_4$ cup extra-virgin olive oil
Salt and freshly ground black pepper
4 large cloves garlic, coarsely chopped
Water

1. Preheat the oven to 450°F. Arrange the onion pieces cut sides up in a large shallow pan (such as a half-sheet pan or broiler pan). Tear apart the thyme branches and scatter over the onions, along with the rosemary leaves. Tuck the broken bay leaves here and there. Sprinkle with the fennel and crush the tomatoes over the onions. Moisten the wedges with the wine and olive oil and season liberally with salt and pepper.

2. Roast about 1 hour, basting with the pan juices several times. After about the first 20 minutes, add the garlic. If the pan juices threaten to burn, add $^1/_3$ to $^1/_2$ cup water and scrape up any brown glaze with a spatula. Baste the onions with it. They're done when they are tender when pierced with a knife but still hold their shape. Serve hot, warm, or at room temperature, basted with any of their pan juices.

MARGHERITA'S CRUSHED BUTTERMILK POTATOES

Purea di Patate alla Margherita

Serves 4; doubles easily

Creamy with a subtle tang, these potatoes are from the high mountains of northern Italy's Alto Adige region, and specifically the cowherd's hut called Malga Sonen, where hikers stop to eat. Sonen's mistress, Margherita, uses the buttermilk left over from churning butter to cook her potatoes. Like every farmwoman in the area, she has more buttermilk than she can ever use. When simmered in buttermilk, potatoes are transformed into amazingly fine eating. One secret of this wonderful dish is using waxy-style potatoes with buttery flavors. And don't skimp on the browned butter—it tastes like toasted hazelnuts.

➤ *Cook to Cook:* These potatoes taste even better the second day. Reheat them as described below. Protect the sweetness that sets apart waxy-style potatoes (Yellow Finns, Desirees, Red Bliss and the like) by storing the new potatoes in the refrigerator, where their sugars will not turn to starch. Punch holes in their bag for air circulation. They will keep well up to 2 weeks.

2 pounds buttery waxy potatoes (such as Yellow Finn, Red Bliss, red-skinned San Luis Valley, or Desiree), peeled and thinly sliced	2 cups buttermilk, or more as needed 2 cups water Salt and freshly ground black pepper 4 tablespoons unsalted butter

1. Place the potatoes in a 4-quart saucepan with the buttermilk, water, a little salt, and pepper to taste. Bring to a simmer, cover, and cook 25 minutes, or until the potatoes are tender but not falling apart. Check for scorching, adding equal parts buttermilk and water if necessary to have the consistency of a thick stew.

2. Uncover and cook down the liquid, stirring and crushing the potatoes until creamy and thick, 5 to 10 minutes. Season to taste. (They can be set aside, covered, for an hour or more. Reheat in the saucepan over low heat, stirring constantly.)

3. While the potatoes simmer, slowly cook the butter in a small skillet until a rich golden brown. Set aside until needed.

4. Serve the hot potatoes mounded in a warmed bowl, pouring the reheated browned butter over them.

LAKE GARDA POTATOES

Patate alla Lago di Garta

Serves 4

Potatoes no bigger than shooter marbles simmer in white wine, herbs and a little olive oil until tender and glazed in this dish from Lake Garda. On its eastern shore, where sunlight shines longer and stronger than on the western one, the first small potatoes are dug from home gardens in late spring. These wine-glazed potatoes, mounded on paper plates, were being sold by the local equivalent of the women's auxiliary at a street fair in Bardolino, the elegant old wine town on the lake shore. According to Giorgio Erbifori, chef-owner of Bardolino's Ristorante Aurora, cooking potatoes in wine relates to the custom on Lake Garda of preserving tiny lake fish and other foods in wine vinegar and herbs.

➤ *Cook to Cook:* Yellow Finn or red-skinned potatoes are excellent done this way. If larger than 1¹/₂ inches in diameter, cut them into 1-inch pieces.

1¹/₂ pounds 1- to 1¹/₂-inch-diameter Yellow Finn or red-skinned potatoes	6 fresh sage leaves
1 tablespoon robust extra-virgin olive oil	3 large cloves garlic, sliced
1 branch fresh mint	²/₃ cup dry white wine (such as Pinot Grigio, Soave, or Sauvignon Blanc)
A 2-inch branch fresh rosemary	Salt and freshly ground black pepper
	Water

1. In a 10-inch sauté pan, combine the potatoes with all the remaining ingredients, including a little salt and pepper, and enough water to cover them generously. Bring to a simmer, cover, and cook about 10 minutes. Uncover and continue simmering, turning the potatoes often, until they are easily pierced with a knife but not falling apart.

2. If the pan liquid has not reduced to a glaze, lift the potatoes out of the pan and boil down the liquid to a syrup. Return the potatoes to the pan and stir to coat with the glaze. Enjoy them hot or at room temperature. (They can be kept warm in the covered pan up to 20 minutes.)

ROMAGNA ROAST POTATOES

Patate alla Romagnola

Serves 4 to 6

Country women in Romagna used to bake these potatoes each week along with their homemade bread. Cloaked in olive oil and flavored with bits of cured pork, rosemary, garlic and tomatoes, the potatoes roasted near the opening of the big bread ovens, where the women could easily turn and baste them with the pan juices. The feast of the day was the crusty potatoes, fresh baked bread and homemade wine. Not a bad idea today, but these roasted potatoes are good with nearly everything—from a green salad (page 299) to chicken to seafood.

Extra-virgin olive oil
2¹/₂ to 3 pounds medium Yellow Finn
   or red-skinned potatoes
2 thick slices (about 2 ounces)
   cotechino sausage, soppressata, or
   pancetta, chopped

Leaves from a 6-inch branch fresh
   rosemary
Salt and freshly ground black pepper
1¹/₂ cups halved cherry tomatoes
6 cloves garlic, coarsely chopped

1. Preheat the oven to 425°F. Generously oil a large shallow baking pan (such as a half-sheet pan or broiler pan). Cut the potatoes in half or into quarters and place them in the pan, rolling the pieces around to coat with oil, ending cut side up. Make sure they are in a single layer and barely touching. Drizzle the potatoes with another tablespoon of oil, then sprinkle with the cured meat, rosemary, and salt and pepper.

2. Roast 30 minutes, turning once or twice. Blend in the tomatoes and garlic. Roast about another 40 minutes, basting with the pan juices and turning for even browning. Once the potatoes are crisp and easily pierced with a knife, they're done. Serve them hot or warm.

TWICE-BAKED POTATOES WITH WILD MUSHROOMS

Patate Ricotte ai Funghi

Serves 4 to 8

Baked potatoes stuffed with cheese and wild mushrooms used to be a second breakfast for Maria Fedrizzi when she was growing up on a farm in the mountains of the Trentino region's Sole Valley. Just mentioning potatoes got her talking. "After the men milked the cows and let them out to pasture, my mother used to set out plates of these potatoes. She took potatoes left over from supper, split them, worked in buttermilk or cream and some of our cheese. Sometimes she had leftover mushrooms too—wild ones my grandmother always gathered. I still have the reflector oven she used in front of the fire to bake the potatoes." With Maria's recipe and mushrooms gathered in the supermarket, I make them for supper for my husband.

➤ **Cook to Cook:** You could make the potatoes just the way Maria's mother did—with leftovers—or you could start from scratch several hours ahead. Hold them at room temperature. Bake at 350°F for about 45 minutes to heat the potatoes all the way through.

4 large Yukon Gold or red-skinned potatoes
Extra-virgin olive oil
1/4 cup buttermilk or cream
2 tablespoons unsalted butter
1 1/2 cups (6 ounces) freshly grated Grana del Trentino, Parmigiano-Reggiano, or Asiago cheese
Salt and freshly ground black pepper
2 tablespoons unsalted butter or extra-virgin olive oil
6 ounces portobello mushrooms, cleaned and cut into 1 by 1/2-inch pieces
6 ounces oyster mushrooms, cleaned and cut into 1 by 1/2-inch pieces

1 medium red onion, cut into 1/4-inch dice
1 tightly packed tablespoon fresh basil leaves, chopped
1/8 teaspoon dried thyme
2 cloves garlic, minced
2 canned plum tomatoes, drained, seeded, and chopped
1 teaspoon tomato paste, diluted in 2 tablespoons water
1/2 cup dry white wine

1. Preheat the oven to 400°F. Rub the potatoes with a bit of oil. Prick all over with a fork. Bake 1 hour, or until tender when pierced with a knife. Cool about 10 minutes. (Leave the oven on.)

2. Cut the potatoes lengthwise in half. Spoon out the flesh into a medium bowl, leaving a 1/4-inch-thick shell. With a fork, mash in the buttermilk or cream, the 2 tablespoons butter, half the cheese, and salt and pepper to taste.

3. Heat the remaining 2 tablespoons butter or oil in a 12-inch skillet over high heat. Stir in the mushrooms and onions. Sauté 3 minutes, or until the onions are softened and browned. Stir in the basil, thyme, garlic, and plum tomatoes. Sauté over high heat about 1 minute. Blend in the tomato paste mixture, cooking until reduced to almost nothing. Stir in half the wine, scraping up any brown bits from the bottom of the pan. Boil down to a glaze at the bottom of the pan. Repeat with the rest of the wine. Season to taste with salt and pepper. Remove from the heat.

4. Lightly oil a 9 by 13-inch baking pan. Set aside one third of the potatoes. Lightly fold the mushrooms into the rest of the potatoes. Stuff this mixture tightly into the potato shells. With a knife, cover each stuffed potato with a layer of plain mashed potatoes, as though you were frosting a cake. Set the potatoes in the pan. Turn the oven down to 375°F. Bake 30 minutes, or until heated through. Sprinkle the potatoes with the remaining cheese and bake another 5 minutes. Serve hot.

POTATO "GATTO"

"Gattó" Di Patate

Serves 6 to 8

This is like a lasagne of mashed potatoes—crushed potatoes mixed with Parmigiano, salami and peas, layered in a casserole with a filling of mozzarella and browned onion. Not to miss any opportunity for more big flavors, the whole thing is topped with coarse-cut, toasted garlic bread crumbs. What a dish for supper! No one can stop eating it. Serve the potatoes with a tart, vinegary salad of sturdy greens like the one on page 299.

A dish from the Naples countryside, the *"gattó"* comes from the French *"gâteau,"* meaning cake—a layered cake of potatoes. The French occupied Naples in the late eighteenth century and left behind a strong influence on local dishes.

3 pounds Yellow Finn or red-skinned potatoes	4 tablespoons unsalted butter
Water	1 cup freshly grated Parmigiano-Reggiano cheese
Extra-virgin olive oil	1/3 cup milk
1 medium onion, cut into 1/4-inch dice	5 1/8-inch-thick slices (1/4 pound) soppressata or other good-tasting salami, cut into 1/4-inch dice
Salt and freshly ground black pepper	
1 large clove garlic, peeled	
1 large clove garlic, minced	1 1/3 cups tiny frozen peas, defrosted
3 to 4 1-inch-thick slices country bread, torn into bite-sized pieces	1/2 pound fresh mozzarella in liquid, drained and sliced 1/4 inch thick

1. Place the potatoes in 4-quart pot, cover with water, and simmer 25 minutes, or until tender.

2. While the potatoes cook, lightly film a 10-inch skillet with olive oil and heat over medium-high heat. Quickly brown the onion, seasoning with salt and pepper. Take off the heat and turn the onions into a bowl. Wipe out the skillet with a wad of paper towels and set aside.

3. Turn on the food processor, drop in the garlic, then the bread, and process until the bread is in coarse crumbs (about 1/2-inch pieces). Film the skillet again with oil. Add the bread and stir over medium heat, sprinkling with salt and pepper, about 5 minutes, or until pale gold. Turn out onto a sheet of foil and cool.

4. Preheat the oven to 400°F. Oil an 8-inch square baking dish or pan. Slice the butter into a large bowl. Drain the potatoes, peel, and add to the bowl. Mash with a large fork, blending in the Parmigiano, milk, and salt and pepper to taste. The potatoes should be lumpy. Fold in the salami and half the peas. Spread half the potatoes in the baking dish. Top with the remaining peas and the onions, then the sliced mozzarella. Cover with the rest of the potatoes. (At this point, you can cover and refrigerate the casserole overnight. Bring to room temperature before baking.)

5. Bake about 30 minutes, or until the casserole is hot. Top with bread crumbs, pressing them into the potatoes a bit. Bake another 10 minutes. Serve hot, cutting into 8 or more squares.

CRISP POTATO "PIZZA"

"Pizza" di Patate

Serves 3 to 4 as a side dish or antipasto

When time is short and you want a
dynamite potato dish, try this one. I've watched Italian home cooks speed up
cooking potatoes for supper by thinly slicing them and spreading out the pieces
in a single layer on a baking sheet, so they look like a pizza crust. After about
twenty minutes in a hot oven, you have cooked potatoes. This recipe takes the
idea to a new level—toss the slices with orange zest, onion rings, garlic, black
olives and spices and bake them fast so some of the potato browns and crisps and
some turns creamy. It's almost better than pizza. Serve the potatoes with poached
fish or roasted poultry. Then try them on their own for supper with solely a salad.

2 large cloves garlic

3 tightly packed tablespoons fresh
Italian parsley leaves

1 1/2 pounds small red-skinned potatoes,
sliced 1/16 to 1/8 inch thick

1 medium red onion, sliced into very
thin rings

3 tablespoons extra-virgin olive oil

1/2 teaspoon dried oregano

1/8 teaspoon hot red pepper flakes

Shredded zest of 2 large oranges

1/3 cup oil-cured black olives, pitted
and coarsely chopped

Salt and freshly ground black pepper

1. Preheat the oven to 500°F. Oil a 14-inch pizza pan or a cookie sheet. Mince
together the garlic and parsley. Place in a large bowl with the potatoes and onion. Fold
in the olive oil, oregano, hot pepper, half the orange zest, and half the olives, along with
generous sprinklings of salt and black pepper. Toss everything to coat the potato slices.

2. Spread the potatoes out in an even single layer on the pan. Bake 20 minutes,
then sprinkle with the remaining orange zest and olives. Bake another 10 minutes, or
until the potatoes are speckled with golden brown and the zest has darkened. To get
the top to brown to a rich gold, it may be necessary to broil the "pizza" for 2 to 3 minutes. Remove from the oven and serve right away. Slice into wedges (or squares) and
lift off the pan with a spatula.

SALAD OF TART GREENS
AND RED ONION

Insalata Verde

Serves 4

This is the kind of salad I was raised on and later discovered was eaten on just about every farm I visited. Every night we had a big bowl of mixed greens—tart and mild, changing with what my mother found in the market. On farms I stayed at in Italy, the greens came from the garden, or were foraged from the fields. Dressing the salad was a ritual always done at the table. First, my mother sprinkled it with some dried basil, salt and pepper. She tossed the greens with only enough olive oil to give them a little gleam. She sprinkled a little vinegar in and tossed again. Then she always tasted a leaf, thought for a moment and added a little more salt, or oil or vinegar. Another taste, and finally she let us take the salad.

➤ *Cook to Cook:* Pair this salad with the braised beans of Tuscan Mountain Supper (page 186), Potato "Gattó" (page 296) and just about any roasted, grilled or braised meat. This is the classic Italian green salad, good on its own but readily setting off the character of other foods.

1 medium red onion, cut into thin rings	1 small head red leaf or Bibb lettuce
Ice water	Salt and freshly ground black pepper
Pale green inner leaves from 1 large head curly endive, frisée, or other tangy greens	1/2 teaspoon dried basil
	2 to 3 tablespoons robust, peppery extra-virgin olive oil
Pale inner leaves from 1 large head escarole or 1 small head oak leaf lettuce or green radicchio	About 2 tablespoons red wine vinegar

1. Combine the onion and ice water to cover in a bowl and refrigerate 30 minutes.

2. Wash and thoroughly dry the greens. Tear into bite-sized pieces. Turn into a big salad bowl.

3. Just before serving, drain the onions and pat dry. Sprinkle the greens with salt and pepper, the basil, and the drained onions. Don't dress the salad until you're ready to serve it.

4. At the table, toss with enough oil to barely coat the greens, about 2 tablespoons. Toss with vinegar to taste, starting with 2 tablespoons. Taste for balance, making sure the vinegar is assertive but not harsh. Serve the salad immediately.

WILTED DANDELION SALAD

Insalata di Dente di Leone

Serves 4

Sauté pancetta and soppressata until crisp in olive oil with garlic and simmer in some vinegar, pour the hot dressing over tart greens and you are eating the salad that means spring has finally come to the high mountains of the Trento region. This recipe is from Maria Fedrizzi, a vibrant woman in her sixties who guided me through Malé village's museum of country life in the Valley of the Sun. She grew up on a mountain farm, where this salad was eaten nearly every night in warm weather. She's a born storyteller—by the time Maria finished telling me about her life, I felt I'd grown up with the salad too.

➤ ***Cook to Cook:*** Try this salad with any grilled or roasted dishes, especially Crisp Potato "Pizza" (page 298). Gather dandelion greens that show no signs of flowers, and be sure they haven't been treated with chemicals. Or use a mix of organic greens from the market.

8 loosely packed cups tiny dandelion greens or mesclun	2 thin slices pancetta
2 tablespoons fruity extra-virgin olive oil	1 medium red onion, sliced into thin rings
2 thin slices soppressata or cacciatori salami	2 large cloves garlic, minced
	3 tablespoons red wine vinegar
	Salt and freshly ground black pepper

1. Wash the greens thoroughly, checking for grit. Dry thoroughly, then place in a shallow salad bowl.

2. Heat the oil in a 10-inch skillet over medium heat. Sauté the meats until barely colored. Stir in the onions, barely wilting them over high heat. Turn the heat to low, add the garlic, and cook a minute or two. Blend in the vinegar and boil down only a few seconds. Pour over the greens, season with salt and pepper, and toss until blended. Serve the salad immediately.

MARIA FEDRIZZI: GROWING UP ON A MOUNTAIN FARM

Maria Fedrizzi grew up on a mountain farm above the village of Malé in the Swiss-Italian Alps. Today, it's a ninety-minute drive west and north of Trento. In her childhood, it was a day's journey. She told me that when spring finally came each year, it was like being released from prison. "We could visit each other again, and get outside to work. The cows were usually so weak from a winter in their stalls the men joked about carrying them to pastures. But in a week, you could see how strong they were getting from eating the new grass. We made cheese, we grew potatoes and greens and we always gathered wild greens and mushrooms. We had polenta too, from the Veneto. Everyone kept a pig. The men hunted. People say we were poor, but when you never know anything different, you're not poor. I loved our life up there."

Maria now lives in Malé and has grandchildren. Her greatest pride, after them, is Malé's new museum of country life, which she helped create and now runs. On the museum's wide hearth, Maria showed me how to make the dressing for Wilted Dandelion Salad (page 300) in a long-handled black steel skillet over the fire. "We always ate wilted salad with a potato pancake. It cooked on the fire too. That was our supper almost every night in spring and summer. No one had stoves then. I still do it that way sometimes."

At every display, she had another recollection to share. Lifting an old inkwell from a desk, she explained, "In some ways, this was the heart of our lives. Important people used inkwells—the teacher who taught us to read and write and the lawyer everyone went to to have their will made. You know, we're different here from Italians south of us. The law said we had to learn to read and write, and we could not divide up our land. We had to will our land to one person. So there was always enough money to support a family and pay taxes. The boys who didn't inherit became cheese makers or other things. That was the law made when we were still part of the Hapsburg Empire in the last part of the 1700s. So all we farmers were helped by someone with an inkwell."

FRESH FAVA SALAD WITH MINT AND YOUNG SHEEP CHEESE

Insalata di Fava

Serves 3 to 4

When the first spring grasses and wild flowers are blooming, shepherds herd their flocks into hill meadows. At the same time fava beans are ripening in farmhouse gardens to that piercing green color of new spring leaves. Farmers say the first wild flowers and greens give spring sheep's milk its unique sweetness—a perfect match for the tender young fava. No wonder, in Italy, this salad *is* spring. The fava beans are lightly cooked to help slip off their skins. If your fava are sweet and tender with their skins, skip that step. Serve it with coarse country bread for lunch as a first course, and do take it on picnics.

➤ *Cook to Cook:* Fava beans, especially when young and fresh, taste mildly sweet, almost meaty. Sometimes called broad or horse beans, find fresh fava in co-ops, specialty stores and produce departments in early spring. Fresh fava beans are sold in their pods and need to be shelled before cooking. Choose those that aren't bulging (this indicates age). Most have a tough outer skin that will need to be slipped off. The easiest way is to drop them in boiling water for a few minutes.

In this recipe, use any of these young sheeps' milk cheeses: Cacio Romano, young pecorino Toscano, pecorino Sardo, pecorino Sienese, Sini Fulvi Sini or Lago Monate young pecorino, Cacio Romano, or artisan-made American sheep cheeses.

2½ to 3 pounds fresh fava beans (2 cups shelled)
1 quart boiling water
1 clove garlic, split
3 tablespoons white wine vinegar
3 tablespoons minced onion

Salt and freshly ground black pepper
2 ounces young sheep cheese (see Cook to Cook), shaved into long furls
1 to 1½ tablespoons extra-virgin olive oil
1 tightly packed teaspoon fresh mint, torn

1. If the raw fava are sweet and tender, use them raw. Otherwise, in the boiling water, boil the fava 5 minutes, or until barely tender. Drain, rinse with cold water, and cool. Slip off the skins by making a small slit with a paring knife and gently squeezing out the bean. You will have about 2 cups peeled beans.

2. Rub a serving bowl generously with the split garlic. Add the fava, vinegar, onion, salt, and pepper. Let stand about 15 minutes. Strew cheese furls over the beans. Drizzle with olive oil and gently combine. Taste for seasoning, scatter the mint over the beans, and serve at room temperature with a rustic bread.

GRILLED LETTUCES
Insalata alla Griglia
Serves 2 to 3; doubles easily

Taking the mild and tart greens we usually tear into a salad bowl and lightly caramelizing them over heat opens up a whole new taste experience. This salad could be a meal unto itself with some bread and cheese. The greens complement other grilled foods, like fish and poultry. This is the green salad that can be done ahead and will not wilt while waiting to go to the table.

1 head Bibb lettuce
1 head romaine lettuce
1 head curly endive or escarole
Extra-virgin olive oil

3 cloves garlic, thinly sliced
Salt and freshly ground black pepper
Lemon wedges or wine vinegar

1. Discard any bruised outer lettuce leaves. Keep the heads intact as you wash them by immersing in a sinkful of cold water. Cut each into quarters. Wash again if the insides of the lettuces appear to be gritty. Drain thoroughly. Wrap in paper towels and chill several hours.

2. Spread the wedges of greens on a platter, cut side up, and sprinkle lightly with olive oil and the garlic, turning to coat. Sprinkle with salt and pepper.

3. To cook the lettuces on the stovetop, heat a large griddle, ridged pan, or sauté pan over medium-high heat. Arrange the lettuces about an inch apart (do in two batches if necessary) in the pan and brown on all sides. Then lower the heat and cook about 5 minutes. The greens should be caramelized at their edges but still somewhat crisp at their centers. Remove from the heat and taste for salt and pepper. Or, to cook on an outdoor grill, burn the coals until they're covered with gray ash. Have the rack about 4 inches from them. Grill the lettuces over the hot coals, turning them to be sure the edges of their outer leaves become flecked with brown. Then shift them on the grill to cook farther away from the hottest coals. Once they're browned but still crisp at their centers, remove from the grill.

4. Arrange the wedges of greens on a platter and serve warm or at room temperature. Sprinkle with lemon or wine vinegar at the table.

TREVISO POTATO SALAD
Insalata di Patate alla Trevisana

Serves 4 to 6

When you taste potato salad with radicchio you'll probably react the way I did—why didn't anyone think of this before? The radicchio makes the potatoes taste wonderful. In Italy's radicchio capital, the elegant town of Treviso, twenty minutes north of Venice by train, someone did think of it—a long time ago. There the salad is made with waxy potatoes, olive oil, vinegar and the long narrow leaves of Treviso's own style of radicchio.

It's a favorite snack in the old wine taverns that are part of a Treviso tradition. Called *osterie,* the taverns serve local wines, usually Prosecco, and always have food out on the bar. People in Treviso end their workday by dropping into one or two of their favorite places, knowing they'll find their friends there. Small plates and bowls line the narrow bars in each osteria, filled with this salad, maybe rosy goose prosciutto, grilled radicchio, tiny fried fish and slices of salami. There are no plates, no forks; only toothpicks, fingers and napkins. Never elaborate, these are the same dishes that years ago were served *"in umbra,"* an expression heard constantly in Treviso. Literally, "in the shade," it means a place to relax, have something to eat, sip a glass of wine and take time with friends.

➤ *Cook to Cook:* Treviso's long-leafed radicchio rarely gets as bitter as the ball-shaped purple-red radicchio sold in most of our markets. It's hard to find, but when you do, be sure the long narrow leaves are unwilted and their cream and maroon coloring is bright. When it's not available, substitute Belgian endive for Treviso radicchio.

2 pounds (about 15 to 20) small buttery, waxy potatoes (such as Yellow Finn, Red Bliss, red-skinned San Luis Valley, Desiree, or Yukon Gold)

Water

1/2 medium red onion, cut into thin slivers

1/4 cup plus about 3 1/2 tablespoons red wine vinegar

Salt and freshly ground black pepper

3 tablespoons extra-virgin olive oil

1 1/2 heads (8 to 10 ounces) long-leaved Treviso radicchio or Belgian endive, cut into 1/2-inch pieces

1 tightly packed tablespoon fresh Italian parsley leaves, chopped

1. Combine the potatoes with enough water to cover in a 6-quart pot and simmer 15 to 20 minutes, or until tender with a little firmness at the center. Drain, peel, and cut into ½-inch pieces. Turn into a large bowl.

2. Gently fold in the onion, ¼ cup of the vinegar, salt and pepper to taste, and the oil. Let stand 30 minutes.

3. Just before serving, gently fold in the radicchio or endive and the remaining vinegar to taste. Season with salt and pepper, then fold in the parsley. Serve at room temperature on clusters of radicchio or endive leaves.

Oil and Vinegar

Olive oil and wine vinegar, along with salt and pepper, dress foods, especially vegetables, everywhere in Italy. It is a deceptively simple way of seasoning. Instead of everything tasting the same, oil and vinegar exploit the individuality of each ingredient.

How much oil to how much vinegar is determined by what is being seasoned and the taste of the cook. For example, I tasted a fennel salad in Marche where a cook pointed up the fennel's sweetness with more vinegar than oil. In contrast, a friend in the Veneto shuns vinegar, using only a little of the flowery fruity oil from Lake Garda to emphasize the gentleness of fennel. If fresh fennel needs a fruity olive oil and maybe only a whisper of vinegar, cooked dried beans and potatoes want more vinegar and less oil, because their starches absorb and mute flavorings.

Then we have to consider that not all olive oils and wine vinegars are alike. Which ones to pair with which foods is often answered in Italian kitchens by what is harvested or made nearby. When the oil and vinegar and foods to be dressed all come from the same land, there is an intrinsic rightness to the combination. Italians describe this perfectly. *"Si sposa,"* they say. "It marries."

THE SEED MAN OF VICENZA

Three generations of the seed man's family have sold seeds from this counter in the store on Vicenza's main square. It is tidy, the wooden shelves painted a fresh white, the seed drawers clearly labeled. The seed man is a hardy sixty, straight, generous in build and amused by my questions. We talk radicchio. This is the Veneto region, home of Italy's four types of red radicchio. The seed man explains that the father of them all is the famous radicchio of Treviso, with long tongue-shaped leaves of maroon and cream that cluster into narrow heads.

Treviso is an elegant medieval town directly north of Venice—no more than twenty minutes away by train. Each December, Treviso has a radicchio festival. Restaurants serve radicchio in everything from antipasto to dessert. There actually is a sweet radicchio tart: boiled radicchio, caramelized and buried in pastry cream, baked in a sweet crust. In meetings and seminars, growers discuss the fine points of horticulture, marketing and uses. Folklorists argue that new growing techniques for making radicchio milder and more appealing insult Treviso's heritage. The new radicchio designed for export to foreign markets compromises the integrity of one of Italy's most distinguished towns.

Market stalls are heaped with piles of radicchio. Everyone buys it. Purists insist you can eat it raw, you can eat it in risotto, you can eat it grilled and you can eat it marinated in vinegar. You do not eat it in some of the absurd dishes restaurant cooks seemed driven to create. The expression *troppo lavorato*, "overworked," is one of Italy's damning observations. You hear it often in Treviso at this time of year.

By Christmas, all four kinds of radicchio are overwhelming Treviso's shoppers. The seed man calls it the radicchio invasion. Each of the four is distinctive. Treviso's long-leafed heads could be crisp porcelain sculptures with their spear-like leaves. The mild Castelfranco looks like out-of-control cabbage roses, with wide ruffled leaves of pale creamy green spattered with deep claret spots. Verona radicchio's chunky oval heads resemble stubby heads of romaine lettuce with leaves the color of watered-down Chianti ribbed bright white. The fourth type of radicchio is the tight maroon

Treviso radicchio.

purple ball we see most often in America. It comes from a peninsula on the Adriatic tipped with the fishing and farming village of Chioggia, which gives the little heads their name, rosso di Chioggia.

According to the seed man, the same kind of radicchio can taste strong or mild depending on how it's raised. *Radicchio* is the generic Italian name for all chicories. Though chicories are ancient, growing all over Europe, the reddish radicchi aren't accidentally cultivated wild plants. Farmers and botanists set out to create them. Treviso's long-leafed variety came first, in the mid-1800s. From there, all other red radicchi evolved—the Castelfranco from crossing Treviso with a member of the escarole family; rossi di Chioggia, which we know so well, spawned by Castelfranco; and finally the Verona, a direct descendant of the father red of Treviso.

Innocently, I asked the seed man, why not just one kind of radicchio? All these towns are close to each other, why can't they all grow the same kind? When he stopped laughing, he responded, "You expect Italians living in different places to share anything that might be interpreted as being the same? Impossible! Never! Take Chioggia, the radicchio you know in America. The people of Chioggia are famous for being irreverent and knowing how to have a good time. When they make a little money fishing or growing radicchio, they enjoy it, usually with their friends and their family. Go across Chioggia's bridge into what seems a little suburb, and the people are entirely different. They think the Chioggiotti are insane, stupid. They won't part with a lira, and they would never let their neighbors know anything good has happened—they might hit them up for handouts.

"You know, Chioggia is down the coast from Venice and was under its power for a long, long time." He went to the door, gesturing for me to follow. We stepped out into Vicenza's main square. Nearby was a column several stories high, with a lion on top. One of its front paws was resting on a propped-up open book. It looked familiar. "That is the lion of Venice," the seed man explained. "You've seen it in the Piazza San Marco in Venice and in every town square that was under the rule of the Venetian Republic.

"When the book is open, it means the town willingly accepted Venice's rule. When it is closed, they didn't. On Chioggia's column, the book is closed. They call Venice's lion the alley cat. And when they walk under the lion column in the Piazza San Marco, they always say, 'Here kitty kitty, here kitty kitty'!"

Vegetables and Salads

ORANGE SALAD WITH BLACK OLIVES AND RED ONION

Insalata di Arance alla Siciliana

Serves 4 to 6

A Sicilian classic, this salad looks stunning on a buffet table and tastes wonderful. A little sugar and vinegar brings our fruit closer to the intensely flavored oranges that Sicilian farmers pick fresh from their trees. When blood oranges are available, from February to May, blend them with the navels, slipping slices in here and there in a random pattern.

Exotic with exciting contrasts of sweet, salt and savory, this salad reminds us that the Arab world of North Africa is only ninety miles south of Sicily's coast. The salad could come straight from Morocco, Tunisia, or the Middle East. I've always wondered if it is another dish that first came to the island with the Arab invaders who dominated Sicily from the ninth to the fifteenth centuries.

➤ *Cook to Cook:* Thinly slice half a small bulb of fresh fennel over the oranges for another traditional version of this salad.

1 small or $1/2$ medium red onion, sliced into thin rings	About 2 tablespoons extra-virgin olive oil
Ice water	1 tablespoon red wine vinegar
5 large navel oranges or 3 navel oranges plus 2 or 3 blood oranges	$1/4$ to $1/2$ teaspoon sugar
5 herbed or oil-cured black olives, pitted and coarsely chopped	Salt and freshly ground black pepper

1. Immerse the onions in a bowl of ice cubes and cold water. Refrigerate 30 minutes to several hours.

2. Peel the oranges, trimming away all the white pith. Slice into rounds between $1/8$ and $1/4$ inch thick, saving their juice. (The oranges can wait, covered, for several hours at room temperature.)

3. Overlap the orange slices on a large platter. Drain the onions and tuck the rings here and there between the orange slices. Scatter the olives on top. Sprinkle with the olive oil, vinegar, sugar, and reserved orange juice. Season with a little salt and a generous amount of black pepper. Serve soon, to experience the full crispness of the onions.

GRILLED SCALLIONS AND ASPARAGUS

Scalogno e Asparagi Grigliati

Serves 4

Few of us think of scallions as a vegetable, but through the ultimate wisdom of a cook in Tuscany who made this dish one spring, I found they are wonderful grilled, especially when accompanied by asparagus. The vegetables can be made three hours or more before serving and held at room temperature with no problem. Their finish could be fresh lemon, or balsamic vinegar.

3/4 to 1 pound pencil-slim asparagus, trimmed of tough stems

3 bunches scallions, trimmed of root ends and green tops cut to about 4 inches long

About 2 tablespoons extra-virgin olive oil

Generous pinch of sugar

Salt and freshly ground black pepper

2 to 3 tablespoons high-quality commercial balsamic vinegar or fresh lemon juice

1/4 cup finely diced red onion

1/4 cup pine nuts, toasted

1. Up to 3 hours before serving, gently combine the asparagus and scallions with the olive oil, sugar, and salt and pepper to taste.

2. Grill the scallions in one or two batches on an outdoor grill, or in a griddled skillet, on a griddle, or in a sauté pan over medium-high heat, until browned on all sides and tender-crisp, about 3 minutes. Remove to a platter.

3. Repeat the process with the asparagus; it takes 4 to 5 minutes.

4. Arrange the two vegetables on a serving platter, sprinkling with the balsamic or lemon juice, onion, and pine nuts. Serve at room temperature.

FOCACCIA, PIZZA AND BREADS OF INGENUITY

No grain has been more important in Italy than wheat. Money may have been kept under mattresses, but in Sicily, the tall chest that held the year's wheat harvest was not in the barn, nor even the kitchen. It stood in the corner of the farm overseer's bedroom, next to his side of the bed. Anyone trying to reach it had to deal with the overseer first. Since before the rise of ancient Rome, bread made of wheat has been at different times a dream, a meal, a symbol and a celebration.

Years ago, practically everyone who lived on the land ate bread baked by someone in the family. These days few farmers bake their own bread. But if they do still bake at home, usually they make the kinds of breads you'll find in this chapter—what I call the "Breads of Ingenuity."

Ingenuity is the soul of country food everywhere. You take what the land gives and make something of it. All over Italy, country people have traditionally embellished the breads they baked for their families with what they had in their pantries and gardens, turning them into breads that were meals unto themselves or into celebration food. These are the sweetened holiday breads and the pizzas, focacce and pizza rustica and sweetened holiday breads.

Maybe it's because these breads deliver so much good eating for the time spent making them. Certainly they're the party food of choice for country gatherings, especially with young people, who some old-timers claim are turning all of Italy's restaurants into pizzerias. More ordinary focacce and pizzas can hold almost anything you like to eat. In these recipes, find the classic tomatoes with mozzarella, or fresh greens and black olives or rings of red onion with arugula and hot chiles. Two-crusted pizza rustica, filled with tomatoes, onions, olives and currants, could just as easily hold ham, cheeses and roasted peppers. "Cook with what you have" was always the guiding force behind these breads. With a glass of wine and some fruit for dessert, we can serve the country meal Italian farmers ate in the fields during harvests and at night at the kitchen table in front of the fire.

Celebrations and holidays always meant enriching the bread dough made each week with the ingredients that meant special occasions on the farm—sugar or honey, candied fruits, spices, eggs and butter. Everyday bread doughs became Little Easter Loaves in the mountains northeast of Milan, or the Sweet Pumpkin Bread made for All Souls' Day in a fishing town on the Adriatic or Lucca's anise-and-currant-flavored Buccellato that's eaten whenever there's any excuse for celebration.

Mulling over the ingenuity of bread leads to a question—how do you turn a stalk of wheat into the flour that you mix with water, ferment and finally fashion into a loaf of bread? This is neither logical nor easy. How wheat is processed is at the heart of how most Italian farmers worked. Everyone living where wheat could grow raised it at one time or another, with the goal of making bread to feed their family. Wheat's high value on the market sometimes drove landowners to find ways of feeding their workers and/or families with wheat substitutes, like fava beans in the south and polenta in the north. In difficult times, wheat bread became dream food—unobtainable except by the very well off. Even now, in the Puglia countryside around the town of Otranto, farmers and their wives go out into the wheat fields in May when the wheat is turning from green to gold. They kneel and pray, "Give us this day our daily bread. . . ." The women touch the earth and kiss their hands as a symbol of thanks for the fertility that brings their bread to them.

How the wheat stalk became flour wasn't clear to me until I met a retired schoolteacher turned museum guide at a little country folklife museum near the town where Prosecco wine comes from—Conegliano—about an hour's drive north of Venice. Pietro Cescin showed me how he explains it to schoolchildren. He took a stalk of wheat, pointing out the rows of kernels at its top, and said, "You have to figure out a way to remove the coarse outer coatings from these kernels because they're indigestible. This is called threshing." First the children would try to peel or pick away the coating with their fingers, with no success. Then Cescin vigorously rubbed the kernels between his palms, and the tough coating, or chaff, was freed from the grain. The next step is called winnowing— separating the chaff from the grain. Cescin gently blew over the grain, and the chaff piled in his open palms and floated away while the grain barely moved. The wheat was ready for grinding into flour.

Today machines do the work of hands. In the millennia before machines, farmers worked something like this: They loosened the chaff by beating or rubbing heads of wheat in an area of flat, hard dirt or tightly paved stones called the *aia*. If grains scattered here, they couldn't be lost in crevices. To get rid of the chaff, the farmers waited for a day when breezes were soft, then scooped the grain and chaff into wide shallow baskets and carefully tossed the grain into the air. With luck, the breezes carried away the chaff and the grain fell back into the basket. Imagine doing this for enough grain for a year's worth of bread for a large family. No wonder farmers were always trying new methods.

From the aia, the wheat was stored until it was needed for flour. An old saying instructs, "Grind your corn once a week, but your wheat once a month." Farmers took wheat to a local mill, or the women ground it at home in small hand-operated mills called *querns*. Flour was usually stored in a *madia*, which looks like a sideboard and is similar to the Hoosier cabinets popular in our Midwest. Almost every farm kitchen had one, and today collectors and bread bakers treasure old madias. The madia's top is hinged. When you lift it, there is a wide, shallow trough where the women mixed and kneaded their bread dough. They stored the baked bread under the lid, along with a piece of unbaked dough for leavening the next batch. Beneath the trough is a cupboard where utensils and flour were kept. In the Romagna region, farmwives carved a line inside the madia's flour bin. If the flour's level fell beneath the line before Easter, there wouldn't be enough to last until the June wheat harvest. Short supplies always spur ingenuity. Women stretched the wheat by not sifting out as much bran and germ from their ground flour, making darker, denser, more filling loaves. Some flattened their loaves into what we think of as focaccia, garnishing them with generous amounts of salt and oil. Eating a little of this filled you up. Pizza was and is a delicious way of turning a little bit of dough into a meal for a family, especially if there's a flourishing garden outside the kitchen door that supplies toppings for free.

I sometimes find myself thinking of all this when I bake these breads. Probably farmwomen who baked bread week after week didn't marvel at the wonder of it all, but they never wasted a crumb. No one threw bread away. Farmwomen still revive a several-day-old loaf that's beginning to dry up the way my grandmother did—rub the crust with water and warm the bread near the fire, or in the oven. Try this trick for bringing a dry loaf back to life. All over central and southern Italy, cooks simmer hard stale bread with water, salt, garlic and hot pepper, finishing the dish with olive oil. This is soup—good soup at that. In a Sicilian home, I saw in practice what Sicilian food historian Mary Taylor Simeti describes in her writings—when a piece of bread fell on the floor, it was immediately picked up and kissed in apology. In Puglia, it's bad luck if a dropped loaf of bread lands upside down. And the number of bread crumbs you drop predicts the number of years you'll spend in Purgatory.

No wonder bread is such a revered canvas for embellishments and improvisations, and the centerpiece of celebrations. Bread is a celebration. It's a miraculous food. Mix flour, water and leavening and you have a dough that responds to you—push it and it comes back to you. Leave it to rest and, seemingly by magic, the dough grows—you can smell the wheat and yeast ripening.

Bread welcomes a world of flavorings and foods before it's baked and afterward. Once you put it in the oven, the lump of dough is transformed into a loaf of bread—food you could live on. I hope you enjoy these breads. They're a telling part of a delicious legacy.

The Five-Ounce Cup

The recipes in the bread and dessert chapters use a 5-ounce (by weight) cup of flour, measured by scooping a dry measuring cup down into a sack of flour and leveling it off with a straight edge. There is no tapping or tamping. Another name for this method is "dip and sweep." For absolute accuracy, weigh the flour.

FOCACCIA

Makes 1 18 by 13-inch focaccia

This focaccia is different. With its fragrant, nutty flavors and chewy crust, it has more heft and substance than most—it's the kind of bread you build a meal around. And with any of the toppings from the recipes that follow, it could become a meal in itself. The bread comes from the mountains where Tuscany and Liguria meet.

Within this focaccia's ingredients and method lie two secrets to bringing depth and character to homemade breads. By blending white and whole wheat flours to re-create the home-ground, coarse-sifted flours country people have baked with for centuries, we achieve especially nutty flavors. Giving the dough time to ripen opens up more of its wheaten character. Blend and knead the bread the night before you want to serve it. Let it mature overnight in the refrigerator, and ripen it with a slow rise the next day. There's no extra work, but by making time your ally, you'll have a bread of exceptional depth with a dense, nutty-tasting crumb.

➤ ***Cook to Cook:*** If possible, make the focaccia with organic flours, always sniffing them for freshness before buying. There should be no stale or "off" aromas. Often organic all-purpose unbleached white flours are flecked with whole wheat or wheat germ—all the better for this bread. I like the flavor of sea salt in my breads—use it if possible. If not, use regular salt, cutting back one eighth on the quantity. This dough will be softer and stickier than most bread doughs, and this is as it should be.

1 1/2 teaspoons active dry yeast
2 2/3 cups warm water (100°F)
3/4 cup (4.5 ounces) whole wheat bread flour (preferably organic)
4 1/2 cups (about 22 ounces) unbleached all-purpose flour (preferably organic), plus an additional 1/2 to 1 cup

3 1/2 teaspoons fine sea salt
1 to 2 tablespoons extra-virgin olive oil
About 1 tablespoon coarse sea salt

1. Start the focaccia a day ahead: In a large bowl, or the bowl of a heavy-duty mixer, dissolve the yeast in 1/3 cup of the water, along with 1 tablespoon of the whole wheat flour. Let stand until bubbly, about 5 minutes. With a wooden spoon or the paddle attachment, beat in the remaining 2 1/3 cups water, the remaining whole wheat flour, the 4 1/2 cups white flour, and the fine sea salt. Beat by hand or at medium-low speed into a soft, sticky, very elastic dough, about 5 minutes.

2. If making the dough by hand, turn it out onto a floured board and work in another ½ cup to ¾ cup flour, then knead it with floured hands until soft, sticky, and very elastic. If using a mixer, switch to the dough hook. Knead 10 minutes, adding ½ to ¾ cup flour so that the dough cleans the sides of the bowl, but about a third of it puddles on the bottom.

3. To finish the dough made by either method, knead in a few more tablespoons of flour to reduce its stickiness. It will be soft and should be a little sticky. Place in a large oiled bowl. Cover with plastic wrap and refrigerate 8 to 12 hours. (It will not rise; don't worry.)

4. Turn the dough out onto a lightly floured surface and knead a few times. Set it back in the bowl and let it rise at room temperature about 4 hours, or until tripled in bulk.

5. Knead the dough down with floured hands (it will be soft and sticky). Oil an 18 by 13-inch sheet pan or 3 9-inch square cake pans. Stretch the dough to fill the sheet pan, or divide into 3 pieces and spread in cake pans. It will be about ½ inch thick. Cover with a towel and let rise at room temperature 1½ to 1¾ hours, or until doubled in bulk.

6. During this last rise, preheat the oven to 400°F. Drizzle the dough with the olive oil and sprinkle with the coarse salt, or top with any of the suggested toppings in the recipes that follow. Bake about 40 minutes, or until the focaccia is a rich golden brown. With oven mitts and a spatula, slip it out of the pan(s) directly onto the oven rack and bake another 5 minutes, or until hollow-sounding when tapped on its underside. Serve warm or at room temperature.

A Tuscan mountain farm.

FOCACCIA BY ANY OTHER NAME

Tearing off a piece of focaccia, I reach for the platter of salami. Coarse salt and olive oil cover the bread's crust. Flecks of whole wheat color its crumb. The bread and salami could make a meal. No doubt this was often a meal for people here in Tuscany. Months later and over a thousand miles to the south, in Siracusa's market on the Sicilian coast, a farmwoman sells me her homemade turnover of semolina bread stuffed with tomato, potato and cheese. She calls it focaccia. Sicilian recipes for focaccia confuse any definition of focaccia even further—I find several in Sicily for double-crusted pies, and another for a flat round dough with a topping, just like pizza. Across the Italian peninsula, in southern Puglia, a double-crusted pastry tart stuffed with onion, olives and currants is called focaccia in one town and pizza rustica in another. Focaccia is also the name of a Puglia concoction of sliced cornmeal bread topped with roasted olives, and of little round flatbreads baked with tomato sauce.

So what is focaccia? In my Italian dictionary, similar words reveal an intriguing pattern. *Focolaio* means focus, hotbed, center of all. *Focolare* is hearth, fireplace, home *and* focus. In Italy, they say, "I return to my hearth," when telling of going back home. The word *focaccia* can embrace all low breads and tarts, leavened or unleavened, that are baked on a griddle like a pancake, baked in shallow pans buried in embers on the hearth or baked in the oven.

A revealing instruction I find over and over again in old Italian cookbooks describes how hearth breads have been baked for thousands of years: ". . . and bake with fire on the bottom and fire on the top. . . ." Italian country people still use this system today. Shallow clay or metal pans heat on the hearthstone in a bed of hot coals. The focaccia is placed in the pan. A domed lid that has been heating over the fire is set over the pan. Coals are heaped on the lid, creating what is called a pot oven—the classic example of fire on the bottom and fire on the top, and the answer to baking bread with far less fuel than what's needed to fire up a large bread oven.

The most fascinating of focaccia-type breads baked with this old method is a near cousin to pasta, the testaroli of Liguria and the Lunigiana—a great round pancake-like bread no more than a quarter inch thick, and a specialty mastered by every home cook there. This local name comes from the *testo*—the flat griddle or wide shallow pan the bread cooks on.

The testaroli's loose flour-and-water batter bakes in shallow lidded pans, or terra-cotta forms, usually with fire on the top and fire on the bottom. When cooks bake them to crisp and cratered, testaroli are eaten as bread. When baked to soft and spongy (a state reached in several different ways, each traditional to its own area), testaroli straddle the line between bread and pasta. Sliced into strips, these testaroli simmer briefly in water, then are drained and sauced with pesto of fresh basil. And yes, some people refer to them as focaccia.

PORTOBELLO MUSHROOM AND CRISP SAGE FOCACCIA

Focaccia ai Funghi e Salvia

Makes 1 18 by 13-inch focaccia (makes enough topping for 2 12- to 13-inch pizzas)

Wine Suggestion: A red Friuli Refosco or Piemontese Barbera d'Asti

3 tablespoons extra-virgin olive oil
30 fresh sage leaves
1¼ pounds portobello mushrooms, stemmed, cleaned, and coarsely chopped

2 large cloves garlic, thinly sliced
Salt and freshly ground black pepper
1 unbaked Focaccia (page 316), about halfway through the final rise

1. Preheat the oven to 400°F degrees. Film the bottom of a 12-inch sauté pan with 2½ tablespoons of the olive oil. Set over medium heat. Add the sage leaves. Sauté 2 to 3 minutes, or until crisp. Immediately remove with a slotted spoon and reserve. Turn the heat to high. Add the mushrooms, tossing until coated with oil then quickly brown them. Add the garlic and cook 30 seconds. Remove the pan from the heat and let cool. Season to taste. By the time the mushrooms are close to room temperature, the focaccia will be fully risen.

2. Spread the mushrooms on the focaccia dough. Sprinkle with the sage leaves and a little salt and pepper. Drizzle with the remaining ½ tablespoon olive oil. Bake 40 minutes, or until the dough is a rich golden brown. With oven mitts and a spatula, slip the focaccia out of the pan directly onto the oven rack and bake another 5 minutes, or until hollow-sounding when tapped on its underside. Serve warm or at room temperature.

The Sage Bush

I can't separate sage from my personal sense of Italianness. There's not a time I can remember when any woman on the Tuscan side of my family lived without a sage bush in the garden. The herb went into everything, especially chicken and root vegetables. What the ubiquitous fig tree was for southern Italian immigrants—legendary in families for being nurtured and kept alive in hostile American climates as a treasured remnant of the homeland—so the sage bush was for my relatives. The sage bush endured in their new land and was a way back to the kitchens and gardens left behind.

TOMATO, ONION AND PARMIGIANO-REGGIANO FOCACCIA

Focaccia con Pomodoro, Cipolle e Parmigiano

Makes 1 18 by 13-inch focaccia (makes enough topping for 2 12- to 13-inch pizzas)

Wine Suggestion: A red Barbera d'Asti

3 to 4 large ripe, delicious tomatoes, sliced about 1/4 inch thick

1 unbaked Focaccia (page 316), ready for baking

1 medium onion, cut into 1/4-inch dice

2 tightly packed tablespoons *each* fresh basil and Italian parsley leaves, chopped

1 1/2 teaspoons fresh marjoram leaves, chopped

2 cloves garlic, minced

2 1/2 tablespoons extra-virgin olive oil

Salt and freshly ground black pepper

1/4 cup freshly grated Parmigiano-Reggiano cheese, young sheep cheese, or Fontinella or about 1/2 cup thinly sliced fresh mozzarella

1. Preheat the oven to 400°F. Arrange the tomato slices on the focaccia dough. Top with the chopped onion, herbs and garlic. Drizzle with the olive oil. Sprinkle with salt and pepper.

2. Bake 40 minutes, or until the dough is a rich golden brown and the tomatoes and onions appear slightly withered. With oven mitts and a spatula, slip the focaccia out of the pan directly onto the oven rack, sprinkle with the cheese, and bake another 5 minutes, or until hollow-sounding when tapped on its underside. Serve warm or at room temperature.

RED ONION, ARUGULA AND PEPERONCINO FOCACCIA

Focaccia con Cipolla Rossa

Makes 1 18 by 13-inch focaccia (makes enough topping for 2 12- to 13-inch pizzas)

Wine Suggestion: A crisp, white Frascati Superióre

1½ medium red onions, thinly sliced into rings

½ cup Kalamata olives, pitted and finely chopped

1 large clove garlic, minced

2 tightly packed cups arugula leaves, coarsely chopped

1 teaspoon dried oregano

2 loosely packed tablespoons fresh basil leaves, chopped

Shredded zest of 1 medium orange

1 medium hot chile (such as peperoncino, Cubanelle, hot Hungarian wax, or jalapeño), seeded and thinly sliced

Salt and freshly ground black pepper

2 tablespoons extra-virgin olive oil

1 unbaked Focaccia (page 316), ready for baking

1. Preheat the oven to 400°F. In a bowl, combine all the ingredients except the oil (and focaccia) and toss with 1 tablespoon of the olive oil. Spread the topping over the dough, pushing some of it in with your fingers. Drizzle with the remaining 1 tablespoon oil.

2. Bake 40 minutes, or until the dough is a rich golden brown. With oven mitts and a spatula, slip the focaccia out of the pan directly onto the oven rack and bake another 5 minutes, or until hollow-sounding when tapped on its underside. Serve warm or at room temperature.

OVEN-SEARED RADICCHIO AND ASIAGO FOCACCIA

Focaccia con Radicchio e Asiago

Makes 1 18 by 13-inch focaccia

If the radicchio in your market tastes bitter, substitute Belgian endive or curly endive.

Wine Suggestion: A red Piemontese Dolcetto di Dogliani or d'Alba

1 pound radicchio, curly endive, or escarole, separated into leaves
6 quarts boiling salted water
2 cloves garlic, minced
3 tablespoons fresh basil leaves, minced

Salt and freshly ground black pepper
2 tablespoons extra-virgin olive oil
1 unbaked Focaccia (page 316), ready for baking
1/3 cup shredded Italian Asiago cheese or domestic Asiago

1. Preheat the oven to 400°F. Drop the radicchio or other leaves into the boiling water. Cook 3 minutes, uncovered. Drain immediately in a colander, rinse with cold water, and squeeze dry. Coarsely chop.

2. In a bowl, toss together the blanched leaves, the garlic, and basil. Season lightly with salt and pepper.

3. Drizzle 1 tablespoon of the olive oil over the dough. Spread the radicchio mixture over the dough. Sprinkle with the remaining 1 tablespoon oil. Bake 40 minutes, or until the dough is a rich golden brown. With oven mitts and a spatula, slip the focaccia out of the pan directly onto the oven rack and bake another 5 minutes, or until hollow-sounding when tapped on its underside. Sprinkle the cheese over the focaccia and remove from the oven. Serve warm or at room temperature.

RAISIN-ROSEMARY FOCACCIA

Focaccia al Rosmarino e Uvetta

Makes 1 18 by 13-inch focaccia (makes enough topping for 2 12- to 13-inch pizzas)

Raisins and rosemary are a wonderful play of sweet and savory, and the browned raisins look like tiny olives baked on top of this focaccia. This Tuscan snack bread was taken to the fields and eaten along with wine that had been cooling in the well for a merenda, or snack break, in the heat of the day. Serve this focaccia cut into small squares with drinks or wine.

1 unbaked Focaccia (page 316), ready for baking
1 ½ tablespoons extra-virgin olive oil
1 tablespoon sugar
½16 teaspoon salt

½ cup raisins, soaked in hot water and drained
2 tablespoons fresh rosemary leaves, chopped

1. Preheat the oven to 400°F. Poke the dough with your fingers and spread with the olive oil. Sprinkle with the sugar, salt, raisins, and rosemary. With a sharp knife, cut into 3-inch squares in the pan.

2. Bake 40 minutes, or until the dough is a rich golden brown. With oven mitts and a spatula, slip the focaccia out of the pan directly onto the oven rack and bake another 5 minutes, or until hollow-sounding when tapped on its underside. Serve warm or at room temperature.

A CRUST FOR PIZZA

Pasta per Pizza

Makes 1 12- to 13-inch pizza crust, serving 2; doubles easily

One of the secrets of Italy's irresistibly light pizzas is a thin crisp crust like this one; another is not overloading the pie with toppings—less is definitely more on pizza. This dough goes together easily and can be used after a single rise. If time is very short, blend, knead and rest it for thirty minutes, then roll it out.

➤ ***Cook to Cook:*** No baking stone is needed, since you slip the crust out of the pan and crisp it directly on the bottom rack of the oven during the last several minutes of baking. Use this crust for any pizza topping, and do make it with organic ingredients if at all possible.

$^1/_2$ cup warm water (about 100°F)	1 to 1$^1/_4$ cups unbleached all-purpose
Heaping $^1/_2$ teaspoon active	flour (5 to 6 ounces) (preferably
dry yeast	organic), plus more as needed
Pinch of sugar	$^1/_2$ teaspoon salt

1. Pour $^1/_4$ cup of the water into a measuring cup. Stir in the yeast, sugar, and 1 teaspoon of the flour. Bubbles should form on the surface in about 8 minutes. If not, the yeast is past its prime—start again with fresher yeast.

2. In a medium mixing bowl or a food processor, combine 1 cup of the flour and the salt. Blend in the yeast mixture and the remaining $^1/_4$ cup water. Beat with a spoon 2 minutes, or process with on-off pulses 20 seconds. The dough should be soft and sticky. If it's very soft, work in more flour by the tablespoonful until it is some-what sticky, soft, and very elastic. Knead by hand 5 minutes, or process another 5 seconds.

3. Oil a medium bowl, put in the dough, and cover with plastic wrap. Let it rise at room temperature until it is nearly tripled in bulk, about 2 hours. If you are not ready to bake, keep the dough covered and hold up to 4 hours in all. About 20 minutes before baking, punch it down and knead a minute, then form it into a ball and cover.

4. Set an oven rack in the lowest position and preheat the oven to 500°F. Roll the dough out on a floured surface to a 13-inch round about $^1/_8$ inch thick. Set on an oiled baking sheet or pizza pan. Let rest 10 minutes.

5. Top the pizza as desired (see the following recipes). Bake 10 minutes. Using a spatula and a thick oven mitt, slip the pizza off the pan onto the oven rack. Bake another 2 to 3 minutes. Slip back onto the pan and serve hot.

WHOLE WHEAT PIZZA CRUST

Substitute 1/2 cup whole wheat flour or whole wheat graham flour (coarser grind) for 1/2 cup of the all-purpose flour.

THE EVIL EYE

Farmers in the Lunigiana Mountains carry a little sack on a cord around their necks. It holds three grains of wheat to ward off the "evil eye." It hangs between a medal of the Madonna and a medal of the farmer's patron saint. This is called not taking any chances—pagan and Christian beliefs together on a single cord, hanging over the heart.

PIZZA OF TOMATO, CHEESE AND ARUGULA

Pizza ai Pomodori, Mozzarella e Rucola

Makes 1 12- to 13-inch pizza, serving 2; doubles easily

This is the classic pizza of chewy crust, garlicky tomato sauce and creamy mozzarella, with a final touch so dear to the hearts of Pugliese cooks—as the pie emerges from the oven, farmers and pizza makers in Puglia top it with a handful of local wild arugula. For us, the greens can be young arugula or the salad mixes found in our markets. So many of the farms I visited had pizza ovens. From Tuscany down to Sicily, pizza is party food in the countryside. For our own parties, do what Italian farm cooks do—double, triple or even quadruple the crust recipe. As one pizza bakes, invite guests to top the next one, improvising with the suggested variations. Pizzas bake so fast, you can easily keep fresh pizza coming for a crowd.

Wine Suggestion: A red Brigaldara Valpolicella Classico

1 cup Oven-Roasted Canned Tomatoes (page 29) or Tomato Sauce IV (page 128)

OR

TOMATO SAUCE

1 tablespoon extra-virgin olive oil

1 clove garlic, minced

6 large fresh basil leaves, chopped

1 tightly packed teaspoon fresh Italian parsley leaves, chopped

Salt and freshly ground black pepper

1 14-ounce can whole tomatoes

1 Crust for Pizza (page 324), ready for baking

TOPPING

5 to 6 ounces fresh mozzarella, sliced about 1/4 inch thick

2 generous pinches dried oregano

Salt and freshly ground black pepper

About 2 tablespoons extra-virgin olive oil

1/4 tightly packed cup young arugula leaves or organic mesclun mix, coarsely chopped

1. If making the tomato sauce, heat the oil in a 2-quart saucepan over medium heat. Sauté the garlic and herbs a few seconds, seasoning with salt and pepper. Add the tomatoes with their liquid, crushing them with your hands as they go into the pan. Cook, uncovered, at a lively simmer over medium to medium-low heat 20 minutes, or until thick, scraping down the sides of the pan and stirring frequently. Set aside,

covered, for 15 minutes. Season to taste. (The sauce can be refrigerated up to 2 days.) Bring to room temperature before using.

2. Set an oven rack in the lowest position and preheat the oven to 500°F. Spread the roasted tomatoes or tomato sauce over the pizza dough. Scatter the mozzarella over it and lightly sprinkle with the oregano, salt and pepper, and olive oil. Bake 10 minutes, or until the crust is golden brown and the cheese is molten.

3. Using a spatula and a thick oven mitt, slip the pizza off the pan onto the oven rack. Bake another 2 to 3 minutes; don't let the mozzarella brown. Slip the pizza back onto the pan, top with the arugula, and serve hot.

MORE POSSIBILITIES

Improvise with the recipe above: Sprinkle one or two of the following ingredients over the tomato sauce before topping with the cheese: 3 or 4 fresh basil leaves, torn; 3 to 4 anchovies, chopped; 1 tablespoon capers; 1/3 cup sliced onions; 1/4 cup thinly sliced pepperoni; 1/4 cup thinly sliced prosciutto; 1/4 cup pitted olives; 1/2 cup olive oil–packed tuna; and/or 1/2 cup whole-milk ricotta.

Farmer Mimmina bakes bread at Il Frantoio in Puglia.

PIZZA OF CHEESE AND FRESH GREENS

Pizza al Formaggio e Verdure

Makes 1 12- to 13-inch pizza, serving 2; doubles easily

A pizza without tomatoes—instead, a blend of fresh and ripened cheeses finished with fresh herbs, greens and olive oil that takes no time to assemble.

Wine Suggestion: A simple Chianti by Santa Cristina

½ pound fresh mozzarella, sliced
   ¼ inch thick
1 Crust for Pizza (page 324), ready for
   baking
½ cup (2 ounces) freshly grated
   Parmigiano-Reggiano cheese or
   medium-aged sheep cheese (Pecorino
   di Pienza, Pecorino Toscano,
   Pecorino Pugliese, or Fiore Sardo)

6 large fresh basil leaves, torn
Generous pinch of hot red pepper
   flakes
⅓ tightly packed cup chopped greens
   (such as Swiss chard leaves, young
   arugula, mesclun, or dandelion
   greens)
Salt and freshly ground black pepper
About 3 tablespoons extra-virgin olive oil

1. Set an oven rack in the lowest position and preheat oven to 500°F. Scatter the mozzarella over the dough. Sprinkle it with the grated cheese, basil leaves, hot pepper, and greens. Lightly season with salt and pepper and moisten the greens with oil.

2. Bake 10 minutes, or until the crust is golden brown and the cheese is molten. Using a spatula and a thick oven mitt, slip the pizza off the pan onto the oven rack. Bake another 2 to 3 minutes; don't let the mozzarella brown. Slip the pizza back onto the pan and serve hot.

FRESH TOMATO AND BLACK OLIVE PIZZA

Pizza con Pomodori Freschi e Olive Nere

Makes one 12 to 13-inch pizza, serving 2; doubles easily

Another Puglia-inspired pizza, for when you find great-tasting little tomatoes like Sweet 100's, Red Currant or grape tomatoes, Sun Golds and the like.

$\frac{1}{2}$ pound delicious cherry tomatoes (see above), quartered

1 Crust for Pizza (page 324), ready for baking

$\frac{1}{4}$ cup Sicilian black olives or Kalamata olives, pitted and coarsely chopped

2 generous pinches dried oregano

Salt and freshly ground black pepper

2 to 3 tablespoons extra-virgin olive oil

1. Set an oven rack to the lowest position and preheat the oven to 500°F. Scatter the tomatoes over the dough. Sprinkle with the olives, oregano, salt and pepper, and olive oil.

2. Bake 10 minutes, or until the crust is golden brown. Using a spatula and a thick oven mitt, slip the pizza off the pan onto the oven rack. Bake another 2 to 3 minutes. Slip the pizza back onto the pan and serve hot.

PIZZA RUSTICA

Serves 6 as a light supper, 8 to 12 as an antipasto or first course

This isn't a typical pizza rustica. Then again, little of Puglia's vegetable cooking is typical—there's always an original twist that coaxes out more flavor. With this double-crusted pie, a tender, melting crust envelops a filling of browned onion and tomato—two big flavors that could stand on their own. But there's more—a play of sweet and savory, a little vinegar in the onions, along with olives and currants. The pizza is a meal in itself. Have it for supper with a salad, or serve it the way its creator does. On her Puglia farm, Rosalba Ciannamea cuts the pie into dainty bite-sized diamonds and serves it as antipasto. I like it that way with drinks. To totally confuse etymologists, the Pugliese call their double- and single-crusted pies pizza rustica, pizza and even focaccia.

➤ **Cook to Cook:** This pie recipe is a lot simpler than it looks. Make the pastry up to a day ahead, and store it in the refrigerator. Bake the tart several hours ahead of time, then warm it in a 350°F oven for about 10 minutes before cutting and serving.

Insure tender pastry by remembering a simple rule: Whenever pastry is worked (mixed or rolled out), give it a rest in the refrigerator for a minimum of 30 minutes.

PASTRY

2 cups (10 ounces) unbleached all-purpose flour (preferably organic)

1 cup (5 ounces) cake flour (preferably organic)

1 1/2 teaspoons baking powder

1 teaspoon salt

6 tablespoons cold unsalted butter, cut into small pieces

3 tablespoons extra-virgin olive oil

1/2 cup plus 3 tablespoons ice water

FILLING

2 tablespoons extra-virgin olive oil

3 medium onions (2 pounds), cut into 1/2-inch dice

Salt and freshly ground black pepper

4 canned whole tomatoes, drained, seeded, and chopped

2 teaspoons red wine vinegar

1/3 cup Kalamata olives, pitted and chopped medium-fine

1 generous tablespoon currants or raisins, soaked in hot water 10 minutes and drained

1/2 cup freshly grated Parmigiano-Reggiano cheese

1 large egg, beaten

1. Make the pastry by blending the flours, baking powder, and salt in a food processor or large bowl. Thoroughly work in the butter and oil by processing a few seconds, until the mixture looks like coarse meal. Or, by hand, work in with your fingertips. Sprinkle the water over the dough and blend in with a few pulses of the machine, or toss with a fork. Blend only until the dough is evenly moistened and in small clumps. Shape the dough into 2 round patties, wrap in plastic, and chill 30 minutes to 24 hours.

2. Lightly oil a 14- to 16-inch pizza pan or a large cookie sheet. Roll out one half of the pastry on a floured surface to a 14- to 16-inch round if using a pizza pan, or a 12 by 14- to 15-inch rectangle if using a cookie sheet. It will be a little less than 1/8 inch thick. Place on the pan and cover with two overlapping pieces of foil. Roll out the remaining pastry and place on top of the first one. Refrigerate 30 minutes, or more.

3. Heat the oil in a 12-inch skillet over medium-high heat. Quickly sauté the onions to golden brown, sprinkling with salt and pepper. Stir in the tomatoes and cook 4 to 5 minutes, to very thick. Cool.

4. Set an oven rack in the lowest position and preheat the oven to 400°F. Stir the vinegar into the onions and taste for seasoning. Lift the pastry on the foil off to the side. Spread the onions over the bottom pastry, leaving a 1 1/2- to 2-inch border all around. Sprinkle with the olives, currants or raisins, and cheese.

5. Brush the beaten egg over the border of dough. Top with the second sheet of pastry, sealing the edges. Trim the pastry to an even border, roll it up, and crimp. Brush the top of the pie with the beaten egg and pierce all over with a fork. Bake 1 hour, or until browned and crisp. Serve warm (or rewarmed), cut into small diamonds (about 1 inch) as an antipasto, or larger pieces as a light supper.

SWEET PUMPKIN BREAD

Pane Dolce di Zucca

Makes 3 7-inch round loaves

These little round loaves are more like coffee cake than bread. They're the color of dark amber. Sweet pumpkin, honey and raisins make them moist and dense. Lemon and rosemary bring an elegant, exotic quality to the breads even though they're the essence of farmhouse baking. Whenever home bakers in the country wanted something special, they just amended their everyday bread doughs with sweeteners and flavorings they had on hand—like grape syrup, honey, sweet squash and rosemary.

This pumpkin bread is a speciality of Chioggia, a town of farmers and fishermen on the Adriatic coast below Venice. They eat it on November 2, All Souls' Day. A lot of people keep pumpkin bread on the sideboard, wrapped in a linen napkin, ready to be sliced and served to callers along with homemade sweet wine. I serve the bread for brunch with a selection of jams, butter and cream cheese. It makes a great house gift. Toasted and buttered, this is the best late afternoon snack.

➤ *Cook to Cook:* From start to finish, and with little actual effort, sweet pumpkin bread takes about 5 hours. It could be started in the evening, refrigerated overnight during its first rise and finished by early afternoon the next day. Tightly wrapped, the breads freeze well up to 3 months. Use organic ingredients for this bread if at all possible.

2 pounds sugar pumpkin or butternut squash

2 tablespoons extra-virgin olive oil

Shredded zest of 4 large lemons

3 tightly packed tablespoons fresh rosemary leaves, chopped

1½ tablespoons (2 envelopes) active dry yeast

1 cup water, at room temperature

1 cup honey

1 cup milk, at room temperature

1 cup (5 ounces) whole wheat bread flour (preferably organic)

1 tablespoon salt

6 to 7 cups (30 to 35 ounces) unbleached white bread flour (preferably organic)

1 cup golden raisins, soaked in warm water 10 minutes and drained

About 3 cups cornmeal

3 cups ice cubes

1. To roast the pumpkin or squash, preheat the oven to 400°F. Cut the pumpkin or squash lengthwise in half and scoop out the seeds. Cover a cookie sheet with foil and lightly oil it. Roast the pumpkin or squash flesh side down 1 hour, or until easily pierced with a knife. Cool.

2. Scoop out the pumpkin or squash flesh. Puree in a blender or food processor. Measure out $1^1/_2$ cups of puree.

3. In a small skillet, combine the olive oil, lemon zest, and rosemary and warm over medium heat only long enough to be aromatic, 2 to 3 minutes. Immediately remove from the heat and cool.

4. In the bowl of a heavy-duty mixer or other large bowl, combine the yeast, a little of the water, and a few drops of the honey. Let stand until bubbly, about 5 minutes. Then add the remaining water and honey, the milk, the herb blend, whole wheat flour, the pumpkin or squash puree, salt, and $2^1/_2$ cups of the white flour (the raisins go in before the final rise). Beat with the paddle attachment 8 minutes at low speed, or beat with a spoon. Gradually work in another 3 to 4 cups white flour. When the dough becomes too heavy to stir, switch to the dough hook, or turn the dough out onto a floured board and knead in the flour with the help of a pastry scraper. Work in enough flour to make a soft (but not slack), very elastic dough with some stickiness. (Better a too soft dough than a too heavy one.)

5. Continue to knead 15 minutes by machine or by hand. The dough will still be sticky. Set the dough in a large oiled bowl, cover with plastic wrap, and let rise at room temperature until tripled in bulk, about 3 hours.

6. Punch down the dough and knead in the drained raisins. Shape the dough into 3 balls of equal size. Generously cover a baking peel or cookie sheet with half the cornmeal and set the breads on it, spacing them 2 inches apart. Sprinkle with a few spoonfuls of white flour and cover with a towel. Let rise only until $1^1/_2$ times their original size, 45 minutes to 1 hour. Sprinkle a large cookie sheet generously with the remaining cornmeal and set aside.

7. Meanwhile, slip a large shallow pan onto the oven's bottom rack. Set a second rack above it. Preheat the oven to 400°F.

8. Gently slip the risen breads onto the prepared cookie sheet. With a sharp paring knife, cut an X into each loaf. Set them in the oven. Turn the ice cubes into the hot shallow pan, stand back, and immediately close the oven door. Bake 30 minutes. Turn the heat down to 350°F, and bake 20 minutes more. With oven mitts, lift the breads off their sheet and set them directly on the oven rack. Bake another 15 minutes, or until the bottoms of the loaves sound hollow when tapped. Cool breads on a rack. You can hold them at room temperature several days, loosely wrapped.

BUCCELLATO
Buccellato alla Moda di Taddeucci

Makes 1 large loaf, serving 8 to 10

Anise and currants flavor this legendary bread of Lucca. Shaped in the form of a ring, this golden bread isn't quite like Italy's other yeasted sweet breads. Instead of being rich and cake-like, Buccellato is lightly sweetened and spiced—an appealing chewy white bread with a dense, lean crumb. I like Buccellato's simplicity. It tastes like homemade farmhouse bread spiffed up for company with currants and sugar. It's superb with any sweet wine.

In Lucca, no celebration happens without Buccellato and glasses of the sweet Vin Santo. When family comes from far away, Buccellato is served. At a christening for a new baby, Buccellato is served. Youngsters plead with parents, "Aunt Amelia is here [from across town], can't we have Buccellato?" But it's never just *any* Buccellato. The one true Buccellato comes from Taddeucci, the bakery on Piazza San Michele founded by Iacopo Taddeucci in 1882. The stylish old shop has not changed much since then, nor has its Buccellato.

Serve Buccellato sliced thin with glasses of Vin Santo. Toast leftovers for breakfast, or an after-dinner treat with fruit. The Lucchese make a sort of Buccellato strawberry shortcake in berry season, and I think it makes a great bread pudding.

➤ **Cook to Cook:** A heavy-duty electric mixer is handy here, as the dough is a dense one. Its beating bruises the currants, slightly darkening the dough but spreading their flavor through the bread. Certainly a wooden spoon will accomplish the same thing, but it takes much more elbow grease. Use an organic bread or high-protein flour if at all possible. Anticipate about 7 1/2 hours to make the bread. If more convenient, the first rise of 4 hours can be stretched to overnight in a cool place.

Wine Suggestion: A sweet Tuscan Vin Santo

2 1/4 teaspoons (1 package) active dry yeast

2/3 cup warm water (90°F)

About 5 cups (25 ounces) unbleached white bread flour (preferably organic)

1 1/4 cups milk, at room temperature

1 tablespoon anise seeds, bruised with the side of a knife

2 teaspoons salt

3/4 cup (5.25 ounces) sugar

1 cup (about 1/4 pound) currants, soaked in hot water 15 minutes and drained

GLAZE

1 tablespoon sugar

1 tablespoon water

1 large egg

1. In the bowl of a heavy-duty mixer or another large bowl, dissolve the yeast in half the water, with a pinch of the flour. Let proof 10 minutes, or until bubbly. With the paddle attachment at low speed, or by hand, beat in the rest of the water, the milk, anise seeds, salt, sugar, and currants. Slowly beat in 4 cups of the flour, until a soft dough has formed.

2. Replace the paddle with the dough hook and knead at medium-low speed 15 minutes, adding an additional cup of flour a tablespoon at a time, for a soft, sticky dough. Remove the dough to a floured work surface. Knead by hand 2 minutes to form a soft, very elastic dough that is barely sticky. Or, if working by hand, stir in flour until the dough is too heavy to handle. Turn it out onto a floured surface and knead in the remaining flour until the dough is soft, extremely elastic, and barely sticky. Place the dough in an oiled bowl. Cover with plastic wrap and let rise at room temperature 4 hours, or until almost tripled in bulk.

3. Oil a large cookie sheet or pizza pan. Knead down the dough. It will be sticky. Shape the dough into a 24-inch-long log. Bring the ends together, forming a ring, pinch ends to seal, and set it on the pan. Place an oiled upside-down custard cup or ramekin (about 3 inches in diameter) in the center to maintain the shape of the ring as the dough rises. Cover and let rise at room temperature 1 1/2 to 2 hours, until barely doubled.

4. Preheat the oven to 375°F. In a small bowl, beat together the glaze ingredients. Brush generously over the dough. Bake 50 to 55 minutes, or until the bread is a deep mahogany brown and sounds hollow when its bottom is thumped. Cool on a rack. Buccellato keeps several days at room temperature, if well wrapped.

RAISINS, SAINTS AND SHARECROPPERS

In Siena, to the south of Lucca, raisins are baked into a bread similar to Buccellato. It's called "Bread with Saints" (*Pan co' Santi*) and is always baked for St. Martin's Day on November 11. In northern and central Italy, St. Martin's Day closes the farm year, since by this time all the important harvests are in—wheat, hay, corn, produce, fruits and wine. So November 11 became the day for sharecroppers and landowners in those areas to renegotiate their yearly contracts or sever them, with the sharecropper and his family moving on to another post. Bonfires in village squares often mark St. Martin's Day. Farmers feed the blaze with tokens of their harvests—bundles of wheat and hay, bunches of grapes and cuttings from gardens, all symbolizing the cleansing of the land so it will be ready in spring to take seeds and give back food. In Siena, the dried wine grapes that are the raisins in Bread with Saints are part of this idea of consuming the harvest to make way for rebirth. In local lore, the raisins *are* the saints. Eating them in the bread is looked upon as an act of faith that new crops will flourish the following year.

In the Modena area of northern Italy, this commemorating of the harvest is expressed another way. Country people there say about a farmer whose husbandry they admire that he has "put the pig in the shade," meaning he's attended to the four necessities: a year's worth of wood to warm the house and cook meals, enough grain for plentiful bread, enough wine to nourish his family (in Italy, wine was and is seen as food, not solely a beverage) and enough cured pig to feed them or be sold through the year as each part of the preserved animal matured.

Eating saints, putting pigs in the shade and purifying harvests with fire all express that dual philosophy every farmer knows—to be as smart as possible and have faith.

TALE OF THE EASTER BREAD
OF VAL CAMONICA

Giorgio Gaioni writes about the folklore and history of his home, the mountains of the northern end of the Camonica Valley, in the Lombardy region. Gaioni says the following fairy tale is what everyone there tells their children at Eastertime.

The story goes that Rosa the baker was the greediest, tightest woman in the village of Monno. Never had she given away a single loaf of bread, not even to the neediest of the mountain people. Her sole purposes in life were baking and collecting money for her loaves. Everyone in the high valley knew this, so no beggar stopped at her bakery.

On the day before Easter, called the Easter Vigil, rain deluged the village. Rosa was peering out the door when out of the shadows a beggar appeared. "Happy Easter, Rosa," he whispered. Rosa jumped back, frightened. "Tomorrow is Easter," the soft voice continued. "Have you forgotten?" In a trance, Rosa invited the beggar in and gave him a loaf of bread.

Now what do you think happened? Rosa got so dizzy that she staggered back against the counter. Suddenly she had the strangest but most wonderful feeling. She was warm all over, and so happy. The feeling began to go away and the stranger had disappeared. But peering in the window was Widow Menica's little boy. Rosa had never liked him. He always looked so needy. She hated poor people. Let them get jobs and not bother her.

Yet without thinking, Rosa gave the little boy the biggest loaf in the shop. The good feelings came back. Soon her doorway was crowded with the needy of the mountainside—like Peter the cripple; old Martin, who couldn't remember his own name; and Julia, the orphan no one liked. Each and every one left with a loaf of bread for Easter.

By the time everyone left, it was dark outside. The big bread trough held only one tiny loaf for Rosa to eat the next morning in celebration of the Resurrection. Then, another beggar was in the doorway. "Oh, you poor soul," exclaimed Rosa, "you've come too late. There is only one small loaf left, not enough for your Easter, but here, please take it."

The beggar said, "Turn around, Rosa, and see." Before her eyes, the long wooden trough filled with one loaf after another, more bread than she had ever baked at one time. And this wasn't the simple bread she made each day from flour, water, and yeast; these loaves shone with golden crusts of sugar. Inside, they had nuggets of candied fruits and tasted of butter. Frightened, Rosa fell to her knees, pleading, "Who are you?" "Don't be frightened, Rosa," said the beggar. "I am Peter the cripple, old Martin, Julia and all the others."

When she finally looked up, he was gone. The bells of Easter were ringing through the village. Midnight had come. Christ had risen. That golden bread came to be known as "La Spongada Dulcia di Pasqua," or Easter Sweet Bread. The mountain people bake it every year.

LITTLE EASTER LOAVES
La Spongada Dulcia di Pasqua

Makes 10 rolls

These rolls are packed with everything that symbolizes Easter and celebration. They're as good as cake—little golden loaves shining with sugar glaze, plied with butter, eggs and candied fruits.

In the northern Camonica Valley, where everyone has them for Easter, farmers eat the breads two ways—at the beginning of Easter dinner with slivers of prosciutto of chamois antelope, and after dinner with cups of espresso. On Monday of the Angel (Easter Monday), mountain families picnic outside. They toast slices of the Easter rolls over outdoor fires and spread them with butter or homemade jam. For an unusual opening to a spring dinner, serve the rolls with a platter of prosciutto and salami.

➤ *Cook to Cook:* The generous quantity of yeast that gives this egg-and-butter-rich dough its lift also makes it turn stale quickly. So either bake and serve the bread on the same day or bake, cool and freeze it up to 3 months. Use an organic bread or high-protein flour if at all possible.

Plan on a total of 8½ hours for the bread, but stagger it over 2 days. Do the 4-hour sponge in the refrigerator overnight.

SPONGE (BIGA)
2¼ tablespoons (1 package) active dry yeast

1½ cups (7.5 ounces) unbleached white bread flour (preferably organic)

1½ cups warm water (90°F)

DOUGH, FIRST RISE
The sponge (from above)

½ cup warm water

2 teaspoons salt

½ cup plus 1 tablespoon (4 ounces) sugar

1 tablespoon active dry yeast

3 cups (15 ounces) unbleached white bread flour (preferably organic)

DOUGH, SECOND RISE
4 tablespoons (½ stick) very soft unsalted butter

¼ cup (1.75 ounces) sugar

2 large eggs, beaten

1 tablespoon vanilla extract

1¾ cup (about 8 ounces) unbleached white bread flour (preferably organic)

½ well-packed cup finely chopped mixed candied fruit

GLAZE
1 large egg

1½ tablespoons sugar

1 tablespoon water

1. To make the sponge, in the bowl of a heavy-duty mixer or another large bowl, mix together the yeast, a pinch of the flour, and $1/2$ cup of the water. Let stand until bubbly, about 8 minutes. Beat in the remaining water and flour until a very elastic dough forms. Cover with plastic wrap and let stand at room temperature 4 hours, or refrigerate overnight. If the sponge has been refrigerated, let it come to room temperature, about an hour, before continuing.

2. For the first rise, stir the sponge mixture down and add the water, salt, sugar, yeast, and $2^1/2$ cups of the flour. Beat at medium speed with paddle attachment 3 minutes, or by hand, until very elastic. Gradually mix in remaining $1/2$ cup flour, using the dough hook, or kneading it in by hand. Work the dough about 7 minutes. Place in an oiled bowl, cover, and let rise at room temperature $1^1/2$ hours, or until fully doubled in volume.

3. For the second rise, in a medium bowl, beat together the butter and sugar. Add the eggs and the vanilla. Knead down the risen dough and transfer it to the bowl of a heavy-duty mixer. With the paddle attachment, beat in the butter mixture at low speed until thoroughly blended. Add the flour $1/2$ cup at a time, beating until a soft, sticky dough forms. Add the candied fruit. Knead with the dough hook or by hand 8 to 10 minutes, or until smooth and elastic. Place in an oiled bowl and let rise at room temperature $1^1/2$ hours, or until fully doubled.

4. For third and final rise, punch down the dough, divide it into 10 pieces, and shape into balls. Place on two oiled cookie sheets and cover loosely with a towel. Let rise at room temperature 35 minutes, or until nearly doubled. Meanwhile, preheat the oven to 375°F.

5. Using a sharp knife, cut each roll nearly in half. Stir together the glaze ingredients and brush over the rolls. Bake 45 minutes, or until they're a deep golden brown and sound hollow when thumped on the bottom. Cool on a rack.

DESSERTS

Expect the unexpected. This chapter embraces generations of imagination. Basil and rosemary flavor a pear pizza. Black pepper brings an exclamation point of spice to a jam of plums and wine. Taste candied citron in an apple turnover for the Epiphany and imagine how good it could be in an American apple pie. See how polenta and chocolate, the first humble, the other suave and audacious, couple in a sumptuous pudding cake. Crushed toasted almonds in a sweet tart crust turn it into a crunchy shortbread and a far more distinctive foil for fruit fillings than the usual sugared pie dough. Green tomatoes, with healthy shots of lemon and cinnamon, are jam and spoon sweet at the same time. In Italian country homes, desserts are not everyday dishes, so when cooks make sweets, they create them in a spirit of playfulness and celebration.

Sugar may have been a luxurious ingredient for some country people in the past, but that never stifled ingenuity. In fact, many cherished old dishes keep their popularity today because they rely on sweeteners far more interesting than sugar. Clever farm women caramelized sweet squash, boiled down the juices of ripe wine grapes into a sweet syrup, collected honey and captured the sweetness of pears, peaches and figs by drying them in haylofts and attics.

The dividing line between home desserts and those in the *pasticceria* is dramatic. Neither tries to imitate the other, and each has its significance. When I was invited by eighteen-year-old Cattia to see her uncles make cheese in a mountain village near Palermo, lucky inspiration sent me to one of the city's elegant pastry shops for a selection of small tarts. I knew Cattia Cannelle's mother was a fine baker, but I took a chance anyway. The gift was perfect. It honored the mother, complimenting her connoisseurship, suggesting that I knew she would appreciate such refinement.

She, in turn, honored me by insisting we take coffee together. Setting out the silver tray from her display cupboard, she spread an intricately crocheted doily over it. The work of her mother, she explained; the whole village had admired her crocheting and weaving. The tartlets, in their fanned paper liners, were carefully arranged on the doily. She made coffee. We'd begun the dance of civility. Whatever Cattia's mother's plans were for that afternoon, they were set aside. My gift had to be acknowledged and shared. And we must all take coffee together, a kind of communion. No matter how pressed by time or business, I had to accept. Coffee equals welcome. It is pivotal.

Coffee holds a special place in country life, far more a restorative and status symbol than we can imagine. Up until several decades ago, many country people couldn't afford to drink it every day; instead, they drank (and many still do) a brew of toasted barley called orzo, Italian for barley. Yet a tin of coffee beans and a hand grinder were fixtures on farmhouse mantels. When anyone important came to call, coffee was made. When a disaster befell the family, coffee was made. And coffee equated with status. I remember the old woman in Lombardy who nodded proudly as she assured me her aunt had married well by saying, "She served the best coffee in the village, and she never skimped on it."

If the place of coffee in country life seems new to us, so will one of the oldest ingredients in the Western world, almond milk. Almonds were pounded, infused in hot liquid, strained and simmered into a delicious cream used with savories and sweets. In parts of southern Italy, where fragrant almonds grow in many a back garden, almond milk was easy treasure, much better suited to hot climates than dairy cream. In this chapter, find it in a sweet pasta and on its own as it is enjoyed during Puglia winters, served hot in demitasse cups, or cool as a creamy dessert.

Each of these recipes invites you into a different facet of Italian country life, from afternoon coffee with friends to holidays. For instance, the rustic Sweet Rosemary-Pear Pizza's lineage goes back centuries with its spicing of rosemary, basil and orange. It is pure country family food, often eaten on bread-baking day. The big round pizza looks so generous, I serve it at impromptu autumn and winter parties. Easter Ricotta Tart is a classic holiday treat found in Italian pastry shops and home kitchens. Everyone in Italy eats ricotta tart at Easter, but try this particular version, with its crackly meringue topping, whenever you want an elegant but unusual finish to a meal. *Elegant* also brings to mind Panna Cotta, probably the lushest cream dessert to come out of the Piedmont region's dairy country. Whenever I need something that's fast to make and stunning to serve, this, or one other dessert, Iced Summer Peaches, is my first choice. Summer for me is Iced Summer Peaches. This dish captures all the lusciousness of my favorite fruit. Serve the peaches after any kind of food, from American barbecue to Thai.

I think you get the idea—take these desserts and weave them into your life. Make them your own just as Italian cooks have for a very long time.

Measuring Techniques and Tips

Though many Italian home cooks measure by the infamous "handful," "pinch" and knowing when "enough is enough," for those of us new to a recipe, more exact quantities make a difference, especially in dessert making.

➤ Flour: A single measuring cup can hold from 3 to 6 ounces in weight of flour, depending upon how the flour is measured. All the bread and dessert recipes in this book use a 5-ounce cup by weight, measured by scooping a dry measuring cup (metal or plastic, not glass) down into the sack of flour and leveling it off with a straight edge. There is no tapping or tamping. This is also called the "dip and sweep" method.

　　For absolute accuracy, however, weigh your flour. If we could step into the kitchen of any home baker in Italy, we would see a scale on the sideboard. Measuring by weight is accurate and it makes the task much easier. Instead of fiddling with cups, you pour the ingredients on the scale and it's done.

➤ Cornmeal and Sugar: Measured by cup, these do not vary as flour does. One cup of sugar weighs 7 ounces, 1 cup of cornmeal weighs $5^1/2$ ounces.

➤ Nuts: With whole nuts such as almonds and walnuts, 1 cup weighs about 4 ounces. When the nuts are chopped, add another $^1/2$ to 1 ounce per cup. One cup of pine nuts weighs 6 ounces.

➤ A Pinch of Salt: No doubt there is an Italian cook who might have taught me this trick, but it actually came from friend and cooking teacher Lois Lee, who helped in testing these recipes. She always adds a pinch of salt to any sweet recipe. The salt makes something good a little better—it nudges flavors out into the open.

➤ Black Pepper: Black pepper in sweet dishes surprises many modern cooks, but the trick comes straight out of the Italian Renaissance and was, no doubt, used long before. Pepper sparks fruits, chocolate, coffee and vanilla. Use it sparingly, but do use it.

➤ Citrus Zest: Lemon and other zests act much like pepper, lifting and punctuating flavors. Use organic fruit and scrub the rind first. A zester, a gadget with a short handle and a metal blade with a row of tiny holes, is invaluable for removing zest.

CHOCOLATE COINS

Monete di Cioccolato

Makes about 80 small cookies

These tiny, intense cookies are packed with chocolate and pine nuts, while a little rum gives them a pleasant bite. Called "Fava of the Dead" in Rome, they mark All Souls' night. Their dark, almost black color gives the little coins a threatening edge. In the Rome of the Caesars, people believed fava beans held the souls of the dead. Dark little cookies shaped like fava beans play with the same idea. I think they're the soul of all dark, deep chocolatey flavors and were really created to nibble on with espresso, creamy Panna Cotta (page 366) or vanilla ice cream.

2¹/2 cups (11 ounces) pine nuts, toasted
1 cup (7 ounces) sugar
2 tablespoons unbleached all-purpose flour
Generous pinch of salt

5 large egg yolks
¹/4 cup dark rum
2 ounces bittersweet chocolate, melted
3 tablespoons unsweetened cocoa
2 teaspoons vanilla extract

1. Preheat the oven to 350°F. Cover a cookie sheet with parchment paper or butter and flour it. (The cookies bake in three batches. Spooning the dough out onto three sheets of parchment makes the process easier.) In a food processor, grind 1¹/2 cups of the pine nuts with the sugar and flour to a fine paste. Add the salt, egg yolks, rum, melted chocolate, cocoa, and vanilla, and process until combined. The dough will be very soft. Turn into a bowl and stir in the remaining pine nuts.

2. Drop the dough by ¹/2 teaspoonfuls onto the prepared cookie sheet and, if you have parchment, onto two more, spacing the cookies ¹/2 inch apart. Bake the first batch 12 minutes. The cookies will still be soft when pressed. Remove from the oven and cool the cookies completely on the parchment paper on a rack. Set another parchment sheet of cookies on the cookie sheet and bake; then bake the final batch. Store in airtight containers at room temperature up to a week.

PINE NUT AND ALMOND SHORTBREAD

Frollino di Pignoli e Mandorle

Makes about 15 pieces or 1 tart, serving 6 to 8

In the Reggio countryside, in northern Italy's Emilia-Romagna region, this is called the five-minute dessert, for the amount of time it takes to mix the ingredients and get them in the oven. A cross between shortbread and marzipan, this cookie-like sweet is studded with almonds and pine nuts. Serve it cut into small diamond shapes with coffee, or top it with fruit or jam and slice into squares.

Wine Suggestion: A bright, grapy Lambrusco di Sorbara or Lambrusco Grasparossa di Castelvetro

²/₃ cup (3.33 ounces) unbleached all-purpose flour (preferably organic)

²/₃ cup (3.33 ounces) cake flour (preferably organic)

1 cup (7 ounces) sugar

Generous pinch of salt

1¹/₃ cups (5.5 ounces) unblanched whole almonds, toasted

¹/₂ cup (2.5 ounces) pine nuts

1³/₄ sticks (7 ounces) cold unsalted butter

1 large egg

1 tablespoon vanilla extract

¹/₂ teaspoon almond extract

2 tablespoons Amaretto liqueur

About 3 tablespoons powdered sugar

1. Preheat the oven to 375°F. Butter and flour a 9-inch square cake pan. In a large bowl, whisk together the flours, sugar, and salt. In a food processor or blender, finely chop two thirds of the almonds, adding the remaining third toward the last moment so they are only coarsely chopped. Stir into the dry ingredients along with the pine nuts.

2. By rubbing with your fingertips, blend in the butter until it is the size of small peas. In a small bowl, beat together the egg, extracts, and liqueur. Toss with the dry ingredients only long enough to moisten them. The dough should be rough, with big crumbs. Lightly pack it into the pan, without smoothing the top.

3. Bake 40 minutes, or until a knife inserted in center comes out with a crumb or two. Cool 10 minutes in the pan, then turn out onto a rack, top side up, by first inverting the pan on to a plate. Place a rack on the inverted shortbread and flip it over right

side up. Serve the shortbread warm or at room temperature. Wrapped airtight, it will keep 2 to 3 days at room temperature.

4. To serve, sift the powdered sugar over the pastry and cut into 1-inch diamonds. Or leave the shortbread whole and cover with Soft Plum Jam (page 354), Soft Green Tomato Jam (page 355), or Iced Summer Peaches (page 372), then cut into squares.

NONNO AND THE PINECONE

We never knew where he got them, but every Thanksgiving, my Tuscan grandfather (*nonno*) brought a green pinecone to dinner. It went into the oven as the turkey came out, and roasted through the meal. Aromas of pine and resin became, for me, as much a part of Thanksgiving as the first bites of turkey. By the time the dessert plates appeared, the cone was on the table—hot and opened up, looking like a Christmas tree, each of its "petals" holding a pine nut. It was tricky work, cracking the tiny nuts' shells between your teeth to get at that perfumy-tasting meat without burning your tongue.

Nonno was always bringing treats to the holiday table: For Easter, he presented grand baskets of fantastical panorama sugar eggs and little boxes of Torroni Ferrara nougat candy. At Christmas he had hard candies filled with liqueur, never a favorite of mine and my kid cousin, yet the grown-ups loved them. But Thanksgiving was the pinecone. I wonder if it brought back memories of his home in Tuscany.

Only recently, I realized the pinecones of his childhood probably came from the stone pine, an umbrella-shaped pine growing wild throughout the Mediterranean, and around the seaside resort of Viareggio where his family had property. In America, pine nuts come from the cones of the two-leafed pine growing in the Southwest. How Nonno got green pinecones is still a mystery.

Desserts

APRICOT-PISTACHIO POCKETS

Ravioli Dolci

Makes about 40 cookies

These little round stuffed cookies are no more than three bites each. I can never decide which gives me more pleasure—their crust tasting of almonds, lemon and orange or their filling of apricot and pistachios. Luckily, you have both in every mouthful. Every country cook has her own version of sweet turnovers. They're always called by names we associate with pasta—sweet ravioli, sweet tortelli or sweet cappelletti. Add them to holiday cookie trays, or offer them with coffee for a light finish to a big dinner. On special occasions, sprinkle the baked cookies with Galliano or a sweet grappa di Moscato.

PASTRY

1³/4 cups (8.75 ounces) unbleached all-purpose flour (preferably organic)

1³/4 cups (8.75 ounces) cake flour

¹/2 cup (2 ounces) blanched whole almonds, finely ground

1 cup (7 ounces) sugar

1 teaspoon baking powder

¹/4 teaspoon salt

2 sticks (8 ounces) unsalted butter, softened

Shredded zest of ¹/2 lemon

Shredded zest of ¹/2 orange

2 tablespoons light corn syrup

2 to 3 large eggs

FILLING

Generous ¹/2 cup (¹/4 pound) dried apricots

2 tablespoons sugar, or more to taste

Pinch of salt

Shredded zest of ¹/2 lemon

²/3 cup water

¹/4 cup dry Marsala

3 generous tablespoons shelled salted pistachios, coarsely chopped

1 large egg, beaten for glaze

¹/3 to ¹/2 cup Galliano or grappa di Moscato (optional)

1. In a large mixing bowl, thoroughly blend the flours, almonds, sugar, baking powder, and salt. Add the softened butter and citrus zests and with your fingertips, rub together the ingredients until they resemble coarse meal. In a small bowl, beat together the corn syrup and 2 eggs. Using a fork, toss with the flour mixture until the dough is moistened and clumps together. If it seems dry, beat the remaining egg and toss with the dough to moisten. Gather the dough into a ball, wrap in plastic, and chill 30 minutes to overnight.

2. Meanwhile, in a small saucepan, combine the apricots, 2 tablespoons sugar, the salt, lemon zest, water, and Marsala. Cook over low heat, covered, until the apri-

cots are soft and the mixture is thick, 20 to 30 minutes. If mixture is still very liquid, uncover and cook down. Taste for sweetness, stirring in more sugar if needed. Remove from the heat and cool.

3. Puree the apricot mixture in a food processor. Stir in the pistachios.

4. Preheat the oven to 350°F. Cover a cookie sheet with parchment paper, or butter it. On a floured surface, roll out the pastry 1/16 inch thick. Cut into rounds with a 2½-inch scalloped biscuit cutter, or a drinking glass. Place half of the rounds on the cookie sheet (you may need to do this in 2 batches) and top each round with ½ to ¾ teaspoon of filling. Moisten their rims with water. Top with the remaining rounds and seal the edges. Brush with the beaten egg.

5. Bake 12 to 15 minutes, or until golden brown. Lift off the sheet and cool on racks. Store the cookies up to 10 days in a sealed tin in a cool place. To finish with liqueur, sprinkle each cookie with about ¼ teaspoon liqueur just before setting out.

After dessert at a harvest party at my cousin Edda's in
Tuscany, the singing begins.

Desserts

SWEET ROSEMARY-PEAR PIZZA

Pizza alle Pere e Rosmarino

Makes 1 14- to 16-inch pizza, serving 8 to 10

The wedges of pear on this big farmhouse pizza are sprinkled with rosemary, basil, cinnamon, sugar and orange zest. Such uncommon spicing steps straight out of centuries-old recipes for sweet pizzas.

Sweet pizzas are new to us, but in central and southern Italy, they used to be commonplace. There, the word *pizza* describes all sorts of pies, turnovers and flavored flatbreads—both savory and sweet, made with leavened dough or pastry, as in this pizza. Farmwomen used to bake them as a once-a-week family treat. Usually they slipped the pizzas into their bread ovens after they had removed a week's worth of baked loaves of bread. Don't be put off by the sprinkling of olive oil—it has long been used in sweet dishes and adds just the right fruity note to the pizza.

Wine Suggestion: A modest Tuscan Vin Santo

PASTRY

1½ cups (7.5 ounces) unbleached all-purpose flour (preferably organic)

Generous ¼ teaspoon salt

1½ teaspoons sugar

1 stick (4 ounces) cold unsalted butter, cut into chunks

1 large egg, beaten

2 to 3 tablespoons cold water

TOPPING

4 (1½ to 2 pounds) firm-ripe Bosc pears (preferably organic)

½ lemon

Shredded zest of 1 large orange

1 tablespoon fresh basil leaves, chopped

1 teaspoon fresh rosemary leaves, finely chopped

1 teaspoon ground cinnamon

¼ teaspoon freshly ground black pepper

½ cup sugar

2 tablespoons extra-virgin olive oil

1. For the pastry, combine the dry ingredients in a food processor or large bowl. Cut in the butter with rapid pulses in the processor, or rub between your fingertips until the butter is the size of peas. Add the egg and 2 tablespoons of water. Pulse just until the dough gathers in clumps, or toss with a fork until evenly moistened. If the dough seems dry, blend in another ½ to 1 tablespoon water.

2. Oil a 14- to 16-inch pizza pan. Roll out the dough on a floured board to an extremely thin 17-inch round. Place on the pan. Don't trim the excess pastry—fold it over toward the center of the pie. Refrigerate 30 minutes to overnight.

3. Set an oven rack in the lowest position and preheat the oven to 500°F. Take the dough out of the refrigerator. Peel, core, halve, and stem the pears. Slice vertically into ½-inch-wide wedges, about 14 slices per pear. Moisten with a little lemon juice. Fold back the dough's rim so it hangs over the edge of the pan. Arrange the pear slices in an overlapping spiral on the dough, starting right at the rim of the pan. Sprinkle with the orange zest, basil, rosemary, cinnamon, pepper, sugar, and oil. Flip the overhanging crust onto the pears.

4. Bake 20 to 25 minutes, or until the pears are speckled golden brown and the crust is crisp. Cover the crust's rim with foil if it browns too quickly. Remove the pizza from the oven and serve hot, warm, or at room temperature.

*Corner of a nineteenth-century kitchen
in the Garfagnana Folklife Museum.*

Desserts

PLUM-RICOTTA TART IN AN ALMOND CRUST

Torta alle Prugne con Crosta alla Mandorle

Makes 1 9-inch tart, serving 6 to 8

This tart has everything—a crisp crust shot with crushed almonds, a creamy ricotta filling and a topping of ripe plums that have been cooked down to plump bits in spiced wine. *Spoon sweet* is an old-fashioned term for any dessert you'd eat with a spoon, like this one. Zdena Lancellotti, of the Lancellotti family of farmers turned restaurateurs in Emilia-Romagna, taught me the trick of filling fruit tarts with pureed ricotta instead of cooked pastry cream (it's definitely faster and fresher tasting). When Zdena has mascarpone on hand, she folds it into the ricotta instead of the whipped cream. Try this tart when you want something different that's not taxing to make. For a spicy variation, use Soft Green Tomato Jam (page 355) instead of the plums.

➤ *Cook to Cook:* Plum jam freezes well for several months. Bake the pastry shell anywhere from an hour to 2 days ahead. If holding it more than a day, wrap it in plastic wrap and store in the refrigerator. The ricotta filling is best made shortly before serving the tart. Find high-quality ricotta in Italian groceries and specialty food stores. Or, in supermarkets look for the Polly-O brand. Sound ricotta is made with milk, vinegar or another form of acid and salt—never with gelatin or other additives.

Wine Suggestion: A sweet white Albana di Romagna Passita

CRUST
1 cup (5 ounces) unbleached all-purpose flour (preferably organic)
1/2 cup (2 ounces) blanched whole almonds, toasted
3 tablespoons sugar
1/8 teaspoon salt
5 tablespoons (2.5 ounces) cold unsalted butter
1 large egg
1/4 teaspoon almond extract
1 tablespoon cold water

FILLING
3/4 cup high-quality whole-milk ricotta
1/2 vanilla bean, split, or 1 teaspoon vanilla extract
Pinch of salt
3 tablespoons sugar, or to taste
1/3 cup heavy whipping cream or 1/2 cup mascarpone cheese
1 1/4 cups Soft Plum Jam (page 354)
5 or 6 fresh mint leaves, for garnish

1. For the crust, butter a 9-inch fluted tart pan with a removable bottom. In a food processor or medium bowl, combine the flour, almonds (if working by hand, first chop them fine), sugar, and salt. By machine, process until the almonds are finely chopped; by hand, blend well. Add the butter, pulsing with the processor or working it into the dry ingredients with your fingertips until it is the size of small peas. Beat together the egg, extract, and water. Add to the dough, pulsing or tossing with a fork, only long enough for it to form many clumps. Gather the dough into a ball.

2. Roll the dough out on a generously floured surface to a circle ¼ inch thick and about 11 to 11½ inches in diameter. This dough is too fragile to lift in one piece; cut it into 4 wedges. Using a spatula or pastry scraper, lift each into the pan. Press into place, sealing the sections together, forming an even crust that comes up the sides of the pan. It should be about ¼ inch thick all around. Trim edges of any excess dough. Chill 1 to 12 hours.

3. Place an oven rack in the lowest position and preheat the oven to 375°F. Prick the crust all over with a fork. Line with foil or parchment and weight with dried beans. Bake 15 minutes. Remove from the oven and gently lift the foil or parchment and weights out of the crust, taking care not to burn yourself. Bake another 10 minutes, or until the crust is pale gold and looks dry. Cool on a rack.

4. Fill the tart shell no more than an hour before serving. Puree the ricotta until smooth in a food processor and transfer to a bowl, or press it through a fine sieve into a bowl. Scrape the seeds from the interior of the vanilla bean into the ricotta, or add the extract, along with the salt and sugar to taste. If using cream, whip it to soft peaks. Fold in the cream or mascarpone. Spread the filling in the tart shell. Cover it with the Soft Plum Jam. Garnish with a scattering of mint leaves. Serve at room temperature.

SOFT PLUM JAM
Conserva di Prugne

Makes 2²/₃ cups, serving 6 to 8

The color of shiny garnets, this is a soft jam of ripe plums simmered down in red wine that's been infused with bay leaves, anise, black pepper and cinnamon. Serve it on its own in long-stemmed wineglasses with dollops of whipped cream, spread it on a tart of ricotta cream in almond pastry (see page 352) or simply slather it on toast in the morning.

➤ *Cook to Cook:* To bring out the rich fruitiness of the plums, be careful to cook them only long enough to thicken the syrup, without allowing it to caramelize. Because the jam is low in sugar, it may spoil if canned, but it can be frozen up to 6 months or refrigerated up to 2 weeks.

2 cups Barolo or Zinfandel
1¹/₂ cups (10.5 ounces) sugar
Pinch of salt
1 heaping teaspoon black peppercorns, bruised with a mortar and pestle or the bottom of a heavy pot
1¹/₂ teaspoons anise seeds, bruised with a mortar and pestle or the bottom of a heavy pot

8 bay leaves, broken
6 whole cloves
1 4-inch cinnamon stick, broken
2³/₄ to 3 pounds mixed ripe flavorful plums (such as Queen Rosa, Italian Prune, or Casselman)

1. In a 12-inch skillet, combine the wine, sugar, and spices. Simmer, uncovered, about 10 minutes, or until syrupy. Turn off the heat, cover, and let steep 20 minutes.

2. If the plums' skin taste very tart, peel them. Cut each plum into sixths.

3. Strain the syrup through a fine sieve and turn it back into the skillet. Set over high heat and bring to a boil. Add the plums, lowering the heat to medium. Simmer gently, uncovered, stirring frequently, 20 minutes, or until the plums are softened and breaking down. Turn the heat to high and cook rapidly about 8 minutes, or until the bubbles become large and a foam forms. Take care not to burn or caramelize the syrup.

4. Test the jam for doneness by dragging a wooden spatula through the mixture; it should leave a path that stays cleared. Or test the temperature with a candy thermometer; it should be 200° to 225°F. When it is done, immediately turn the jam out of the pan to cool. Store it in sealed containers in the refrigerator or freezer. Serve at room temperature.

SOFT GREEN TOMATO JAM

Conserva di Pomodori Verdi

Makes 1¹/₂ cups, serving 4 to 5; doubles easily

This recipe from the Puglia region proves that green tomatoes have a more important destiny than merely turning into red tomatoes. Some of the late-summer harvest deserves to be simmered into the colorful, spicy-sweet cross between a thick compote and a soft jam that country people eat on its own as dessert, or use just like jam. Dollop it over grilled polenta, spread it on toast or a tart (page 352), serve with pound cake, ice cream or mascarpone cheese.

> ➤ *Cook to Cook:* Having the tomatoes and sugar stand for 24 hours before cooking allows the sugar to draw out the tomatoes' juices, so they stay crisper in cooking and their syrup is more flavorful. Actual simmering takes about 40 minutes. Insure bright contrasts of tart-sweet fruit and spice by cooking the jam only long enough for it not to run when spooned onto a chilled plate (210°F on a candy thermometer). Beyond this, flavors flatten. Because the jam is low in sugar, it may spoil if canned, but it freezes well for 6 months, or keeps in the refrigerator up to 2 weeks.

2 pounds green tomatoes (preferably organic), cored and cut into ¹/₂-inch pieces (reserve juices and seeds)
1³/₄ cups (10 ounces) sugar
2 medium lemons (preferably organic)
Pinch of salt
Generous pinch of freshly ground black pepper
1 3-inch cinnamon stick, broken

1. In a glass or china bowl, toss together the tomatoes, their juices and seeds, and the sugar. Lightly cover with plastic wrap and leave at room temperature 24 hours.

2. Turn the tomatoes into a 4-quart saucepan. Scrub the lemons if they are not organic. With a zester, shred the zest of both lemons into the tomatoes. Cut away and discard the white pith. Cut the lemon's flesh into small pieces, removing the seeds. Stir into the tomatoes, along with the salt, pepper, and cinnamon stick.

3. Bring to a boil, uncovered, over high heat. Reduce the heat so the jam cooks at a moderate simmer. Simmer, uncovered, about 40 minutes, or until a candy thermometer set into the jam reads 210°F. Or, test by spooning a little jam onto a chilled plate—it should not run. Do not overcook. Turn the jam into a bowl to cool. Refrigerate or freeze. For fullest flavor, eat this spoon sweet at room temperature.

APPLE-CITRON TURNOVER

Torta della Befana

Makes 1 large turnover, serving 6 to 8

This big half-moon-shaped turnover is bursting with chunks of apples, raisins and tiny pieces of citron. When you taste what candied citron does for the apple filling, you may want to try some in your next apple pie. High-quality candied citron, the kind that comes in big pieces, always makes me think of a lemon that's been dipped in allspice and sugar. But even supermarket citron is good in this tart. Hill farmers make it in the Versilla area of northern Tuscany on January 6, the Epiphany, which in Italy is the Day of the Befana, when everyone gets presents.

The night before, children leave bread and cheese on the tables and hay on the windowsills for the Befana, a legendary old woman who travels on her white donkey bearing gifts. The next morning, the little ones race through the house, checking inside their shoes and under beds, hoping for toys and dreading the lumps of coal she leaves behind if they've misbehaved.

➤ *Cook to Cook:* Bring the pastry dough to room temperature before filling the turnover, or it will break when you lift it over the apple filling to make the half-moon-shaped tart.

Wine Suggestion: A simple Vin Santo

PASTRY

1³/₄ cups (6.25 ounces) unbleached all-purpose flour (preferably organic)

Pinch of salt

1 tablespoon sugar

Shredded zest of 1 medium lemon

7 tablespoons (3.5 ounces) cold unsalted butter, cut into small pieces

2 tablespoons extra-virgin olive oil

1 large egg yolk

¹/₄ cup cold water

FILLING

²/₃ cup raisins, soaked in hot water 10 minutes, drained, and dried

3 large (1¹/₂ pounds) apples (preferably organic; use Granny Smith, Braeburn, Keepsake, Liberty, or Haralson, or a blend of several), peeled, cored, and thinly sliced

7 tablespoons (3 ounces) sugar, or to taste

¹/₂ teaspoon ground cinnamon

Generous pinch of freshly ground black pepper

¹/₃ cup finely snipped candied citron

Shredded zest of 1 large lemon

1 tablespoon unsalted butter, thinly sliced

1. To make the pastry, in a food processor or bowl, combine the flour, salt, sugar, and lemon zest. Add the butter and olive oil, pulsing until the mixture resembles very coarse meal. Or rub the ingredients between your fingertips. Add the yolk and water, pulsing or tossing until the dough forms moist clumps. Gather it into a ball.

2. Butter a 16-inch pizza pan or a large cookie sheet. On a floured surface roll out the dough to an 18-inch circle and fit it into the pan, trimming away overhang if using a circular pan. Chill 30 minutes.

3. Preheat the oven to 400°F. Bring the pastry to room temperature. Meanwhile blend the filling ingredients in a large bowl and let stand at room temperature 30 minutes.

4. With a slotted spoon, spoon the filling over half the dough (reserve its juices), leaving a 1½-inch border at its rim. Moisten the edges of the dough with water. This dough is fragile—lift it carefully over the filling, forming a half-moon. If it tears, simply press the torn edges together. Seal the edges and crimp.

5. Brush the crust with the reserved filling liquid and cut 3 slashes in the top. Bake 50 minutes to 1 hour, or until the pastry is a rich brown color and crisp. The apples should be soft when pierced with a knife through one of the vent holes. With two spatulas, gently slide the tart onto a large oval platter. Cool, then cut across the tart's width into slices.

EASTER RICOTTA TART

Torta di Pasqua

Makes 1 10-inch tart, serving 8

What a tart! Streaked with crisp meringue, the heart of this tart is creamy ricotta studded with nubs of chocolate and candied fruit. Everything is cradled in a crust that is more cookie than pastry. At Easter ricotta tarts are eaten all over Italy, but few are as tantalizing as this one by Roberto Martinelli, who bakes and cooks in his parents' food shop in the Tuscan village of Pieve Fosciana. Serve it with small glasses of Vin Santo or Asti Spumante.

➤ *Cook to Cook:* Sweet-tasting, creamy whole-milk ricotta is essential to this tart. Find it in Italian groceries and specialty food stores. Taste before buying. If only supermarket brands are available, look for Polly-O. Sound ricotta is made with milk, vinegar or another form of acid and salt—never with gelatin or other additives. The pastry can be made 2 days ahead, prebaked the next day and then filled and baked the day of serving.

Wine Suggestion: A fine Asti Spumante like Gancia Mon
Grande Cuvee or Giuseppe Contratto Asti de Miranda

PASTRY

1¼ cups (6.25 ounces) unbleached all-purpose flour (preferably organic)

¼ cup (1.25 ounces) cake flour (preferably organic)

⅛ teaspoon salt

3 tablespoons sugar

Shredded zest of 1 medium lemon

6 tablespoons (3 ounces) cold unsalted butter, cut into small pieces

2 large egg yolks

2 teaspoons fresh lemon juice

3 to 5 tablespoons cold water

FILLING

3¼ cups (about 30 ounces) high-quality whole-milk ricotta

¼ cup heavy whipping cream

1 large egg, separated

2 large egg yolks

½ cup (3.5 ounces) plus 3 tablespoons sugar

1 tablespoon Galliano liqueur

1 tablespoon vanilla extract

pinch of salt

⅓ cup (1.5 ounces) mixed candied fruit, cut into ¼-inch dice

2 ounces bittersweet chocolate, cut into ½-inch pieces

1 tablespoon pine nuts or coarsely chopped blanched almonds

1. To make the crust, butter a 10-inch metal pie pan. Mix the dry ingredients in a large bowl or a food processor. With your fingertips or pulsing by machine, work in the butter until it is the size of small peas. In a small bowl, beat together the yolks, lemon juice, and 3 tablespoons of the water. Add to the dry ingredients, tossing with a fork or pulsing only until the pastry forms small clumps; another 1 to 2 tablespoons of water may be needed. Shape the dough into a ball.

2. On a floured surface, roll out the pastry to a 15-inch circle about $1/8$ inch thick. Fit it into the pie pan and trim the edges to a 1-inch overhang. Roll the rim under itself and flute it into a high border standing on the pie pan's rim. Chill 1 hour or up to overnight.

3. Preheat the oven to 400°F. Line the pastry shell with foil or parchment, weight with dried beans, and bake 15 minutes. Gently remove the liner and weights and bake another 2 minutes, or until the crust is firm. Cool on a rack.

4. Preheat the oven to 350°F. Puree the ricotta in a food processor and transfer to a bowl, or pass it through a fine sieve into a bowl. Blend in the cream, yolks, the $1/2$ cup of sugar, the Galliano, vanilla, and salt. Stir in the fruit. Turn the ricotta into the pastry shell. Tuck the chocolate pieces in here and there.

5. In a medium bowl, beat the egg white until foamy. Gradually beat in the remaining 3 tablespoons sugar and continue to beat the meringue until it is the consistency of very thick cream—not quite to soft peaks. With a spoon, make a zigzag stripe of meringue thickly over the filing, not covering it completely. Sprinkle the nuts over the meringue.

6. Make a foil ring and cover the pastry rim with it. Place the tart in the oven and turn the heat down to 325°F. Bake 40 minutes. Remove the foil rim and bake another 15 to 20 minutes, or until a knife inserted an inch from the rim comes out with a few streaks. The filling will jiggle a little when shaken, but will set up in cooling. Remove the tart to a rack and cool.

7. If there's time, cover and chill the tart an hour or so—its flavors seem to open up with this step. But bring it to room temperature before serving, cut into narrow wedges. The tart keeps well, covered, in the refrigerator for 2 to 3 days, but it is absolutely prime the day it's made.

CHOCOLATE POLENTA PUDDING CAKE

Budino di Polenta e Cioccolata

Makes 1 8-inch cake, serving 8 to 10

This is a dessert you'll not easily forget—chocolate, scented with cinnamon and orange, moist, with a creamy center and studded with little pockets of pure chocolate. They're practically molten when the cake is served warm. That comforting quality corn has was meant to be paired with the brazen lushness of chocolate.

Sweet polenta is nothing new in Italy's corn country. Honey, sugar and grape syrup made polenta a special treat even in the times when families lived on it day after day. The chocolate here is pure opulence, a wonderful foil for the humble polenta. The cake brings together rich man's and poor man's food.

➤ *Cook to Cook:* Coarse cornmeal makes a difference in the cake, so do seek it out. Freshness and a minimum of processing are the two qualities most important in a cornmeal. Be sure it smells appealing and has no acidic or stale aroma. Mail-order Giusto's superb coarse-ground organic cornmeal (see page 394 for source information). Keeping a supply in the freezer means having some of the best cornmeal in the country ready whenever you need it.

Wine Suggestion: A red Recioto della Valpolicella

2¹/₂ cups whole milk

³/₄ cup (4.25 ounces) coarsely ground cornmeal

¹/₂ cup (3.5 ounces) plus 3 tablespoons sugar

¹/₂ teaspoon salt

8 ounces bittersweet chocolate (such as Lindt Excellence, Valrhona Grand Cru, or Callebaut bittersweet)

Shredded zest of ¹/₂ large orange

1¹/₂ teaspoons ground cinnamon

Generous ¹/₈ teaspoon freshly ground black pepper

4 large eggs, separated

1 tablespoon vanilla extract

¹/₂ cup heavy whipping cream

TOPPING

1 tablespoon unsweetened cocoa

1 tablespoon sugar

Powdered sugar for dusting

OPTIONAL GARNISH

1 cup heavy whipping cream

1 tablespoon sugar

1. In a 2-quart saucepan bring the milk to the boil. Meanwhile, combine the cornmeal, the ½ cup sugar, and the salt in a medium metal bowl. Whisk in the hot milk until smooth.

2. Wash out the saucepan, fill it two thirds full of water, and bring it to a simmer. Cover the bowl with foil, set it over the water, and cook 40 minutes; the polenta will be thick and stiff. Stir three or four times as it cooks and add water to the pan if necessary.

3. Meanwhile, preheat the oven to 350°F. Butter an 8-inch springform pan. Finely chop three quarters of the chocolate and cut the rest into generous 1-inch pieces.

4. When the polenta is cooked, remove the bowl (or pan) from the water. Blend in the finely chopped chocolate, the orange zest, cinnamon, pepper, yolks, and vanilla. Place 1 cup of this mixture in another bowl and stir the cream into it. Set aside.

5. In a large bowl, whip the egg whites until frothy. Beat in the remaining 3 tablespoons sugar, then whip to soft peaks. Fold a quarter of the whites into the non-cream chocolate-polenta mixture to lighten it. Then fold in the rest, leaving a few white streaks. Fold in the chocolate chunks with one or two strokes. Pour half the batter into the prepared pan. Using a spoon, hollow out the center of the batter so the polenta-cream mixture will sit in a pocket, and add the cream mixture. Cover with the rest of the batter. Sift the cocoa over the top, then sprinkle with the sugar.

6. Bake 1 hour, or until a knife inserted at the edge of the pudding comes out with moist crumbs on it, but when put into the center, comes out with creamy streaks. Cool on a rack 15 minutes.

7. Meanwhile, if desired, make the optional garnish by whipping the cream with the sugar until just thickened. Release the sides of the pan and set the cake on a plate. Serve warm or at room temperature, dusted with powdered sugar. Spoon some of the optional cream beside each slice.

Desserts

APPLE CAKE WITH A CRACKLY MERINGUE

Torta di Mele

Makes 1 9-inch cake, serving 10 to 12

This cake delivers so much elegance for a minimal amount of effort. It's fluffy yet buttery with moist chunks of apple, a cap of crackly meringue and, at its base, a thin crust of rich pastry. To make the pastry, all you do is rub together flour, sugar and butter until it's crumbly and pat some of it into the bottom of the cake pan. The rest becomes the cake's batter when you add eggs, milk, apples and lemon. Top it with a soft whipped meringue and bake. The genius behind this creation is Roberto Martinelli, who bakes in the village of Pieve Fosciana in Tuscany's Garfagnana Valley. His customers put the cake out after Sunday dinner, or keep it wrapped in a tea towel in the cupboard for afternoon coffee with neighbors.

Wine Suggestion: A sweet white Moscato from the Piedmont

2 cups (10 ounces) plus 3 tablespoons unbleached all-purpose flour (preferably organic)

1 1/2 cups (10.5 ounces) plus 2 tablespoons sugar

Generous pinch of salt

1 1/2 sticks (6 ounces) cold unsalted butter, cut into small pieces

3/4 cup milk

2 large eggs

1 teaspoon vanilla extract

Shredded zest of 1 large lemon

1 tablespoon baking powder

2 large (about 1 pound) apples (Granny Smith, Braeburn, or Gala), peeled, cored, and cut into 1/2-inch pieces

1 large egg white

1. Place a rack in the center of the oven and preheat to 375°F. Grease and flour a 9-inch springform pan. In a large bowl, with your fingertips, rub together the 2 cups flour, the 1 1/2 cups sugar, the salt, and butter until crumbly. Remove 1 cup of the crumbs and press them over the bottom and about 1/2 inch up the sides of the springform pan, making a crust about 1/8 inch thick.

2. Make a well in the remaining crumb mixture. Add the milk, eggs, vanilla, lemon zest, the remaining 3 tablespoons flour, and the baking powder. With a whisk, blend this mixture thoroughly *without* incorporating the crumbs. Then, with a wooden spoon stir in the crumbs until well blended but still a little lumpy. Fold in the apples. Scrape the batter into the pan.

3. In a small bowl, beat the egg white until foamy. Beat in the remaining 2 tablespoons sugar and beat until the whites barely stand in peaks. Spread over the top of the batter.

4. Bake 65 to 75 minutes or until a knife inserted in the center comes out clean. Remove from the oven and cool 30 minutes on a wire rack.

5. Slip off the sides of the pan and finish cooling the cake. Serve at room temperature. Covered in plastic wrap, the cake holds well at cool room temperature up to 2 days. It keeps a week in the refrigerator. Either way, warming it in the oven makes it even tastier.

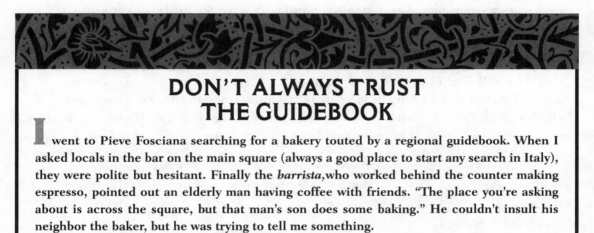

DON'T ALWAYS TRUST THE GUIDEBOOK

I went to Pieve Fosciana searching for a bakery touted by a regional guidebook. When I asked locals in the bar on the main square (always a good place to start any search in Italy), they were polite but hesitant. Finally the *barrista,*who worked behind the counter making espresso, pointed out an elderly man having coffee with friends. "The place you're asking about is across the square, but that man's son does some baking." He couldn't insult his neighbor the baker, but he was trying to tell me something.

The old man practically carried me down the street to a little shop. We would call it a delicatessen. There's at least one of these in every Italian town. Cooked foods and sweets were displayed in the big glass case. The shop's own homemade sausage and hams hung over the counter. Next to the front door was a little espresso machine and a table covered with a white cloth edged in some kind of embroidery. On it sat a tray holding glasses and homemade liqueurs, a Saturday morning welcome to customers: Have a coffee, chase the chill with a little drink—stay and talk.

The old man's son, Roberto, looked like a benevolent bear with a black beard and pink cheeks. He was handing out slivers of ricotta tart to everyone. Cronies and neighbors crowded the store. Saturday morning shopping in small Italian towns is as much catching up on local news as it is stocking the larder, especially now that so many couples both work fulltime jobs. Two people bought a tart immediately. It tasted like a dream. Then he cut into the apple cake. This was even better. Forget guidebooks. This is what I came for.

TIRAMI-SU

Serves 8 to 10

In this Tirami-sù, a blend of mascarpone and zabaglione is slathered between layers of sponge cake that have been moistened with espresso-rum syrup. During the 1970s and '80s, Tirami-sù became the darling of Italy's home cooks. It's irresistible to anyone having company, because you must make it ahead and everyone always raves over it. Each cook has her favorite recipe, especially those living in mascarpone country—the Lombardy region around Milan. This was my first Tirami-sù, tasted in 1981 at a country house near Milan, where it was prepared with locally produced mascarpone. The zabaglione and rum were my hostess's own touches. I've tried others, but keep coming back to this one.

➤ **Cook to Cook:** Mascarpone comes two ways—a firm cheese or a soft one with the consistency of cake frosting, which is the type needed for this recipe. It is sold in bulk and in plastic tubs, imported from Italy or made in Wisconsin. Galbani makes a good one. Some specialty shops make their own mascarpone, which can be superb. Taste for deep, lush sweet cream flavors with no sourness or "cooked" qualities. If mascarpone taste like evaporated milk, don't buy it.

Wine Suggestion: A rich white Sicilian Moscato Passito di
Pantelleria or Maculan's Torcolato

**ZABAGLIONE (MAKE UP TO
2 DAYS AHEAD)**
6 large egg yolks
Scant 1/2 cup (3 ounces) sugar
1/2 cup dry Marsala

**TIRAMI-SU (MAKE 4 TO
24 HOURS AHEAD)**
1 pound soft mascarpone
2/3 cup heavy whipping cream, chilled

6 tablespoons sugar
Pinch of salt
2 9-inch round sponge cake layers
   (store-bought is fine)
1/3 cup very strong espresso
1/4 cup dark rum
1 teaspoon vanilla extract
About 1/4 cup unsweetened cocoa
1 tablespoon powdered sugar

1. To make the zabaglione, half-fill a 4-quart saucepan with water and bring to a simmer over medium-high heat. In a large metal bowl, whisk together the yolks, scant 1/2 cup sugar, and Marsala until foamy. Set the bowl over the simmering water, making sure the bowl doesn't touch it, and keep whisking 5 minutes, or until the cream is thick and reads 170°F on an instant-read thermometer; it will thickly coat a spoon when it's ready. Quickly scrape it into a storage container. Cool, cover, and refrigerate 1 hour to 2 days.

2. About 4½ to 24 hours before serving, stir the mascarpone in a large bowl to loosen it. In a chilled medium bowl, beat the cream with 3 tablespoons of the sugar and the salt to soft peaks. Fold it into the mascarpone, then fold in the cold zabaglione, keeping the mixture light. Chill until ready to assemble the dessert.

3. Have a shallow 2½-quart baking dish handy. Slice each cake horizontally into 2 1-inch-thick layers. Cut into pieces so half the cake covers the bottom of the dish. Mix together the espresso, rum, vanilla, and the remaining 3 tablespoons sugar. Moisten the cake with half the liquid. Cover it with half the mascarpone mixture. Top with another layer of cake. Moisten with the rest of the espresso blend. Cover with the remaining mascarpone cream. Cover and chill at least 4 hours.

4. Just before serving, dust the dessert with sifted cocoa, then sift the powdered sugar over it. Serve cool, but not ice-cold, cut into small squares.

The Original Tirami-sù?

Supposedly the first dessert called Tirami-sù was created during the 1960s at Ristorante Beccherie in the town of Treviso, just north of Venice. Whipped egg yolks and sugar were blended with mascarpone cheese and layered between savoiardi biscuits (hard ladyfingers) that had been soaked in strong espresso. Experts have attributed its creation to other restaurants in Treviso, but local food authorities insist that this is where it began as an improvisation on the popular trifle-like Italian dessert, Zuppa Inglese.

PANNA COTTA

Serves 8; doubles easily

This Panna Cotta is like eating vanilla ice cream. Although *panna cotta* translates as "cooked cream," in fact, you heat the heavy cream only long enough to dissolve the sugar and a little gelatin. To bring the dessert to the consistency it achieves with the superthick cream of the Piedmont region's dairy country where it was born, I stir in sour cream before pouring it into small molds for chilling.

Chefs often dress up Panna Cotta with complicated sauces. I like it on its own, or the way it's eaten in homes, with fresh fruit—cherries when they come into season, then strawberries, raspberries and finally peaches and pears. The boiled-down juice of fresh-pressed wine grapes (Vin Cotto, page 96, or saba), an old country substitute for sugar, sometimes sauces Panna Cotta. Find imported saba from Modena in some fancy food stores. Balsamic vinegar isn't a Piemontese tradition, but the thick liqueur-like artisan-made balsamic (Aceto Balsamico Tradizionale di Modena or Aceto Balsamico Tradizionale di Reggio-Emilia) is fabulous over Panna Cotta.

➤ **Cook to Cook:** Use organic cream if possible and be sure the sour cream contains only cream and culture, no other additives. This recipe unmolds with a soft, creamy finish. For a firmer panna cotta, increase the gelatin to $1^3/_4$ teaspoons.

Wine Suggestion: A lush, sweet red Recioto della Valpolicella
Classico La Roggia by Fratelli Speri

$1^1/_2$ teaspoons unflavored gelatin
2 tablespoons cold water
3 cups heavy whipping cream
$^1/_2$ cup (3.5 ounces) sugar, or more to taste
Pinch of salt
$1^1/_2$ teaspoons vanilla extract
1 cup (8-ounce container) sour cream

OPTIONAL TOPPING
2 cups pitted fresh cherries, strawberries, raspberries, or sliced peaches or pears

OR

$1^1/_2$ to 2 tablespoons artisan-made balsamic vinegar

OR

2 to 3 tablespoons saba syrup or Vin Cotto (page 96)

1. Sprinkle the gelatin over the cold water. Let stand for 5 minutes. In a 3-quart saucepan, warm the cream with the sugar, salt, and vanilla over medium-high heat.

Do not let it boil. Stir in the gelatin until thoroughly dissolved. Take the cream off the heat and cool about 5 minutes.

2. Put the sour cream in a medium bowl. Gently whisk in the warm cream a little at a time until smooth. Taste for sweetness. It may need another teaspoon of sugar. Rinse 8 $^2/_3$-cup ramekins, custard cups, or coffee cups with cold water. Fill each one three-quarters full with the cream. Chill 4 to 24 hours.

3. To serve, either unmold by packing the molds in hot towels and then turning each out onto a dessert plate, or serve in their containers. Serve alone or with the fruit, or drizzle each portion with about $^1/_2$ teaspoon artisan balsamic vinegar or saba.

In the kitchen of a mountain farmer.

ALMOND MILK DEMITASSE

Latte di Mandorle

Makes 5 cups, serving 8 to 10

This thick cream, an infusion of crushed almonds simmered with sugar and almond syrup, is a wonderfully warming old-fashioned drink of generations ago. Chill it and spoon it up like a soft custard, or sip it hot with cookies and cakes, as women still do when they take a break from morning shopping in Puglia's cafés. What hot chocolate is to much of the rest of Italy, almond milk made from local almonds is to southern Italy. By the way, the cream in the recipe is one Puglia cook's addition to traditional almond milk. She insists her mother and grandmother never used it. Certainly it can be left out, but it does help bring our almonds closer to the rich sweet character of those of Puglia.

➣ *Cook to Cook:* Almond milk is traditional in a number of dishes, including Puglia's Christmas treat, Orzo in Swallow's Milk (page 378). Thickened by an additional several minutes of simmering, cream of almond is superb spooned over fruits, cakes, chocolate ice cream and other sweets. Use it warm or cold. Keep cooked almond milk covered and chilled, but know it loses its goodness within about 24 hours.

Since some almonds can be bland, try to taste before purchasing.

1 pound flavorful blanched whole almonds	Pinch of salt
About 6 cups hot water	1 or 2 3-inch cinnamon sticks
6 tablespoons almond syrup (called orgeat, orzo, or orzata)	¼ cup heavy whipping cream (optional)
½ to 1 cup (3.5 to 7 ounces) sugar, or to taste	Ground cinnamon for garnish

1. In a food processor or blender, grind the almonds to a paste with about ½ cup of the hot water. In a medium bowl, blend the almonds with 2½ cups of the hot water, cover, and let stand 30 minutes at room temperature.

2. Line a strainer with a double thickness of cheesecloth or a thin kitchen towel, set it over a bowl, and pour in the almond mixture. Wring out all the liquid and reserve it. Put the almond pulp back into the first bowl, stir in 3 more cups hot water, and steep 30 minutes. Wring out as before into the first batch of almond milk. You'll have 5 to 6 cups.

3. Pour the almond milk into a 4- to 5-quart saucepan. Stir in the syrup, sugar (start with $^1/_2$ cup), salt, and cinnamon stick(s). Bring to a simmer. Simmer, partially covered, 10 minutes. Uncover and simmer another 10 minutes to reduce by about $^1/_2$ cup. Stir frequently and watch for boiling over. Taste for sweetness, adding more sugar as needed. If using cream, stir it in now. Taste again for sweetness.

4. Spoon the almond milk into individual demitasse or full-sized coffee cups, or into small wineglasses. Serve it warm, at room temperature, or chilled, lightly dusted with cinnamon.

ESPRESSO-RICOTTA CREAM WITH ESPRESSO CHOCOLATE SAUCE

Crema di Ricotta all'Espresso

Serves 6 to 8

This cool dessert is silky-sweet ricotta flavored with espresso coffee and spices. The cheese is packed into a pie dish, chilled and then unmolded onto a cake plate. Serve it the way they do at the hill-country trattoria on the Tuscan-Romagna border called Croce Daniele—cut into wedges and streaked with a warm Espresso Chocolate Sauce.

Croce Daniele Trattoria sits on a mountainside with barely any identification. It looks like what it is—a farmhouse where a local family started serving meals years ago and later added more space for a larger dining room. It takes a miracle to find the house, but locals and people from Brisighella and Faenza down on the plain have no trouble. The kitchen is gradually passing from mother to son-in-law, whose passion makes the elderly woman proud. He travels around the area gathering recipes from the old women and men. As with so many places like Croce Daniele, there is no menu. What comes into the kitchen from nearby farms determines what is put before you in the dining room.

➤ **Cook to Cook:** Find high-quality ricotta in Italian groceries and specialty food stores, or use the Polly-O brand. Sound ricotta is made with milk, vinegar or another form of acid and salt—never with gelatin or other additives.

Wine Suggestion: Sambuca liqueur

RICOTTA CREAM

1 1/2 teaspoons unflavored gelatin

1 tablespoon cold water

1/4 cup very strong espresso

1/8 teaspoon ground cinnamon

2 teaspoons vanilla extract

1 pound high-quality whole-milk ricotta

1/3 cup sugar

2 ounces bittersweet chocolate, chopped into 1/4-inch chunks

1/4 cup heavy whipping cream, whipped to soft peaks and chilled

CHOCOLATE SAUCE

2 teaspoons instant espresso powder

1/4 cup hot water

2 tablespoons unsweetened cocoa

1/2 ounce bittersweet chocolate

1/3 to 1/2 cup sugar

1/2 cup half-and-half

1 teaspoon vanilla extract

1. Line an 8-inch pie pan with plastic wrap. Combine the gelatin and cold water in a small saucepan. Let stand 5 minutes. Add the espresso and cinnamon. Stir over medium heat to dissolve the gelatin. Remove from the heat and add the vanilla.

2. Puree the ricotta in a food processor, or press it through a fine sieve. Turn it into a medium bowl and stir in the espresso mixture, sugar, chocolate, and cream. Mix well. Spread in the pie pan, tapping to settle. Cover and chill 8 to 24 hours.

3. To make the sauce, combine the espresso powder with the hot water in a small saucepan. Stir to dissolve. Blend in the cocoa, chocolate, and $1/3$ cup sugar. Stir over low heat until the chocolate melts. Add the half-and-half and heat until an instant-read thermometer reads 100°F. The sauce should be the consistency of thin cream. Remove from the heat and add the vanilla. Taste for sweetness, adding more sugar to taste. The sauce holds well, covered, for an hour or two. Stir as you rewarm it over medium heat before serving.

4. Serve the ricotta cream cool, not cold, sliced into wedges. Drizzle each portion with 2 tablespoons of the warm sauce.

ICED SUMMER PEACHES

Pesche Estive

Serves 4 to 6

Slices of cool fresh peaches are served in wineglasses with a nectar-like wine syrup and surprisingly concentrated flavors. This is one of the more intriguing fruit desserts you'll taste, and there's nothing to it—merely peaches, sugar, wine and an interesting technique. Some country people still use this old trick for making decent fruit taste better and superb fruit luscious. Macerating sliced peaches with sugar permeates them with sweetness and concentrates their flavors while drawing out their juices and turning them into a nectar-like syrup. Then, marinating the fruit in wine releases still more tastes, because certain flavors are soluble only in alcohol. Farmers may not have known the science of this technique, but they knew a day of steeping in sugar and wine in a cool cellar gave the family splendid fruit for after supper.

➤ *Cook to Cook:* If peaches are ripe, often peeling is simply a matter of pulling back their skin with a sharp knife. If need be, dip peaches very briefly in boiling water. The goal is solely to loosen their skins, never to cook the fruit at all, as its character would change drastically. Nectarines can be used instead of peaches.

Wine Suggestion: A fruity Moscato d'Asti

4 large ripe, fragrant peaches or nectarines, peeled, pitted, and sliced into about 8 wedges each

5 to 8 tablespoons sugar

About 1 cup dry white wine (such as Pinot Grigio, Sauvignon Blanc, or Arneis)

4 to 6 sprigs fresh mint or lemon verbena

1. Layer the peaches or nectarines in an attractive glass serving bowl, sprinkling each strata with a tablespoon or so of sugar. (Use less sugar rather than more.) Cover with plastic wrap and refrigerate 2 to 3 hours.

2. Taste the peaches for sweetness, adding more sugar as needed. Pour in wine to barely cover, turning the fruit gently with a spatula to blend. Cover again and refrigerate 4 to 6 hours.

3. Take the fruit out of the refrigerator 30 to 45 minutes before serving. Present the peaches by spooning them and their liquid into wineglasses and finishing with sprigs of mint or lemon verbena.

CARAMELIZED CHESTNUTS

Mondine Quasi Caramellate

Serves 4

In the Versilla Mountains of Tuscany, roasted chestnuts are taken hot from the fire, moistened with wine, shelled, sugared and soaked in rum and vanilla. For a flamboyant finish, they are flamed at the table, turning the sugar into a dark, sticky caramel.

Signore Frati, who created what he claims is Italy's only chestnut museum, shared this recipe in explaining how chestnuts were the bread, sweets and sometimes even meat of Tuscan hill farmers. Although he's an engineer who lives and works in Lucca, his museum is an hour's drive north of town, in the mountaintop village of Colognora di Pescaglia where he grew up, and where everyone still gathers chestnuts every autumn.

Wine Suggestion: A sweet red vermouth on ice

1 pound fresh chestnuts	1/4 cup dark rum
2/3 cup sweet red vermouth	1 vanilla bean, split
1/3 cup dry white vermouth	1/2 pound fresh ricotta or 1/2 cup heavy
2 1/2 tablespoons sugar	cream, whipped and chilled

1. Preheat the oven to 400°F. Make a shallow cut two thirds of the way around each chestnut. Roast in a shallow pan 45 minutes to 1 hour, or until the interior is tender when pierced with the tip of a knife.

2. Immediately turn the hot chestnuts into a deep bowl and add the two vermouths. Cover tightly with a cloth and let stand 20 minutes.

3. Drain the chestnuts, reserving the wine. Shell the nuts, removing their inner skins as well as their outer shells. Turn them back into the bowl. Heat the wine and pour it over the nuts. Cover and marinate another 20 minutes.

4. Drain the chestnuts, discarding the wine. Turn them into a 10-inch skillet. Sprinkle with the sugar and rum. Scrape the seeds from the inside of the vanilla bean over the chestnuts. Gently warm the chestnuts over medium heat. Have a long-handled spoon handy. Stand away as you light the rum. Turn the chestnuts with the spoon until the flames die down, then boil down the liquid until thick, just a few minutes.

5. Spoon the hot chestnuts into four small dessert dishes, then top them with a generous dollop of ricotta or, for an American touch, whipped cream.

FIGS IN HONEYED WINE

Fichi al Miele e Vino

Serves 6 to 8

Dried figs plump as they simmer in this ancient Mediterranean blend of wine, honey, bay, fennel, orange, cloves, cinnamon and black pepper.

The figs improve when prepared a day ahead, with the fruit absorbing more of the syrup's flavors. For a luxurious finish, dollop mascarpone or creamy ricotta next to the fruit. I serve the figs at the end of a big meal, especially during the holidays as a respite from rich desserts.

➤ *Cook to Cook:* When fresh figs are available, simmer the syrup without them and strain. Cut the ripe fruits in half and serve napped with the syrup.

Wine Suggestion: Sicily's sweet Moscato Passito di Pantelleria

2 bottles dry white wine (such as Soave Classico, Pinot Grigio, or Sauvignon Blanc)

2 cups water

1 cup honey, or more to taste

4 bay leaves

1/2 cup (3.5 ounces) sugar

1 tablespoon fennel seeds, pounded fine

Shredded zest of 1 large orange, cut in large strips

2 whole cloves

Generous 1/4 teaspoon freshly ground black pepper

1 4-inch cinnamon stick, broken

1 pound dried figs

1. In a 4- to 5-quart saucepan, combine all the ingredients except the figs. Boil, uncovered, 8 minutes, or until reduced by half. Taste for sweetness, adding more honey if necessary. Add the figs and simmer, uncovered, 20 minutes, or until the figs are softened but hold their shape. (The figs can be kept in their syrup up to 6 hours at room temperature, or overnight in the refrigerator.)

2. To serve the dessert, the syrup can be strained, but it is more traditional and interesting with all the ingredients. Lift out the figs with a slotted spoon and set aside. Boil the syrup again, reducing it by about half, or until it is thickened, and intensely flavored. Put the figs back in the syrup. Remove from the heat and cool to room temperature.

3. Serve the figs on small dessert plates, allowing 2 figs per serving, and spoon the syrup over them. Serve with small dollops of mascarpone or fresh ricotta, if desired.

A TRIBUTE OF WHITE FIGS

Years ago, Tuscan sharecroppers used to split open the ripe figs of late summer, sprinkle them with crushed anise seeds and set them out to dry on twig racks in the sun. People used to say the dried fruit brought sweetness and the feel of summer to winter tables, especially when sugar was expensive.

The farmwomen always held back the whitest figs. These weren't for the family. They were carefully arranged in small wooden boxes lined with white paper. At Christmas, the sharecropper presented these to the landowner, a small lagniappe beyond the capons and other foods demanded by their contract. Perhaps the figs were a political ploy as well, part of the constant game between the landowner and the sharecropper over who could outsmart the other in the division of crops and goods. A box of white figs might distract from a short weight of grain.

THE TWO MISTRESSES
OF IL FRANTOIO

I went to Il Frantoio for one night and stayed ten. Almost as soon as I stepped through the big iron gate into the courtyard, Rosalba Ciannamea, Il Frantoio's new owner, seemed to know instinctively what I was looking for. We were drawn to the same things. When I explained that I hoped to understand the area's foods by understanding the ways its country people had lived from the land, she sat me down in the shade, brought me a cool drink and set in my lap a large old scrapbook. She'd found it in the attic. The book had belonged to Signora Bimbi, Il Frantoio's mistress from sometime around 1910 until the late 1930s.

Signora Bimbi's scrapbook reveals life on the estate at the beginning of the century and the tastes of a woman Rosalba never met. She is restoring Il Frantoio back to that period, and Signora Bimbi has become her guide. The estate is a typical *masseria*, a fortress farm of the south, with vast tracts of olive trees, wheat fields, white-washed buildings and a drive that winds for half a mile from the highway before reaching the gates to the main compound. These estates were worlds unto themselves. Everyone from stable boy to landowner lived behind their high walls, some from birth to death. The masseria system of farming and many of Puglia's existing estates trace their origins to ancient Roman rule.

Today Il Frantoio belongs to Rosalba and her husband, Armando. They're a middle-aged city couple who moved from Bari, fifty miles away, into the country when they fell in love with Il Frantoio. Their goal is making the farm self-sufficient again by taking in guests and improv-

ing how the land is used. They now produce their own oil instead of selling their olives to a cooperative, as was done before they took over. They joined a new regional program that is attempting to raise the standards of local olive oils, and Armando trained as an olive oil taster for the project. As part of a volunteer team, he samples oils to determine if they fit the regional taste profile being developed for Puglia. Now they follow cultivation methods prescribed

by the program—using far fewer chemicals, with more hand tending of the trees. Rosalba hopes all this results in better, more saleable oils.

Although to me it seemed that olive trees cover every inch of their land, Armando and Rosalba also raise wheat and try to grow much of the produce and herbs they use to feed the guests they take in. Il Frantoio is part of Italy's new Agritourism movement, the government program encouraging farmers to take in guests. They're not taxed the way hotels, inns and restaurants are. Rosalba and Armando have taken Il Frantoio beyond a guest farm. It is more like an elegant country inn in New England or California. Antiques, huge beds and old linens furnish the rooms. Dinner and breakfast are included in the daily charges, along with kitchen privileges in the old main-house kitchen that's straight out of the turn of the century. You will never go hungry at Il Frantoio.

Ninety years ago, Signora Bimbi supervised work at Il Frantoio, but now the mistress herself, Rosalba, chips away cheap tiles to reveal the original flagstones in the granary as she turns it into a bedroom suite with the furniture and linens of Signora Bimbi's time. She puts up all the preserved vegetables and fruits that are served each night at dinner in the converted chapel. Rosalba grows heirloom strains of wheat because she loves how they make Il Frantoio's homemade bread taste. She restored the old walled and terraced citrus garden, and planted the courtyard's flowers and palm trees. Elegant, dark-haired and cordial as she is, it's easier envisioning Rosalba as a "lady who lunches" than in an apron cooking many-course dinners for a hundred people every Sunday.

Rosalba calls her kitchen in the chapel her playground for grown-ups. Every afternoon, she writes the evening menu on a chalkboard hung on the white tile wall. Then the women of Il Frantoio gather. They live with their families within the compound walls. There is Thea, Rosalba's sister-in-law; the teenage Croatian refugee now living with the family; and Mimmina and her daughter, the schoolteacher.

Mimmina and her family were the resident *contadini*, or farmers, living within the walls of the compound when Rosalba and Armando purchased Il Frantoio. Their arrangement began long ago with Signora Bimbi's descendants and continues today. The kitchen is off-limits to guests—even those, like me, with a passion for local foods and traditions. Only aromas and muffled banter cross the threshold to the courtyard and my chair in the shade, where I read Signora Bimbi's scrapbook.

CHRISTMAS ORZO IN SWALLOW'S MILK

Orzo di Natale

Serves 8 to 10

This is a pasta dish guaranteed to draw attention, and to please everyone. Pasta shaped like rice grains cooks in fragrant sweet almond milk in this traditional opening in the Lecce area of Puglia to Christmas or New Year's Eve. Sweet pastas always mean celebration in Italy. I serve up Orzo in Swallow's Milk in small bowls for dessert, dusting each portion with cinnamon.

With the region's hot climate and limited grazing that supports very few cows, "swallow's milk" is Puglia whimsy to describe the infusion of ground almonds and hot water that tastes like cream. It is actually almond milk, which dates back at least a thousand years and is made all over the Mediterranean. The late Puglia food authority Luigi Sada told me it symbolizes the sweet milk of the Virgin Mother that nourished the Baby Jesus. It reminds me of the thick creamy custards my mother used to make in winter, only it's more opulent and grown-up. Do try this for dessert—it won't disappoint.

➤ *Cook to Cook:* **Make the almond milk up to 6 hours ahead, holding it covered and chilled. Since some almonds are bland, try to taste before buying. Often organic almonds have better flavor. Organic or not, cut or slivered almonds have less almond taste than whole ones. You can boost the almond character with a little more almond syrup and a few drops of almond extract.**

Wine Suggestion: A fine Asti Spumante like Fratelli Mon
Grande Cuvee or Giuseppe Contratto Asti de Miranda

1 pound flavorful blanched whole
    almonds
About 6 cups hot water
6 tablespoons almond syrup (orgeat,
    orzo, or orzata), or more to taste
1/2 to 1 cup (3.5 to 7 ounces) sugar, or
    to taste

Pinch of salt
1 or 2 3-inch cinnamon sticks
Generous 1/2 cup rice-shaped pasta
    (orzo or meloni) or broken vermicelli
1/4 cup heavy whipping cream
Ground cinnamon for garnish

1. In a food processor or blender, grind the almonds to a paste with about $\frac{1}{2}$ cup of the hot water. In a medium bowl, blend the almonds with $2\frac{1}{2}$ cups of the hot water, cover, and let stand 30 minutes at room temperature.

2. Line a sieve with a double thickness of cheesecloth or a thin kitchen towel. Set over a bowl. Pour in the almond mixture. Wring out all the liquid and reserve it. Put the almond pulp back into the first bowl, stir in 3 more cups of hot water, and steep 30 minutes. Wring out as before into the first batch of almond milk. There should be about 5 cups.

3. Pour the almond milk into a 4- to 5-quart saucepan. Stir in the almond syrup, $\frac{1}{2}$ cup sugar, salt, and cinnamon stick(s). Bring to a simmer. Add the pasta and simmer, partially covered, 15 to 20 minutes, until the pasta is just tender. Stir frequently and watch for boiling over. Taste for sweetness as the pasta cooks and add more sugar as needed. Stir in the cream.

4. Turn into a $1\frac{1}{2}$-quart serving bowl (cut glass is lovely here), or into eight to ten small bowls. Serve the pasta warm or at room temperature, with a dusting of cinnamon. Spoons are the best way to eat it.

MENUS

QUICK WEEKNIGHT SUPPERS

Roman Salad (page 42)
Sicilian Farmer's Bruschetta (page 34)
Fresh Fruit

Grilled Lettuces (page 303)
Uncooked Tomato Sauce for Fusilli
(page 122)
Fresh Peaches with Mascarpone Cheese

Shepherd's Salad (page 46)
Fresh Berries with Cream

Grilled Lamb Chops with Onion and
Oregano (page 253)
Grilled Leftover Polenta (page 36)
Fresh Tomatoes
Nectarines and Apricots with Young
Asiago Cheese

CASUAL DINNERS

Grilled Lettuces (page 303)
Seafood Sauté with Stubby Pasta
(page 84)
Iced Summer Peaches (page 372)

Signora Bimbi's Peppers (page 26)
Spiced Cauliflower with Ziti (page 138)
Green Salad
Almond Milk Demitasse (page 368)

Wilted Dandelion Salad (page 300)
Risotto in the Style of Milan (page 156)
Panna Cotta (page 366)

Hot-and-Spicy Eggplant Soup (page 202)
Balsamico Roast Chicken and Potatoes
(page 224)
Simplest-of-All Green Beans (page 276)
Grilled Scallions and Asparagus (page 309)
Sweet Rosemary-Pear Pizza (page 350)

Tomato-Mozzarella Salad with Pine Nuts
and Basil (page 41)
Tuscan Pork Ribs (page 238)
Crusty Potatoes with Wilted Arugula
(page 49)
Figs in Honeyed Wine (page 374)

Salad of Tart Greens and Red Onion
(page 299)
Tyrolean Pot Roast (page 262)
Margherita's Crushed Buttermilk Potatoes
(page 291)
Pine Nut and Almond Shortbread (page 346)

DINNER PARTIES

Linguine with Pistachio-Almond Pesto
(page 72)
Leg of Lamb Glazed with Balsamic and
Red Wine (page 256)
Simplest-of-All Green Beans (page 276)
Chocolate Polenta Pudding Cake (page 360)

Cantaloupe with Black Pepper, Oil and
Vinegar (page 37)
Fresh Cheese Ovals with Herbs and Spices
(page 40)
Wine-Glazed Chicken (page 230)
Boiled New Potatoes
Tirami-sù (page 364)

Baked Maccheroni with Sunday Ragù
(page 146)
Home-Style Cauliflower and Red Onions
(page 279)
Chocolate Coins (page 345)
Almond Milk Demitasse (page 368)

Sweet-Tart Salad of Apples, Basil and
Sorrel (page 44)
Artichoke Wedding Timbale (page 100)
Espresso-Ricotta Cream (page 370)

CHRISTMAS DINNER

Farmhouse Sunday Soup (page 194)
Harvest Capon (page 228)
Melting Tuscan Kale (page 277)
Romagna Roast Potatoes (page 293)
Orange Salad with Black Olives and Red
Onion (page 308)
Roasted Chestnuts
Christmas Orzo in Swallow's Milk
(page 378)
Apricot-Pistachio Pockets (page 348)

A NEARLY MEATLESS PUGLIA SUPPER PARTY

Mozzarella Bundles (page 56)
Oven-Candied Summer Tomatoes
(page 27)
Fava Puree, Puglia-Style (page 182)

Whole Pan-Roasted Peppers (page 184)
Sautéed Greens (page 184)

Raw Radishes
Fresh Tart Salad Greens
Chocolate Coins (page 345)
Almond Milk Demitasse (page 368)

DINNER FROM THE TUSCAN HILLS

A Medium-Aged Tuscan
Sheep Cheese
Bruschetta with Garlic and Olive Oil
(page 34)
Tuscan Mountain Supper (page 186)
Apple Cake with a Crackly Meringue
(page 362)

PICNICS

Signora Bimbi's Peppers (page 26)
Roasted Roman Artichokes (page 55)
Sicilian Farmer's Bruschetta (page 34)
Grilled Chicken Pieces in Sicilian Mint
Sauce (page 48)
Trout Marinated with Sweet Onions
(page 264)
Treviso Potato Salad (page 304)
Iced Summer Peaches (page 372)

Fresh Greens for Salad
The Puglia Streetwalker (page 132)
Raisin-Rosemary Focaccia (page 323)
Plum-Ricotta Tart in an Almond Crust
(page 352)

INGREDIENTS

You'll find almost all the ingredients for the recipes in this book at your local markets. Capture the best these recipes have to offer by buying in season in farmers' markets and places selling artisan-made and organic foods. When an imported Italian ingredient isn't available, look to local sources, since that's exactly where Italy's farmhouse cooks turn when something they want to cook with isn't coming from their own gardens or pantries.

I've suggested substitutions and included mail-order sources (page 394) for those living in areas where selection is limited.

A Tasting Trick

Whenever possible, taste before you buy. To fully evaluate the quality of any cured or fermented food like cheese, cured meats, wine, balsamic vinegar and bread, try this: After swallowing, count to ten. A food might taste fine initially but have an unpleasant aftertaste. If so, don't buy it. That aftertaste will linger in your cooking and on your palate. Aftertaste can reveal how a food's been stored, careless production or foods going from mature to over the hill.

Anchovies

Both salt-cured and oil-packed anchovies are used throughout Italy. Salt-packed whole anchovies taste meatier than those packed in oil.

Buying, Storing and Using Anchovies   Find them in specialty stores and Italian groceries sold by the piece, or in cans of 1 pound and larger. Salted anchovies hold a year in the refrigerator. To store, remove the anchovies from the can and brush off the salt. Pack them in glass jars, layering them between 1/4- to 1/2-inch-thick layers of fresh sea salt. Bone by opening the anchovy like a book and lifting out the spine and bones. Trim off the head, tail and fins. To diminish salt, soak up to 15 minutes.

Buying, Storing and Using Oil-Packed Anchovies   Buy flat-packed anchovy fillets in olive oil. Store up to 1 year in a cool dry cupboard. To mellow anchovy's aggressiveness, either rinse or soak up to 10 minutes.

Substitute Two oil-packed anchovy fillets for 1 whole salted anchovy.

Balsamic Vinegar

There are two kinds of balsamic vinegar: artisan-made and commercial.

Artisan-Made Balsamic Vinegar   More liqueur and sauce than vinegar. It can be so complex and luscious that it is sometimes sipped from a spoon. Two consortiums of producers and Italian federal law regulate it heavily to insure quality. True balsamic vinegar by law and tradition is produced only where balsamic vinegar originated—in the adjoining provinces of Modena and Reggio, in northern Italy's Emilia-Romagna region. It is made by families who boil down the juice (called grape must) of fresh-pressed wine grapes and then, over years, pass it through a series of wood barrels in the airy attics of their homes. Artisan balsamic contains no wine vinegar. I described the process in detail in my book *The Splendid Table*.

What to Buy   The most reliable sources for true artisan-made balsamics are those bottled by two consortiums, one in Modena, the other in Reggio, after blind tastings to decide on the best. The key word to look for on a label is *"tradizionale,"* as in "Aceto Balsamico Tradizionale di Modena" or "Aceto Balsamico Tradizionale di Reggio-Emilia." Modena's vinegars are either *"Vecchio,"* for twelve-year-old vinegar, or *"Extra Vecchio,"* for twenty-five-year-old. In Reggio, "tradizionale" has three levels of quality—red label, silver and gold. Three-and-one-half-ounce bottles of artisan-made balsamic range from $60 to $250. No two taste alike, because of countless variables—the ages of the wood barrels, the grape blends and each family's style and techniques. Some names to look for: Biancardi, Carandini, Cavalli, Delizia Estense, Leonardi, Malpighi and Pedroni.

Using Artisan-Made Balsamic   Artisan-made balsamic is a concentrated syrupy sauce for seasoning cooked foods, not a vinegar for salad dressings and marinades. Drizzle small amounts over finished dishes—simple pastas, polenta (page 172), risotto (page 154), roasted and grilled vegetables, meat and seafood. Sprinkle it over fruit, chocolate pound cake, creamy desserts (page 366) and vanilla ice cream. **There are no substitutes.**

Commercial Balsamic Vinegar   Few regulations govern commercial balsamic's origins, production or age. The best ones are blends of young artisan-made balsamic or boiled-down grape must and good wine vinegar. Balsamic vinegar makers have always used blends like this for everyday cooking. Lesser commercial balsamics are made of inferior wine vinegar, colored and flavored with caramel. They possess all the goodness of paint remover. Price often doesn't indicate quality.

Using Commercial Balsamic   Use for salads, marinades and simmering into sauces, as well as drizzling over finished dishes. Enrich commercial balsamic with a generous pinch of dark brown sugar per each tablespoon of vinegar. Restaurant chefs in America boil down commercial balsamic to a syrup as a stand-in for "tradizionale." Although not approaching artisan balsamic's finesse, the syrup is good on composed salads and the like.

What to Buy   Malpighi, Cavalli, Mamma Balducci, Elsa, Giusti, La Casa del Balsamico, Due Frati, La Vecchia Dispensa and Manicardi.

Two Exceptions   Noé by Carandini, carried by Balducci's (see mail-order sources, page 394), falls between syrupy artisan-made and commercial balsamic vinegar—a splendid vinegar for about $50 for 8 ounces.

   "Saba" Il Dolce Sapore Degli Estensi di Modena by Giuseppe Leonardi is available from Zingerman's (see mail-order sources, page 395) and in specialty food stores. Saba is the syrup of boiled-down grape must made for more than a millennium all over the Mediterranean as a sweetener from the times when sugar was affordable only to the wealthy. In southern Italy, saba is called Vin Cotto (page 96). Some historians in Modena and Reggio believe saba that was stored in old vinegar barrels became the first balsamic vinegars over a thousand years ago. Use saba as you would artisan balsamic vinegar.

Beans, Dried

See page 181.

Capers, Salted

As big as the tip of a pinky finger, these are the flower buds of the *Capparis sicula* bush, cured in a cloak of salt crystals. They taste of exotic flowers and herbs, far more intriguing than those packed in vinegar.

Buying, Storing and Using Salted Capers   Some of the most prized come from the island of Pantelleria, between the coasts of Sicily and Africa. Find them in specialty food shops and Mediterranean groceries. Rinse well before using. Store in sealed containers in a cool dark place up to a year.

Substitute   Rinsed vinegar-packed capers.

CHEESES

Corrado Barberis, president of Italy's National Institute of Rural Sociology stated, "Cheese is a village's calling card to the world." The skill of the cheese maker certainly shapes a cheese's character. But so does the microclimate it comes from and the mentality and customs of its place of origin. Try to make the same cheese away from its home, and it changes. So there's logic to saying every area of Italy has its own individual cheeses. Many never leave their valley or village. For this reason, when calling for a cheese in a recipe, I've suggested several possibilities of both Italian and domestic examples available in the United States. I've always kept in mind the character of the original cheese and respected that in recommending others. Just remember, the best cheeses are produced by artisans, not factories. Always taste before buying.

Mozzarella

Mozzarella makers say, "Mozzarella has twenty-four attributes and it loses one each hour." Freshness is paramount in mozzarella; better to buy a fresh domestic mozzarella than an old import.

Buffalo milk mozzarella (*mozzarella di bufala*), imported from the Naples area, is famous for its robust grassy, gamy flavors. Cow's milk mozzarella (also called *fiore di latte*) is sweeter and milder.

What to Buy   Look for mozzarella packed in liquid that is soft and chewy, but not rubbery, with a milky center and tasting of fresh milk, with a pleasant hint of sourness. The mozzarella frozen in its liquid now appearing in markets is a respectable stand-in for fresh. The brick-like cheese labeled "low-moisture mozzarella" has nothing to do with true mozzarella. It is not a substitute. Store fresh mozzarella in its liquid in the refrigerator for no more than a day or two.

Using Mozzarella   Obviously on pizzas, with pasta and with tomatoes (page 41). Fresh mozzarella is a course unto itself. Drizzle slices with good olive oil, fresh herbs, salt and pepper and serve at the beginning or end of a meal.

Ricotta

Fresh ricotta is lumpy, with soft, creamy curds tasting almost sweet. Ricotta is made with cow's, sheep's, or goat's milk. Sheep's milk ricotta is favored in southern Italy.

What to Buy   Since freshness is essential, domestic whole-milk ricotta is usually the best choice. Taste before buying if possible for creamy, soft curds tasting of fresh sweet milk. Sheep and goat ricottas taste bigger and nutty-sweet. Reject ricotta with a grainy texture or flat, lean character and any containing preservatives or gelatin. If you can't get premium ricotta, whole-milk Polly-O, available in many supermarkets, is a respectable cheese. Old Chatham Sheepherders in Old Chatham, New York, produces a sound sheep's milk ricotta.

Parmigiano-Reggiano

The king of Italian cheeses. Not *a* Parmesan, Parmigiano-Reggiano is *the* one and only Parmesan cheese; anything else bearing that name is an imitation. By law and the nature of its microclimate, Parmigiano-Reggiano can be produced only in the provinces of Parma, Reggio, Modena and part of Bologna province in the Emilia-Romagna region, as well as in a small part of neighboring Lombardy. Parmigiano-Reggiano cheese makers apprentice between ten and fourteen years.

What to Buy   Try to buy from a newly opened cheese. Look for vertical stenciling on the rind repeating the words "Parmigiano-Reggiano." "Export" branded into the side of an eighty-pound wheel assures double testing for soundness. Older is *not* better. Most Parmigiano is in its prime at 2 years. Find the cheese's month and date of production on the rind. I prefer cheeses not packed in Cryovac. It seems to smother the life out of the cheese—flavors are never as fine with Cryovac.

Taste for big, full flavors that keep opening up and changing as you chew. The cheese turns creamy and crackly on the tongue. It should never be dry, like sawdust. You may find hints of herbs, cream, hay, flint, flowers, earthiness and even a suggestion of roasted meat. Parmigiano's aftertaste is most telling; it should leave you with a desire for more. Winter cheeses tend to taste velvety and rich; summer cheeses can be more flowery, sweet and delicate.

Sharpness, saltiness and bitterness are all signs of careless production and handling, or of a cheese that is too old.

Buy only chunks, never grated cheese. Loosely wrap the cheese in waxed paper and then plastic wrap. Store up to a month in the vegetable section of the refrigerator. If the cheese seems to be drying out, loosely wrap it in moistened cheesecloth or a thin towel, rewrap in plastic and refrigerate 2 days to remoisten. Cut and grate Parmigiano-Reggiano as needed.

Using Parmigiano-Reggiano   Serve chunks of the cheese at room temperature before a meal or for dessert. Parmigiano-Reggiano is never cut, but "opened" in a way to release its shale-like structure. An almond-shaped Parmigiano knife is ideal, but prying away chunks (instead of cutting into the cheese) with a regular knife accomplishes nearly the same thing.

Substitutions   Nothing equals a great Parmigiano, but if not to be had, use Grana Padano or domestic Vella Dry Jack or Asiago. American-made Parmesan is inedible. Never use it.

Sheep Cheese (Pecorino)

Cheeses of sheep's milk or sheep's and cow's milk blends tend to be made in areas where cattle grazing is difficult—mainly, but not exclusively, in central and southern Italy. The variety of Italian pecorino cheeses exported to the United States increases each year, but many of those I've sampled in Italy rarely travel to the next province, never mind across an ocean. Easy substitutions are found in the increasing number of sound Italian and American sheep cheeses that are available in our shops.

Always taste before buying. Remember, just because it's imported doesn't mean it's good. Trust your palate. Better a good American cheese than a mediocre Italian one. Many of our artisan-made cheeses share a kindred character and spirit with cheeses produced by Italian shepherds and cheese makers.

Sheep's Milk Ricotta   See Ricotta above.

Ricotta Salata   This is pecorino ricotta that is salted and pressed. It tastes clean and milky, with pleasing saltiness.

Substitutions   Young Cacio Romano, Marzolino and any firm fresh cheese with character similar to ricotta salata.

Medium-Aged Sheep Cheeses   Usually squat cylinders weighing 3 to 6 pounds and generally aged 3 to 6 months, these cheeses each reflect the micro-climate where they're made. They're as good for eating as for cooking.

Tasting   Medium-aged pecorino can taste of nuts, hay, grass, herbs; have a pleasingly earthy tang; be full-flavored and almost fruity; or taste almost primitively fresh and milky. Poor ones are salty, sharp and/or sour, with an unpleasant bite in their aftertastes.

What to Buy   When a recipe calls for medium-aged sheep cheese, all of these will work: Pecorino Toscano, Pecorino di Pienza, Fiore Sardo, Crete Senesi, Canestrato Pugliese, Casciotta d'Urbino, Cacio Romano, Puglia Cacioricotta, Pecorino Sardo Dolce and Pecorino Siciliano. Two sound brands to look for on sheep cheeses: Sini Fulvi Sini and Lago Monate.

Substitutions   Substitute American artisan-made sheep cheeses for Italian, but taste before you buy. Also try cow's milk cheeses with nutty flavors: from California, the Vella cheese company's Dry Jack, Fontinella and Asiago, and Yerba Santa Alpine's cheeses; Wisconsin's Love Tree Farms sheep cheeses, Bass Lake sheep cheeses and Stella Fontinella. Find the last in many supermarkets.

Aged Pecorino

Pecorino Romano is the most common of these and the most bastardized. Domestic examples are terrible—bitter, sharp and like eating a block of salt. Taste for big, bold, tangy flavors with no bitterness or overwhelming sharpness.

What to Buy   The best Italian aged pecorino I've tasted in America is made by Sini Fulvi Sini and imported. It's found in many cheese shops and specialty stores.

Substitutions   Sharp provolone, aged Fiore Sardo, Pecorino Siciliano and Sicily's Canestrato.

Farro

This whole grain from central Italy looks like wheat kernels but cooks faster, with a lighter, more delicate flavor. (See page 160.) Store either in the freezer or in an open container at room temperature up to 1 year. Look for the botanical designation *Triticum dicoccum*.

Substitutions   Kamut, barley or whole wheat kernels (wheat berries).

OLIVE OILS

Olive oils are graded according to the amount of acid they contain and whether they're processed with heat and with or without chemical solvents.

"Extra-virgin" describes oil with the least amount of acid, less than 1 percent, that is processed without heat and/or solvents.

"Virgin," "fine virgin" and **"semi-fine virgin"** are oils with higher acid levels but that have not been treated with heat or solvents.

"Pure," "pomace" and only the words **"olive oil"** on the label all describe oils treated with solvents, and in some cases heat.

"Light" is a marketing ploy. It has the same calorie count as other oils, but the oil is treated to remove taste and color. Don't waste your money or your palate on it.

What to Know

Buy extra-virgin oils for the purest expression of the olive, but remember "extra-virgin" describes a process, not a quality of flavor.

Fresher is better. Olive oil is in its prime in its first year of life, so when buying premium oil (almost always expensive), look for a harvest date—in Italian, *"raccolta da," "annata,"* or *"annata di produzione."* Olives are harvested and pressed from October to March, depending on where they grow in Italy. Don't be fooled by a bottling date (*"imbottigliato," "in bottiglia"*). Producers can hold oils a year or more before bottling. Lacking a harvest date, check the "best by" or "best before" date, usually set 2 years after harvest. Don't buy premium oils without any indication of the year of production.

Color is no indication of quality.

Store olive oil away from heat and light.

Some Italians save expensive premium oils for seasoning cooked dishes and salads. They cook with cheaper extra-virgin oils that are inoffensive.

Premium oils are as distinctive as wines. No two are exactly alike, and many change with each year's harvest, and certainly with their place of origin. The only way to know an oil is to sample it.

How to Taste Olive Oil

Never sample olive oil with bread, which always improves its flavor. Evaluate olive oil by tasting it from a spoon, rolling the oil around in your mouth to fully savor it. Then suck air over the oil to break down its flavor elements. After you swallow, wait for the aftertaste. For example, Tuscan and Umbrian oils might leave behind lots of pepper in your throat, while the gentler oils of, say, Liguria, can taste like butter.

Then decide if you like the oil. Is the oil flat, dull and merely "oily"? Or is it lively and full of fruit? Maybe it's mellow with subtle buttery flavors or tastes of nuts, cheese and vegetables. Olive oils have a vast range of possibilities.

What to Buy

Buy for flavor. If you don't like an oil, don't use it. One of the great pleasures of Italian cooking is gradually collecting a "wardrobe" of oils for different-style dishes. The following recommendations are some of my favorites. Perhaps they'll be a starting point for your own experiments.

For Cooking   Some oils with good balance and flavor are Carapelli, Bella, Carli, Fabri, Colavita and Sciabica from California.

For Seasoning   A twirl of distinctive oil over a dish brings flavors into focus much the way salt and pepper do. For me, olive oils fall into three categories. Here are some I like for seasoning. I cook with them when I am feeling flush.

Buttery, Gently Fruity   Ardoino "Fructus" (an oil I keep coming back to), Frantoio Borgomaro di Laura Marvaldi and Roi's Carte Noire are my favorites for basil pesto (page 74), and any dish where herbs and cheese dominate, as well as most green salads. In the "not as distinctive but quite fine" category are Rainieri, Crespi and Isnardi.

Fruity, Full-Flavored, Some Pepper   For seafood dishes (pages 264–270) and nut pesto (page 72), and for drizzling over cheeses, potatoes (page 50), bread and vegetables, I like Ravida, Laudemio Frescobaldi (both favorite all-around oils), Olio Verde of Gianfranco Becchina and Lila Jaeger and McEvoy olive oils of California.

Robust, Peppery, Aggressive   For minestrone (page 210), bean soups (page 200), robust pastas and salads and bruschetta (page 34), or with cooked dried beans (pages 182 and 185), potato salads (page 304) and grilled meat and fish, try Castello di Ama, Capezzana, Laudemio Poppiano, Trevi, Biondi Santi, Col d'Orcia, and Magni.

CURED PORK

Most important of all when buying cured meats is to taste, then wait ten seconds after swallowing for the aftertaste. If you like what you're eating and there's no unpleasant aftertaste, it's worth purchasing.

Serving or Cooking

For antipasto, figure $^1/_2$ to 1 ounce cured meats per person. In cooking, an ounce or so goes a long way in bringing more character to a dish.

Coppa, Cappricola and Capocollo   All these are the same cuts—pork shoulder or neck in a solid piece—cured in different styles depending upon where their makers are in Italy. Taste coppa for big meaty flavors, subtle spicing and not too much salt. Cappricola or capocollo is sold sweet or hot, spiced with fennel and maybe hot pepper. They, too, should taste harmonious and never salty. Use for big meaty flavors in pasta sauces and braised dishes.
Recommended Brands: Volpi, Rapelli and Oldani.

Ingredients

Pancetta This bacon cut is cured with salt, pepper, bay leaves and cloves, rolled into a cylinder and aged several months. It is safe to eat raw. Pancetta tastes intensely meaty and delicately salted; its fat has an appealing satiny quality. Pancetta brings body and robustness to dishes. In these recipes, pancetta often stands in for Italian salt pork, as our salt pork is quite different. Pancetta's delicacy works well in these dishes. Freeze pancetta up to 6 months. **Recommended Brands:** Molinari and Rapelli.

Prosciutto Ham cured solely with salt, usually air-dried and aged more than a year, Italy's prosciutti are not equaled by any American-made prosciutto. They possess incredible finesse. Serve fine prosciutto without melon or other embellishments. Anticipate 3 thin slices per person. Prosciutto fat is one of the world's great cooking mediums. Do try it.

Recommended Prosciutti Prosciutto San Daniele or Prosciutto di Parma. (Parma ham maker Tosini's exceptional 600-day-old prosciutto can be found in some shops). Prosciutto di Carpignana is the country cousin—a more robust ham.

Salami Like cheese, nearly every area of Italy has its own individual salami. Keep sampling new ones as you find them. Some to look for are cacciatori, Toscano, Veneta, soppressata, salame Milano and Genoa. **Recommended Brands:** Volpi, Rapelli and Oldani.

Pasta, Dried

See page 64.

Polenta

See page 172.

Porcini Mushrooms

Dried porcini are more easily had than fresh ones. This is the *Boletus edulis* mushroom. The best dried porcini are in big pieces and smell of loam, roasting meat and the forest. They are usually dark-colored. Inferior porcini smell like weak bouillon cubes. Store sealed in a cool dark place and use within a year.

Fresh porcini should not have any bruising or signs of rotting. Use quickly, with grilling being a favorite way of cooking.

Rice

See page 155.

Sea Salt

Often sea salt is intensely salty, so a little goes a long way. Trace minerals give varying nuances of flavor to sea salt, depending on its source. Because they are inconsistent (some are actually unpleasant), I have not specified sea salt in the recipes. When you find one you like, do use it.

What to Buy I like two salts from Sicily: Borrometi and Ravida. Taste sea salts before stocking up.

Tomatoes

See pages 113 and 115.

Wines

Obviously, cook with wines you enjoy drinking—and know modest-priced wines are ideal.

What to Buy For dry white wine, use a Pinot Grigio or Sauvignon Blanc. For dry red, try a Montepulciano d'Abruzzo or Zinfandel. Girelli's Canaletto wines are my particular favorites, for their extremely reasonable pricing and respectable quality.

Wine Vinegar

Buy red and white wine vinegars in small quantities to taste for distinctive character beyond the vinegar's acidity. Once you find one you like, stock up and store in a cool dark cupboard. I like these brands: Steff, Colavita, Badia di Coltibuono and the orange-scented Aspretto di Arancio by Rossana Rosini.

MAIL-ORDER SOURCES

Food Sources

BALDUCCI'S
424 Sixth Avenue
New York, NY 10011
Phone: (800) 225-3822
Fax: (516) 843-0383
Website: www.balducci.com
Catalog available
Full line of Italian foods, including Noé balsamic vinegar.

CORTI BROTHERS
5810 Folsom Blvd.
Sacramento, CA 95819
Phone: (800) 509-3663
Free newsletter available
Premium balsamic vinegars, olive oils and selected Italian products.

DAIRY FRESH CANDIES
57 Salem Street
Boston, MA 02113
Phone: (800) 336-5536
Fax: (617) 742-9828
Candied citron by the chunk and other candied and dried fruits.

DEAN & DELUCA
560 Broadway
New York, NY 10012
Phone: (800) 221-7714
Website: www.dean-deluca.com
Catalog available
Balsamic vinegars, cheeses, oils, pastas, cured meats and other Italian products.

GIUSTO'S
344 Littlefield Avenue
South San Francisco, CA 94080
Phone: (888) 873-6566
Fax: (650) 873-2826
Product information available
Cornmeal for polenta, grains and flours for baking.

LOVE TREE FARMS
12413 County Road Z
Grantsburg, WI 54840
Phone: (715) 488-2966
Sheep cheeses.

JAMISON FARM
171 Jamison Lane
Latrobe, PA 15650
Phone: (800) 237-5262
Website: www.jamisonfarm.com
Catalog available
Free-range, antibiotic- and hormone-free lamb, shipped fresh or frozen.

MOZZARELLA COMPANY
2944 Elm Street
Dallas, TX 75226
Phone: (800) 798-2954
Fax: (214) 741-4076
Website: www.foodwine.com/ (then click on Mozzarella)
Catalog available
Fresh mozzarella and other handmade additive- and preservative-free fresh and aged cheeses.

PENZEYS SPICES

Post Office Box 933
Muskego, WI 53150
Phone: (414) 679-7207
Fax: (414) 679-7878
Website: www.penzeys.com
Catalog available
Wide variety of spices and seasonings.

SUMMERFIELD FARM

10044 James Monroe Highway
Culpeper, VA 22701
Phone: (800) 898-3276
Website: www.summerfieldfarm.com
Top-quality veal.

VELLA CHEESE COMPANY

Post Office Box 191
Sonoma, CA 95476
Phone: (800) 848-0505
Fax: (707) 938-4307
Website: www.vellacheese.com
Catalog available
Dry Jack and Fontinella cheeses.

VERMONT BUTTER AND CHEESE COMPANY

Pitman Road, Box 95
Websterville, VT 05678
Phone: (800) 884-6287
Website: www.vtbutterandcheeseco.com
Catalog available
Mascarpone cheese.

VERMONT SHEPHERD

RFD 3, Box 265
Putney, VT 05346
Phone: (802) 387-4473
Fax: (802) 387-2041
E-mail: vtsheprd@sover.net
Brochure and price list available
Aged sheep's milk cheese.

WAR EAGLE MILL

Route 5, Box 411
Rogers, AR 72756
Phone: (501) 789-5343
Website: www.wareaglemill.com
Catalog available
Stone-ground certified organic flours and grains.

WHITE MOUNTAIN FARM

890 Lane 4 North
Mosca, CO 81146
Phone: (719) 378-2436
Brochure available
*Certified organically grown potatoes,
    including Yellow Finns.*

ZINGERMAN'S

422 Detroit Street
Ann Arbor, MI 48104
Phone: (888) 636-8162
Fax: (734) 769-1260
Website: www.zingermans.com
Catalog available
*Select group of balsamic vinegars, olive oils
    and other Italian products, including
    Ravida olive oil and Rustichella pasta.*

Seed Sources

SEEDS OF CHANGE
Post Office Box 15700
Santa Fe, NM 87506-5700
Phone: (888) 762-7333
Fax: (888) 329-4762
Website: www.seedsofchange.com
Catalog available
Organic heirloom, traditional and native varieties.

JOHNNY'S SELECTED SEEDS
Foss Hill Road
Albion, ME 04910
Phone: (207) 437-4301
Fax: (800) 437-4290 (US only)
Website: www.johnnyseeds.com
Catalog available
Excellent tomato selection.

THE COOK'S GARDEN
Post Office Box 535
Londonderry, VT 05148
Phone: (800) 457-9703
Fax: (800) 457-9705
Website: www.cooksgarden.com
Catalog available
Organic vegetables and herbs, heirlooms.

SHEPHERD'S GARDEN SEEDS
30 Irene Street
Torrington, CT 06790
Phone: (860) 482-3638
Fax: (860) 482-0532
Catalog available
Vegetables and herbs.

WHEN IN ITALY

These are some of my favorite guest farms, country life museums and restaurants. Accommodations on guest farms are usually very simple—a clean bedroom and bath with no telephone or television in the rooms (I've eliminated any falling below this standard). Staying on a farm with an Italian family can be one of the richest experiences you'll have as a traveler. In Italy the guest farm movement is called "Agriturismo" and you will find numerous guidebooks there. Do explore beyond this list. Get out into the countryside and experience Italian country life firsthand.

Since opening times, ownership and services can change, please always call or write ahead to check prices and verify the information below. When calling from outside Italy, the telephone country code is 39. Drop the 39 when calling from within the country.

LOMBARDY REGION

Museo Lombardo di Storia dell'Agricoltura e Museo del Pane
(Museum of country life on the Lombardy plain and a bread museum)
Castello Morando Bolognini
Via C. Battisti
S. Angelo Lodignano (near Lodi)
Phone: 39.0371.211.140

Museo Agricolo Ricci-Curbastro
(A museum of farm equipment)
Owner: Gualberto Ricci-Curbastro
Villa Evelina
Via Adro 37
25031 Capriolo (Brescia)
Phone: 39.030.736.094
The Ricci-Curbastro family also have guest facilities. I have not stayed here, but know the family has high standards of hospitality. Four apartments for 2 to 6 people, open all year; no meals. Wine production and organic polenta.

Agriturismo Le Frise
(A goat farm on a mountainside in the Camonica Valley—see page 38)
Owners: Emma Rota and Gualberto Martini
Rive dei Balti
25040 Artone (Brescia)
Phone and fax: 39.0364.598.298
Three rooms with private bath and breakfast. Restaurant open for dinner Saturday evening and Sunday noon.

Ristorante Due Colombe
Owners: The Cerveni family—Giuseppe, Clara and Stefano
Via Bonomelli 17
25038 Rovato (Brescia)
Phone and fax: 39.030.772.1534

Ristorante La Dispensa
Owners: Sergio and Nicla Zarattini, with sons Leonardo and Simone
Via Castello 19-21
Castellaro Lagusello
46040 Mozambano (Mantova)
Phone: 39.0376.88.850

EMILIA-ROMAGNA REGION
Ristorante Croce Daniele
Owners: Giovanna Montevecche and son-in-law Luciano Gentilini
Via Monte Romano 43
48010 Brisighella (Ravenna)
Phone: 39.0546.87.019

Ristorante Lancellotti (see page 94)
Owners: Ida and Camillo, with sons Emilio, Angelo and Francesco Lancellotti
Via Achille Grandi 120
41019 Soliera (Modena)
Phone: 39.059.567. 406
Fax: 39.059.565.431

Villa Gaidello (see page 131)
Owner: Paola Bini
Via Gaidello 18
41013 Castelfranco Emilia (Modena)
Phone: 39.059.926.806
Fax: 39.059.926.620
Six apartments. Dinner served by reservation on weekends and occasionally during the week.

Ristorante La Buca
Via Ghizzi 6
Zibello (Parma)
Phone: 39.0524.99.214

TUSCANY REGION
Il Museo Etnografico di San Pellegrino in Alpe
(Rural life in the Garfagnana area of Tuscany, depicted in a large, well-arranged collection in a beautiful mountain setting)
San Pellegrino in Alpe (Lucca)
Phone: 39.0583.64.9072 or 68.604

Hotel Il Casone
(A simple country hotel in the Garfagnana area of northern Tuscany, see page 187, near the top of the Apennine Mountains and the museum mentioned above)
Owners: The Rigoli family
Via Statale 324
Casone di Profecchia (Lucca)
Phone: 39.0583.649.030
Thirty rooms with private baths. Meals available—good local food.

Museo del Castagno
(Italy's only chestnut museum in a tiny mountain village north of Lucca)
Contact: Signore Frati
55060 Colognora di Pescaglia (Lucca)
Phone: 39.0583.954.465 or 358.004

Hotel Il Chiostro di Pienza
Corso Rossellino 26
Pienza (Siena)
Phone: 39.0578.748.400
Fax: 39.0578.748.440

MARCHE REGION
Agriturismo Locanda Alce Nero (Black Elk)
(Italy's oldest organic farming cooperative)
Gino Girolomoni
Via Valli 18
61030 Isola del Piano
Phone: 39.0721.720.126

PUGLIA REGION
Ristorante al Fornello da Ricci
Owners: Dora and Angelo Ricci, with daughters Antonella and Rossella
Contrada Montevicoli
72013 Ceglie Messapica (Brindisi)
Phone and fax: 39.0831.377.104

Trattoria Delle Ruote
(A farmhouse restaurant)
Owner: Peppino Ceci
Via Ceglie, Est 4.5 km
74015 Martina Franca
Phone: 39.080.483.7473

Il Frantoio (see page 376)
Owners: Rosalba Ciannamea and Armando
Balestrazzi
S.S. 16 km 874
72017 Ostuni (Brindisi)
Phone and fax: 39.0831.330.276
This guest farm is more like staying
in a country house hotel. Guest rooms
are furnished with antiques, good beds and
well-equipped baths. Breakfast and a
multi-course dinner are included in the
room rate.

Ristorante Locanda del Gallo
Owners: The Sozzo family
Piazza Castello 1
Acaya (Vernole)
Phone: 39.0832.861.102

Trattoria Casareccia
Owner: Concetta Cantoro
Via Col. Costadura 19
Lecce
Phone: 39.0832.245.178

Pizzeria Bruna
Owner: La Bruna
Via Risorgimento
S. Donato di Lecce
Phone: 39.0832.658.207

SICILY
Azienda Agricola il Limoneto
(see page 247)
Owners: Adelina Norcia and Alceste Moscati
Via del Platano 3
Siracusa Canicattini Bagni
96100 Siracusa
Phone and fax: 39.0931.717.352
This guest farm has bedrooms with private
baths. Meals available.

Ristorante Monte S. Giuliano
Owners: Andrea di Coppola and Giurlanda
Matteo
Vicolo San Rocco 7
Erice (Trapani)
Phone: 39.0923.869.595

Museo Etnografico Siciliano G. Pitre'
(One of Italy's most important, and most
neglected, collections of folklife and folk art)
Palazzina Cinese
Via Duca Degli Abruzzi 1
90416 Palermo
Phone: 39.091.740.4893

Museo i Luoghi del Lavoro Contadino
(This country life museum is a collection
of buildings spread through the country
town of Buscemi)
Contact: Rosario Acquaviva
Corso Vittorio Emanuele 25
96100 Buscemi (Siracusa)
Phone and fax: 39.0931.878.528

TRENTINO–ALTO ADIGE REGIONS
Hotel Accademia
Franca and Giovanna di Fambri
Vicolo Colico 4–6
38100 Trento
Phone: 39.0461.233.600
Fax: 39.0461.230.174

When in Italy

Osteria Le Due Spade (restaurant)
Owner: Pompeo Peterlana
Via Don Arcangelo Rizzi 11
38100 Trento
Phone: 39.0461.23443

Museo Della Civilta' Solandra
Contact: Maria Fedrizzi
Via Trento 13
38027 Malé (Trento)
Phone: 39.0463.91.272

Museo Degli Usi e Costumi Gente Trentina
(One of Italy's important folklife museums)
Via Mach S. Michele
88010 S. Michele all'Adige (Trento)
Phone: 39.0461.650.314

Museo Etnografico Provinciale
(Italy's only outdoor country life museum, with farm buildings spanning several centuries collected from all over the region)
Via Duca Teodone 24
39031 Teodone-Brunico
Phone: 39.0474.552.087

Malga Sonen
Alpe di Siusi
Castelrotto
(A cowherd's hut where meals are served, reached only on foot. Local tourist board has directions and information on hours)

Hotel Cavallino d'Oro
Krausplatz
I-39040 Castelrotto
Sudtirol
Phone: 39.0471.706.337
Fax: 39.0471.707.172

VENETO REGION
Museo della Vita Agricola
Contact: Pietro Cescin
Via Barriera
31058 Susegana
Phone: 39.0438.738.610

Trattoria Toni del Spin
Via Inferiore 7
Treviso
Phone: 39.0422.543.829

Osteria dal Dante
Piazza Garibaldi 6
Treviso
Phone: 39.0422.51897

Antico Ristorante Beccherie
Owners: The Campeol family
Piazza Ancillotto 11
Treviso
Phone: 39.0422.540.871

A PARTIAL
BIBLIOGRAPHY

Acquaviva, Rosario. *Gli Abiti dei Contadini e della Borghesia Rurale dell'Altipiano Ibleo Tra '800 e '900*. Edizioni Lussografica. Caltanissetta, 1990.

Alberini, Massimo. *Maccheroni e Spaghetti*. Casale Monferrato: Edizioni Piemme s.p.a., 1994.

Amaradio, Ida, Tommaso D'Alba, and Guido Di Prima, editors. *La Cucina Tradizionale dell'Ennese*. Seconda edizione. Paprio Editrice Enna, 1986.

Biagioni, Pietro Lugi. *Il Museu Etnografico di San Pellegrino in Alpe*. Maria Pacini Fazzi Editore, Lucca.

Bugialli, Giuliano. *Foods of Tuscany*. New York: Stewart, Tabori & Chang, 1992.

Camporesi, Piero. *Alimentazione Folcolre Societa*. Parma: Pratiche Editrice, 1980.

Casa Editrice Bonechi. *Cultura Contadina in Toscana*. Two volumes. Casa Editrice Bonechi, 1989.

Casa Museo di Antonino Uccello, *La Roba della Sposa*. Palazzo Acreide, 1988.

Cavalli, Germano. *Note di Etnografla e di Folklore La Castagna*. Estratto da Studi Lunigianesi Anno 12–13, 1982–1983. Artigianelli, Pontremoli, 1984.

Codacci, Leo. *Civilta della Tavola Contadina*. Firenze: G. C. Sansoni Editore Nuova s.p.a., 1981.

Correnti, Pino. *Il Libro d'Oro della Cucina e dei Vini di Sicilia*. Milano: Úgo Mursia Editore s.p.a., 1976.

Corsi, Guglielma. *Un Secolo di Cucina Umbra*. Assisi: Edizioni Porzluncola, S. Maria degli Angeli, 1976.

Del Conte, Anna. *Gastronomy of Italy*. New York: Prentice Hall, 1987.

Downie, David. *Enchanted Liguria*. New York: Rizzoli, 1997.

Ferrante, Maria Pignatelli. *La Cucina delle Murge*. Padova: Franco Muzzio Editore, 1991.

Field, Carol. *Celebrating Italy*. New York: William Morrow, 1990.

Gaioni, Giorgio. *Leggende di Val Camonica e Val di Scalve*. Seconda edizione. Edizioni Quetti—Artogne/Brescia, 1990.

Gaudenzio, Francesco. *Il Pan Unto Toscano*. Bologna: Arnaldo Forni Editore, 1990.

Giardelli, Paolo. *Il Cerchio del Tempo, Le Tradizioni Popolari dei Liguri*. Sagep Editrice, 1991.

Griefsmair, Hans. *Il Museo etnografico di Dietenheim*. Casa Editrice Athesia, Bolzano/Bozen, 1986.

Grillli, Dino. *I Lucchesidi Una Volta*. Lucca: Maria Pacini Fazzi Editore, 1988.

Gurrieri, Francesco, and Gianluca Belli. *La Casa Colonica in Italia*. Firenze: Ponte alle Grazie s.p.a., 1994.

Istituto Nazionale di Sociologia Rurale. *Atlante dei Prodotti Tipici: I Formaggi*. Seconda edizione. Franco Angeli, 1991.

Jenkins, Nancy Harmon. *Flavors of Puglia*. New York: Broadway Books, 1997.

Lera, Guglielmo. *Antiche Botteghe di Lucca*. Lucca: Publilucca Editrice, 1990.

Lucchesi, Emiliana. *La Cucina della Lucchesia*. Franco Muzzio Editore, 1989.

Marchese, Salvatore. *La Cucina di Lunigiana*. Franco Muzzio Editore, 1989.

Morresi, Nicla Mazzara. *La Cucina Marchigiana*. Edizioni Aniballi, 1992.

Pavan, Camillo. *Raici*. Treviso, 1992.

Pellizzari, Camillo, editor. *La Cucina Bresciana*. Editore Fausto Sardini, 1976.

Picchi, Graziella, editor. *Atlante dei Prodotti Tipici: Le Conserve*. Istituto Nazionale di Sociologia Rurale, Franco Angeli, 1993.

Plotkin, Fred. Recipes from Paradise. Little, Brown and Company, 1997.

Pomar, Anna. *L'lsola dei Sapori*. Palermo: Edizioni Good.

Prato, Caterina. *Manuale di Cucina*. Liberia "Styria" Editrice, 1906.

Sada, Luigi. *Il Sacro e Il Profano nella Cucina Pugliese*. Edizione speciale per il trentennale de "La Taberna." Bari/Santo Spirito: Edizioni del Centro Librario, 1989.

Sada, Luigi. *La Cucina della Terra di Bari*. Padova: Franco Muzzio Editore, 1991.

Scheuermeier, Paul. *Il Lavoro dei Contadini*. Two volumes. Milano: Longanesi & C., 1980.

Simeti, Mary Taylor. *Pomp and Sustenance*. New York: Alfred A. Knopf, 1989.

Stanziano, Angelina, and Laura Santoro. *Puglia, la Tradizione in Cucina*. Schena Editore.

Uccello, Antonino, editor. *Del Mangiar Siracusano*. Seconda edizione. Ente.

Uccello, Antonio. *La Casa-Museo di Palazzolo Acreide* (catalog). Siracusa, 1978.

Verardi, M. Letizia Troccoli. *I Misteriosi Simboli dei Trulli*. Seconda edizione. Bari: Mario Adda Editore, 1984.

de Zuliani, Mariu Salvatori. *A Tola Coi I Nostri Veci: La Cucina Veneziana*. Milano: Franco Angeli, 1993.

INDEX

Page numbers in *italics* refer to illustrations.

oven-seared radicchio and Asiago focaccia, 322

P

pancetta, 392
  in mozzarella bundles, 56
  in roasted Roman artichokes, 55
pan co'santi, 336
pancotto al pomodoro, 204–5
pane dolce di zucca, 332–33
panna cotta, 343, 366–67
Pantelleria, capers from, 385
pappa al pomodoro, 204
Parma, country life museum in, 13–15
Parmesan cheese, *see* Parmigiano-Reggiano cheese
Parmigiano knives, 32, 387
Parmigiano-Reggiano cheese, 386–87
  Guatelli's peppers and onions with, 288–89
  in minestrone, 213
  pizza with fresh greens and, 328
  polenta with balsamic vinegar and, 175
  in potato "gattó," 296–97
  in rich man's antipasto, 32–33
  rind of, for seasoning, 191, 201, 210, 213
  tagliarini with fresh artichokes, lemon and, 82–83
  tomato, and onion focaccia, 320
"passed" sauce, 119
pasta, 59–63
  artichoke wedding timbale, 100–103
  baked maccheroni with Sunday ragù, 146–47
  broken bridegrooms with roasted tomatoes, 139
  in broth, 190
  bucatini with Amatriciana sauce, 144–45
  buying, 64–65
  cheese-filled, 194–95
  chopped chive "pesto" on perciatelli, 76–77

pasta *(cont.)*
  with Christmas orzo in swallow's milk, 378–79
  cooking and serving, 59, 65–68
  cuts, shapes and sizes of, 60, 70
  Ettore Guatelli's soffritto with tomatoes for, 178–79
  fresh vs. dried, 64, 71
  Friday night spaghetti with tuna and black olives, 88–89
  gemelli with roasted peppers and greens, 78–79
  of the grape harvest, 96–97
  homemade, 69–71, 195
  with king of pestos, 74–75
  lasagne, Nonna's home-style, 148–49
  leftovers, 68
  linguine with nut pesto, 72–73
  little handkerchiefs with portobello mushrooms, 98–99
  little parcels of sweet squash, 104–5
  in minestrone, 213
  in mother's broth, 196–97
  orecchiette, with ninth-night lamb, 250–51
  penne with Sicilian shepherd's sauce, 136–37
  Puglia streetwalker sauce for, 132–33
  saucing, 66–68
  sausage, peppers and shells, 142–43
  seafood sauté with stubby, 84–85
  Siracusa market, 80–81
  spaghetti alla carbonara, 90
  spaghettini with shrimp, chickpeas and young greens, 86–87
  tagliarini with fresh artichokes, parmigiano and lemon, 82
  tagliatelle with chicken ragù and asparagus, 92–93
  white point of, 68, 73
  see also tomato sauce(s); ziti
pasta alla gricia, 145
pasta alla moda del mercato di Siracusa, 80–81

pasta casalinga, 69–71
pasta col pesce, 84–85
pasta della vendemmia, 96–97
pasta di San Giovanni, 130–31
pasta machines, 87, 87
pasta per pizza, 324–25
pasta puttanesca pugliese, 132–33
pastry:
  for apple-citron turnover, 356–57
  Easter ricotta tart, 358–59
patate alla Lago di Garta, 292
patate alla romagnola, 293
patate con rucola, 49
patate ricotte ai funghi, 294–95
patate schiacciate con acciughe, 50–51
peaches, iced summer, 372
pear, sweet rosemary-, pizza, 350–51
peas:
  in home-style osso buco, 258–59
  in potato "gattó," 296–97
  sweet, "in their jackets," 282
  Vicenza sweet, soup, 216–17
pecorino, *see* sheep cheese
Pedreschi, Enzo, 265
pelati al forno, 29
pellagra, 171
penne dei pastori siciliani, 136–37
penne with Sicilian shepherd's sauce, 136–37
peperoncino, red onion, and arugula focaccia, 321
peperoni della Signora Bimbi, I, 26
peperoni e cipolle alla Guatelli, 288–89
pepper(s):
  baking day chicken with black olives and red, 226–27
  braised pork with three, 240–41
  gemelli with greens and roasted, 78–79
  Guatelli's, with onions, 288–89
  sausage and shells with, 142–43
  Signora Bimbi's, 26
  whole pan-roasted, 184

potato(es) *(cont.)*
  warm crushed, with anchovies,
    50–51
  wine-glazed, Lake Garda, 292
potato salad:
  anchovy dressing for, 42
  Treviso, 304–5
pot oven, 318
pot roast, Tyrolean, 262–63
pots and pans, for sauces, 118
poultry broth, pasta in, 194–95
pounded wheat, 165, 167
prosciutto, 392
  broth with, 197
  in tagliarini with fresh arti-
    chokes, Parmigiano and
    lemon, 82–83
pudding cake, chocolate polenta,
    360–61
Puglia region, 11–12, 16, 314,
    398–99
  goats and sheep of, 252
  hanging winter tomatoes, 134
  masseria farming system, 376
  Saturday market in Ostuni,
    205
  wheat and olive trees, 287
  wheat farming in, 313
Puglia-style:
  almond milk, 343, 368–69
  antipasti, 24
  calamari mixed grill, 268–69
  Christmas dinner, 61
  Christmas orzo in swallow's
    milk, 378–79
  farro, 162
  fava beans, 181, *181,* 183
  fava puree, 153, 180, 182–83
  fish soup, 189
  focaccia, 318
  fresh tomato and black olive
    pizza, 329
  green tomato sauce, 130
  lamb ragù with wheat, 166–67
  lamb stew, 222–23
  menu, 381
  ninth-night lamb, 250–51
  pizza of tomato, cheese and
    arugula, 326–27
  pizza rustica, 330–31
  pounded wheat, 165
  Signora Bimbi's peppers, 26

Puglia-style *(cont.)*
  soft green tomato jam, 355
  streetwalker's pasta sauce,
    132–33
  tomato paste, 129
  tomato sauce, 126
  wheat, 152
pumpkin bread, sweet, 332–33
puntarelle, 42–43
purea di patate alla Margherita, 291
purè di fave, 182
puree:
  fava, Puglia-style, 180, 182–83
  salsa, 127
  tomato sauce, 119–20
  white bean, 31

Q

quaglie al melograno, 236–37
quail in pomegranate sauce,
    sautéed, 236–37

R

rabbit with black olives and red
    peppers, baking day,
    226–27
radicchio, 306–7, *306*
  focaccia with Asiago, oven-
    seared, 322
  mushrooms stuffed with Asiago
    and, 52–53
  in Treviso potato salad, 304–5
ragù:
  baked maccheroni with
    Sunday, 146–47
  Puglia lamb, with wheat,
    166–67
  stufato, 280–81
ragù pugliese, 166–67
raisin(s):
  in bread with saints, 336
  -rosemary focaccia, 323
Rastelli, Enrico, 157
ravioli dolci, 348–49
red onions:
  arugula and peperoncino focac-
    cia with, 321
  home-style cauliflower with,
    279
  orange salad with black olives
    and, 308
  roasted, wedges, 290

red onions *(cont.)*
  salad of tart greens and,
    299–300
  Tuscan white beans and salami
    with, 30–31
red peppers:
  baking day chicken with black
    olives and, 226–27
  braised pork with three pep-
    pers, 240–41
  gemelli with greens and
    roasted, 78–79
  in Guatelli's peppers with
    onions, 288–89
  sausage and shells with,
    142–43
  in Signora Bimbi's peppers, 26
  whole pan-roasted, 184
red wine, leg of lamb glazed with
    balsamic and, 256–57
red wine vinegar, 393
  see also wine vinegar
restaurant guide, 397–400
ribs, Tuscan pork, 238–39
Ricci-Curbastro family, 241,
    397
Ricci family, 134, 398
  tomato sauce, 112, 126
rice, 152
  in minestrone, 213
  see also risotto
rich man's antipasto, 32–33
ricotta, 135, 386
  espresso-, cream with espresso
    chocolate sauce, 370–71
  in penne with Sicilian
    shepherd's sauce, 136–37
  -plum tart in an almond crust,
    352–53
  salata, 387
  in Sicilian farmer's bruschetta,
    34–35
  tart, Easter, 343, 358–59
  wheat berries with honey and,
    170
Rigoli, Riccardo, 187
risotto, 152, 155
  farmwoman's, 154–55
  farro, with chickpeas, orange
    and sage, 163–64
  with sea scallops and balsamic
    vinegar, 158–59

Index

Tuscan-style (cont.)
  green beans, 276
  grilled scallions and asparagus, 309
  kale, melting, 277
  Lucchese veal chops, 260
  minestrone, 213
  mountain supper, 186
  pine nuts, 347
  pork ribs, 238–39
  raisin-rosemary focaccia, 323
  spaghettini with shrimp, chickpeas and young greens, 86–87
  supper soup of sweet squash, farro and beans, 218–19
  tomato sauce, 114
  trout, 223
  white beans with red onion and salami, 30–31
Tuscany, 11, *317*, 398
  bread ovens of, 28
  grape harvest in, 19–21
twice-baked potato with wild mushrooms, 294–95
Tyrolean pot roast, 262–63

U

Uccello, Antonino, 12
Umbrian-style:
  farro, 162
  minestrone, 213
  pasta sauce, 62
  roasted porcetta, 222, 242–43

V

veal:
  chops, Lucchese, 260
  in home-style osso buco, 258–59
vegetable(s), 273–75
  broth, hearty, 198–99
  early autumn, roast, 286–87
  raw, white bean puree for, 31
  stufato, 280–81, *281*
  see also specific vegetables
Veneto region, 400
Veneto-style radicchio, 274

verdure al forno, 286–87
Vicenza, seed man of, 306–7
Vicenza-style, sweet pea soup, 216–17
Villa Gaidello, Modena, 14, 131, 398
vin cotto, 96
  cuccía with, 170
  farro with, 161
  over *panna cotta*, 366–67
vinegar, *see* balsamic vinegar; wine vinegar

W

warm crushed potatoes with anchovies, 50–51
wedding foods:
  artichoke timbale, 100–103
  pasta, 63
  sausage, peppers and shells, 142–43
  soup, 193
wheat, 60–61, 109, 152, 165, 167, 311–13
  cuccía, 165
  in golden gnocchi, 168–69
  pounded, 165
  Puglia lamb ragù with, 166–67
wheat berries with ricotta and honey, 170
white bean(s), 181
  puree, 31
  Tuscan, with red onion and salami, 30–31
white wine:
  -glazed chicken, 230–31
  in Lake Garda potatoes, 292
white wine vinegar, 393
  cantaloupe with black pepper, oil and, 37
whole pan-roasted peppers, 184
whole wheat pizza crust, 325
wine(s):
  for cooking, 393
  figs in honeyed, 374
  red, leg of lamb glazed with balsamic and, 256–57
  see also white wine

wine vinegar, 305, 393
  red, for lamb in chile-vinegar sauce, 254–55
  white, cantaloupe with black pepper, oil and, 37
winnowing, wheat, 313
winter tomatoes, 134

Y

yellow peppers:
  braised pork with three peppers, 240–41
  in Guatelli's peppers with onions, 288–89

Z

zabaglione, for *tirami-sù*, 364–65
Zarattini, Nicla and Sergio, 25, 397
  little parcels of sweet squash, 104–5
  warm crushed potatoes with anchovies, 50–51
zest, citrus, 344
zester, 344
zita con pomodori, capocollo e mozzarella, 140–41
ziti:
  broken bridegrooms with roasted tomatoes, 139
  spiced cauliflower with, 138–39
  with tomatoes, capocollo and diced mozzarella, 140–41
ziti con cavolfiore piccante, 138–39
ziti con pomodori arrostiti, 139
ziti di ceci tutti santi, 214–15
zucca con polenta, 176–77
zuppa di bisi in tecia, 216–17
zuppa di Maria Lembi, 218–19
zuppa inglese, 365
zuppa piccante alle melanzane, 202–3